EMOTION AND PROACTIVITY AT WORK

Prospects and Dialogues

Edited by
Kelly Z. Peng and Chia-Huei Wu

With a Foreword by
Sharon K. Parker

BRISTOL
UNIVERSITY
PRESS

First published in Great Britain in 2021 by

Bristol University Press
University of Bristol
1–9 Old Park Hill
Bristol
BS2 8BB
UK
t: +44 (0)117 954 5940
e: bup-info@bristol.ac.uk

Details of international sales and distribution partners are available at bristoluniversitypress.co.uk

British Library Cataloguing in Publication Data
A catalogue record for this book is available from the British Library

ISBN 978-1-5292-0830-6 hardcover
ISBN 978-1-5292-1263-1 ePub
ISBN 978-1-5292-1265-5 OA PDF

Cover design: Clifford Hayes
Front cover image: Group of multi-ethnic designers brainstorming
© Rawpixel.com
Bristol University Press uses environmentally responsible print partners.
Printed and bound in Great Britain by CPI Group (UK) Ltd,
Croydon, CR0 4YY

Contents

List of Figures and Tables

Figures

Tables

Notes on Contributors

Neal M. Ashkanasy OAM, PhD is Professor of Management at the UQ Business School (University of Queensland). He studies emotion, leadership, culture, and ethical behaviour. He has published over 100 refereed articles and was Editor-in-Chief of the *Journal of Organizational Behavior*. In 2019, he was the MOC Division Distinguished Scholar.

Uta K. Bindl is Reader in Organizational Behaviour at King's Business School. Uta earned her PhD from the Institute of Work Psychology at the University of Sheffield. Her research interests are: (1) motivation in organizations, and (2) employee well-being and affect regulation; and has published in the *Journal of Management*, the *Journal of Applied Psychology*, *Human Relations* and others. She also serves as an editorial board member of the *Academy of Management Review*, the *Journal of Applied Psychology* and the *Journal of Organizational Behavior*. Uta has been an award-winning teacher at the London School of Economics, and is currently an elected Representative-At-Large at the Organizational Behavior Division of the Academy of Management.

Francesco Cangiano is Assistant Professor of Management at the Bond Business School. Francesco received his PhD in Organizational Behaviour at the University of Western Australia Business School. Francesco's main research areas include proactive work behaviour, employee well-being and motivation.

Zhijun Chen is Academic Director of the MBA programme and Head of the Department of Human Resources Management at the Shanghai University of Finance and Economics and a professor of the department. Zhijun is interested in studying employee proactive behaviour, coworker influence, and different forms of leadership styles. He has published in the *Journal of Applied Psychology*, *Organization Science*, *Personnel Psychology*, and others. He is Associate Editor of *Human Relations* and the Representative-At-Large for the International

Association of Chinese Management Research. He also sits on the editorial review board of the the *Asian Pacific Journal of Management* and the *Journal of Business Research*.

Nai-Wen Chi is Distinguished Professor of Graduate Institute of Human Resource Management, National Sun-Yat Sen University. He completed his PhD at the Department of Business Management, National Cheng Chi University. His research areas include emotions at work, employee attitudes and behaviours, and team management. His papers have been published in the *Journal of Applied Psychology, Journal of Management, Organizational Behavior and Human Decision Processes, Personnel Psychology*, the *Journal of Organizational Behavior*, the *Journal of Vocational Behavior, Human Relations*, the *Journal of Service Research*, the *Journal of Business Research, Group & Organization Management*, the *Journal of Occupational and Organizational Psychology*, and other outlets.

Emily Guohua Huang (PhD, Hong Kong University of Science and Technology) is Associate Professor in the Department of Management at the Hong Kong Baptist University. She is interested in studying employee responses to stress and uncertainties at the workplace. Specific research interests include job insecurity, emotion in organizations, counterproductive behaviours at work, and team process. Her work has been published at management journals such as the *Journal of Applied Psychology*, the *Journal of Management, Organizational Behavior and Human Decision Processes*, and the *Journal of Organizational Behavior.*

Shunhong Ji is a PhD student at the College of Business of the Shanghai University of Finance and Economics. His research interests include motivation, proactive behaviour and work design. His recent research explores the emotional outcomes of employee proactive behaviour and also the underpinning mechanisms. In addition, he is strong in methodology and statistical analysis.

Daniya Kamran-Morley is a doctoral candidate at the Katz Graduate School of Business, University of Pittsburgh. Her research interests include work engagement, passion, and ideologies of work and management.

R. David Lebel is Associate Professor of Organizational Behavior at the University of Pittsburgh. He received his PhD from the Wharton School of the University of Pennsylvania. His current research interests include proactivity, voice, innovation, and the influence of emotions on behaviour at work.

Cynthia Lee (PhD University of Maryland) is Group Chair and Professor, Management and Organizational Development, D'Amore-McKim School of Business, Northeastern University. Professor Lee's research interests include managing and leading change, creativity and innovation, employment relationships including the understanding the changing nature of psychological contracts, workplace justice, and the effects of job insecurity. Her work publishes in the *Academy of Management Journal*, the *Academy of Management Review*, the *Journal of Applied Psychology*, *Organization Science*, the *Journal of International Studies*, the *Journal of Management*, the *Journal of Organizational Behavior*, among others.

Chenwei Li is Associate Professor of Management at the Lam Family College of Business, San Francisco State University. She received her PhD from the University of Alabama. Her primary research interests focus on leadership, employee voice and creativity. Her work has been published in the management field's premier journals such as the *Journal of Management*, the *Journal of Organizational Behavior*, the *Journal of Business Ethics*, among others. Chenwei received the 2020 Ascendant Scholar Award from the Western Academy of Management. She teaches Leadership and Influence Skills and Human Resource Management courses and conducts leadership training workshops for managers of different levels in companies.

Wanlu Li holds a post-doctorate fellowship at the Business School, Sun Yat-sen University. She worked as a research assistant at the Department of Business Administration, Shue Yan University, in 2019. She received her doctoral degree from the Education University of Hong Kong in 2019. Her research interests are proactivity and teacher behaviours.

Zhenyu Liao is Assistant Professor in the D'Amore-McKim School of Business at Northeastern University. His research primarily focuses on leadership behaviour, behavioural ethics, social biases, and algorithmic labour. Prior to his professorship, he was a post-doctoral fellow at Washington University in St Louis after he obtained PhD at the National University of Singapore.

Wu Liu is Professor in the Faculty of Business at the Hong Kong Polytechnic University. His research interests include leader–member and team dynamics on extra-role behaviours, emotion, and cross-cultural conflict resolution. He received his PhD in organization studies at Vanderbilt University.

Hector P. Madrid is Assistant Professor of Organizational Behavior in the Management School at Pontificia Universidad Católica de Chile. He earned his PhD at the Institute of Work Psychology, University of Sheffield. His research interests are about affect in the workplace in relation to creativity, innovation, and proactivity.

Sandra Ohly has been Professor in Business Psychology at the University of Kassel since 2010. She received her PhD from the Technical University of Braunschweig in 2005, and completed her habilitation at the Goethe University Frankfurt in 2010. Her research focuses on well-being, creativity and proactive behaviour at work. She is also interested in affective and motivational processes, oftentimes using diary methods. She is also Editor-in-Chief of the *European Journal of Work and Organizational Psychology*, and on the editorial board of the *Journal of Applied Psychology*, the *Journal of Business and Psychology* and the *Journal of Occupational and Organizational Psychology*.

Kan Ouyang is Associate Professor in the Department of Human Resource Management at the College of Business of Shanghai University of Finance and Economics. She received her PhD in management from the Hong Kong Polytechnic University. Her research interests include employee proactivity, work recovery, and leadership.

Malcolm Patterson is Senior Lecturer at the Management School, University of Sheffield. He has research interests including the relationships between work conditions, employee well-being (emotion, moods, stress, engagement) and behaviour at work (for example, pro- and anti-social behaviour).

Kelly Z. Peng (PhD, Chinese University of Hong Kong) is Associate Professor at the Department of Business Administration, Hong Kong Shue Yan University. Her research interests include emotions in management, proactive behaviour, employment relationship, and career development. She has published in the *Journal of Management, Human Resources Management,* the *Journal of World Business*, among others. She also serves on the editorial review broad of the *Asia Pacific*

Journal of Management (APJM, as recognized as Best Reviewer of APJM in 2017), and the *Journal of Managerial Psychology*.She was appointed Chair Professor under the Feitian Scholars Schema of Gansu Province, China in 2019.

Laura Venz has been Assistant Professor in Work and Organizational Psychology at the Leuphana University of Lüneburg since 2019. She received her PhD from the University of Mannheim in 2015. Her research focuses on affective well-being and social relationships at work. She is also interested in studying affective processes in relation to enacted work behaviours, oftentimes using experience sampling methods.

Fenghao Wang is a doctoral candidate in the Department of Management and Marketing at the Hong Kong Polytechnic University. His research interests include emotion, social hierarchy, and voice behaviour. His work appeared in *Academy of Management Best Paper Proceedings*.

Chia-Huei Wu is Professor in Organizational Psychology at the University of Leeds. He received his PhD from the University of Western Australia and holds an MPhil from the University of Sheffield and an MSc and BSc from the National Taiwan University. His research interests include proactivity at work, work and personality development, and subjective well-being. Chia-Huei has published his work in leading journals, including the *Academy of Management Journal*, the *Journal of Applied Psychology* and the *Journal of Management*, among others. He is the author of the book, *Employee Proactivity in Organizations: An Attachment Perspective*, and currently serves as an associate editor for the *Journal of Management*.

Bingjie Yu is a PhD student in the Department of Management at Hong Kong Baptist University. Her current research interests include job insecurity, self-concept and discretionary behaviours. She has published research papers in journals such as the *Asian Pacific Journal of Management* and *Personnel Review*.

Hannes Zacher is Professor of Work and Organizational Psychology at the Institute of Psychology – Wilhelm Wundt, Leipzig University. In his research programme, he investigates aging at work, career development, and occupational well-being; proactivity, innovation, leadership, and entrepreneurship; and pro-environmental employee behaviour.

Acknowledgements

This edited book was incubated by an Hong Kong international symposium on emotion and proactivity in May 2019. We would like to thank all the speakers, Chen Zhijun, Huang Guo-hua. Emily, Jiang Yan, Lam Chak Fu, Li Wendong, Liang Jian, Liu Wu, Neal Ashkanasy, Ronald Humphrey, Wen Shanshan, Wu Chia-huei, Zhang Lingling, for their encouragement in proposing this book. And five out of 12 speakers are chapter contributors. The event and open access of this edited book are all supported by grants from IIDS–RGC Grant on 'Fueling the Proactivity by Emotions "Energy": Through Understanding the Functions of Discrete Emotions in Different Social Settings (UGC/IIDS15/B01/18)' awarded to Kelly Z. Peng as principal investigator.

Foreword

Sharon K. Parker

COVID-19 sharpened unexpectedly and lasted longer than we supposed. This situation has brought many changes to the working lives of almost everyone in the world. Organizations have needed to rapidly pivot their operations in the light of supply chain disruptions, new opportunities, and altered demands. Individuals, too, have needed to take on new tasks, or even new jobs entirely, and have often have to creatively and rapidly implement new ways of doing things during this time. At this time, employees' proactivity – or their self-initiated, future-focused and change-oriented work behaviour – is crucial for success. More perhaps than ever before, we need employees and managers alike to be voicing suggestions, implementing new work methods, and coming up with creative ideas.

What motivates employees to be proactive? In our 'can do, reason to, and energized to' model of proactive motivation (Parker, Bindl, and Strauss, 2010), we theorized that employees need to believe they can be proactive (such as having self-efficacy); they need to have an internalized reason to do so (such as seeing it as part of their role); and they will benefit from positive feelings of activation. The first two of these processes, can do and reason to, have had quite some focus in research. But the role of positive emotions in energizing proactivity has only recently started to get the attention this motivational pathway deserves.

Consequently, I am delighted to see this book focusing on emotions and proactivity. The 12 chapters across three parts offer a comprehensive review on emotion and proactivity from different angles. The chapters also provide insights for how we can extend current research to enrich our understanding on the relationship between emotion and proactivity.

The first part of the book starts with a chapter offering a systematic view of what we already know based on existing research on emotion and proactivity (Chapter 1). This is followed by a chapter that reviews and reflects on the motivational function of emotion in energizing proactivity and the need to extend the scope of studies on emotion and proactivity (Chapter 2).

The second part contains eight chapters discussing different subjects on the role of emotion in shaping proactive behaviour. Chapter 3 offers a multilevel lens to the study of emotion and proactivity. The following seven chapters then discuss different topics that map onto different levels, including: work affective events (Chapter 4) and cross-domain influences at the within-person level (Chapter 5); job insecurity and its resulting emotions at the between-person level (Chapter 6); other-praising emotions (Chapter 7) and leaders' anger expression (Chapter 8) at the interpersonal or relationship level; and group affective tone (Chapter 9 and 10) at the team level.

The third part gives attention to the emotional consequences of proactivity; an emerging topic in the literature. Specifically, this part contains a chapter discussing the impact of proactivity on individual well-being (Chapter 11) and emotional experiences (Chapter 12).

The discussion of emotion and proactivity will be enriched after the publication of this volume. It provides a comprehensive overview for anyone wanting to get up to speed on this topic, and is a terrific source of new ideas for budding PhD students or other scholars looking for new inspiration. And just as important as its academic contribution, the book provides a rich and informative source of practical guidance for managers, consultants, and others seeking to foster more proactivity among workers. It is a true pleasure to recommend this important and timely book.

References

Parker, S. K., Bindl, U. K., and Strauss, K. (2010). Making things happen: A model of proactive motivation. *Journal of Management*, 36, 827–56.

Emotion and Proactivity at Work: Where Are We Now?

Kelly Z. Peng and Chia-Huei Wu

Due to globalization and technology innovation, the business environment has become more complex and uncertain. To cope with such a changing environment effectively, employees are expected to be proactive, to respond to and master changes effectively, instead of waiting for their supervisors or organizations to instruct them what to do (Griffin, Neal, and Parker, 2007). Being proactive is about taking control to make things happen rather than watching things happen. To date, scholars in the field of organizational behaviour have invested lots of effort to study employee proactive behaviour (proactivity in brief), that is, self-initiating, future-oriented behaviour aiming to improve the work situations or oneself (Parker, Bindl, and Strauss, 2010). Proactivity is initiated by employees themselves owing to their interests, motivation or beliefs, instead of instructions or demands from others. Proactivity is future-oriented, as it is strongly based on anticipating and thinking about the longer-term future. Proactivity is change-oriented as it acts to address those anticipated challenges by improving or altering the status quo. It involves aspiring and striving to bring about change in the environment and/or oneself to achieve a different future (Grant and Ashford, 2008). That is, being proactive requires more motivational energy.

As a result, scholars have invested lots of effort to identify motivational forces that can drive proactive behaviour (for example, Parker, Bindl, and Strauss, 2010). As Mitchell and Daniels (2003) indicated, employees' behaviour can be driven by cold (or cognitive) processes as well as hot (or affective) processes. Employee proactivity is also driven by cognitive factors such as self-efficacy, an individual's belief in his or her capacity to execute behaviours necessary to achieve specific goals (Bandura, 1994), as well as affective factors such as one's positive emotions or feelings at work (see Cai, Parker, Chen, and Lam, 2019; Cangiano, Bindl, and Parker, 2016, for reviews). Nevertheless, research so far has paid much more attention to cold (or cognitive) processes than hot (or affective) processes in driving proactivity.

Indeed, emotion at the workplace is attracting more and more attention in management research. Inspired by the affective revolution in organizational behaviour (Barsade, Brief, and Spataro, 2003), emotions have not been considered as barriers to rationality at work (for example, Barsade and Gibson, 2007). Instead, positive emotion can broaden and build our cognitive horizon, which in turn leads to an enlarged action repertoire and behaviour change (Fredrickson, 2001) while also being a source of energy to support the individual to engage and sustain contribution at work (Bakker, 2019; Quinn, Spreitzer, and Lam, 2012). At the same time, emotions could provide social cues for behavioural options (for example, Schwarz, 2011; van Kleef, 2009). Specifically, positive emotions signals that things proceed smoothly and the environment is safe, which can also be a source of energy in initiating proactive actions and helps them deal with any risks or obstacles that occur during the proactive process. For negative emotions, it reveals there is a problematic situation and changes are needed, which may also serve as 'a priming energy' to be proactive. In short, emotions could provide motivational energy in priming, driving, and/or sustaining proactivity in various forms and mechanisms (for example, Bindl et al, 2012; Lebel, 2016; 2017; Sonnentag and Starzyk, 2015).

The revolution also goes beyond the traditional approach to classifying moods/emotions as either positive or negative (Brief and Weiss, 2002) by differentiating individual affective experiences in a circumplex model (Russell, 1980; 2003) and draw attentions to directly studying discrete emotion (Brief and Weiss, 2002), a particular subjective feeling toward a certain target (for example, Izard, 1991), to understand 'the processes and the different outcomes resulting from that particular discrete emotion' (Ashkanasy and Dorris, 2017, p 70). Discrete emotion literature mainly adopts the functional perspective that each emotion bears a unique functional, adaptive, and relational meaning (for example, Izard, 1991; Lazarus, 1991). As a result, each emotion should link to specific functions and thus lead to specific behavioural tendencies (for example, Frijda, 1987; Izard, 1991; Lazarus, 1991; Levenson, 1994). Researchers have found that different discrete emotion (for example, fear or anger) exert differential effect or go through differential mechanisms to the proactive process. Owing to the affective revolution in organizational behaviour, we now have rich pool emotional mechanisms to understand the relationship between emotions and proactivity.

Neverthless, studies on emotion and proactivity are ongoing yet there is a lack of synergy to link both fields to move forward. This edited book is aimed to disseminate new thinking in synergistic interaction of emotion and proactivity to advance the understanding of the emotional process of proactivity and forward-looking future research revenues. Starting from this motive, our book is organized into three parts: In Part I, contributors discuss and review why and how should we study proactivity from an emotion lens, offering a foundation for the basic research motive in the topic of emotion and proactivity. In particular, how emotion contributes to proactive process and what works are needed in the specific literature. In Part II, contributors discuss how emotions can shape employees' proactivity at different levels/contexts. This part addresses issues such as how emotional experiences can shape employees' proactivity at different levels (events, daily, or team), how different emotions can influence employees' proactivity (that is, positive affect against negative affect; or the various discrete emotions, like anger, fear, or pride), and how the emotions or emotion expression motivate or inhibit proactivity in an interpersonal context, and how the spillover effects of emotional experiences on proactivity occur across work and non-work domain. Finally, in Part III, the chapters discuss how proactivity can shape employees' emotional experiences and subjective well-being afterwards, a research avenue that has only attracted attention in very recent years. Below we briefly introduce each chapter in this book.

Part I: Emotion and Proactivity – Why and How it Matters

Chapter 1, by Peng, Li, and Bindl, provides a detailed quantitative and qualitative overview of 30 years (up to 2020) of published research on how emotion has been conceptualized and examined in proactivity literature to show a full picture of the 'hot' side of proactivity. Different from the previous review (Cangiano, Bindl, and Parker, 2016) that mainly relied on qualitative approaches, Peng, Li, and Bindl add bibliometric analysis (for example, Antonakis et al, 2016; Chatterjee and Sahasranaman, 2018) to visualize the evolution of affect and proactivity literature. They found that the research so far is dispersed and much more systematical effort is required. The chapter further offers a qualitative review of evidence regarding how positive and negative affect and discrete emotions both influence, or derail, proactive behaviour at work, which is an indispensable topic in proactivity literature. Peng and her colleagues further outline future research avenues in four aspects: (1) discrete emotions and proactivity; (2) affective consequences of proactivity; (3) a dynamic/reciprocal process of emotions and proactivity; and (4) the multilevel process of emotions on proactivity. These research calls all receive echoes from the other chapters in the book.

Chapter 2, by Lebel and Kamran-Morley, adds conceptual development to indicate how we can advance studies on emotion and proactivity. They firstly review how the emotion has been conceptualized in the proactivity literature and specifically focus on how emotions have been studied under the 'energized-to' mechanism, proposed by Parker, Bindl, and Strauss (2010). They identify the limitations of the existing conceptualization and investigation and indicate potential avenues for future research. Specifically, they advocate that future research should focus on how discrete emotions may impact proactivity (for example, Bindl, 2019; Lebel, 2017), especially when and why specific negative emotions, in addition to positive emotions, can motivate proactivity (Lebel, 2016; Oh and Farh, 2017). Meanwhile, they discuss why work engagement, a concept that involves cognitive, physical, as well as emotional energy for employees (Rich, Lepine, and Crawford, 2010) should not be used as an indicator to understand emotion and proactivity. Such clarification facilitates greatly for relevant research to specifically focus on emotions instead of related but non-emotion concepts.

Part II: The Role of Emotion in Shaping Proactivity in Different Contexts

As a leading chapter in this part, in Chapter 3 Ashkanasy firstly brings a multilevel model for how we can analyze the impact of emotion on employees' proactivity at different levels. The model includes five levels of analysis: (1) within-person temporal variation in emotions; (2) between-persons individual differences in experiencing and expressing emotions; (3) perception and communication of emotions in interpersonal relationships; (4) emotions in groups and teams; and (5) emotional culture and culture at the organizational level of analysis. Such a multilevel framework is both dynamic and interactive in organizational dynamics. Emotions, behaviours, and attitudes at each of the five levels, can vary moment by moment or day by day and intricately relate to corresponding variables across every level of the model. This framework helps guide future studies on emotion and proactivity and links to other chapters discussing emotion and proactivity at the work event level (Chapter 4), a within-person, cross-domain (work versus non-work) level (Chapter 5), a between-individual level (Chapter 6), and interpersonal relationship level (Chapters 7 and 8), and a team level (Chapters 9 and 10).

In Chapter 4, Ohly and Venz build a novel framework at the event level by combining the theoretical approaches of affective events theory (AET) and motivation for proactive behaviour, 'can do', 'reason to' and 'energized to'. The chapter first provides a short overview of affective events theory and previous research linking affective events to proactive behaviorbehaviour. Grounding on the overview, they incorporate the three motivationational mechanisms and the newly developed extension of AET with taxonomy of work evernt (Ohly and Schmitt, 2014 to discuss additional mechanisms on how various types of affective events can be linked to proactive behaviour via several affective states. It is because different event types are likely to foster different appraisal processes, that they may not only spur 'energized-to', but also 'reason-to' and 'can-do' motivation. More interestingly, the proposed framework also discusses how different event types affect the three motivational mechanisms and how various proactive behaviours affect the affective states in different ways. The chapter has developed novel process on how affective events can foster proactive behaviour, believe it provides a starting point for future research at event level in the emotion and proactivity field.

In Chapter 5, Ouyang focuses on employee proactivity by looking at the cross-domain interface between work and non-work. She mainly reviewed studies in two categories of non-work factors: one is off-job experiences (employees' experiences after work) and sleep. More importantly, Ouyang proposes and develops the cross-domain interplay through the emotional energy perspective. Specificially, such non-work-related factors likely influence individuals' affective experiences, which in turn act as energetical activation for employees to engage in proactive behaviour. This theoretical development provides insight into understanding the non-work antecedents of proactivity in the workplace through emotional mechanism, which is relatively overlooked in the past literature. It also expands the scope of this book to the non-work context.

In Chapter 6, Huang, Yu, and Lee focus on job insecurity (JI) (that is, the perceived powerlessness to maintain desired continuity in a threatened job situation) to understand how employees react proactively when they perceive JI and the psychological mechanisms explaining the effects. Based on the appraisal theories of emotion, people react differently to similar situations based on their appraisals of the situation and each specific emotion has specific behavioural response components (for example, Roseman, 2013) that predict actions. Thus, understanding the four discrete emotions triggered by JI – anger, frustration, fear, and shame – offers us a lens to make sense of employee proactive behaviours, together with other discretionary behaviours, when perceived JI. This conceptual work contributes our knowledge on future research directions for studying JI and employee behaviour relationships from the perspective of discrete emotions.

In Chapter 7, Wu and Li focus on how discrete other-praising emotions (that is positive emotional responses elicited by exemplary others) can shape different types of proactive behaviour. In brief, they introduce four other-praising emotions – gratitude, elevation, admiration, and awe – and elaborate on how each emotion can drive employees to engage in proactive prosocial, moral, learning and self-transcendent behaviour, respectively. Their chapter illustrates the merits of studying the role of discrete emotions in driving specific forms of proactive behaviour because it not only advances the understanding of each emotion but also enriches the differentiation of different forms of proactive behaviours. In addition, the focus on other-praising emotions helps unpack the role of exemplary others in inspiring an individual's proactive behaviour at work, contributing to the understanding of social, interpersonal influence processes in driving employees' proactivity.

In Chapter 8, Liu, Wang, and Liao explore whether and why a leader's display of anger influences employee voice and share their research journey to address this research question. Based on emotion as social information theory (van Kleef, De Dreu, and Manstead, 2010), they differentiate two types of anger: anger towards tasks (that is, task-focused anger), and anger towards employees (that is, person-focused anger). They acquired empirical evidence and found that task-focused anger signals the leader's dissatisfaction with tasks or current situations, and it would motivate employees to reflect the status quo, thus leading to upward voice. By contrast, person-focused anger signals the leader's dominance and status, and it would threaten employees' self-esteem, thus discouraging voice. In this chapter, they have elaborated on their research journey in conducting an empirical test and indicated potential puzzles for future research. Such sharing will benefit researchers who are interested in this topic.

In Chapter 9, Madrid and Patterson expand the scope of the affect and proactivity relationship to a multilevel perspective, that is, how the individual level influences the team level through interpersonal mechanisms and social integration processes. Specifically, based on the proposed process models of teamwork, affective tones and team proactive behaviours are emergent states and behavioural processes respectively, which facilitate and contribute to team performance and building the job attitudes of their members. The model contributes to our knowledge that the construction of team-level affect are those associated with the composition of individual differences, like team members' skills and personality trait. Fruthermore, the behavioural process, including voice and innovation, could construct team-level affect and reinforce each other to achieve team effectiveness. This work could be valuable for promoting intervention of teamwork processes in organizations and increasing the possibility of functional team outcomes.

In Chapter 10, Chi moves the focus to group level by focusing on group affective tone (GAT – homogeneous affective reactions within a group) and creativity, a specific form of employee proactivity. The group affective tone can be positive (PGAT) or negative (NGAT). This chapter provides a comprehensive review of the studies on GAT and reviews the theoretical foundations, empirical evidence, and unaddressed questions regarding PGAT and NGAT on team creativity. To integrate the divergent results regarding the GAT–team creativity association, Chi proposes a dual pathway model to highlight the potential mechanisms (that is, promotion- and prevention-focused actions) and boundary conditions (that is, task complexity and team supportive context) of PGAT and NGAT on team creativity. In addition to proposing the theoretical framework, the chapter offers conceptual and methodological suggestions to improve the research on GAT and team creativity in the future.

Part III: The Emotional Consequences of Proactivity

Proactive behaviours are not routine behaviours, regularly displayed during one's workday. Rather, proactivity can be considered as a deliberate self-regulatory process involving considerable volition (Bindl et al, 2012). Therefore, proactivity is not only driven and stimulated by affective states but can also likely elicit intense emotional reactions. In this part, we have one chapter focusing on the impact of proactivity on employees' well-being specifically and the other chapter framing the emotional consequences of proactivity more broadly.

In Chapter 11, Ji, Chen, and Cangiano extend the conversation to discuss how proactivity can bring consequences on employees' well-being that involves one's emotional responses to their proactive actions at work. An overview of the contemporary research on the association between proactive behaviour and well-being outcomes are started with a scientific mapping of this field of research to identify key clusters and topics. Based on two well-established perspectives adopted in this field, namely the developmental perspective and the resource-depletion perspective, the chapter summarizes the key findings concerning moderators, dynamic spirals, and alternative pathways. The journey of being proactive needs further exploration, by including more contingency factors, especially the contextual factors.

In Chapter 12, Zacher addresses the affective consequences of employees' proactive personality and behaviour. He introduces a conceptual model on the proximate consequences of (change in) proactive personality and behaviour (that is, change in the self and/ or work environment), more distal psychological consequences (that is, change in resources, need satisfaction, goal progress), and affective outcomes. Additionally, the roles of potential boundary conditions, including individual and contextual demands, resources, and barriers, as well as trait affectivity are outlined in the conceptual framework. The chapter further discusses central differences between a within-person perspective (that is, intraindividual change in proactivity and affective experiences over time) and a between-person perspective (that is, individual differences in proactive personality and behaviour and affective experiences) specifically. This work has definitely outlined a full process of how and when proactive behaviour will induce emotional consequences. These theoretical efforts are further strengthened by reviewing conceptual and empirical articles that have examined the affective consequences of different forms of proactivity.

Altogether, this book addresses issues on emotion and proactivity that have not been systematically studied and offers prospective future research directions and agenda. We believe our collection of chapters will inspire more ideas and future research to unpack the emotional journey in driving proactivity and the proactive journey in shaping emotions.

References

Antonakis, J., Bastardoz, N., Jacquart, P., and Shamir, B. (2016). Charisma: An ill-defined and ill-measured gift. *Annual Review of Organizational Psychology and Organizational Behavior*, 3, 293–319.

Ashkanasy, N. M. and Dorris, A. D. (2017). Emotions in the workplace. *Annual Review of Organizational Psychology and Organizational Behavior*, 4, 67–90.

Baker, W. E. (2019). Emotional energy, relational energy, and organizational energy: toward a multilevel model. *Annual Review of Organizational Psychology and Organizational Behavior*, 6, 373–95.

Bandura, A. (1994). Self-efficacy. In V. S. Ramachaudra (ed), *Encyclopedia of Human Behaviour*, vol 4, New York: Academic Press, pp 71–81.

Barsade, S. G., Brief, A. P., and Spataro, S. E. (2003). The affective revolution in organizational behavior: The emergence of a paradigm. In J. Greenberg (ed), *Organizational Behavior: The State of the Science*, Mahwah, NJ: Lawrence Erlbaum Associates, pp 3–52.

Barsade, S. G. and Gibson, D. E. (2007). Why does affect matter in organizations? *The Academy of Management Perspectives*, 21, 36–59.

Bindl, U. K. (2019). Work-related proactivity through the lens of narrative: investigating emotional journeys in the process of making things happen. *Human Relations*, 72(4), 615–45.

Bindl, U. K., Parker, S. K., Totterdell, P., and Hagger-Johnson, G. (2012). Fuel of the self-starter: How mood relates to proactive goal regulation. *Journal of Applied Psychology*, 97(1), 134–50.

Brief, A. P., and Weiss, H. M. 2002. Organizational behavior: Affect in the workplace. *Annual Review of Psychology*, 53(1), 279–307.

Cai, Z., Parker, S. K., Chen, Z., and Lam, W. (2019). How does the social context fuel the proactive fire? A multilevel review and theoretical synthesis. *Journal Of Organizational Behavior*, 40(2), 209–30. doi: 10.1002/job.2347.

Cangiano, F., Bindl, U. K., and Parker, S. K. (2016). The 'hot' side of proactivity: Exploring an affect-based perspective on proactivity in organizations. In S. K. Parker and U. K. Bindl (eds), *Proactivity at Work*, New York: Routledge, pp 355–84.

Chatterjee, D. and Sahasranamam, S. (2018). Technological innovation research in China and India: A bibliometric analysis for the period 1991–2015. *Management and Organization Review*, 14(1), 179–221.

Fredrickson, B. L. (2001). The role of positive emotions in positive psychology: The broaden-and-build theory of positive emotions. *American Psychologist*, 56(3), 218–26.

Frijda, N. H. (1987). Emotion, cognitive structure, and action tendency. *Cognition and Emotion*, 1, 115–43.

Grant, A. M. and Ashford, S. J. (2008). The dynamics of proactivity at work. *Research in Organizational Behavior*, 28, 3–34.

Griffin, M. A., Neal, A., and Parker, S. K. (2007). A new model of work role performance: Positive behavior in uncertain and interdependent contexts. *Academy of Management Journal*, 50, 327–347. doi: http://dx.doi.org/10.5465/AMJ.2007.24634438.

Izard, C. E. (1991). *The Psychology of Emotions*. New York: Plenum.

Lazarus, R. S. (1991). Progress on a cognitive-motivational-relational theory of emotion. *American Psychologist*, 46, 819–34.

Lebel, R. D. (2016). Overcoming the fear factor: How perceptions of supervisor openness lead employees to speak up when fearing external threat. *Organizational Behavior and Human Decision Processes*, 135, 10–21.

Lebel, R. D. (2017). Moving beyond fight and flight: A contingent model of how the emotional regulation of anger and fear sparks proactivity. *Academy of Management Review*, 42(2), 190–206.

Levenson, R. W. (1994). Human emotion: A functional view. In P. Ekman and R. J. Davidson (eds), *The Nature of Emotion: Fundamental Questions*, Oxford: Oxford University Press, 123–6.

Oh, J. K. and Farh, C. I. (2017). An emotional process theory of how subordinates appraise, experience, and respond to abusive supervision over time. *Academy of Management Review*, 42(2), 207–32.

Ohly, S. and Schmitt, A. (2014). What makes us enthusiastic, angry, feeling at rest or worried? Development and validation of an affective work events taxonomy using concept mapping methodology. *Journal of Business and Psychology*. doi: 10.1007/s10869-013-9328-3.

Mitchell, T. R. and Daniels, D. (2003). Motivation. In W. C. Borman, D. R. Ilgen, and R. J. Klimoski (eds), *Handbook of Psychology: Industrial and Organizational Psychology*, vol 12, Hoboken, NJ: John Wiley & Sons Inc, pp 225–54.

Parker, S. K., Bindl, U. K., and Strauss, K. (2010). Making things happen: A model of proactive motivation. *Journal of Management,* 36, 827–856. doi: https://doi.org/10.1177/0149206310363732.

Quinn, R. W., Spreitzer, G. M., and Lam, C. F. (2012). Building a sustainable model of human energy in organizations: Exploring the critical role of resources. *The Academy of Management Annals*, 6(1), 337–96.

Rich, B. L., Lepine, J. A., and Crawford, E. R. (2010). Job engagement: Antecedents and effects on job performance. *Academy of Management Journal*, 53(3), 617–35.

Roseman, I. J. (2013). Appraisal in the emotion system: Coherence in strategies for coping. *Emotion Review*, 5(2), 141–9.

Russell, J. A. (1980). A circumplex model of affect. *Journal of Personality and Social Psychology*, 39, 1161–78.

Russell, J. A. (2003). Core affect and the psychological construction of emotion. *Psychological Review*, 110, 145–72.

Schwarz, N. (2011). Feelings-as-information theory. *Handbook of Theories of Social Psychology*, 1, 289–308.

Sonnentag, S. and Starzyk, A. (2015). Perceived prosocial impact, perceived situational constraints, and proactive work behavior: Looking at two distinct affective pathways. *Journal of Organizational Behavior*, 36, 806–24.

van Kleef, G. A. (2009). How emotions regulate social life: The emotions as social information (EASI) model. *Current Directions in Psychological Science*, 18, 184–8.

van Kleef, G. A., De Dreu, C. K. W., and Manstead, A. S. R. (2010). An interpersonal approach to emotion in social decision making: The emotions as social information model. *Advances in Experimental Social Psychology*, 42: 45–96.

PART I

Emotion and Proactivity – Why and How It Matters

1

Feeling Energized to Become Proactive: A Systematic Literature Review of the Affect-Proactivity Link

Kelly Z. Peng, Wanlu Li, and Uta K. Bindl

There is "the affective revolution in organizational behaviour" (Barsade, Brief, and Spataro 2003, p 3) occuring early this century, which transforms the earlier belief by managers that emotions are barriers to rationality at work (for example, Barsade and Gibson, 2007). It is well-accepted that employees' behaviour at work, including proactive behaviour, is shaped by both 'cold' cognitive motivational processes as well as 'hot' affective motivational processes (Mitchell and Daniels, 2003). However, proactivity research to date has mainly focused on the 'cold' side (Parker, Bindl, and Strauss, 2010), and recently more attention is called to draw to the 'hot' side (for example, Cai et al, 2019; Cangiano, Bindl, and Parker, 2016). The increasing importance and interest in the 'hot' side affect[1] and proactivity link at work is reflected in the descriptive statistics offered by the Web of Science database (shown in Figure 1.1 and 1.2) in the past 30 years with its highest citation frequency captured in 2019. In this chapter we review the role of affective experiences – particularly, (core) affect/mood and (discrete) emotions – in shaping proactivity (detailed definitions are summarized in Table 1.1), generally defined as self-initiated action to bring about change in oneself, team, and/or the organization (Grant and Ashford, 2008).

In proactivity literature, Parker, Bindl, and Strauss (2010) identified three motivational processes that can promote proactive

Figure 1.1: Annual count of total publications that mentioned both proactive behaviours and positive/negative affect over the past 15 years

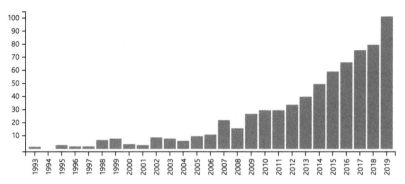

Figure 1.2: Annual counts of total publications that mentioned both proactive behaviour and emotions over the past 15 years

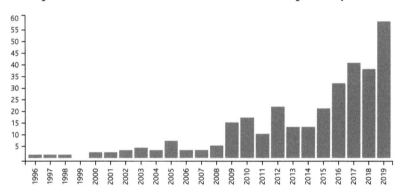

behaviours: 'can do,' 'reason to,' and 'energized to', where 'can do' and 'reason to' map onto the aforementioned 'cold' cognitive motivational pathways (Mitchell and Daniels, 2003), whereas 'energized to' captures the influence of 'hot' affective processes on proactivity. In line with the idea of the 'energized to' pathway, Quinn and Dutton (2005) defined energy (or energetic activation) as a feeling that one is eager and being vitalized to act, which serves as a motivational factor that induces the direction of human action at work. Individuals who feel emotionally energized are more engaged in their work, which has been shown to inspire employees to engage in a wide variety of proactive behaviours. For example, experiencing positive affect facilitates taking charge (Fay and Sonnentag, 2012; Zhou, Liu, Li, Cheng, and Hu, 2018) and proactivity (Cullen-Lester, Leroy, Gerbasi, and Nishii, 2016). Apart from the effect of positive feelings, the effect of negative affect is not conclusive in the literature and many scholars call for more attention (for example, Cangiano et al, 2016; Lebel and Kamran-Morley, in press; Sonnentag and Starzyk, 2015), not to say the variety of negative (discrete) emotions. As a whole, we still have limited knowledge about this 'hot' side of being proactive at work.

This chapter aims to summarize and consider future directions of literature that has focused particularly on the 'energized to' motivation to become proactive, including both (core) affect/ mood and (discrete) emotions. We build from, and substantially extend, Cangiano and colleagues' (2016) review, which unraveled 'an affect-based perspective on proactivity in organizations'. Although their review has been invaluable for scholars to understand the development of the topic, it has primarily relied on qualitative approaches for reviewing the content and topics of the extant literature. We believe that, apart from additional research published since this initial review, more knowledge may be gained from adapting systematic, quantitative-based review approaches, especially, a new method – bibliometric analysis (for example, Antonakis, Bastardoz, Jacquart, and Shamir, 2016; Chatterjee and Sahasranamam, 2018). Thus, firstly we employed this method to provide a quantitative visualization of the evolution of affect and proactivity literature according to the time sequence through 30 years (with the first publications appearing in 1989, until 2019 from the Web of Science database). After tracing the evolutionary pathway of the topic visually then we further provide a qualitative-based overview of the highly relevant and frequently cited papers and summarize the research findings on the topic. Finally, by integrating our quantitative review and qualitative summary of the topic, we provide a roadmap for future affect and proactivity research.

A quantitative-based review of the affect–proactivity link

We adopted Citespace, a Java-based visualization software created by Chen (2004), to generate bibliometric maps of the existing literature. The bibliometric maps are generated based on published articles and references cited by these published articles. By analyzing the co-cited references and their authors, there is document co-citation and author co-citation figures respectively. Further, by analyzing the citing documents, there is the keyword co-occurrence figure. Specifically, there are three resulting figures: (1) document co-citation figures (each node represents a cited document and the larger the node is, the more frequently the document has been cited); (2) author co-citation figures (each node represents a cited author and the linkages between the nodes mean that one citing document cited these two authors simultaneously and called author co-citation); (3) keywords co-occurrence figures (visualizes the most frequently occurring patterns of keywords to show the evolving research themes of this field across time) (Xie, 2015; Zhu, Song, Zhu, and Johnson, 2019).

Sample and procedure

We collected data from the Web of Science core collection database from the year 1989 to 2019 in the two key research areas of 'Management' and 'Psychology Applied', without restrictions on journal selection within these areas. We firstly identified three keywords in affective experiences: affect, emotion, and mood. We then followed the categorization by Parker and Collins (2010) to determine proactive behaviours[2]: four types of proactive work behaviours (refers to taking control of, and bringing about change within, the internal organizational environment) and another four types of proactive person–environment fit (P–E fit) behaviours[3] (refers to changing oneself or the situation to achieve greater compatibility between one's own attributes and the organizational environment) (see Table 1.1 for detailed definitions for eight types of behaviours). For each search, we combined and paired keywords from two types: one type of affective experience with one type of proactive behaviour. In sum, our sample includes 537 citing documents with 28,060 cited (secondary) documents. Following Zhu et al (2019), we also adopted five years as a slice, six slices as a whole (1990–2019) to generate findings in the context of affect and proactivity research.

Affect–proactive work behaviour link

We firstly zoom in on proactive work behaviours, including taking charge, voice, problem prevention, and personal initiatives, and their relationships with affect. As shown in Figure 1.3, *voice* is an overriding proactive work behaviour that receives the most attention from scholars over the years. Few most frequently cited papers are worth being mentioned. On the one hand, Morrison (2011) integrated previous definitions of voice and identified essential motivating factors, such as: the motives to help the organization or unit, perceived safety,

Table 1.1: Definitions of affective and proactive constructs in this chapter

	Constructs	Definition
Affect	(Core) Affect	A neurophysiological state that is consciously accessible as a simple, non-reflective feeling that is an integral blend of valence (pleasure–displeasure) and activation (sleepy–activated) values. Combinations of activation and valence result in four distinct quadrants: high-activated positive affect, low-activated positive affect, low-activated negative affect, and high-activated negative affect (Russell, 2003).
	(Discrete) Emotion	Begins with an individual's assessment of the personal meaning of some antecedent event and triggers a cascade of response tendencies which manifest across a loosely coupled component system (Fredrickson, 2001).
	Mood	Prolonged core affect with no object (simple mood) or with a quasi-Object (Russell, 2003). It is frequently categorized as positive and negative mood.
Proactive work behaviours	Taking charge	Discretionary behaviour intended to effect organizationally functional change (Morrison and Phelps, 1999).
	Voice	Discretionary communication of ideas, suggestions, concerns, or opinions about work-related issues with the intent to improve organizational or unit functioning (Morrison, 2011).
	Problem prevention	Self-directed and anticipatory action to prevent the reoccurrence of work problems (Frese and Fay, 2001).
	Personal initiative	A work behaviour that is self-starting and proactive that overcomes barriers to achieve a goal (Frese and Fay, 2001).
Proactive person-environment fit behaviours	Career initiative	Individual's active attempts to promote his or her career rather than a passive response to the job situation as given (Seibert, Kraimer, and Crant, 2001).
	Job change negotiation	A form of proactive socialization in which individuals attempt to change their job so that it better fits their skills, abilities, and preferences (Ashford and Black, 1996; Parker and Collins, 2010).
	Job crafting	The physical and cognitive changes individuals make in the task or relational boundaries of their work (Bindl et al, 2019; Wrzesniewski and Dutton, 2001).
	Feedback-seeking	Individual actions to gather information relevant to one's own behaviour; two methods are identified as inquiry and monitoring (Ashford, Blatt, and Van de Walle, 2003; Anseel et al, 2015).

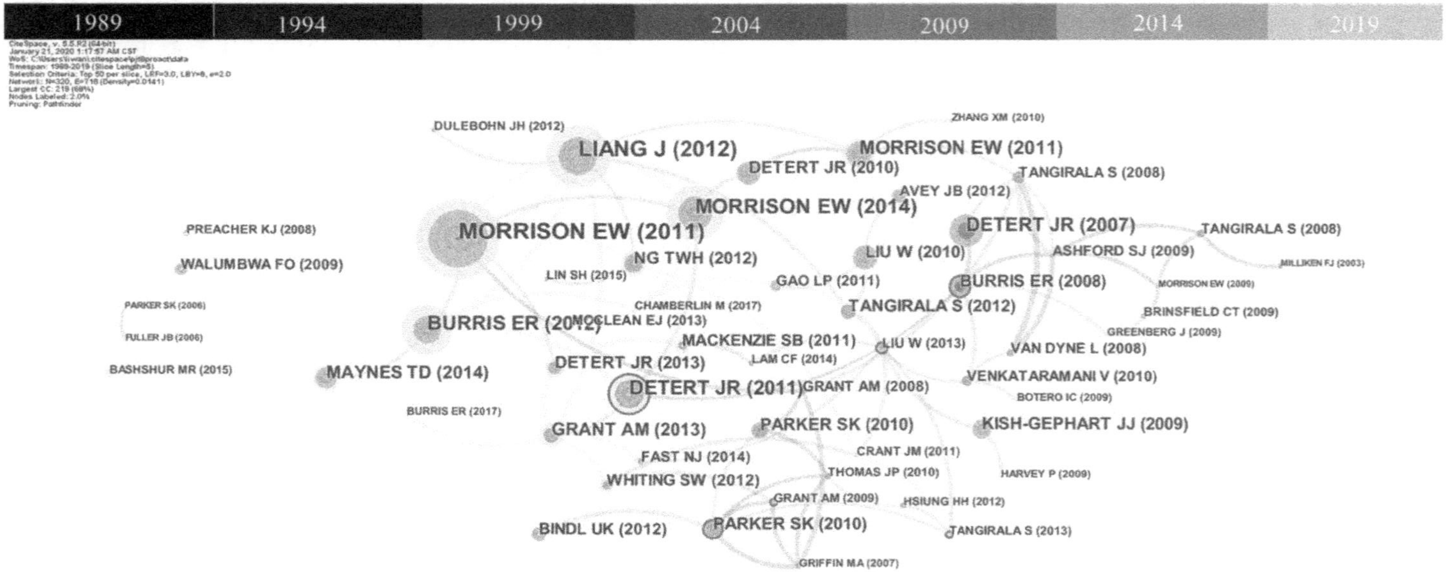

Figure 1.3: Document co-citation of proactive work behaviour and affective constructs

efficacy of voice, and potential affective motivational factors (fear, anger, anticipatory emotions, etc). Following this review, she then specified that anger may serve as a motivator that drives individuals to speak up, but that fear inhibits one to voice (Morrison, 2011; 2014). During the same period, Liang, Farh, and Farh (2012) distinguished promotive and prohibitive voice and suggested that psychological antecedents have different effects on these two different types of voice. Although this article does not directly focus on the affect and proactivity link, it sheds light on future study in choosing emotional antecedents for these two types of voice (for example, Qin, DiRenzo, Xu, and Duan, 2014 illustrated that a curvilinear relationship exists between emotional exhaustion and prohibitive voice, from a resource perspective).

On the other hand, Detert and Burris (2007) propose that voice is a risky behaviour and employees need to build psychological safety to overcome the fear and uncertain feelings in performing such behaviours. Further, Burris, Detert, and Chiaburu (2008) indicated that psychological attachment to the organization (measured as affective commitment) is unable to predict employees' voice behaviour, but detachment with the organization reduced voice to supervisor. After those initial explorations of the affect and voice link, Detert and Edmondson (2011) also added by suggesting that affect can serve as situation (information) cues for one to interpret whether it is safe to speak up based on self-protective implicit voice theories. More recently, Liu and his colleagues research (Liu et al, 2017; Liu et al, 2015) extends this idea by examining the effect of leaders' negative and peers' positive affect on focal employees' voice. This stream of researchers identified that the different emotions from different parties in the organization may have different impacts on proactive voice behaviours of focal employees. It contributes to the literature from a relational perspective on affect–proactivity link and specifically focuses on discrete emotions rather than core affect.

Although overridden by voice research, the affect–proactive work behaviours link is significantly advanced by Parker, Bindl, and Strauss (2010) to a great extent. They identified 'energized-to' as a key motivational state that enhances proactive goal generation (that is, the setting of proactivity-related goals) and sustains goal striving (that is, the implementation of proactive action at work), over and above two cognitive motivational pathways to proactivity: 'can do' and 'reason do'. Following this conceptual work in explicitly discussing the role of affect for proactivity, by way of the 'energized to' motivational mechanism, research attention shifted to focusing on various affect–proactive work behaviour links, other than the affect–voice link, especially taking positive affect into account as a key antecedent of proactive behaviours (Lam, Spreitzer, and Fritz, 2014; Bindl et al, 2012).

In Figure 1.4, the five most cited authors that have, at least briefly, discussed the affect–proactive work behaviour link, are all in voice topic, including Morrison, Van Dyne, Detert, Milliken, and LePine. In particular, Morrison, Detert, and Milliken all focused their attention on voice (or silence) behaviour as we have already reviewed in the previous section, while Van Dyne and LePine focus on voice and helping as kinds of extra role behaviour in early literature (Van Dyne and LePine, 1998). They discuss the role of emotion in voicing in different ways. Morrison (2014) suggested that fear hinders employees to speaking up, while Van Dyne Ang, and Botero (2003) indicated that fear leads to defensive voice. More recently, voice can also be identified as promotive and prohibitive voice (Liang, Farh, and Farh, 2012). In this sense, given the different nature of different types of voice, we may expect there would be differential affect–voice links, especially concerning various discrete emotions (for example, Kiewitz et al, 2016; Liu et al. 2015; Lebel, 2016; Lebel, 2017), which can also be observed in the next figure as the trend shown after 2010.

In line with Figure 1.3 and 1.4, Figure 1.5 also indicates that voice is the most studied proactive work behaviour from an affective perspective.[4] Before 2010, voice frequently co-occurred with judgment, organizational justice, and satisfaction directly. After 2010, focus turns more to discrete emotions: anger and anxiety in particular are two main emotions that have been linked with proactive behaviours in the network. For instance, from a functional perspective of emotions, anger provides an assessment of the injustice issue (Keltner and Haidt, 1999), which triggers speaking up behaviours in the organization (for example, Edwards, Ashkanasy, and Gardner, 2009; Harvey, Martinko, and Douglas, 2009). In addition, depression, positive affect and positive emotion as independent nodes isolate from the major network. This suggests that these are still inconclusive and wait to be further explored in this field.

Affect–proactive person–environment fit behaviour link

We now turn to proactive P–E fit behaviours, including job crafting, feedback-seeking, job change negotiation, and career initiative behaviours, and their relationship with affect. Both document (Figure 1.6) and author co-citation figures (Figure 1.7) indicate that, although this topic has received less attention (the highest co-citation frequency of key references is 13 and no burst paper[5] was found in

Figure 1.4: Author co-citation of proactive work behaviour and affective constructs

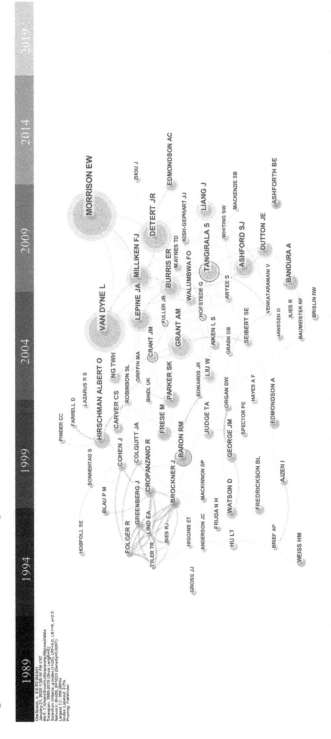

Figure 1.5: Keyword co-occurrence of proactive work behaviour and affective constructs

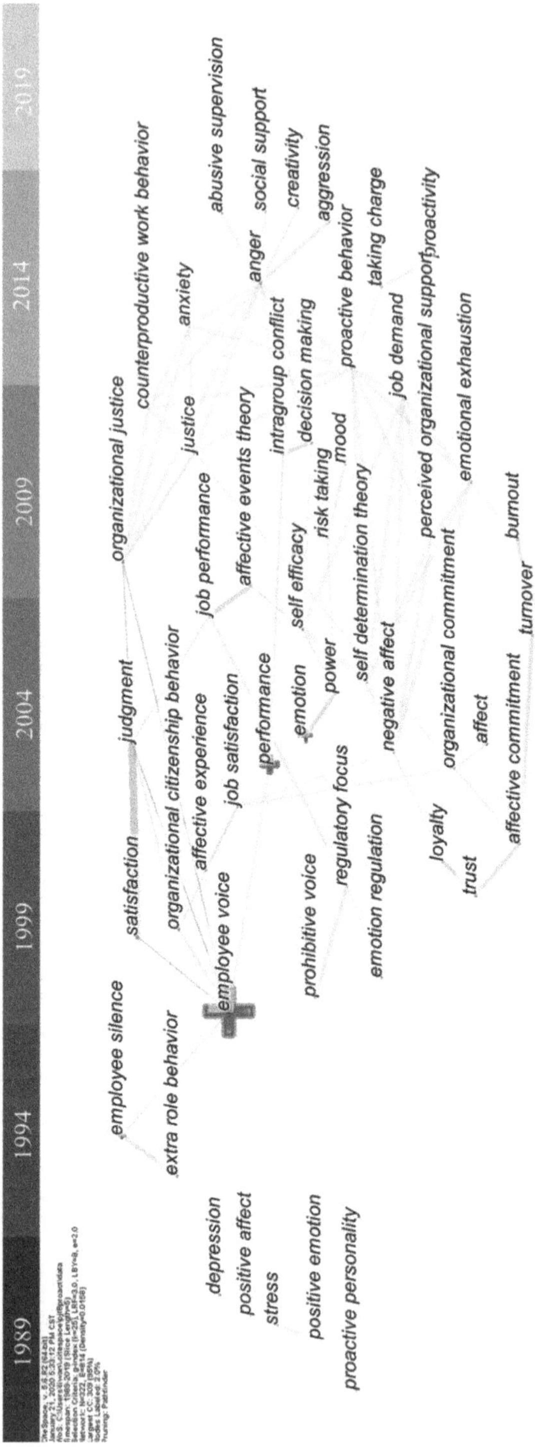

Figure 1.6: Document co-citation of proactive P–E fit behaviours and affective constructs

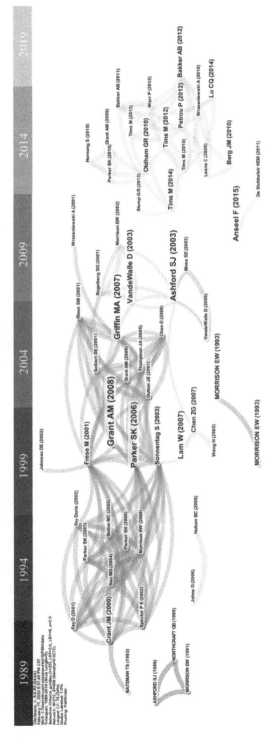

this category in the latter qualitative review), researchers have mainly studied this topic from 1995 until 2014, with less linkage shown in more recent research. The major part of the network represents the development of feedback-seeking behaviours, which are defined as the conscious devotion of effort towards determining the correctness and adequacy of behaviours for attaining valued end states (Ashford, 1986). From Figure 1.6, we can infer that Grant and Ashford (2008) is one of the most critical nodes that summarized previous literature and offered a new direction for future research.

According to Figure 1.7, two important landmark authors in this field are Ashford and Morrison. Ashford is the most significant researcher in the proactive behaviour field, especially feedback-seeking behaviour. She suggests feedback is evaluative information about the self, so that it is more emotionally charged (Ashford, Blatt, and Van de Walle, 2003). Meanwhile, Morrison also concentrated on feedback- and information-seeking among newcomers, and their socialization process (for example, Morrison, 1993a; 1993b; Morrison, Chen, and Salgado, 2004). These results showed an initial connection between negative discrete emotions, such as fear, and feedback-seeking behaviour. For example, seeking feedback requires individuals to cope with their emotions for potential negative information afterwards, such as fear and depression (for example, Pettit and Joiner, 2001). Thus, current literature, which is yet very limited, mainly focuses on affective consequences of proactivebehaviours, which we will discuss in more detail in the qualitative review section.

According to Figure 1.8, feedback-seeking behaviour is still the central topic discussed under this category. Despite this, the figure shows that before 2000 this proactivity literature tended to discuss the negative affective constructs, including anxiety, shyness, depression, shame, and guilt (as shown on the left side of the network), while there were few direct investigations on the specific affect–feedback-seeking behaviour link. In the next ten years (1999–2009) affective constructs, such as depression, anxiety, guilt, and shame, appear as node, they are not directly linked with feedback-seeking behaviours (or job crafting). Instead, these emotions are linked to affective responses to feedback, say affective consequence of sought feedback, which is consistent with our observation as above. As a whole, there is much less research focus on P–E fit proactive behaviour and their association with affective experience, compared to proactive work behaviours' literature.

Figure 1.7: Author co-citation of proactive P–E fit behaviours and affective constructs

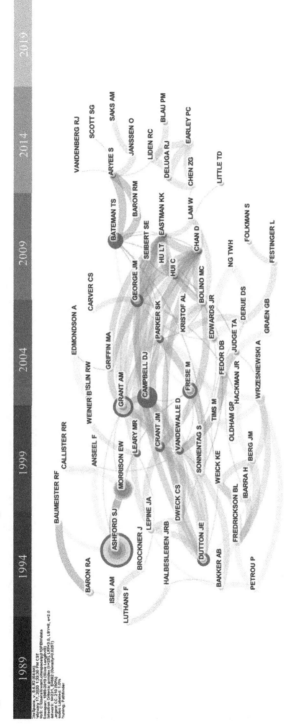

Figure 1.8: The keywords co-occurrence of proactive P–E fit behaviour and affective constructs

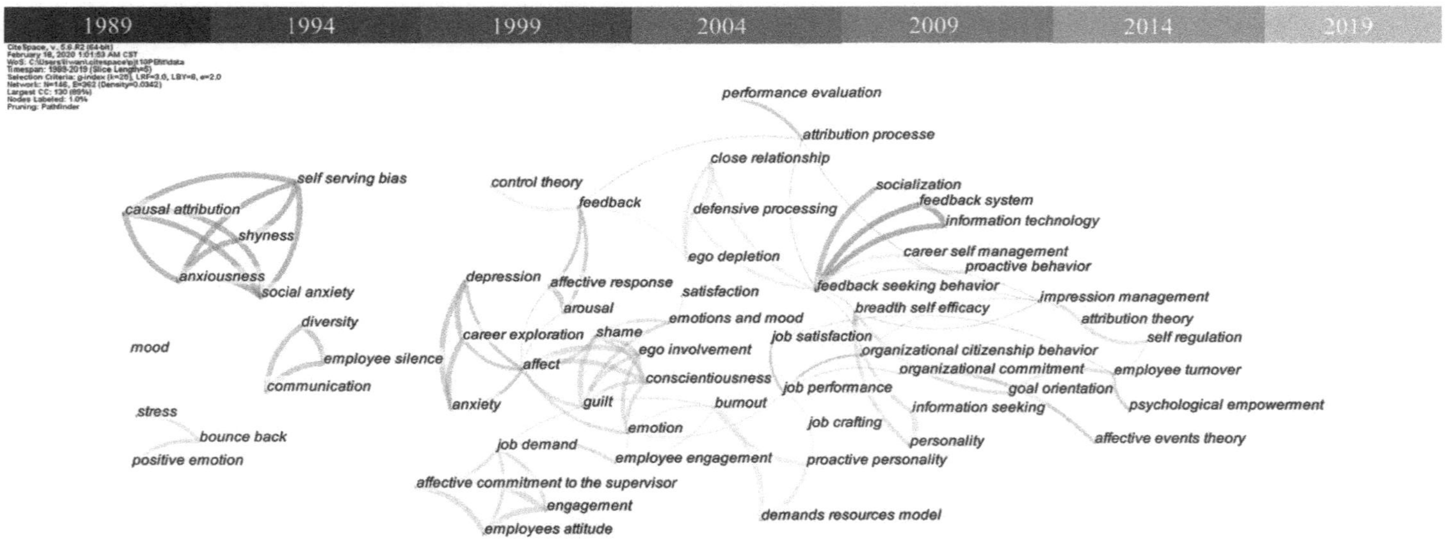

Qualitative-based review on highly relevant and frequently cited papers

To get more overarching insights into the affect–proactivity link, we further focus on those highly relevant and frequently cited papers (updated to July 2020) from the quantitative review. Following the guidance of the quantitative visualization results, we narrowed our focus on those papers that (1) directly tested the relationship between proactive behaviours and affective constructs; and (2) had a citation frequency of larger than or equal to 2. As a result, 30 papers in proactive work behaviour and 13 papers in proactive P–E fit behaviours are presented in Tables 1.2 and 1.3. In the following sections, we will firstly critically review and summarize the major theoretical lens in the affect–proactivity link. Then, by zooming in on different types of affect, we will provide a review of the articles that directly focused on positive and negative affect and proactivity, and ones that directly focused on (discrete) emotions and proactivity respectively. Then, there is a review of articles that focused on affective consequences of proactivity, which is a more emerging topic in the literature. Lastly, we will briefly discuss the articles that involve emotional regulations, say ability in handling emotions, and study its role in proactivity, which could also inform the affect–proactivity link.

Theoretical lenses in the affect–proactivity link

There are two major theoretical lenses to understand the affect–proactivity link: the energy perspective and the information perspective. The first lens considers positive affect or emotions as resources that energize proactivity. Conservation of resources theory (Hobfall, 1989) and job demands-resources model (Demerouti et al, 2001) both indicate the importance of owning enough resource, such as energies (Hobfoll, 1989), for employees to be proactive (Ouyang et al, 2019; Parker et al, 2006). Emotional resource is recognized by the theories that are essential factors and in turn stimulate proactivity. Broaden-and-build theory (Fredrickson, 2001; Conway et al, 2013) offers a more specific explanation as it suggests that positive emotions broaden our mind, which in turn leads to an enlarged action repertoire and behaviour change. More recently, Quinn, Spreitzer, and Lam (2012) integrate six related theories, including the above-mentioned perspectives, to describe the causal loops of the dynamic of human energy. The energy perspective provides a useful theoretical framework that, along with the 'energized to' mechanism (Parker et al, 2010), can explain the role of affect in motivating proactivity, especially positive affect. According to Figures 1.1 and 1.2, research on the affect–proactivity link got more attention in the last five to ten years (including a dramatic increase since 2015), which happens to be in co-occurrence with receipt of most research attention in the energy perspective since 2015 and 2016 (Baker, 2019). This co-occurrence may imply that not only will there be more research on affective experiences in proactivity, but that the energy perspective may become one of the dominant theoretical frame in this topic.

The second theoretical lens focuses on the information conveyed in one's feelings, regarded as social cues (called information perspective hereafter). Feeling-as-information theory proposes that different feelings convey different information, which then impact on judgment (Schwarz, 2011). Specifically, positive affect signals that things proceed smoothly and the environment is safe, while negative affect reveals the judgment of a problematic situation in intrapersonal context. The former signals could either demotivate to be proactive as 'everything goes alright' and it is nature to keep status quo (e.g. Lam, et al, 2014); or motive to be proactive (Sonnentag and Starzyk, 2015) as it increases employees' confidence in initiating proactive actions and helps them deal with any risks or obstacles that occur during the proactive process (Foo, Uy, and Baron, 2009). The latter signals, theoretically, may motivate one to act. However, empirically, that still waits to be answered, as studies on negative affect reported mixed findings, which will be elaborated in the next section. Different from feeling-as-information theory, which focuses on intra-personal effect, affect/emotion-as-social-information focused interpersonal effect, in particular the social-function of others' emotional expression (van Kleef, 2009). Observing the displayed emotions, the observer processes this cue through affective reactions and inferences, and decides on the following behaviours. For example, a partner's display of anger might serve as a sign that the observer did something wrong, and he/she might subsequently have reflections on his/ her recent behaviours. Additionally, affective event theory (Weiss and Cropanzano, 1996) is another frequently adopted theory to explain how affective events at the workplace, both intra-personal and interpersonal events, have effects on job outcomes. As a whole, all three theories together explain why and how others' (discrete) emotions (such as those of peers or leaders) may impact on employee's proactive behaviours.

Positive and negative affect and proactivity

Theories of (core) affect describe emotional experience as falling along two dimensions: valence (pleasant versus unpleasant feelings) and activation (high versus low), from which results four quadrants (Russell, 2003). The majority of research focuses on individuals' valence of affective experience, while some studies may indicate that activation level of affect may play a role (for example, Bindle et al, 2012; Hsiung and Tsai, 2017; Ouyang et al, 2019). Another recent review, in book chapter, reveals that proactivity research has primarily focused on only two of these quadrants: activated positive and activated negative affect; with the majority of this research focused on positive (core) affect (Cangiano et al, 2016). To better examine the relationship between core affect and various proactive behaviours, the following section reviews the most relevant studies by distinguishing the two categories of proactive behaviours.

Proactive work behaviours

With a comprehensive review on 30 papers (see Table 1.2), we will summarize both the intra-personal versus interpersonal perspective and the positive versus negative affect. Intra-personally, it is well established that state positive affect is positively related to engaging in proactive behaviours, including job crafting and personal initiative (for example, Den Hartog and Belschak, 2007; Fay and Sonnentag, 2012; Fritz and Sonnentag, 2009; Kwon, Kim, and Kim, 2019). According to energy perspective, positive affect, as a kind of resource, enlarges one's repertoire of attention, cognition, and action (Fredrickson, 2001) to go beyond routine behaviour and being proactive (Den Hartog and Belschak, 2007; Fay and Sonnentag, 2012; Fritz and Sonnentag, 2009). According to information perspective, positive affect also serves as a cue of a safety environment and leads to more initiative behaviours (for example, Fay and Sonnentag, 2012). Nevertheless, too much positive affect might indicate a signal of change that the status quo is unnecessary, which could lead to less proactive behaviour. That is, there could be an inverse effect on proactive behaviours (Lam et al, 2014).

However, the role of negative affect in predicting proactive work behaviours is much more inconclusive. Den Hartog and Belschak (2007) reported a positive association between negative affect and personal initiative behaviours (yet Study 2 received no significant support). Later on, researchers considered activation level of affect to further investigate the effect of negative affect. Still, mixed findings were found.[6] Bindl et al (2012) found that low-activated negative affect correlated with envisioning

Table 1.2: The 30 highly relevant and frequently cited articles and book chapters during 1990–2020 of proactive work behaviour with affective constructs

Proactive behaviours	No. of articles	Key references	Overarching theoretical framework	Major affect-related constructs investigated	Types of evidence	The role of the affective constructs
Proactive behaviour	10	Barclay and Kiefer (2019)	Appraisal theory	Anxiety	ESM	Me
		Bindl et al (2012)	Broader affect–behaviour links	High/low-activated positive/negative mood	Cross-sectional and longitudinal survey	IV
		Fay and Sonnentag (2012)	Broaden-and-build model and the mood-as-information approach	Positive state affect/negative trait affect	ESM	IV
		Grant, Parker, and Collins (2009)	Attribution theory	Low negative affect	Dyadic cross-sectional survey	Mo
		Jiang et al (2020)	Affect-as-information theory	Leader positive/negative affect presence	Cross sectional survey	IV
		Lam, Spreitzer, and Fritz (2014)	Broaden-and-build and emotion-as-information theories	Positive affect	Dyadic cross-sectional and cross-lagged survey	IV (Curve)
		Lebel (2017)	Discrete perspectives on emotion	Anger and fear	Theoretical paper	IV

Table 1.2: The 30 highly relevant and frequently cited articles and book chapters during 1990–2020 of proactive work behaviour with affective constructs (continued)

Proactive behaviours	No. of articles	Key references	Overarching theoretical framework	Major affect-related constructs investigated	Types of evidence	The role of the affective constructs
		Liu et al (2020)	Activity theory and Broaden-and-build theory	Happiness	Cross-sectional survey	IV
		Ouyang et al (2019)	Conservation of resources theory	High-activated positive affect	ESM	Me
		Wu and Chen (2019)	Social learning theory and conservation of resources theory	Collective thriving	Cross-lag survey	Me
Voice	13	Kish-Gephart, Detert, and Trevino (2009)	Functional perspective in discrete emotion	Fear	Theoretical	IV
		Grant (2013)	Emotion regulation theory	Emotion regulation	Cross-lag survey	IV
		Milliken, Morrison, and Hewlin (2003)	N/A	Fear	Qualitative	IV
		Xu, Loi, and Lam, (2015)	Conservation of resources theory	Emotional exhaustion	Two-wave survey	Me
		Liu et al (2017)	Emotion-as-social-information perspective	Leaders' negative affect	ESM	IV

(continued)

Table 1.2: The 30 highly relevant and frequently cited articles and book chapters during 1990–2020 of proactive work behaviour with affective constructs (continued)

Proactive behaviours	No. of articles	Key references	Overarching theoretical framework	Major affect-related constructs investigated	Types of evidence	The role of the affective constructs
		Liu et al (2015)	Affect-as-social-information perspective	Peers' positive mood	Scenario and round-robin survey	IV
		Madrid, Patterson, and Leiva (2015)	Core affect and cognitive appraisal theories	High/low activated negative core affect (within-person)	Diary study	IV
		Chamberlin, Newton, and Lepine (2017)	N/A	Fear	Meta-analysis	IV
		Harvey, Martinko, and Douglas (2009)	Attribution theory	Anger/pity/compassion	Theoretical	Me
		Lebel (2016)	Functional view of emotion	Fear (external threat)	Dyadic cross-sectional and cross-lag survey	IV
		Michalak, Kiffin-Petersen, and Ashkanasy (2019)	Affective events theory	Fear	Qualitative	IV
		Hsiung and Tsai (2017)	Dual-pathway model of mood and social information processing theory	Activated negative mood	Cross-lag survey	Mo
		Xu et al (2020)	Cost-benefit framework	Manager's positive mood	Cross-lag survey	Mo

Table 1.2: The 30 highly relevant and frequently cited articles and book chapters during 1990–2020 of proactive work behaviour with affective constructs (continued)

Proactive behaviours	No. of articles	Key references	Overarching theoretical framework	Major affect-related constructs investigated	Types of evidence	The role of the affective constructs
Personal initiative	4	Den Hartog and Belschak (2007)	Broaden-and-build model	Positive affect	Cross-sectional survey	IV
		Hong et al (2016)	Theory of proactive motivation	Activated positive affect	Cross-lag survey	Me
		Schraub et al (2014)	Affective events theory	Leaders' emotion Management-employee affective well-being	Cross-lag survey	IV-Me
		Zacher et al (2019)	Control-process theory on affect	Positive/negative mood-emotional engagement/exhaustion	Three-waves longitudinal	Me-DV
Taking charge	3	Bal, Chiaburu, and Diaz (2011)	Psychological contract breach	Emotional regulation	Cross-sectional survey	Mo
		Fritz and Sonnentag (2009)	Broaden-and-build theory	Positive and negative affect	ESM	IV
		Müceldili and Erdil (2016)	N/A	Workplace fun	Cross-sectional survey	IV

Note: IV = independent variable; Mo = moderator; Me = mediator; DV = dependent variable; ESM = experience sampling method.

element of proactivity only, rather than other element, especially the enacting one. However, low-activated negative affect associated with silence at work, as it enhanced reflection over behaviour (Madrid, Patterson, and Leiva, 2015). More recently, Sonnentag and Starzyk (2015) found negative affect only relates to issue identification, pointing out the potential problem at work, rather than change implementation. In this sense, what matters is the specific types of proactive behaviour. Besides the main effect, negative affect may serve as a moderator. For example, activated negative affect together with voice climate jointly serve as moderators that reduce the negative impact of power distance orientation on voice (Hsiung and Tsai, 2017). Another example, employees' expression of low negative affect helps to get credit from supervisors for performing proactive behaviours in performance appraisal (Grant, Parker, and Collins, 2009). The studies show that the effects of negative affect are more complicated and/or subtle, and need more future research.

Apart from intra-personal perspective, researchers also found that positive or negative affect of others plays an important role in interpersonal influence on proactive behaviours. Yet, these are very initial efforts mainly based on information perspective. There is research that investigated how others' affect had an impact on focal proactive work behaviours, such as leaders and peers (for example, Jiang et al, 2020; Liu et al, 2015; Liu et al, 2017, Xu et al, 2020). Specifically, they followed the affect-as-social-information perspective (van Kleef, 2009) and suggested that peers' positive mood display offered focal employees' psychological safety and may lead to voice. Liu et al (2017) also found that although leader's both positive and negative affect can boost subordinates' voice behaviour, the mechanisms are different. Such relationship in positive affect could be accounted for through employees' psychological safety directly via emotional contagion mechanism (through employees' own positive affect). For negative affect, both the emotional contagion mechanism and the informational perspective does not work, which is interesting to further explore. As a whole, along with our observations in intrapersonal perspective, we still know very little about how negative affect works on motivating proactivity at work.

Proactive personal–environment fit behaviours

The 13 researches that focus on proactive P–E fit behaviour and affect are centered on feedback-seeking behaviours and job crafting. On the one hand, the focal employee's positive affect are shown to play an important role in promoting one's job crafting behaviours (for example, Kwon, Kim, and Kim, 2019; Mäkikangas., Bakker, and Schaufeli, 2017;

Rogala and Cieslak, 2019). Positive affect could also promote feedback-seeking behaviours, yet through taking the available information be perceived as useful for realistic self-assessment and potential long-term improvement afterwards (Gervey, Igou, and Trope, 2005). On the other hand, concerning feedback-seeking behaviours in particular, feedback provider's affect state, such as leader, may also influence the proactive P–E fit behaviour of the focal employee (for example, Makikangas et al, 2017). It is easy to understand that the perceived positive affect from the feedback giver positively relates to employees' feedback-seeking behaviours, whereas negative mood prohibits feedback-seeking behaviours (Ang et al, 1993; Trope and Neter, 1994; as shown in Table 1.3). Additionally, positive affect could be the consequence/responses to feedback (Christensen-Salem et al, 2018), which will be discussed in the 'emotional consequence of proactivity' section specifically. In short, consistent with our observation in quantitative review, the direct investigation on the positive/negative affect–P–E fit proactive behaviour is very much limited and we know very little in the literature, especially for negative affect.

Discrete emotions and proactivity

In understanding the role of discrete emotion in proactivity, researchers mainly adopt the functional perspective (as shown in Tables 1.2 and 1.3), which concentrates more on the nature and functions of emotions. Unlike the dimensional approach to affect, which oversimplifies as positive and negative dimensions (for example, Russell and Carroll, 1999; Watson, Clark, and Tellegen, 1988), the discrete approach appreciates the complexity of discrete emotions and addresses their nuanced meanings (for example, Arnold, 1960; Lazarus, 1966, 1968; Roseman, 1984; Roseman, Spindel, and Jose, 1990). They argue that emotion is not a general subjective feeling, but instead that each emotion bears a unique functional, adaptive and relational meaning (for example, Izard, 1991; Izard, Ackerman, Schoff, and Fine, 2000; Lazarus, 1991). As a result, each emotion should link to specific functions and thus lead to specific behavioural tendencies (for example, Fredrickson, 2001; Frijda, 1987; Frijda, Kuipers, and Ter Schure, 1989; Izard, 1991; Izard et al, 2000; Lazarus, 1991; Levenson, 1994; Oatley and Jenkins, 1996; Tooby and Cosmides, 1990). In application in the emotion–proactivity link, interestingly, the functional perspective is twisted with either energy or informational perspective, or both. Some (discrete) emotion may serve as energy (for example, joy, vitality, etc), some may serve as information (for example, fear, shame, etc) or social cues (for example, leaders' anger) to show their differential functions.

Table 1.3: The 13 influential articles during 1990–2019 of proactive P–E fit behaviours

Proactive behaviours	No. of articles	Key References	Overarching theoretical framework	Major affective constructs investigated	Types of evidence	The role of the affective construct
Feedback-seeking	7	Qian et al (2016)	Social cognitive theory	Emotional regulation	Dyadic cross-sectional survey	Mo
		Trope and Neter (1994)	N/A	Feedback provider's positive/negative affect	Experiment	IV
		Ang et al (1993)	Control theory	Feedback provider's affect	Experiment	IV
		Gervey, Igou, and Trope (2005)	Mood-as-resource approach	Focal positive/neutral mood	Experiments	IV
		Pettit and Joiner (2001)	Self-verification theory	Depressed	Experiment	DV
		Christensen-Salem et al (2018)	Affective events theory	Activated positive affect	ESM	DV
		van Hooff and van Hooft (2014)	Job demands–resources model	Boredom	Cross-sectional survey	DV, Mo
Job crafting	5	Makikangas, Bakker, and Schaufeli (2017)	Job demands–resources theory	Team members' positive affect	ESM	IV
		Kwon, Kim, and Kim (2019)	Affective event theory	Daily positive affect	ESM	IV

Table 1.3: The 13 influential articles during 1990–2019 of proactive P–E fit behaviours (continued)

Proactive behaviours	No. of articles	Key References	Overarching theoretical framework	Major affective constructs investigated	Types of evidence	The role of the affective construct
		Pekaar, Bakker, van der Linden, Born, and Sirén (2018)	EI theory	Self/other-focused emotional regulation	Weekly diary	IV and Me
		Rogala and Cieslak (2019)	Broaden-and-build theory	Positive emotions	Cross-lag survey	IV
Career initiative	1	Hardin et al (2007)	Theory of self-discrepancies	Negative / positive affect	Cross-sectional survey	DV

Note: IV = independent variable; Mo = moderator; Me = mediator; + = significantly positively correlated; n.s. = non-significant; DV = dependent variable; ESM = experience sampling method.

We now review findings on discrete emotions and the two types of proactive behaviour. In particular, for proactive P–E fit behaviours, as included in Table 1.3, two researches focused on discrete emotions in this category – depressed and boredom – which are related to feedback-seeking behaviour (Petti and Joiner, 2001) and job crafting respectively. They take discrete emotion, say depression and boredom respectively, as consequence. In this case, the detailed review will be shown in the next section specifically. We will only focus on proactive work behaviour to review as below.

Proactive work behaviour

Among various discrete emotions, anger and fear are two emotions at the centre stage in this field. From a functional perspective, anger serves as a sign of cheating and of harm being inflicted (Levenson, 1999). It also reveals a response to a loss or lack of reward that is contributed to another target, usually due to the target doing something wrong (Schwarz, 2011). That is, individuals who experience anger usually tend to show eagerness to revise or to change the status quo. Empirically, anger is positively related to whistleblowing and voice (Harvey, Martinko, and Douglas, 2009; Lebel, 2017). Fear serves as a sign of danger and threat from the environment and others (Levenson, 1999). High intensity fear tends to lead to an immediate act, for example, speaking up, whereas low intensity fear is prone to link with silence (Mar, Newton, and Lepine, 2017, Kish-Gephart Detert, Trevino, and Edmondson, 2009, Michalak, Kiffin-Petersen, and Ashkanasy, 2019; Milliken, Morrison, and Hewlin, 2003). The targets of the (discrete) emotion also (such as fear of within group threat or outgroup threat) may lead to differential behaviours. For instance, Lebel (2016) suggested that fear of external threat (for example, economic downturn) increases the employee's voice, whereas fear of being viewed and labelled in a negative way may lead to silence (Milliken, Morrison, and Hewlin, 2003).

Apart from anger and fear, other discrete emotions have differential effect on various proactive behaviours. Such as, anxiety that is generated by unfair events triggers problem prevention behaviours as a response (Barclay and Kiefer, 2019); happiness elicits proactivity towards team (Liu et al, 2020); collective positive emotion related to proactive customer service behaviour positively (Wu and Chen, 2019). There is some research that pays attention to some less studied emotion and its effect on different proactive behaviours, such as workplace fun positively related to taking charge (Müceldili and Erdil, 2016).

The emotional consequences of proactivity

Proactivity is not only shaped by affective experience but can also shape one's affective experience afterwards. Research on emotional consequences of proactivity has been rare but started attracting scholars' attention recently. In understanding affective consequence of being proactive, energy perspective provides a useful theoretical lens. Proactive behaviours also work as an approach to create resources or energy into the affective process afterwards through differential mechanisms. For example, job crafting as a tool could boost employees' affective well-being by accumulating job resources through relational mechanisms (for example, the increasing of leader–member exchange), cognitive mechanisms (for example, increasing self-efficacy (Van Den Heuvel, Demerouti, and Peeters, 2015) or reducing self-discrepancy (Hardin, Weigold, Robitschek, and Nixon, 2007)) and affective mechanisms (for example, positive affect (Van Den Heuvel et. al, 2015), such as reducing boredom (Van Hooff and Van Hooft, 2014), and increasing job passion (Teng, 2019)).

Meanwhile, being proactive may also lead to loss of resources or energy, as the actions cost extra efforts and result in more job demands. Two recent articles show that the affective consequences of proactivity could be in dual process, namely change both positive and negative affect afterwards, yet in different ways. Zacher et al (2019) found change in personal initiative negatively predicted change in positive mood directly (independent of perceived organizational support) and, whereas it positively predicted change in negative mood only when perceived organizational support was low. Cangiano, Parker, and Yeo (2019) propose there is energy-generating pathway and strain pathway to explain how proactive work behaviours induced both positive and negative emotional consequences respectively. In the same pattern, daily proactivity will directly and independently fuel daily vitality, while it leads to more end-of-workday anxiety only when employees reported a high level of punitive supervision. Interestingly, for feedback-seeking behaviours, such dual process may depend on the contents of the sought feedback or the coping strategy towards them. Specifically, a diary study suggests that the negative ones among sought feedbacks increase one's depression level (Pettit and Joiner, 2001), while the acceptance of sought feedback can give rise to positive affect and in turn increased creativity (Christensen-Salem et al, 2018). As a whole, it is very likely that the energy-generating pathway towards positive affective consequence will be more salient, while the energy-depletion (strain) pathway towards negative affective consequence is more complicated and more contextual constraints should be taken into consideration.

Emotional regulation and proactivity

For both proactive work behaviour and proactive P–E fit behaviours, other than the direct test of the emotion–proactivity link, it is worth noting the role of the ability of using and managing one's emotions, which mostly play as moderator (for example, Bal, Chiaburu, and Diaz, 2011). More specifically, Lebel (2017) proposed that emotional regulation is an important moderator that may determine whether fear and anger could be transformed as motive into proactivity. Emotional regulation may also serve as an important antecedent. For example, it fosters job crafting and in turn earns higher level of weekly energy (Pekaar et al, 2018); or it predicts to seek more feedback from both supervisors and subordinates (Qian et al, 2016). Although this research is not directly relevant to the affect–proactivity link, it would inform the topic that such ability could also works as resources in being proactive, or help to better utilize the emotional resources to be proactive.

A short outlook

Taking all the above together, we may see that employees should experience an emotional journey in being proactive at work. By understanding affective experiences throughout the full engagement in proactivity at work, we could have rich understandings on the affect–proactivity link. Drawing from qualitative accounts of employees, Bindl (2019) identified three emotional journeys in the process of proactivity (issue identification, implementation, and reflection): proactivity-as-frustration; proactivity-as-growth; and proactivity-as-threat. Across three journeys, employees typically started with negative emotions, such as anger and frustration, induced by the identification of a dysfunctional work situation. However, while employees in the threat journey stopped their proactive efforts due to experienced fear, and employees in the frustration journey remained negative in their accounts of proactive efforts, and reduced their engagement in future proactive behaviours, employees in the growth journey began to experience a shift from negative to positive emotions, such as feeling happy, proud and excited, which helped to boost future proactive behaviours. Such dynamic process should be of great interest and deserves further exploration with different empirical efforts in the future.

Conclusion

Before drawing conclusion from this review, we would also like to note that our review may be limited in two major ways. First, we constrained our database of this review from the year 1990 to 2020 (July), which does not include papers that were published either before 1990 or later than 2020. Hence, it is also important for future researchers to keep up to date if they need to capture the dynamic trend of the affect–proactivity literature. Second, according to our purpose of this review, we separated different types of proactive behaviours into two general categories and reviewed them separately. Hence, this review may lack of knowledge of the connections, links, and interactions between these two categories. For future researchers, an overall review is recommended to show the overall development of the proactivity literature.

Despite these limitations, we are confident to draw several conclusions based on our review. First, there are two major theoretical perspectives guiding research on the affect–proactivity link. The more dominant one is the energy perspective (Quinn and Dutton, 2005): affective experiences, especially positive ones, serve as energy/ resource that is a strong motivator for individuals being 'energized to' be proactive at work. Meanwhile, being proactive may also bring affective consequences through dual-process – either energy-generating or energy-depletion pathway. The other one is the information perspective: it indicates that positive versus negative affect and various discrete emotions convey differential information to self and others, and in turn conveys different 'signals' to proactive behaviour. Basically, this perspective is mainly adopted to explain how negative affect or discrete emotions works for proactive behaviours. Second, the quantitative result indicates that affective experiences, including positive and negative affect/mood, and discrete emotions (for example, fear, anger, and anxiety), began to receive attention from researchers in the last two decades. And, in each category, voice and feedback-seeking behaviour are two behaviours that have been studied most in the affect–proactive link, respectively. The other types of proactive behaviours and overall proactivity, taking as work performance (Griffin et al, 2007), are lacking of investigation in the literature. Third, the qualitative review shows that the valence and activation level of affect shows effects on proactivity differently. Comparably, the valence dimension (positive versus negative) is more salient in affecting proactivity than the activation dimension. Meanwhile, negative affect is still inconclusive no matter as antecedents or consequences of proactivity. Fourth, as both quantitative and qualitative reviews show, discrete emotions and proactivity link is an under-investigated topic, with very limited knowledge. According to the functional perspective of emotion, each discrete emotion should link to specific functions and thus lead to specific behavioural tendencies. Although we have known that anger and fear may lead to voice with boundary conditions, we still know very little about the other emotions and their link with various proactive behaviours.

Future research

Based on our review and major conclusions above, future research is called to expand and advance our knowledge on the role of affect in shaping and being shaped by proactivity. As the above short outlook noted, gaining rich understandings on the affective/emotional journey in dynamic ways will be the final goal of the topic. Here we provide several specific directions for future empirical explorations to contribute and attain the final goal. First, future research in the affect–proactivity link may involve the role of discrete emotion more. Take guilt as an example: in organizations, injustice, work–family conflict, and negative feedback make employees feel guilty, if they believe that they are the cause of the problems, and they may repair the condition by initiating changes (Ilies et al, 2013). In this sense, it will expand our understandings of the motivational process of the affect–proactivity link by going beyond anger and fear, which have been the most widely studied in proactivity research, to gain a more comprehensive insight into human motivation, and its link with proactivity at work. It is also echoed in the 'affective revolution in organizational behaviour' that there should be 'a shift in emphasis to balance the interest in moods with an interest in discrete emotions' (Brief and Weiss, 2002, p 298) and 'the focus would be on what is driving each of the processes and the different outcomes resulting from that particular discrete emotion' (Ashkanasy and Dorris, 2017, p 70). In addition, we also found that there are mixed and inconclusive results of negative affect and negative-natured discrete emotions (the majority in the discrete emotion family) in the literature. This may also imply the necessity for more detailed research into each kind of discrete emotion.

Second, the affective consequences of proactivity need more exploration. The route could be multidirectional; as a very recent attempt by Bindl (2019) has suggested, there are routes to experiencing feelings of growth, frustration, and threat. On the one hand, we need more sense of when and why we will choose a certain route rather than others. Note that, although proactivity has overall been found to be beneficial for organizations, the extent to which any of these implications are relevant for a particular organization may well depend on how ready the organization is to welcome employee initiative. On the other hand, we may focus on the various discrete emotions to disclose the variety and dynamics of the affective consequences of proactive behaviour within various natures and contexts. For example, anxiety may be highly salient in the initial phase of proactivity, in the context of issue identification; while pride may be very salient in the completion phase of proactivity, in the context of issue selling. In this vein, investigating employees' affective experiences of proactivity across behaviour natures and contexts is important.

Third, besides the further investigation of the affective antecedents and consequences of proactivity, we cannot overlook the potential in a reciprocal process of the affect–proactivity link. The hedonic contingency theory (Wegener and Petty, 1994, 1996) is a theory about mood management that suggests that happy individuals are interested in sustaining their positive affect state, whereas sad individuals are interested in affective repair. Employee proactive behaviours as we discussed above could bring about positive or negative results, which may prompt the process to go in different directions. If employees are 'energized to' be proactive by positive affect or a certain positive emotion, they may be more likely to keep feeling happy. Nevertheless, if employees are 'informed by' negative affect to find something wrong, they may resort to proactive behaviour to make change, which may either neutralize or transform the feelings afterwards. In this way, we may outline various affective journeys through a reciprocal perspective. It will be of great value in the within-person context to understand a dynamic process of the affect–proactivity link, rather than the current dominant static view in the literature.

Last but not the least, a multilevel process of the affect–proactivity link would be a promising and important direction. Based on the current review, the energy perspective is becoming a dominant perspective for examining the link. Combined with the recent development in this theoretical perspective, emotion could contribute to individual, team, and organizational level energy (for example, Baker, 2019), which, in turn, could 'energize to' proactivity at various levels. Currently, focus has been very much on the individual level, but team-wide affective processes, or even emotional climate or culture at the organizational level, could all affect this link in different ways. Although multilevel efforts have been made in the proactivity literature (for example, Hong et al, 2016), there is a lack of focus on this in the affect–proactivity link and this perspective will also inform the understanding of the affective/emotional journey of proactivity by including contextual and individual factors at different levels as mentioned.

Notes

[1] Based on our search, we found that articles that focus on mood distinguished into positive and negative mood, and using the PANAS scale as a measurement (for example, Liu et al, 2015; Tsai, Chen, and Liu, 2007, Zacher et al, 2019); for an exception, see Bindl et al (2012) who focused more comprehensively on affective quadrants of the circumplex (Russell, 2003). Therefore, in this chapter, we combined the searching results here and the following quantitative literature review work throughout. As a result, we adopted affect hereafter to include (core) affect and mood.

[2] Innovation and creativity are excluded in this review as they are relatively independent from proactive literature.

[3] Proactive strategic behaviours including issue selling and strategic scanning, refers to taking control of and causing change in the broader organization's strategy and its fit with the external environment (Parker and Collins, 2010), which is excluded in this review due to the limited quantity of research.

[4] It is worthwhile to note, although job performance and job satisfaction are two frequently mentioned outcomes in the figure, the former construct closely linked with OCBs in the years 1995–2000 and co-occurred with voice; the latter one is a more recent studied outcome of voice behaviour. That is, they are not directly related to the relationships of affect and proactivity.

[5] Burst refers to the sharp increase of keywords or references in a specific area, which suggests the emerging trend in the field (Kim and Chen, 2015).

[6] Activation concerns a person's 'state of readiness for action or energy expenditure' (Russell, 2003), and represents 'motivational intensity' or 'the impetus to act' (Gable and Harmon-Jones, 2010). Combinations of activation and valence result in four distinct quadrants (see Table 1.1).

References

Ang, S., Cummings, L. L., Straub, D. W., and Earley, P. C. (1993). The effects of information technology and the perceived mood of the feedback giver on feedback seeking. *Information Systems Research*, 4, 240–61.

Anseel, F., Beatty, A. S., Shen, W., Lievens, F., and Sackett, P. R. (2015). How are we doing after 30 years? A meta-analytic review of the antecedents and outcomes of feedback-seeking behavior. *Journal of Management*, 41, 318–48.

Antonakis, J., Bastardoz, N., Jacquart, P., and Shamir, B. (2016). Charisma: An ill-defined and ill-measured gift. *Annual Review of Organizational Psychology and Organizational Behavior*, 3, 293–319.

Arnold, M. B. (1960). *Emotion and personality*. New York: Columbia University Press.

Ashford, S. J. (1986). Feedback-seeking in individual adaptation: A resource perspective. *Academy of Management Journal*, 29, 465–87.

Ashford, S. J. and Black, J. S. (1996). Proactivity during organizational entry: The role of desire for control. *Journal of Applied Psychology*, 81, 199–214.

Ashford, S. J., Blatt, R., and Van de Walle, D. (2003). Reflections on the looking glass: A review of research on feedback-seeking behavior in organizations. *Journal of Management*, 29, 773–99.

Ashkanasy, N. M. and Dorris, A. D. (2017). Emotions in the workplace. *Annual Review of Organizational Psychology and Organizational Behavior*, 4, 67–90.

Baker, W. E. (2019). Emotional energy, relational energy, and organizational energy: toward a multilevel model. *Annual Review of Organizational Psychology and Organizational Behavior*, 6, 373–95.

Bakker, A. B., Demerouti, E., and Sanz-Vergel, A. I. (2014). Burnout and work engagement: The JD-R approach. *Annual Review of Organizational Psychology and Organizational Behavior*, 1, 389–411.

Bal, P. M., Chiaburu, D. S., and Diaz, I. (2011). Does psychological contract breach decrease proactive behaviors? The moderating effect of emotion regulation. *Group and Organization Management*, 36, 722–58.

Barclay, L. J. and Kiefer, T. (2019). In the aftermath of unfair events: Understanding the differential effects of anxiety and anger. *Journal of Management*, 45, 1802–29.

Barsade, S. G., Brief, A. P., and Spataro S. E. (2003). The affective revolution in organizational behavior: The emergence of a paradigm. In J. Greenberg (ed), *Organizational Behavior: The State of the Science: 3–51*, Mahwah, NJ: Lawrence Erlbaum.

Barsade, S. G., and Gibson, D. E. (2007). Why does affect matter in organizations? *The Academy of Management Perspectives*, 21, 36–59.

Berg, J. M., Grant, A. M., and Johnson, V. (2010). When callings are calling: Crafting work and leisure in pursuit of unanswered occupational callings. *Organization Science*, 21, 973–94.

Bindl, U. K. (2019). Work-related proactivity through the lens of narrative: investigating emotional journeys in the process of making things happen. *Human Relations*, 72, 615–45.

Bindl, U. K., Parker, S. K., Totterdell, P., and Hagger-Johnson, G. (2012). Fuel of the self-starter: How mood relates to proactive goal regulation. *Journal of Applied Psychology*, 97, 134–50.

Bindl, U. K., Unsworth, K. L., Gibson, C. B., and Stride, C. B. (2019). Job crafting revisited: Implications of an extended framework for active changes at work. *Journal of Applied Psychology*, 104, 605–28. http://dx.doi.org/10.1037/apl0000362.

Brief, A. P. and Weiss, H. M. (2002). Organizational behavior: Affect in the workplace. *Annual Review of Psychology*, 53, 279–307.

Burris, E. R., Detert, J. R., and Chiaburu, D. S. (2008). Quitting before leaving: the mediating effects of psychological attachment and detachment on voice. *Journal of Applied Psychology*, 93, 912–22.

Cai, Z., Parker, S. K., Chen, Z., and Lam, W. (2019). How does the social context fuel the proactive fire? A multilevel review and theoretical synthesis. *Journal of Organizational Behavior,* 40, 209–30.

Cangiano, F., Bindl, U. K., and Parker, S. K. (2016). The hot side of proactivity: Exploring an affect-based perspective on proactivity in organizations. In S. K. Parker and U. K. Bindl (eds), *Proactivity at Work: Making Things Happen in Organizations,* New York: Routledge, pp 355–484).

Cangiano, F., Parker, S. K., and Yeo, G. B. (2019). Does daily proactivity affect well-being? The moderating role of punitive supervision. *Journal of Organizational Behavior,* 40, 59–72.

Chamberlin, M., Newton, D. W., and Lepine, J. A. (2017). A meta-analysis of voice and its promotive and prohibitive forms: Identification of key associations, distinctions, and future research directions. *Personnel Psychology,* 70, 11–71.

Chatterjee, D. and Sahasranamam, S. (2018). Technological innovation research in China and India: A bibliometric analysis for the period 1991–2015. *Management and Organization Review,* 14, 179–221.

Chen, C. (2004). Searching for intellectual turning points: Progressive knowledge domain visualization. *Proceedings of the National Academy of Sciences,* 101, 5303–10.

Chen, C. (2006). *Information Visualization: Beyond the Horizon.* New York: Springer Science and Business Media.

Chen, C. (2012). *Turning Points: The Nature of Creativity.* Berlin, Heidelberg: Springer Science and Business Media.

Christensen-Salem, A., Kinicki, A., Zhang, Z., and Walumbwa, F. O. (2018). Responses to feedback: The role of acceptance, affect, and creative behavior. *Journal of Leadership and Organizational Studies,* 25, 416–29.

Conway, A. M., Tugade, M. M., Catalino, L. I., and Fredrickson, B. L. (2013). The broaden-and-build theory of positive emotions: Form, function and mechanisms. *Oxford Handbook of Happiness,* 17–34.

Cullen-Lester, K. L., Leroy, H., Gerbasi, A., and Nishii, L. (2016). Energy's role in the extraversion (dis)advantage: How energy ties and task conflict help clarify the realtionship between extraversion and proactive performance. *Journal of Organizational Behaviour,* 37, 1003–22. https://doi.org/10.1002/job.

Demerouti, E., Bakker, A. B., Nachreiner, F., and Schaufeli, W. B. (2001). The job demands-resources model of burnout. *Journal of Applied Psychology,* 86, 499–512.

Den Hartog, D. N. and Belschak, F. D. (2007). Personal initiative, commitment and affect at work. *Journal of Occupational and Organizational Psychology,* 80, 601–22.

Detert, J.R. and Burris, E.R. (2007). Leadership behavior and employee voice: Is the door really open? *Academy of Management Journal,* 50, 869–84.

Detert, J. R. and Edmondson, A. C. (2011). Implicit voice theories: Taken-for-granted rules of self-censorship at work. *Academy of Management Journal,* 54, 461–88.

Edwards, M. S., Ashkanasy, N. M., and Gardner, J. (2009). Deciding to speak up or to remain silent following observed wrongdoing: The role of discrete emotions and climate of silence. *Voice and Silence in Organizations*, 83–109.

Ekman, P. 1992. An argument for basic emotions. *Cognition and Emotion*, 6, 169–200.

Fay, D. and Sonnentag, S. (2012). Within-person fluctuations of proactive behavior: How affect and experienced competence regulate work behavior. *Human Performance*, 25, 72–93.

Foo, M. D., Uy, M. A., and Baron, R. A. (2009). How do feelings influence effort? An empirical study of entrepreneurs' affect and venture effort. *Journal of Applied Psychology*, 94, 1086–94.

Fredrickson, B. L. (2001). The role of positive emotions in positive psychology: The broaden-and-build theory of positive emotions. *American Psychologist*, 56, 218.

Frese, M., and Fay, D. (2001). Personal initiative: an active work for the 21st century. *Research in Organizational Behavior*, 23, 133–87.

Frijda, N. H. (1987). Emotion, cognitive structure, and action tendency. *Cognition and Emotion*, 1, 115–43.

Frijda, N. H., Kuipers, P., and Ter Schure, E. (1989). Relations among emotion, appraisal, and emotional action readiness. *Journal of Personality and Social Psychology*, 57, 212.

Fritz, C. and Sonnentag, S. (2009). Antecedents of day-level proactive behavior: A look at job stressors and positive affect during the workday. *Journal of Management*, 35, 94–111.

Gable, P. and Harmon-Jones, E. (2010). The blues broaden, but the nasty narrows: Attentional consequences of negative affects low and high in motivational intensity. *Psychological Science,* 21, 211–15.

Gervey, B., Igou, E. R., and Trope, Y. (2005). Positive mood and future-oriented self-evaluation. *Motivation and Emotion, 29*, 267–294.

Grant, A. M. and Ashford, S. J. (2008). The dynamics of proactivity at work. *Research in Organizational Behavior*, 28, 3–34.

Grant, A. M., Parker, S., and Collins, C. (2009). Getting credit for proactive behavior: Supervisor reactions depend on what you value and how you feel. *Personnel Psychology*, 62, 31–55.

Grant, A. M. (2013). Rocking the boat but keeping it steady: The role of emotion regulation in employee voice. *Academy of Management Journal*, 56, 1703–23.

Griffin, M. A., Neal, A., and Parker, S. K. (2007). A new model of work role performance: Positive behavior in uncertain and interdependent contexts. *Academy of Management Journal*, 50, 327–47.

Hardin, E. E., Weigold, I. K., Robitschek, C., and Nixon, A. E. (2007). Self-discrepancy and distress: The role of personal growth initiative. *Journal of Counseling Psychology*, 54, 86–92.

Harvey, P., Martinko, M. J., and Douglas, S. C. (2009). Causal perceptions and the decision to speak up or pipe down. *Voice and Silence in Organizations*, 63–82.

Hobfoll, S. E. (1989). Conservation of resources: A new attempt at conceptualizing stress. *American Psychologist*, 44, 513–24.

Hong, Y., Liao, H., Raub, S., and Han, J. H. (2016). What it takes to get proactive: An integrative multilevel model of the antecedents of personal initiative. *Journal of Applied Psychology*, 101, 687–701.

Hsiung, H. H. and Tsai, W. C. (2017). The joint moderating effects of activated negative moods and group voice climate on the relationship between power distance orientation and employee voice behavior. *Applied Psychology*, 66, 487–514.

Ilies, R., Peng, A. C., Savani, K., and Dimotakis, N. 2013. Guilty and helpful: an emotion-based reparatory model of voluntary work behavior. *Journal of Applied Psychology*, 98, 1051–9.

Izard, C. E. (1991). *The Psychology of Emotions*. New York: Plenum.

Izard, C. E., Ackerman, B. P., Schoff, K. M., and Fine, S. E. (2000). Self-organization of discrete emotions, emotion patterns, and emotion-cognition relations. In M. Lewis and I. Granic (eds.), *Emotion, Development, and Self-Organization: Dynamic Systems Approaches to Emotional Development* (pp. 15–36). New York: Cambridge University Press.

Jiang, J., Dong, Y., Li, B., Gu, H., and Yu, L. (2020). Do feelings matter? The effect of leader affective presence on employee proactive customer service performance. *International Journal of Contemporary Hospitality Management*, 32, 2305–23.

Keltner, D. and Haidt, J. (1999). Social functions of emotions at four levels of analysis. *Cognition and Emotion*, 13, 505–21.

Kiewitz, C., Restubog, S. L. D., Shoss, M. K., Garcia, P. R. J. M., and Tang, R. L. (2016). Suffering in silence: Investigating the role of fear in the relationship between abusive supervision and defensive silence. *Journal of Applied Psychology*, 101, 731–42.

Kim, M. C. and Chen, C. (2015). A scientometric review of emerging trends and new developments in recommendation systems. *Scientometrics*, 104, 239–63.

Kish-Gephart, J. J., Detert, J. R., Treviño, L. K., and Edmondson, A. C. (2009). Silenced by fear: The nature, sources, and consequences of fear at work. *Research in Organizational Behavior*, 29, 163–93.

Kwon, N., Kim, M., and Kim, M. S. (2019). Daily positive affect and job crafting: The cross level moderating effects of individuals' resources. *Sustainability*, 11(16), 4286.

Lam, C. F., Spreitzer, G., and Fritz, C. (2014). Too much of a good thing: Curvilinear effect of positive affect on proactive behaviors. *Journal of Organizational Behavior*, 35, 530–46.

Lazarus, R. S. (1966). *Psychological Stress and the Coping Process*. New York: McGraw-Hill

Lazarus, R. S. (1968). *Emotions and Adaptation: Conceptual and Empirical Relations*. In Nebraska symposium on motivation. University of Nebraska Press.

Lazarus, R. S. (1991). Progress on a cognitive-motivational-relational theory of emotion. *American Psychologist*, 46, 819–34.

Lebel, R. D. (2016). Overcoming the fear factor: How perceptions of supervisor openness lead employees to speak up when fearing external threat. *Organizational Behavior and Human Decision Processes,* 135, 10–21.

Lebel, R. D. (2017). Moving beyond fight and flight: A contingent model of how the emotional regulation of anger and fear sparks proactivity. *Academy of Management Review*, 42, 190–206.

Lebel, R. D. and Kamran-Morley, D. (in press) Clarifying the conceptualization of the Energized-to pathway of proactivity. In K. Z. Peng, and C. H. Wu (eds), *Emotion and Proactivity at Work: Prospects and Dialogues*, Bristol: Bristol University Press.

Levenson, R. W. (1994). Human emotion: A functional view. *The nature of emotion: Fundamental questions*, 1, 123–6.

Levenson, R. W. (1999). The intrapersonal functions of emotion. *Cognition and Emotion*, 13, 481–504.

Liang, J., Farh, C. I., and Farh, J. L. (2012). Psychological antecedents of promotive and prohibitive voice: A two-wave examination. *Academy of Management Journal,* 55, 71–92.

Liu, M. L., Hsieh, M. W., Hsiao, C., Lin, C. P., and Yang, C. (2020). Modeling knowledge sharing and team performance in technology industry: The main and moderating effects of happiness. *Review of Managerial Science*, 14(3), 587–610.

Liu, W., Song, Z., Li, X., and Liao, Z. (2017). Why and when leaders' affective states influence employee upward voice. *Academy of Management Journal*, 60, 238–63.

Liu, W., Tangirala, S., Lam, W., Chen, Z., Jia, R. T., and Huang, X. (2015). How and when peers' positive mood influences employees' voice. *Journal of Applied Psychology*, 100, 976–89.

Madrid, H. P., Patterson, M. G., and Leiva, P. I. (2015). Negative core affect and employee silence: How differences in activation, cognitive rumination, and problem-solving demands matter. *Journal of Applied Psychology*, 100, 1887–98.

Mäkikangas, A., Bakker, A. B., and Schaufeli, W. B. (2017). Antecedents of daily team job crafting. *European Journal of Work and Organizational Psychology*, 26(3), 421–33.

Michalak, R. T., Kiffin-Petersen, S. A., and Ashkanasy, N. M. (2019). 'I feel mad so I be bad': The role of affect, dissatisfaction and stress in determining responses to interpersonal deviance. *British Journal of Management*, 30, 645–67.

Milliken, F. J., Morrison, E. W., and Hewlin, P. F. (2003). An exploratory study of employee silence: Issues that employees don't communicate upward and why. *Journal of Management Studies*, 40, 1453–76.

Mitchell, T. R. and Daniels, D. (2003). Observations and commentary on recent research in work motivation. *Motivation and Work Behavior*, 7, 225–54.

Morrison, E. W. (1993a). Newcomer information seeking: Exploring types, modes, sources, and outcomes. *Academy of Management Journal*, 36, 557–89.

Morrison, E. W. (1993b). Longitudinal study of the effects of information seeking on newcomer socialization. *Journal of Applied Psychology*, 78, 173–83.

Morrison, E. W., Chen, Y. R., and Salgado, S. R. (2004). Cultural differences in newcomer feedback seeking: A comparison of the United States and Hong Kong. *Applied Psychology*, 53, 1–22.

Morrison, E. W. and Phelps, C. C. (1999). Taking charge at work: Extrarole efforts to initiate workplace change. *Academy of Management Journal*, 42, 403–19.

Morrison, E. W. (2011). Employee voice behavior: Integration and directions for future research. *Academy of Management Annals*, 5, 373–412.

Morrison, E. W. (2014). Employee voice and silence. *Annual Review of Organization Psychology and Organization. Behavior*, 1, 173–97.

Müceldili, B. and Erdil, O. (2016). Finding fun in work: The effect of workplace fun on taking charge and job engagement. *Procedia-Social and Behavioral Sciences*, 235, 304–12.

Oatley, K. and Jenkins, J. M. (1996). *Understanding Emotions*. Cambridge, MA: Blackwells.

Ouyang, K., Cheng, B. H., Lam, W., and Parker, S. K. (2019). Enjoy your evening, be proactive tomorrow: How off-job experiences shape daily proactivity. *Journal of Applied Psychology*, 104, 1003.

Parker, S. K., Bindl, U. K., and Strauss, K. (2010). Making things happen: A model of proactive motivation. *Journal of Management*, 36, 827–56.

Parker, S. K. and Collins, C. G. (2010). Taking stock: Integrating and differentiating multiple proactive behaviors. *Journal of Management*, 36, 633–62.

Parker, S. K., Williams, H. M., and Turner, N. (2006). Modeling the antecedents of proactive behavior at work. *Journal of Applied Psychology*, 91, 636–52.

Pekaar, K. A., Bakker, A. B., van der Liden, D., Born, M. P., and Siren, H. J. (2018). Managing own and others' emotions: A weekly study on the enactment of emotional intelligence. *Journal of Vocational Behavior*, 109, 137–51.

Pettit, J., Joiner, T.E. (2001). Negative-feedback seeking leads to depressive symptom increases under conditions of stress. *Journal of Psychopathology and Behavioral Assessment*, 23, 69–74. https://doi.org/10.1023/A:1011047708787.

Qian, J., Han, Z. R., Guo, Z., Yang, F., Wang, H., and Wang, Q. (2016). The relation of feedback-seeking motives and emotion regulation strategies to front-line managers' feedback source profiles: A person-centered approach. *Journal of Management and Organization*, 22, 68–79.

Qin, X., DiRenzo, M. S., Xu, M., and Duan, Y. (2014). When do emotionally exhausted employees speak up? Exploring the potential curvilinear relationship between emotional exhaustion and voice. *Journal of Organizational Behavior*, 35, 1018–41.

Quinn, R. W. and Dutton, J. E. (2005). Coordination as energy-in-conversation. *Academy of Management Review*, 30, 36–57.

Quinn, R. W., Spreitzer, G. M., and Lam, C. F. (2012). Building a sustainable model of human energy in organizations: Exploring the critical role of resources. *The Academy of Management Annals*, 6, 337–96.

Rogala, A. and Cieslak, R. (2019). Positive emotions at work and job crafting: Results from two prospective studies. *Frontiers in Psychology*, 10, 2786.

Roseman, I. J. (1984). Cognitive determinants of emotion: A structural theory. *Review of Personality and Social Psychology*, 5, 11–36.

Roseman, I. J., Spindel, M. S., and Jose, P. E. (1990). Appraisals of emotion-eliciting events: Testing a theory of discrete emotions. *Journal of Personality and Social Psychology*, 59, 899–915.

Russell, J. A. (2003). Core affect and the psychological construction of emotion. *Psychological Review*, 110, 145–72.

Russell, J. A. and Carroll, J. M. (1999). On the bipolarity of positive and negative affect. *Psychological Bulletin*, 125, 3–30.

Schraub, E. M., Michel, A., Shemla, M., and Sonntag, K. (2014). The roles of leader emotion management and team conflict for team members' personal initiative: A multilevel perspective. *European Journal of Work and Organizational Psychology*, 23, 263–76.

Schwarz, N. (2011). Feelings-as-information theory. *Handbook of Theories of Social Psychology*, 1, 289–308.

Seibert, S. E., Kraimer, M. L., and Crant, J. M. (2001). What do proactive people do? A longitudinal model linking proactive personality and career success. *Personnel Psychology*, 54, 845–74

Sonnentag, S. (2003). Recovery, work engagement, and proactive behavior: a new look at the interface between nonwork and work. *Journal of Applied Psychology*, 88, 518–28.

Sonnentag, S. and Starzyk, A. (2015). Perceived prosocial impact, perceived situational constraints, and proactive work behavior: Looking at two distinct affective pathways. *Journal of Organizational Behavior*, 36, 806–24.

Tavares, S. M. (2016). How does creativity at work influence employee's positive affect at work?. *European Journal of Work and Organizational Psychology*, 25, 525–39.

Teng, H. Y. (2019). Job crafting and customer service behaviors in the hospitality industry: Mediating effect of job passion. *International Journal of Hospitality Management*, 81, 34–42.

Tooby, J. and Cosmides, L. (1990). The past explains the present: Emotional adaptations and the structure of ancestral environments. *Ethology and Sociobiology*, 11, 375–424.

Trope, Y. and Neter, E. (1994). Reconciling competing motives in self-evaluation: the role of self-control in feedback seeking. *Journal of Personality and Social Psychology*, 66, 646–57.

Tsai, W. C., Chen, C. C., and Liu, H. L. (2007). Test of a model linking employee positive moods and task performance. *Journal of Applied Psychology*, *92*, 1570–1583.

Van den Heuvel, M., Demerouti, E., and Peeters, M. C. (2015). The job crafting intervention: Effects on job resources, self-efficacy, and affective well-being. *Journal of Occupational and Organizational Psychology*, 88, 511–32.

Van Dyne, L. and LePine, J. A. (1998). Helping and voice extra-role behaviors: Evidence of construct and predictive validity. *Academy of Management Journal*, 41, 108–19.

Van Dyne, L, Ang, S., and Botero, I. C. (2003). Conceptualizing employee silence and employee voice as multidimensional constructs. *Journal of Management Studies*, 40, 1359–92.

van Hooff, M. L. and van Hooft, E. A. (2014). Boredom at work: Proximal and distal consequences of affective work-related boredom. *Journal of Occupational Health Psychology*, 19, 348–59.

van Kleef, G. A. (2009). How emotions regulate social life: The emotions as social information (EASI) model. *Current Directions in Psychological Science*, 18, 184–8.

Watson, D., Clark, L. A., and Tellegen, A. (1988). Development and validation of brief measures of positive and negative affect: the PANAS scales. *Journal of Personality and Social Psychology*, 54, 1063–70.

Wegener, D. T. and Petty, R. E. (1994). Mood management across affective states: The hedonic contingency hypothesis. *Journal of Personality and Social Psychology*, 66, 1034–48.

Wegener, D. T. and Petty, R. E. (1996). Effects of mood on persuasion. Processes: Enhancing, reducing, and biasing scrutiny of attitude-relevant. In L. L. Martin and A. Tesser (eds.), *Striving and Feeling: Interactions Among Goals, Affect, and Self-regulation*, 329–62. Mahwah, NJ: Lawrence Erlbaum.

Weiss, H. M. and Cropanzano, R. (1996). Affective Events Theory: A theoretical discussion of the structure, causes and consequences of affective experiences at work. In B. M. Staw and L. L. Cummings (eds), *Research in Organizational Behavior: An Annual Series of Analytical Essays and Critical Reviews*, 18, 1–74. London: JAI Press.

Wrzesniewski, A. and Dutton, J. E. (2001). Crafting a job: Revisioning employees as active crafters of their work. *Academy of Management Review*, 26, 179–201.

Wu, C. M. and Chen, T. J. (2019). Inspiring prosociality in hotel workplaces: Roles of authentic leadership, collective mindfulness, and collective thriving. *Tourism Management Perspectives*, 31, 123–35.

Xie, P. (2015). Study of international anticancer research trends via co-word and document co-citation visualization analysis. *Scientometrics*, 105, 611–22.

Xu, E., Huang, X., Ouyang, K., Liu, W., and Hu, S. (2020). Tactics of speaking up: The roles of issue importance, perceived managerial openness, and managers' positive mood. *Human Resource Management*, 59, 255–69.

Xu, A. J., Loi, R., and Lam, L. W. (2015). The bad boss takes it all: how abusive supervision and leader-member exchange interact to influence employee silence. *The Leadership Quarterly*, 26, 763–74.

Zacher, H., Schmitt, A., Jimmieson, N. L., and Rudolph, C. W. (2019). Dynamic effects of personal initiative on engagement and exhaustion: The role of mood, autonomy, and support. *Journal of Organizational Behavior*, 40, 38–58.

Zhou, K., Liu, W., Li, M., Cheng, Z., and Hu, X. (2018). The relationship between narcissism and taking charge: The role of energy at work and hierarchical level. *Psychological Reports*, 123, 472–87.

Zhu, J., Song, L. J., Zhu, L., and Johnson, R. E. (2019). Visualizing the landscape and evolution of leadership research. *The Leadership Quarterly*, 30, 215–32.

2

Igniting Initiative: Clarifying the Conceptualization of the Energized-to Pathway of Proactivity

R. David Lebel and Daniya Kamran-Morley

Organizations are increasingly looking for ways to motivate their employees to be self-starting and to act in advance (Campbell, 2000). With increasing uncertainty, technological change, and competition, leaders simply cannot prescribe in advance what employees need to effectively carry out their jobs (Griffin, Neal, and Parker, 2007). Organizational scholars have spent considerable time investigating the antecedents of proactivity, defined as 'anticipatory action that employees take to impact themselves and/or their environments' (Grant and Ashford, 2008, p 8). Parker, Bindl, and Strauss (2010) developed a prominent model guiding research on proactivity, describing can-do, reason-to, and energized-to motivational pathways. The can-do pathway, involving employees' perceptions of whether they feel capable of proactivity, is well established. For example, several studies demonstrate that self-efficacy is a primary antecedent of a wide range of proactive behaviours (for example, Den Hartog and Belschak, 2012; Parker and Collins, 2010; Parker, Williams, and Turner, 2006). Similarly well-established is the reason-to pathway, involving perceptions that being proactive is worthwhile. In particular, studies demonstrate the important role of felt responsibility (Morrison and Phelps, 1999) and organizational commitment (Rank et al, 2007) in motivating proactive behaviour.

However, less is known about the energized-to pathway, which involves the affective energy to be proactive. A recent review found significantly fewer studies on this pathway compared to the can-do and reason-to pathways (Cai et al, 2019). Furthermore, the limited research on the energized-to pathway has produced mixed results. For example, while Bindl at al (2012) found that positive affect predicted multiple aspects of proactive behaviour, Hong et al (2016) found no relationship between positive affect and personal initiative. Not only is there less empirical research on the energized-to pathway, there is also less conceptual development describing why certain energized-to states should impact proactivity. For example, Parker, Bindl, and Strauss (2010) provide substantial detail describing the reason-to pathway via a number of mechanisms, including expectancy and intrinsic motivation, but only describe one theoretical pathway in regard to energized-to motivation (that is, core affect). This limitation significantly narrows the theoretical focus to positive affective states and also ignores alternative theories – such as discrete emotions theory – that can provide additional insights into the energized-to pathway. Because of the mixed empirical results and a lack of conceptual development, we believe that the time is right for a closer examination of why and how the energized-to pathway motivates proactive behaviour.

The purpose of this chapter is to enhance our understanding of proactive behaviour at work by adding more conceptual development to the energized-to pathway. First, we argue that future research should move beyond conceptualizing energized-to motivation as core affect and towards a focus on how discrete emotions may impact proactivity (Bindl, 2019; Lebel, 2017). As argued below, doing so sheds light on a wider range of emotional states, including negative ones, that can motivate proactivity (Lebel, 2016; Oh and Farh, 2017). Second, we argue that the role of work engagement as an energized-to mechanism should be clarified. Work engagement is a major source of cognitive, physical, and emotional energy for employees (Rich, Lepine, and Crawford, 2010), and thus has clear links to the energized-to pathway. However, proactivity scholars have muddied the waters by describing the effect of engagement on proactivity in terms of *both* affect and cognition (for example, Cai et al, 2019). Thus, we examine the link between work engagement and proactivity in greater detail, specifying when engagement supplies the affective or cognitive motivation to be proactive.

In this chapter, we will describe how the energized-to motivational state has been conceptualized in the proactivity literature, briefly review findings from research examining the effects of this 'hot' pathway on proactivity, and then describe potential avenues to enhance theory and research on this topic.

Current conceptualizations of energized-to proactive motivation

Defining affect

Beginning with Parker, Bindl, and Strauss's (2010) model of proactivity, scholars have primarily described energy in terms of affective, or emotional, forces. Affective experience can take a number of forms, including state and trait sources of emotion (Barsade and Gibson, 2007). Feeling states include discrete emotions and moods. Discrete emotions (including anger, fear, guilt, sadness, and happiness) are elicited by a specific cause or event, involve physiological reactions, and are short-lived, relatively intense experiences (Frijda, 1986; Lazarus, 1991). In contrast, moods are relatively more diffuse emotional states involving more global positive or negative feelings (Watson and Tellegen, 1985). Trait affect involves a person's dispositional, or stable, tendency to experience positive and negative emotional states, and is generally referred to as positive and negative trait affect (Barsade and Gibson, 2007). In this chapter, we focus on emotional states, rather than traits. Interested readers can see Cangiano, Bindl, and Parker's (2017) recent book chapter for a review on trait affect and proactivity.

A conceptual focus on core affect

Following Parker, Bindl, and Strauss's (2010) lead, the vast majority of proactivity research examining the energized-to pathway has built on theories of core affect, defined as 'momentary, elementary, feelings of pleasure or displeasure and of activation or deactivation' (Seo, Barrett, and Bartunek, 2004, p 424). Theories of core affect describe emotional experience as falling along two dimensions: valence (pleasant versus unpleasant feelings) and activation (high versus low); crossing these two dimensions results in four quadrants (Russell, 2003). A recent review reveals that proactivity research has primarily focused on only two of these quadrants – activated positive and activated negative affect – and mostly on positive core affect (Cangiano, Bindl, and Parker, 2017).

The role of positive emotional states

Theoretically, proactivity scholars provide a number of reasons why highly positive and activated affective experience should supply the energy to be proactive, or to exhibit self-starting, anticipatory, and persistent behaviour (Frese and Fay, 2001). First, positive core affect activates an approach action tendency (Seo, Barrett, and Bartunek, 2004), which is necessary for employees to be self-starting (Parker, Bindl, and Strauss, 2010). Second, positive emotional states broaden our thought processes (Isen, 2001) and are associated with future-oriented thinking (Foo, Uy, and Baron, 2009), both of which help employees think of ways to act in advance and anticipate changing job demands. Third, being proactive often requires setting challenging goals and then persisting despite obstacles (Frese and Fay, 2001; Parker, Bindl, and Strauss, 2010), which requires high levels of energy. By definition, positive core affect is a highly activated and pleasant state that 'provides the energy necessary for engaging and persisting in proactive work behaviour' (Sonnentag and Starzyk, 2015, p 809), fuelling employees to overcome setbacks and accomplish proactive goals. Fourth, positive affect helps employees view their current course of action in a positive light (Seo, Barrett, and Bartunek, 2004), which energizes them to follow through when obstacles arise during their proactive efforts (Hong et al, 2016).

Research generally supports a positive association between positive affect – in terms of state positive affect – and proactivity (Cangiano, Bindl, and Parker, 2017). These findings appear to be robust; for example, Bindl et al (2012) found that highly activated and positive mood was positively associated with several aspects of the proactivity process – including envisioning, planning, executing, and reflecting on proactive behaviour. Other notable studies have found that feelings of state positive affect increased the time spent on proactive tasks at work (Fay and Sonnentag, 2012) and whether employees implement ideas at work (Sonnentag and Starzyk, 2015). Furthermore, employees' state positive affect stemming from leader behaviour can increase the extent to which employees speak up and take initiative at work (Lin et al, 2016; Liu et al, 2017). In summary, there is both theoretical and empirical support for the argument that positive and high activated emotional experience influences proactivity.

The role of negative emotional states

While positive affect is generally associated with employee proactivity, relatively less is known about how negative affect may shape proactivity.

Theoretically, proactivity scholars have made competing arguments as to the role of negative affect and proactivity. On the one hand, Frese and Fay (2001) argued that it is often negative affect, such as dissatisfaction, that can stimulate a desire to change and challenge the status quo. This follows from theories suggesting that negative affective states signal a need for change and function to motivate behaviour to effectively address a situation (Elfenbein, 2007; George, 2011). In support of this line of thinking, Sonnentag and Staryzk (2012) argued and found that experiencing negative affect is positively associated with proactively identifying work-related issues. However, others have argued that negative affect is likely to reduce employees' proactive efforts. Since the experience of negative affect narrows cognitive processing, it could preclude employees from thinking of ways to anticipate customer needs or proactively find solutions to existing problems (Parker, Bindl, and Strauss, 2010). Additionally, negative affect can elicit an avoidant, rather than approach, orientation, making proactivity less likely (Bindl et al, 2012). Moreover, negative affective experience can exhaust employees and deplete their self-regulatory resources, inhibiting one's physical ability to carry out proactive efforts (Bindl et al, 2012).

Given these competing theoretical arguments, the mixed and inconsistent results from the limited number of studies examining negative affect and proactivity are not surprising. Results from these studies variously suggest a positive relationship (Sonnentag and Staryzk, 2015), a negative relationship (Fay and Sonnentag, 2012), or no relationship (Bindl et al, 2012; Fritz and Sonnentag, 2009) between state negative affect and proactivity. In summary, the role of negative affect in shaping proactivity is less clear than the role of positive affect, from both a theoretical and empirical standpoint.

The role of work engagement

Scholars also argue that work engagement is an energized-to antecedent of proactivity (Fritz and Sonnentag, 2009; Sonnentag, 2003). A primary reason for this is that work engagement, as a 'persistent, positive affective-motivational state of fulfillment' (Maslach, Schaufeli, and Leiter, 2001, p 417) supplies energy, enthusiasm, and vigour to be self-starting and proactive. Empirical research supports this notion as, for example, Salanova and Schaufeli (2008) found that job engagement mediated the relationship between job resources (for example, control and feedback) and personal initiative. Sonnentag (2003) argued and found that employees able to recover from the stress and strain of work felt more engaged at work and thus reported taking more personal initiative at work. Additionally, Den Hartog and Belschak (2012) argued and found that employee work engagement, as a positive emotional state, mediated the relationship between leaders displaying ethical behaviour and employee personal initiative. Making similar arguments, Schmitt, Den Hartog, and Belschak (2016) found that work engagement indirectly mediates the relationship between transformational leadership and proactivity in the form of personal initiative and voice.

While work engagement is frequently linked to proactivity, there is evidence to suggest that work engagement may not be limited conceptually to the energized-to pathway. While noting that work engagement likely drives proactivity via positive emotional forces, Den Hartog and Belschak (2012) and Schmitt, Den Hartog, and Belschak (2016) both argue that engagement can cognitively drive proactivity in the form of absorption and dedication. Furthermore, a recent review of proactive behaviour also suggests that there may be both affective and cognitive components of work engagement that influence proactivity (Cai et al, 2019). This suggests that work engagement may not cleanly link to the energized-to pathway.

Limitations of current conceptualizations of energized-to proactive motivation

While research linking core affect and work engagement to proactivity sheds important light on the motivation for this behaviour, this research is limited in a number of important ways. First, researchers have primarily focused on two dimensions of core affect: high activation positive states and moods (for example, active, energized, and excited) and high activation negative states and moods (for example, distressed, nervous, and hostile). A focus on these two dimensions is incomplete, as there are *four* dimensions of core affective experience (Russell, 2003; Seo, Barrett, and Bartunek, 2004). An important step in correcting this omission comes from Bindl et al (2012), who argue that proactivity scholars should not only consider the valence of the emotion, but also the activation level of the emotion to examine each of the four quadrants. Applying this idea, Bindl et al's research suggests that different quadrants may have distinct effects on proactivity; for example, they found that while high positive affect was associated with proactivity, *low* activated positive affect was not. They also found that low activated negative affect was associated with envisioning proactivity. These intriguing findings suggest that there is theoretical utility in applying the four dimensions of core affect, as a narrow conceptual focus on only two dimensions of activated positive and activated negative affect has likely limited the ability to detect the effects of emotion on proactivity. Because of this, it is important for proactivity scholars to theoretically and empirically specify which quadrant of core affect will impact proactive behaviour.

A second and related limitation is that focusing on core affect lumps together a number of similar, but distinct, positive or negative emotions. For example, most studies (for example, Liu et al, 2017; Sonnentag and Staryzk, 2015) arguing that high activated positive or negative affect impacts proactivity measure emotional experience by employing the PANAS (Watson, Clark, and Tellegen, 1988). This measure lumps together positive emotions such as interest and pride, and negative emotions such as anger and fear, which are similar conceptually in terms of valence and activation, but distinct in a number of ways (Frijda, 1986; Roseman, 2011). More specifically, discrete emotions arise from certain appraisals of events and are accompanied by distinct physiological and behavioural reactions (Shaver et al, 1987; Smith and Ellsworth, 1985). Anger, for example, differs greatly from fear in motivating approach versus avoidant behaviour (Lerner and Keltner, 2001). Similarly, excitement is likely to elicit a different behavioural reaction than pride (Roseman, 2013). Therefore, proactivity scholars lose predictive ability when they lump together negative or positive core affective states, which is likely one major reason why research on negative emotions and proactivity has produced mixed results (Lebel, 2017).

A third limitation is that applications of the energized-to pathway also suffer from unclear theoretical arguments. For example, Hong et al (2016, p 691) classify activated positive affect as an energized-to state and then argue that it 'may influence personal initiative through shaping individuals' expectancy, utility, and process judgment'. This argument clearly confounds the reason-to motivational state based on utility judgments with the energized-to state based on positive emotion. Moreover, a recent review seemed to blur the lines between cognition and affect by describing the effect of engagement on proactivity in terms of emotion, noting that states of engagement 'arguably provide positive and activated affective states that stimulate proactive behaviour' (Cai et al, 2019, p 212). However, these authors then classify engagement as an 'other' mediating mechanism and do *not* classify it as an energized-to motivational force. This classification serves to muddy the waters, as the authors clearly make energized-to arguments based on core affect (for example, 'positive and activated affective states'), but then classify engagement as a motivational force separate from energized-to forces. Given that work engagement is an important driver of proactive behaviour, it is imperative that we correctly classify the mechanisms through which work engagement stimulates proactivity.

Ways forward: Clarifying the energized-to pathway

Given these limitations, we suggest a number of ways to improve theory and research on the energized-to pathway. First, we argue that proactivity scholars should apply discrete emotional theories to capture important nuances among negative and positive emotional states. Second, and similarly, we argue that proactivity scholars should better delineate when and how negative emotional states impact proactivity. And, third, we argue that proactivity scholars should scrutinize the engagement to proactivity link so that it remains theoretically consistent with multidimensional conceptualizations of the construct (for example, Kahn, 1990), and specify which dimensions of the construct do and do not participate in the theorized pathway. See Table 2.1 for a summary of these suggestions.

Table 2.1: Summary of suggestions for future research linking energized-to motivators to proactivity

Limitation	Suggestions for proactivity research
A narrow conceptual focus on two of the four core affective states.	• Examine all four core affective states (for example, Bindl et al, 2012).
Conceptually and empirically lumping together similar, but distinct, emotions.	• Apply discrete emotional theories to predict proactive behaviours.
Competing theoretical arguments for the role of negative emotions on proactivity.	• Focus on contingent effects, rather than main effects. • Clarify which stage of proactivity is most likely to be affected by a specific emotional state (for example, planning, envisioning, or enacting)
Unclear theoretical arguments describing how work engagement is linked to proactivity.	• Specify which dimension of work engagement is of theoretical interest (vigour, absorption, or dedication) and link to the appropriate motivational pathway (energized-to, can-do, or reason-to). • Alternatively, conceptualize work engagement more broadly and consider the role of all three dimensions theoretical development.

Focusing on discrete emotions

One reason for proactivity scholars to utilize discrete emotions is that 'when we theoretically treat all negative (or positive) emotions as functionally the same, we lose sight of the fact that different processes drive each of them, and that different outcomes can result from them too' (Gooty, Gavin, and Ashkanasy, 2009, p 835). Indeed, discrete emotions, in contrast to core affective states and moods, arise from a unique set of antecedents and are associated with distinct motivational, physiological, and behavioural consequences (Ekman, 1992; Lazarus, 1991). Regarding antecedents, how an employee appraises a workplace event determines which discrete emotion they experience (Weiss and Cropanzano, 1996). For example, anger arises when employees are certain about an event's cause and also feel a sense of control, whereas fear arises from perceptions of uncertainty and a lack of ability to do something about the situation (Shaver et al, 1987).

Discrete emotions are also distinct from core affective states and moods because of their corresponding action tendencies, or states of action readiness, which involve motivational goals to address a given situation (Frijda, Kuipers, and ter Schure, 1989; Roseman, Wiest, and Swartz, 1994). Action tendencies prepare a person to take action when necessary, as 'emotions are meant to move us' (Elfenbein, 2007, p 346). Each emotion has a unique behavioural signature, as discrete emotions supply and direct one's energy via specific action tendencies (Frijda, 1986; Lazarus, 1991). For example, anger's action tendency motivates behaviour to change the situation, correct a perceived wrong, or move against a person or situation (Roseman, Wiest, and Swatz, 1994), whereas fear's action tendency motivates behaviour directed at safety from a threat or protection in a situation (Izard and Ackerman, 2000). Thus, discrete emotional theories suggest that even though both anger and fear fall into the same core affective state (that is, negative valence and high activation), they significantly vary in the behaviours they elicit in terms of approach versus avoidance (Lerner and Keltner, 2001).

Following this, we now describe how distinguishing among discrete emotions has important implications for how and when certain emotions may motivate proactive behaviours.

How: Identifying different effects on the form or stage of proactivity

Discrete negative emotional states are likely to motivate different forms of proactivity because of their unique action tendencies, which function to address challenges, stressors, or social situations (Frijda, 1986; Lazarus, 1991). Proactive behaviours can take a variety of forms (Grant and Ashford, 2008), including feedback-seeking, taking charge, and voice. Therefore, we recommend that proactivity scholars clearly specify the action tendency of a particular discrete emotion as it applies to motivating proactive behaviour. For example, anger's action tendency towards approach to move against the source of harm and fear's action tendency to protect by avoiding perceived threat are likely to elicit different proactive behaviours (Lebel, 2017). Anger's energy to correct a perceived wrong is likely to energize employees to speak up and challenge the status quo (Geddes and Callister, 2007). Similarly, employees angered by injustice may be motivated to identify problems and speak up on behalf of others, or blow the whistle on inappropriate work practices (Lindebaum and Geddes, 2016). In contrast, given fear's function to protect the self, employees afraid of losing their job may proactively seek feedback to improve their performance and thus secure their job.

Other negative discrete emotions may also be linked to other forms of proactivity. For example, scholars have suggested that guilt is 'associated with a desire to proactively repair a bad situation' and thus act in advance to prevent a negative result or to improve upon prior mistakes (Bohns and Flynn, 2012, p 1158). In this way, guilt may lead to proactive problem prevention (Parker and Collins, 2010), or feedback-seeking to correct previous mistakes (Roseman, 2011). As another example, frustration with a work process can motivate proactivity because the employee 'wants to change something for the better' (Frese and Fay, 2001). Thus, frustration, with its action tendency to overcome obstacles, is likely to be associated with proactive behaviours such as improving upon, or correcting, existing work practices characteristic of taking charge (Morrison and Phelps, 1999).

The unique action tendencies of discrete emotions also suggest that positive discrete emotions are linked to different forms of proactivity. For example, the discrete emotional state of excitement is associated with an action tendency to move towards an outcome or situation, including instrumental action such as approaching goals and incentives (Roseman, 2011). Therefore, employees in an excited state are energized to think about ways to achieve their proactive goals and take career initiative to move up the corporate ladder (Parker and Collins, 2010). As another example, feeling pride is associated with an action tendency of exhibiting and asserting the self to 'show what you can do' (Roseman, 2011, p 439). Thus, an affective state of pride could motivate an employee to proactively create positive impressions or speak up with new ideas to make themselves look good (Bolino, 1999).

Specific discrete emotions may also have unique effects on different stages of proactivity. When viewed as a process, proactivity can involve envisioning, planning, enacting, and reflecting on this behaviour (Bindl et al, 2012; Grant and Ashford, 2008). Research suggests that the discrete emotions of sadness and despair are associated with employees envisioning proactive behaviours, but not the other stages of proactivity (Bindl et al, 2012). Others suggest that frustration may be crucial to identifying issues and problems to be corrected (Bindl, 2019; Frese and Fay, 2001), and thus important for the planning stage of proactivity. Feelings of regret may also be linked to the planning stage, with employees identifying previous mistakes that could be corrected in the future (Roseman, 2013). Once issues are identified, more highly-activated discrete emotions such as anger or excitement may then drive employees to be proactive in addressing those issues (Kish-Gephart et al, 2009). Taken together, proactivity scholars may benefit from linking specific discrete emotions to a particular stage of proactivity, and/or by developing integrative theoretical models to explain how each stage of proactivity may be influenced by discrete emotions.

When: Focusing on contingent factors linking negative emotions to proactivity

We have described how one solution to addressing the mixed findings from research examining negative emotions and proactivity is to focus on discrete emotional states rather than core negative affect. Another solution is to focus on *contingent* relationships, rather than main effects. Discrete theories of emotion suggest that emotion-driven behaviour is dependent on contextual factors (Frijda, 1986; Parrott, 2001), or 'dependent on the joint occurrence of an emotion and specific external or internal stimulus conditions' (Roseman, Wiest, and Swartz, 1994, p 216). For example, the experience of anger can lead to counterproductive, uncivil, or vengeful behaviour, or to constructive problem resolution (Andersson and Pearson, 1999; Averill, 1982), while fear can lead to withdrawal, silence, or defensive effort (Öhman, 2008). Therefore, the behavioural consequences of discrete emotional experience can vary depending upon the situation, with employees exhibiting a range of behaviours after experiencing negative emotions.

Therefore, the question is not whether, but *when* negative emotions will spark proactivity (Lebel, 2017; Lindebaum and Jordan, 2012). Accordingly, proactivity scholars should adopt functional discrete theories of emotion (for example, Frijda, Kuipers, and ter Schure, 1989) to develop theoretical models describing those conditions under which a particular discrete emotion can spark proactive behaviour. For example, Lebel (2016) argued and found that employees' fear of job loss was positively associated with speaking up, but only when employees also perceived their supervisor as open to input. From a functional perspective, the protective action tendency resulting from fear of job loss motivated action to improve the current state of affairs (speaking up), but only when this action was perceived as leading to change (perceptions of supervisor openness). When employees viewed their supervisors as not open to input, fear of job loss motivated action to protect the self by remaining silent.

Existing theory on proactivity provides a number of other contingent factors that may influence when negative emotions, such as anger and guilt, may result in proactive behaviours. For example, anger's action tendency to correct a perceived wrong is likely to spark employees to speak up about an issue when anger's energy is combined with other-focused, or prosocial, motives (Kish-Gephart et al, 2009; Lindebaum and Geddes, 2016). Taking a functional perspective, these authors argue that when employees are more focused on benefiting others, the tendency of anger to motivate behaviour to lash out or get revenge is weakened, and the tendency to motivate approach-related behaviours to address the situation is strengthened (see also Carver and Harmon-Jones, 2009). Other scholars have argued that employees must regulate their anger to be proactive (Lebel, 2017; Oh and Farh, 2017). From this perspective, anger's high level of negative energy is likely to lead to retaliation when employees are unable to regulate their emotions, but anger's approach-focused energy can produce proactive efforts to secure resources or speak up when employees are able to control and regulate their emotional experience (Grant, 2013). In regard to guilt, Bohns and Flynn (2012) argue that autonomy and the specificity of performance feedback are two important contingent factors shaping when this emotion may spark proactive effort. When employees receive specific feedback or perceive high levels of autonomy, these authors argue, guilt's action tendency to redress a situation takes the form of proactivity, as employees know exactly what needs to be done or feel they have enough control to change their job situation. In contrast, when employees receive vague feedback or perceive low autonomy, their guilt may turn into feelings of confusion and helplessness, lowering proactivity.

There are likely to be a number of additional contingent factors, whether at the individual, group, or organizational level that influence when a particular negative emotion may or may not motivate proactive behaviour. We believe that the time is right to expand on the ideas described above and to explore potential contingencies in greater depth. Applying functional theories of emotion provide a template for future proactivity research. More specifically, a number of scholars have applied a discrete emotion's unique action tendency, and then explain the conditions under which this tendency may be strengthened or weakened (for example, Lebel, 2017; Lindebaum and Geddes, 2016; Oh and Farh, 2017). We believe that following this approach will be fruitful for research on proactivity.

Clarifying how work engagement shapes proactivity

Engagement as more than an energized-to state

As described above, work engagement has been overwhelmingly construed as an antecedent that exclusively utilizes the energized-to pathway. However, this restriction undermines the role of work engagement in enhancing proactivity. Work engagement is not a singularly emotional construct; it has clear cognitive and physical components (Kahn, 1990; Rich, Lepine, and Crawford, 2010). By underutilizing the mechanisms of work engagement, current theorizing of what motivates proactive behaviour among employees and workers remains incomplete.

In Kahn's (1990) seminal work on engagement, he conceptualized engagement as the integration of one's personal self into their work role performances. In a state of engagement, people employ and express themselves physically, cognitively, and emotionally during role performances. In this interpretation, engagement is about psychological presence (Rothbard, 2001), enacted through physical, cognitive, and emotional means. Engagement therefore necessitates strong cognitive and physical considerations; employees must make judgements about the role they wish to play in their work, about the congruence of their and their organization's values, and conduct repeated self-evaluations to match their desired work selves with their current work selves (Rich, Lepine, and Crawford, 2010).

Further research has advanced and clarified Kahn's model, and isolated three main dimensions to the work engagement construct. These are: vigour, dedication, and absorption (Schaufeli et al, 2002). We posit that each dimension of work engagement maps neatly onto each of the three pathways to proactivity; vigour, which is characterized by high levels of energy and mental resilience while working likely operates through the energized-to pathway; dedication, which is characterized by a sense of significance, enthusiasm, inspiration, pride, and challenge, likely operates through the reason-to pathway; and absorption, which is the act of being fully concentrated and deeply engrossed in the work, is likely to operate through the can-do pathway.

Vigour and the energized-to pathway

The energized-to pathway represents a state of activated positive affect, such as feeling enthusiastic, excited, or passionate. Parker, Bindl, and Strauss (2010) suggest that a high degree of activation increases the amount of effort put into a behaviour by increasing the experience of energy. This is consistent with the vigour dimension of work engagement. When an individual demonstrates vigour, they expend large amounts of effort towards their work, sustaining their level of energy and enthusiasm even in the face of difficulties (Schaufeli et al, 2002), and experiencing positive perceptions about their work and their organizations (Salanova, Agut, and Peiró, 2005). Such energy is needed for employees to proactively approach and overcome, rather than avoid, challenges at work (Frese and Fay, 2001). In this way, vigour is compatible with how proactivity scholars have articulated the relationship between work engagement and proactivity (for example, Parker, Bindl, and Strauss, 2010). Given that vigour is a critical dimension of work engagement, it is not wrong to insist that work engagement leads to proactive behaviour through the energized-to pathway. However, it is incomplete to insist that work engagement leads to proactive behaviour solely through the energized-to pathway. As we outline below, the other two dimensions of work engagement are more suited to alternative pathways to proactivity.

Dedication and the reason-to pathway

Proactivity scholars have suggested that intrinsic forces are important drivers of self-directed behaviour, perhaps even more so than external or situational ones (Griffin, Neal, and Parker, 2007). Proactivity implies that the goals one is striving towards are discretionary, with uncertain or ambiguous outcomes, and take place with no strong compulsion from others. In the absence of strong external cues toward action, there must be strong internal reasons why an employee should be proactive. Such intrinsic motivational forces are a primary aspect of reason-to proactive motivation (Parker, Bindl, and Strauss, 2010).

The dedication aspect of work engagement supplies reason-to motivation, involving feelings of task significance and of believing that your job is important, valued, and worth investing time in (Schaufeli et al, 2002). It is the result of an internalization process where individuals feel ownership in their roles, that their personal values align with the tasks that they must accomplish, and that the future success of the task is indicative of a personal success, not just a professional one. Dedication is not simply about the act of being engaged, but about the *choice* to be engaged. This concept explains *why* an individual becomes engaged enough to be proactive, because one's commitment to work is based on autonomous, intrinsic decisions (Salanova and Schaufeli, 2008). When an individual feels dedicated, they feel as though their work is valuable enough to accept risk or ambiguity, that their personal selves are imbued into their work roles, and that the joy or pride they experience in doing the work is sufficient reward (Salanova and Schaufeli, 2008). We therefore suggest that the dedication dimension of work engagement leads to proactive behaviour through the reason-to pathway, where the employee is intrinsically motivated to take action towards a goal.

Absorption and the can-do pathway

The can-do pathway involves perceptions of self-efficacy, as well as appraisals and attributions of control at work (Parke, Bindl, and Strauss, 2010). In order to take proactive action, one must believe that they are physically capable of reaching the desired outcome. Absorption is the state of being engrossed and deeply attached to a work activity (Schaufeli et al, 2002). This involves both physical and cognitive actions, including executing the task itself, carrying out the actions involved in it, and physically interacting with the task with enough frequency that one becomes engrossed in the process (Langelaan et al, 2006;). Absorption is only possible by physically carrying out the work – tackling the task in a tactile and tangible way, with enough repetition the employee increases their sense of competence and self-efficacy in the task at the centre of their engagement. These appraisals of competence and self-efficacy can in turn increase the individual's vigour and dedication, making them even more engaged in their work than they used to be (Rodríguez-Sánchez et al, 2011).

Thus, the physical act of being in charge of and repeating a core work task can foster engagement, such that one feels greater compulsion to indulge in proactive behaviour and increase their confidence in attaining positive outcomes associated with it. We therefore suggest that the absorption dimension of work engagement leads to proactive behaviour through the can-do pathway, where a virtuous cycle of self-efficacy motivates people to pursue proactive goals.

Linking work engagement to proactivity

Moving forward, we recommend that if scholars are interested in exploring how work engagement utilizes the energize-to pathway, they must focus not on work engagement as a whole, but on one property of work engagement: vigour. On the other hand, if scholars are more interested in determining how effective work engagement is as an antecedent to proactive behaviour, they must be prepared to consider proactive action enacted through all three pathways, where the vigour component of work engagement operates through the energized-to pathway, the dedication component of work engagement operates through the reason-to pathway, and the absorption component of work engagement operates through the can-do pathway. By ignoring the cognitive and physical aspects of work engagement, that is, by limiting our view of engagement to its affective constituents, we reduce it to a third of its efficacy, and impose artificial constraints on its propensity towards proactivity. As a broader call to action, we hope that researchers appropriately match the theoretical underpinnings of their constructs of interest to the pathways that motivate proactivity.

Conclusion

Implications and future directions

We hope readers draw a number of conclusions from this chapter. First, that proactivity scholars have generally utilized only half of the model of core affect when linking emotional states to proactive behaviour, focusing on activated positive and/or activated negative affect. In many ways, this is understandable, as a number of studies suggest that activated positive affect is related to proactivity (Cangiano, Bindl, and Parker, 2017). However, recent research suggests that other dimensions of core affect can influence different stages of the proactivity process (Bindl et al, 2012). The solution for proactivity scholars seems clear: to follow Bindl et al's (2012) lead in clearly specifying the role of each aspect of core affect and its relationship to proactive behaviour.

Second, that a focus solely on core affect has limited progress to understand how emotions spark proactivity. This is especially the case in research examining negative emotions and proactivity, which has produced conflicting theoretical arguments and mixed results. Applying theories of core affect lumps together several emotions (such as anger and fear) that are likely to motivate different forms of behaviour (Lerner and Keltner, 2001). Therefore, future research should utilize discrete theories of emotion to better specify the link between specific negative emotions and proactivity (for example, Lebel, 2017; Oh and Farh, 2017). Applying discrete theories of emotion is likely to influence researchers' choices regarding methodology and study design. In particular, discrete emotions, as relatively intense, short-lived emotional experiences, may be best captured with event-sampling designs on a daily or weekly basis (for example, Liu et al, 2017), rather than with cross-sectional surveys, which can lump emotional experience over longer time periods (for example, Lebel, 2016). Alternatively, researchers could utilize qualitative methods to best capture how these more momentary emotional experiences spark proactivity (for example, Bindl, 2019).

Third, that there is ample opportunity to understand the contingent effects of emotions on proactivity. It is our view that one major reason for mixed results in research linking emotions to proactive behaviour is that researchers have focused on main effects and neglected contingent effects. Indeed, discrete theories of emotion explicitly state that emotion-driven behaviour is dependent on situational factors (Frijda, 1986; Roseman, Wiest, and Swartz, 1994). Therefore, our recommendation is to apply discrete theories of emotion to identify the specific contextual factors likely to elicit certain behaviours based on each emotion's action tendency. Such an approach reflects what Weiss and Cropanzano (1996, p 23) had in mind when they advocated for the development of classification schemes to specify environment–emotion–behaviour chains at work. Scholars could also consider employing appraisal theory (Smith and Ellsworth, 1985) to better understand the conditions under which discrete emotional states arise to motivate proactivity. Adopting these approaches provides a clear road map for future proactivity research.

Fourth, any applications or investigations regarding proactivity benefit from consistency and clarification. In particular, scholars are urged to scrutinize the theoretical match between the construct in question and the pathway through which it seems to motivate proactive action. We use the example of work engagement to illustrate that the pathway through which work engagement affects proactivity is likely dependent on the particular dimension of work engagement being activated. We suggest that future studies of work engagement and proactivity specify whether they are conceptualizing the overarching construct of work engagement or more specific aspects of this construct. If scholars wish to study the construct of work engagement as a whole, they must be cognizant of the fact that any combination of all three pathways may activate proactive behaviour, rather than just one. If scholars are focusing on a particular proactive motivational pathway, then they should link their arguments to the appropriate aspect of engagement: vigour (energized-to pathway), dedication (reason-to pathway), or absorption (can-do pathway). Future research may also try to determine whether the various dimensions of work engagement differentially impact proactive behaviour, and whether there is a pattern of activation with the dimensions and their respective pathways indicative of a particular causal ordering.

Summary

The aim of this chapter was to help clarify the role of energized-to motivation in shaping proactivity at work. We first summarized theory and research on the energized-to pathway along with limitations of current conceptualizations of energized-to motivation. We then described a number of ways for proactivity scholars to move beyond and extend existing theoretical approaches to the energized-to- pathway. In particular, we argue that scholars should increasingly use theories of discrete emotion to link specific emotional states to a range of forms and stages of proactive behaviour. We also argue that, given mixed empirical results, proactivity scholars should focus on contingent, rather than main, effects to better understand when discrete emotional states impact proactivity. We then argued that research linking work engagement and proactivity has muddied the waters by making both cognitive and affective motivational arguments, and that future research should theoretically and empirically specify which aspect(s) of work engagement may motivate proactivity. In tandem, adopting these suggestions will help add to theoretical and empirical precision to better understand when emotions do (or do not) motivate proactivity.

References

Andersson, L. M. and Pearson, C. M. (1999). Tit for tat? The spiraling effect of incivility in the workplace. *Academy of Management Review*, 24(3): 452–71.

Averill, J. R. (1982). *Anger and Aggression: An Essay on Emotion*. New York: Springer.

Barsade, S. G. and Gibson, D. E. (2007). Why does affect matter in organizations? *Academy of Management Perspectives*, 21(1): 36–59.

Bindl, U. K. (2019). Work-related proactivity through the lens of narrative: Investigating emotional journeys in the process of making things happen. *Human Relations*, 72(4): 615–45.

Bindl, U. K., Parker, S. K., Totterdell, P., and Hagger-Johnson, G. (2012). Fuel of the self-starter: How mood relates to proactive goal regulation. *Journal of Applied Psychology*, 97(1): 134–50.

Bohns, V. K., and Flynn, F. J. (2012). Guilt by design: Structuring organizations to elicit guilt as an affective reaction to failure. *Organization Science*, 24(4): 1157–73.

Bolino, M. C. (1999). Citizenship and impression management: Good soldiers or good actors? *Academy of Management Review*, 24(1): 82–98.

Cai, Z., Parker, S. K., Chen, Z., and Lam, W. (2019). How does the social context fuel the proactive fire? A multilevel review and theoretical synthesis. *Journal of Organizational Behavior*, 40(2): 209–230.

Campbell, D. J. (2000). The proactive employee: Managing workplace initiative. *Academy of Management Executive*, 14(3): 52–66.

Cangiano, F., Bindl, U. K., and Parker, S. K. (2017). The hot side of proactivity: Exploring an affect-based perspective on proactivity in organizations. In S. K. Parker and U. K. Bindl (eds), *Proactivity at Work: Making Things Happen in Organizations*, New York: Routledge, pp 355–84.

Carver, C. S. and Harmon-Jones, E. (2009). Anger is an approach-related affect: Evidence and implications. *Psychological Bulletin*, 135(2): 183–204.

Den Hartog, D. N. and Belschak, F. D. (2012). Work engagement and machiavellianism in the ethical leadership process. *Journal of Business Ethics*, 107(1): 35–47.

Ekman, P. (1992). An argument for basic emotions. *Cognition and Emotion*, 6(3–4): 169–200.

Elfenbein, H. A. (2007). Emotion in organizations. *Academy of Management Annals*, 1(1): 315–86.

Fay, D. and Sonnentag, S. (2012). Within-person fluctuations of proactive behavior: How affect and experienced competence regulate work behavior. *Human Performance*, 25(1): 72–93.

Foo, M.-D., Uy, M. A., and Baron, R. A. (2009). How do feelings influence effort? An empirical study of entrepreneurs' affect and venture effort. *Journal of Applied Psychology*, 94(4): 1086–94.

Frese, M., and Fay, D. (2001). Personal initiative: An active performance concept for work in the 21st century. *Research in Organizational Behavior*, 23: 133–87.

Frijda, N. H. (1986). *The Emotions*. New York: Cambridge University Press.

Frijda, N. H., Kuipers, P., and ter Schure, E. (1989). Relations among emotion, appraisal, and emotional action readiness. *Journal of Personality and Social Psychology*, 57(2): 212–28.

Fritz, C. and Sonnentag, S. (2009). Antecedents of day-level proactive behavior: A look at job stressors and positive affect during the workday. *Journal of Management*, 35(1): 94–111.

Geddes, D., and Callister, R. R. (2007). Crossing the line(s): A dual threshold model of anger in organizations. *Academy of Management Review*, 32(3): 721–46.

George, J. M. (2011). Dual tuning: A minimum condition for understanding affect in organizations? *Organizational Psychology Review*, 1(2): 147–64.

Gooty, J., Gavin, M., and Ashkanasy, N. M. (2009). Emotions research in OB: The challenges that lie ahead. *Journal of Organizational Behavior*, 30(6): 833–8.

Grant, A. M. (2013). Rocking the boat but keeping it steady: The role of emotion regulation in employee voice. *Academy of Management Journal*, 56(6): 1703–23.

Grant, A. M. and Ashford, S. J. (2008). The dynamics of proactivity at work. *Research in Organizational Behavior*, 28: 3–34.

Griffin, M. A., Neal, A., and Parker, S. K. (2007). A new model of work role performance: Positive behavior in uncertain and interdependent contexts. *Academy of Management Journal*, 50(2): 327–47.

Hong, Y., Liao, H., Raub, S., and Han, J. H. (2016). What it takes to get proactive: An integrative multilevel model of the antecedents of personal initiative. *Journal of Applied Psychology*, 101(5): 687–701.

Isen, A. M. (2001). An influence of positive affect on decision making in complex situations: Theoretical issues with practical implications. *Journal of Consumer Psychology*, 11(2): 75–85.

Izard, C. E., and Ackerman, B. P. (2000). Motivational, organizational, and regulatory functions of discrete emotions. In M. Lewis and J. M. Haviland-Jones (eds), *Handbook of Emotions*, 2nd edn, New York: Guilford Press, pp 253–65.

Kahn, W. A. (1990). Psychological conditions of personal engagement and disengagement at work. *Academy of Management Journal*, 33, 692–724.

Kish-Gephart, J. J., Detert, J. R., Treviño, L. K., and Edmondson, A. C. (2009). Silenced by fear: The nature, sources, and consequences of fear at work. *Research in Organizational Behavior*, 29: 163–93.

Langelaan, S., Bakker, A. B., Van Doornen, L. J., and Schaufeli, W. B. (2006). Burnout and work engagement: Do individual differences make a difference?. *Personality and Individual Differences*, 40(3), 521–32.

Lazarus, R. S. (1991). *Emotion and Adaptation*. New York: Oxford University Press.

Lebel, R. D. (2016). Overcoming the fear factor: How perceptions of supervisor openness lead employees to speak up when fearing external threat. *Organizational Behavior and Human Decision Processes*, 135: 10–21.

Lebel, R. D. (2017). Moving beyond fight and flight: A contingent model of how the emotional regulation of anger and fear sparks proactivity. *Academy of Management Review*, 42(2): 190–206.

Lerner, J. S. and Keltner, D. (2001). Fear, anger, and risk. *Journal of Personality and Social Psychology*, 81(1): 146–59.

Lin, C.-C., Kao, Y.-T., Chen, Y.-L., and Lu, S.-C. (2016). Fostering change-oriented behaviors: A broaden-and-build model. *Journal of Business and Psychology*, 31(3): 399–414.

Lindebaum, D. and Geddes, D. (2016). The place and role of (moral) anger in organizational behavior studies. *Journal of Organizational Behavior*, 37(5): 738–57.

Lindebaum, D. and Jordan, P. J. (2012). Positive emotions, negative emotions, or utility of discrete emotions? *Journal of Organizational Behavior*, 33(7): 1027–30.

Liu, W., Song, Z., Li, X., and Liao, Z. (2017). Why and when leaders' affective states influence employee upward voice. *Academy of Management Journal*, 60(1): 238–63.

Maslach, C., Schaufeli, W. B., and Leiter, M. P. (2001). Job burnout. *Annual Review of Psychology*, 52, 397–422.

Morrison, E. W. and Phelps, C. C. (1999). Taking charge at work: Extrarole efforts to initiate workplace change. *Academy of Management Journal*, 42(4): 403–19.

Oh, J. K., and Farh, C. I. C. (2017). An emotional process theory of how subordinates appraise, experience, and respond to abusive supervision over time. *Academy of Management Review*, 42(2): 207–32.

Öhman, A. (2008). Fear and anxiety: Overlaps and dissociations. In M. Lewis, J. M. Haviland-Jones, and L. F. Barrett (eds), *Handbook of Emotions*, 3rd edn, New York: Guilford Press, pp 709–29.

Parker, S. K., Bindl, U. K., and Strauss, K. (2010). Making things happen: A model of proactive motivation. *Journal of Management*, 36(4): 827–56.

Parker, S. K. and Collins, C. G. (2010). Taking stock: Integrating and differentiating multiple proactive behaviors. *Journal of Management* 36(3): 633–62.

Parker, S. K., Williams, H. M., and Turner, N. (2006). Modeling the antecedents of proactive behavior at work. *Journal of Applied Psychology*, 91(3): 636–52.

Parrott, W. G. (2001). Implications of dysfunctional emotions for understanding how emotions function. *Review of General Psychology*, 5(3): 180–6.

Rank, J., Carsten, J. M., Unger, J. M., and Spector, P. E. (2007). Proactive customer service performance: Relationships with individual, task, and leadership variables. *Human Performance*, 20(4): 363–90.

Rich, B. L., Lepine, J. A., and Crawford, E. R. (2010). Job engagement: Antecedents and effects on job performance. *Academy of Management Journal*, 53(3): 617–35.

Rodríguez-Sánchez, A. M., Schaufeli, W., Salanova, M., Cifre, E., and Sonnenschein, M. (2011). Enjoyment and absorption: An electronic diary study on daily flow patterns. *Work and Stress*, 25(1), 75–92.

Roseman, I. J. (2011). Emotional behaviors, emotivational goals, emotion strategies: Multiple levels of organization integrate variable and consistent responses. *Emotion Review*, 3(4): 434–43.

Roseman, I. J. (2013). Appraisal in the emotion system: Coherence in strategies for coping. *Emotion Review*, 5(2): 141–9.

Roseman, I. J., Wiest, C., and Swartz, T. S. (1994). Phenomenology, behaviors, and goals differentiate discrete emotions. *Journal of Personality and Social Psychology*, 67(2): 206–21.

Rothbard, N. P. (2001). Enriching or depleting? The dynamics of engagement in work and family roles. *Administrative Science Quarterly*, 46(4): 655–84.

Russell, J. A. (2003). Core affect and the psychological construction of emotion. *Psychological Review*, 110(1): 145–72.

Salanova, M., Agut, S., and Peiró, J. M. (2005). Linking organizational resources and work engagement to employee performance and customer loyalty: The mediation of service climate. *Journal of Applied Psychology*, 90(6), 1217.

Salanova, M. and Schaufeli, W. B. (2008). A cross-national study of work engagement as a mediator between job resources and proactive behaviour. *The International Journal of Human Resource Management*, 19(1), 116–31.

Schaufeli, W. B., Salanova, M., González-Romá, V., and Bakker, A. B. (2002). The measurement of engagement and burnout: A two sample confirmatory factor analytic approach. *Journal of Happiness Studies*, 3(1), 71–92.

Schmitt, A., Den Hartog, D. N., and Belschak, F. D. (2016). Transformational leadership and proactive work behaviour: A moderated mediation model including work engagement and job strain. *Journal of Occupational and Organizational Psychology*, 89(3): 588–610.

Seo, M.-G., Barrett, L. F., and Bartunek, J. M. (2004). The role of affective experience in work motivation. *Academy of Management Review*, 29(3): 423–39.

Shaver, P., Schwartz, J., Kirson, D., and O'Connor, C. (1987). Emotion knowledge: Further exploration of a prototype approach. *Journal of Personality and Social Psychology*, 52(6): 1061–86.

Smith, C. A. and Ellsworth, P. C. (1985). Patterns of cognitive appraisal in emotion. *Journal of Personality and Social Psychology*, 48(4): 813–38.

Sonnentag, S. (2003). Recovery, work engagement, and proactive behavior: A new look at the interface between nonwork and work. *Journal of Applied Psychology*, 88(3): 518–28.

Sonnentag, S. and Starzyk, A. (2015). Perceived prosocial impact, perceived situational constraints, and proactive work behavior: Looking at two distinct affective pathways. *Journal of Organizational Behavior*, 36(6): 806–24.

Watson, D., Clark, L. A., and Tellegen, A. (1988). Development and validation of brief measures of positive and negative affect: The PANAS scales. *Journal of Personality and Social Psychology*, 54(6): 1063–70.

Watson, D. and Tellegen, A. (1985). Toward a consensual structure of mood. *Psychological Bulletin*, 98(2): 219–35.

Weiss, H. M. and Cropanzano, R. (1996). Affective events theory: A theoretical discussion of the structure, causes and consequences of affective experiences at work. *Research in Organizational Behavior*, 18: 1–74.

PART II

The Role of Emotion in Shaping Proactivity in Different Contexts

3

A Multilevel Model of Emotions and Proactive Behaviour

Neal M. Ashkanasy

In this chapter, I apply Ashkanasy's (2003) Five-Level Model of Emotions in the Workplace (FLMEW; see also Ashkanasy and Dorris, 2017; Ashkanasy and Humphrey, 2011a) as an overarching framework intended to understand the nexus of emotions and proactive behaviour at different levels of organizational analysis. Consistent with the other chapters in this volume, I utilize the definition of proactivity given in Parker, Williams, and Turner (2006), namely 'self-initiated and future-oriented action that aims to change and improve the situation or oneself' (p 636). This is a broad definition and, as such, covers a wide range of (mostly positive) forms of behaviour in the workplace that occur at every level of analysis. For example, a proactive employee would make constructive suggestions to improve work practices (Ashford, Sutcliffe, and Christianson, 2009; LePine and Van Dyne, 1998); would seek as a new hire to discover information and to build relationships with senior colleagues (Ashford and Black, 1996); or would reach out to employees to assess their needs and to improve team performance (Rank et al, 2007). Bindl and Parker (2010) were the first to outline the multilevel nature and effects of proactive behaviour, including higher performance at the individual level, improved team effectiveness, and improved organizational performance (see also Parker, Bindl, and Strauss, 2010. In the following sections, I first introduce the FLMEW, and then look at the relationship of emotion and proactive behaviour at each of the five levels in the model. I conclude with discussion of how the components of the model fit together to provide an integrated multilevel model of emotions and proactivity in organizations, and suggest some directions for future research on emotions and organizational proactivity at each of the levels of analysis.

The Five-Level Model of Emotions in the Workplace

In this model, Ashkanasy (2003) sets out five distinct but overlapping levels of analysis: (1) within person temporal variability, (2) between-person individual differences, (3) interpersonal interactions, (4) groups and teams, and (5) organization-wide. The first level of the model concerns employees' experience of in-the-moment affect and emotion (Clark, Watson, and Leeka, 1989), focusing on how employees respond to in-the-moment 'affective events' that occur every day in their workplace (Weiss and Cropanzano, 1996). At Level 2, the focus shifts to how emotions are enacted and experienced by different employees. Key variables at this level are trait affectivity (Watson and Tellegen, 1985) and emotional intelligence (Mayer and Salovey, 1997). Level 3 in the model addresses the ways employees communicate and perceive emotions in interpersonal exchanges. Central concepts at this level are interpersonal emotional regulation (Troth et al, 2018; Zaki and Williams, 2013) and emotional labour (Grandey, 2000; Hochschild, 1983). Level 4 in the model focuses on groups, including the concepts of group affective tone (George, 2000), emotional contagion (Hatfield, Caccioppo, and Rapson, 1993) and emotional leadership (Humphrey, 2002). Finally, at Level 5, the model addresses emotional climate (de Rivera, 1992) and organizational culture (Ashkanasy and Härtel, 2014). Importantly, and as Ashkanasy (2003) points out, emotional behaviours and attitudes at each of the five levels, although conceptually distinct, cross the different levels of analysis, resulting in a complex and interconnected picture of organizational functioning. In effect, emotions at the different levels 'cascade throughout the organization, subsequently impacting key organizational variables that underpin organizational performance' (Ashkanasy, Härtel, and Bialkowski, 2020, p 375). In the following sections, I introduce the five levels of analysis and discuss each with particular emphasis on research into employee proactive behaviour.

Level 1: Within person

The central conceptual framework at Level 1 in the FLMEW is Affective Events Theory (AET: Weiss and Cropanzano, 1996). According to these authors, 'affective events' generated within the organizational environment (for example, change, leader behaviour) lead to employees experiencing discrete *emotions* (such as fear, anger, happiness, or sadness) that are acute and object-oriented (for example, fear of a threat or anger when goals are thwarted). These reactions can then become *moods*. These tend not to be object oriented and are longer lasting them emotions (Frijda, 1986).

Weiss and Cropanzano (1996) argue further that these emotional reactions (both emotions and moods) then translate into one of two forms of behaviour. The first is 'affect-driven' behaviour that may be either positive (for example, spontaneously helping a colleague) or negative (for example, shouting at a colleague). This form of behaviour represents a direct response to the event, mediated by the employee's particular emotional or mood state. The second form is 'judgement-driven' behaviour, such as quitting or deciding to be more productive, which come about because of attitudes (for example, job commitment, job satisfaction, anomie) resulting from the affective event (and the subsequent emotional reaction).

With regard to proactive behaviour specifically, it seems that this form of behaviour can be either affect-driven or judgement-driven. Evidence of this may be found in the work of Fritz and Sonnentag (2009), who conducted a study involving 172 clerical assistants in Germany. These researchers asked their study participants to complete diary entries over four days, and found that employees' proactive behaviour often emerged spontaneously in response to their experience of stress related to time pressure, a form of negative affect (see also Fay and Sonnentag, 2002; Lebel, 2017). Over the longer term, however, Fritz and Sonnentag found that study participants' proactive behaviour tended to be associated with positive affect. In other words, while affect-driven proactive behaviour seems to emerge spontaneously in response to negative affective events (time pressure), in the longer term, employees' propensity to engage in proactive behaviour appears to be more likely if the employees are in a positive state. This conclusion would appear to support Morrison and Phelps (1999, p 405), who describe proactive behaviour as a 'calculated, deliberate decision process'.

Level 2: Between-persons

Level 2 of the FLMEW concerns the role of individual differences. Ashkanasy (2003; see also Ashkanasy and Dorris, 2017) examined specifically two emotion-related individual differences: (1) emotional intelligence (Mayer and Salovey, 1997) and (2) trait affect (Watson and Tellegen, 1985). Consistent with Weiss and Cropanzano (1996), Ashkanasy argued that such individual differences serve to moderate the effect of affective events on employees' subsequent emotional reactions. Thus, compared to low emotional intelligence employees, high emotional intelligence employees should be better able to perceive, to assimilate, to understand, and ultimately to manage their emotions. Jordan, Ashkanasy, and Härtel (2002) argue that high emotional intelligence employees can consequently be expected to be less reactive to affective events (such as job loss) than their low emotional intelligence colleagues (see also Lopes et al, 2006). Concerning trait affect, it is axiomatic that high positive affect (PA) individuals should be more likely to experience positive affect in response to positive affective events than their low PA peers, while high negative affect (NA) individuals should be more reactive to negative affective events than their low NA colleagues (compare Dalal et al, 2012).

The particular individual difference relevant to proactive behaviour is trait proactivity (or *proactive personality*, see Bateman and Crant, 1993), which research has found to link to career success (Seibert, Crant, and Kraimer, 1999), job performance (Thompson, 2005), and motivation to learn (Major, Turner, and Fletcher, 2006). More recently, in a field study involving 250 public employees Bhutan et al (2016) found that the relationship of trait proactivity to creativity was related to their study participants' emotional intelligence, such that the relationship between emotional intelligence and creativity was higher for participants with higher trait proactivity.

In another field study, this time involving 200 Chinese employees, Li, Liang, and Crant (2010) found the relationship between proactivity and job satisfaction and organizational citizenship behaviour to be stronger in the presence of a positive organizational climate and positive leader–member relationship quality. I argue that these findings suggest that positivity and, by extension, trait PA acts to facilitate the association between trait proactivity and performance outcomes.

Level 3: Interpersonal relationships

At Level 3 in the FLMEW, Ashkanasy (2003) looks at the means by which organizational employees communicate emotions to others within and without the organization, focusing on *emotional labour*, defined by (Hochschild, 1983) as 'management of feeling to create a publicly observable facial and bodily display' (p 7). Grandey (2000) subsequently made the case that emotional labour is, in essence, a special case of impersonal emotional regulation, in so far as employees seek to communicate particular emotions according to their perception of their organization's mandated display rules (Diefendorff and Richards, 2003). In its classical form, emotional labour can mean either surface acting (where the actor follows organizational display rules and displays emotions that may not represent her or his true feelings) or deep acting (where the actor summons up emotional memories in order to display the mandated emotional expression). The question arises here, however, as to whether an employee needs to engage in proactive behaviour in order to undertake emotional labour appropriately.

In fact, this is what Randolph and Dahling (2013) found in a field study involving 120 employed service workers. Specifically, these authors found that trait proactive employees are especially responsive to organizational display rules, and suffer fewer stressful consequences when doing to. While research with regard to the other forms of interpersonal emotion regulation to data is sparse, there is no reason to doubt that proactive behaviour should not affect these forms any the less than they do in the case of pure extrinsic interpersonal regulation. This would apply especially in the case of co-regulation, which involves both parties actively cooperating to regulate their own and the other party's emotions. In particular, if one of the people involved in the exchange were high on trait proactivity, for example, then it would be expected that s/he would take the lead in this process.

Another aspect where proactivity could play a role at Level 3 concerns the role of emotional regulation in leadership, where Martin, Knopoff, and Beckman (1998) noted that emotional labour represents a means for effective leaders to maximize their relationships with employees. Humphrey, Pollack, and Hawver (2008) subsequently referred to this as 'leading with emotional labour' (see also Ashkanasy and Humphrey, 2011b). Hunt, Gardner, and Fischer (2008) found in particular that, to affect followers' emotions, behaviours and attitudes effectively, leaders need to empathize with their followers; in other words, to feel and to express the emotions perceived by followers. Moreover, surface acting (and the associated feelings of inauthenticity experienced when displaying emotions at odds with felt emotion) can result in stress (Grandey, 2000; 2003).

Taking into account Randloph and Dahling's (2013) findings that trait proactive employees are more comfortable than their less proactive peers when the organization requires them to engage in emotional labour (especially when they employ deep acting), it seems reasonable to conclude that leaders who engage in proactive behaviour should also be more capable of successful 'leading with emotional labour'. Randolph and Dahling explain this in terms of Diefendorff and Gosserand's (2003) 'control theory' of emotional labour, which holds that employees strive to maintain consistency between their felt and displayed emotions.

Level 4: Groups and teams

The fourth level in the FLMEW encompasses group processes and especially team leadership, which Ashkanasy (2003) pitches as a means to facilitate positive group emotions (Krzeminska, Lim, and Härtel, 2018). In this regard, Williams, Parker, and Turner (2010) define *proactive teams* in terms the mean level of proactivity (or proactive personality in a team). George (2000) defines group affective tone in a similar fashion: representing the mean level of a particular affective state among group members. George argues arguing specifically that leaders play a central role in setting a group's affective tone (which is also enabled by processes of emotional contagion, see Barsade, 2002; Sy, Côté, and Saavedra, 2005; Hatfield et al, 1993). Chiu, Owens, and Tesluk (2016) similarly found that team proactivity is associated with team leadership, especially when leadership is shared.

Sy, Côté and Saavedra (2005) found moreover that leaders have a special role to play in engendering a positive emotional tone in a group. In turn, and as Gooty et al (2010) argue, groups whose leaders foster a positive emotional tone become both more cohesive and more effective (see also Humphrey, 2002). More recently, Krzeminska, Lim, and Härtel (2018) found in a study of emergency services teams that leaders who encourage and achieve a positive workgroup emotional tone reduce team members' occupational stress and enhance their psychological capital.

Härtel and Page (2009) subsequently introduced the idea of *discrete emotional crossover*, which they define as 'the transmission of discrete emotions such as anger, joy, contentment, and fear from one individual to another in the same social environment' (p 238). Härtel and Page propose in particular that such crossover is a product of emotional contagion, and also involves importation of emotional experiences from outside the workplace (for example, at home or in social activities).

Petitta, Jiang, and Härtel (2017) later noted that the frequency and intensity of social interactions act as precursors of emotional contagion. Ashkanasy and his associates (2020) extend this notion by observing that 'teams with important and frequent intra-group and leader interactions are likely to "catch" each other's emotions, while teams whose interactions do not meet these criteria may not' (p 378). In this regard, Petitta et al theorized that contagion in work-teams can be a double-edged sword. Thus, positive emotions can act as a positive resource likely to improve team performance, while contagion of negative emotions represents a negative burden on the team likely to result in reduced team performance.

Given that we know from Fritz and Sonnentag's (2009) work that proactive behaviour is associated over the longer term with positive affect, it should also follow that members of groups that possess a leader-facilitated positive affective tone should also display more proactivity. This is indeed what Strauss, Griffin, and Rafferty (2009) found in a study involving 196 Australian public servants. Specifically, these authors found that transformational leadership leads to increased affective organizational commitment (associated with positivity, see Youssef and Luthans, 2007) that in turn leads to team and organizational member proactivity. In another study, Loi, Lam, and Xu (2016) surveyed 258 Chinese hospitality employees nested in 63 teams and found that the high proactivity employees in their study were less likely to quit their jobs in the face of emotional demands within their work team.

Level 5: The organization as a whole

The focus at Level 5 of the FLMEW is on the organizational as a whole and, in particular, the organization's climate and culture. Schneider (2000) defines *organizational climate* as the employees' immediate collective conscious perceptions of their work environment (see also Schneider, Ehrhart, and Macey, 2011). De Rivera (1992, p 2) describes affective climate as 'an objective (emotional) phenomenon that can be palpably sensed'. This is in contrast to *organizational culture*, which Härtel and Ashkanasy (2011) consider analogous to a 'fossil record'. As such, and as Schein (1992) argues, culture derives ultimately from the organization's founder and then evolves from the collective experiences of organizational members. Thus, culture determines the organization's rules and norms of emotional expression (or *display rules*, see Diefendorff and Richards, 2003) and the rules governing social interactions between organizational members. James et al (2008) note in particular that, although organizational culture and climate are distinct constructs, both contain an affective component (see also Ashkanasy, 2007). Thus, while organizational culture sets the norms for display of affect, the actual manifestation of affective climate is reflected in the organization's climate. Thus, as Virtanen (2000) notes, 'climate is … more manifest than culture, and culture more latent than climate' (p 349). Taken together, and as Ashkanasy (2003) and Pizer and Härtel (2005) argue, the means by which organizational members experience the emotional climate of their organization on a daily basis ultimately derives from the organization's culture.

Ashkanasy and Nicholson (2003) examined in particular the 'climate of fear' in organizations and found that such climate was determined by the way organizational units were managed on a day-by-day basis. Ashkanasy and Daus (2002) note further that culture and climate typically combine to determine whether the organization is a source of 'toxic emotions' to its employees (compare Frost, 2007, Leavitt, 2007).

Härtel (2008) coined the term *positive work environment* (PWE) to describe the nature of organizational climate and culture needed to facilitate employee flourishing (see also Härtel and Ashkanasy, 2011. According to Härtel (2008), employees in a PWE view their organization to be 'respectful, inclusive and psychologically safe; leaders and coworkers as trustworthy, fair and open to diversity; and characterized by ethical policies and decision-making' (p 584).

The question that arises at this point is how do PWEs come about? Fujimoto, Härtel, and Panipucci (2005) argue that it comes down to leadership and development of human resource management (HRM) practices that result in a healthy organizational culture and a PWE (see also Dutton and Ragins, 2017). In an empirical test of this notion, Fujimoto and her colleagues found that HRM policies and practices underlie employees' individual and collective positive (versus negative) attitudes to diversity. Building upon this work, Ashkanasy et al (2020) argue that HRM policies and practices play a key role in facilitating a PWE via managing and monitoring the affective experiences of employees, and especially through ensuring that managers are appropriately educated and trained in this regard. Ashkanasy and his colleagues conclude (p 379) this this is achieved via, 'facilitating positive workplace relationships' (Krzeminska, Lim, and Härtel, 2018), constructive conflict management (Ayoko and Härtel, 2002), trust (Kimberley and Härtel, 2007), diversity openness (Härtel and Fujimoto, 2000), and organizational justice (Kimberley and Härtel, 2007).

Turning now to consider the effects of climate and culture on employees' proactive behaviour, and consistent with the position adopted throughout this chapter, it follows that a PWE is a prerequisite – over the longer term – for a climate and culture of proactivity. In this regard, Erkutlu (2012) found in a study of Turkish banking organizations that a positive culture facilitated transfer of shared leadership into employee proactive behaviour that relate, in turn to improved individual and organizational productivity and performance. This result confirms the conclusions reached by Thomas, Whitman, and Viswesvaran (2010) in a meta-analysis: that organizational proactivity links to higher organizational performance.

Finally, as Shirom (2011, p 50) found, a PWE is likely to be associated with a 'vigorous organization', whose managerial apex effectively creates the conditions that generate, maintain, and foster employee (positive affect and) vigour throughout the organization. Such organizational level affective energetic resources should in turn mobilize proactivity across the organization and thereby help to achieve organizational effectiveness.

Summary of the five levels

In this chapter so far, I have addressed the relationship between emotions and proactive behaviour at each of the five levels set out by Ashkanasy (2003) in the FLMEW. At Level 1 (within-person temporal variability), based on Weiss and Cropanzano's (1996) AET, I argued that proactive behaviour can be either affect-driven or judgement-driven. The former is usually in response to a stressful event, where the employee needs proactively to find a solution to a (negative-affect inducing) problem. Over the longer term, however, and as Fritz and Sonnentag (2002) found, accumulating positive affect is a prerequisite to develop the positive attitudes that underlie proactive behaviour. At Level 2 (between-person individual differences), key variables relating to proactive behaviour include (positive) trait affect, emotional intelligence and, especially, proactive personality, which represents a generalized tendency to engage in proactive behaviour leading to improved chances of career success (Seibert, Crant, and Kraimer, 1999) and improved job performance (Thompson, 2005). At Level 3 (interpersonal), the focus shifts to interpersonal emotional exchanges and communication of emotion. In this regard, Randolph and Dahling (2013) found that proactivity is associated with employees' willingness to display emptions consistent with the organization's display rules. I argue further that proactive employees would be likely to take the lead when 'co-regulating' emotions with other parties (Troth et al, 2018).

Levels 4 (groups) and 5 (organization-wide) in the FLMEW refer to collectives within organizations. At Level 4, the focus is on groups and teams, and especially leadership. In this regard, leaders, play a central role in setting a positive affective tone of the group (Sy, Côté, and Saavedra, 2005) leading to reduced stress and enhanced psychological capital (Krzeminska, Lim, and Härtel, 2018). Moreover, research has found that an 'emotionally intelligent group' tends to be more psychologically adjusted (Druskat and Wolff, 2001) and to perform better (Jordan et al, 2002; Offermann et al, 2004) than other groups. Moreover, members of groups possessing positive affective tone tend to be more committed (Youssef and Luthans, 2007) and proactive (Loi et al, 2016). A similar scenario plays out when the organization is considered as a whole, in that a positive work environment tends to be associated with proactivity both as a fact of organizational climate (in the short term) and culture (over the longer term) resulting in tern in higher organizational performance.

A multilevel model of emotions and proactivity

Figure 3.1 shows how the FLMEW can be adapted to reflect proactivity at each of the five levels, based in the foregoing arguments. It is important to note, however, that the levels in the FLMEW do not act completely independently; and nor are they static. Instead, and as Ashkanasy and Dorris (2017) stress, processes within model are inherently interactive and dynamic. In the following, I discuss each of these characteristics in turn.

Figure 3.1: A five-level model of emotions and proactivity in organizations

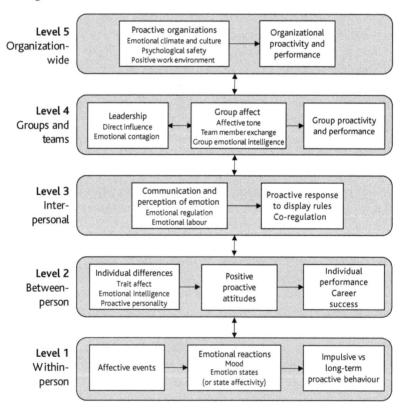

The dynamic nature of the FLMEW

In fact, dynamism is apparent across all five levels in the model. At Level 1, for example, Weiss and Cropanzano (1996) introduced the idea of affective events theory (at Level 1) specifically to deal with the ephemeral nature of emotions and affect (that had previously hindered research on emotions in the workplace, see Ashforth and Humphrey, 1995).

Ashkanasy and Härtel (2014) take this idea a step further and extend it to Level 5 (the organization as a whole). Thus, these authors argue that, just as affect varies moment-by-moment and day-by-day at Level 1, affective climate can likewise be variable (even when the organization's culture is conducive to a PWE). Thus, despite an organization's overall positive leadership and HRM policies, its members can still experience setbacks that result in stress and (state) negativity from time to time. In this instance, a positive culture and a PWE is important to ensure resilience during setbacks In this case, and as Härtel and Ganegoda (2008) note, organizational leaders in PWEs provide positive support to organizational members in order to minimize the effects of negativity and consequent destructive behaviours during difficult periods, resulting in what Shirom (2011, p 50) refers to as a 'vigorous organization'.

With regard to proactive behaviour, an important corollary of this line of argument is that proactive behaviour is not necessarily always associated with positivity. Sometimes, especially during difficult times (for example, having to deal with a pandemic such COVID-19), employees need to engage in proactive behaviour turn the situation around. I alluded to this in my earlier discussion of Level 1, when I cited work by Fritz and Sonnentag (2009) showing that adversity and time pressure can results in (affect-driven) proactive behaviour. A similar pattern was reported by To et al (2012; To, Fisher, and Ashkanasy, 2015) in relation to 'creative effort' (a sister construct to proactivity, see Kim, Hon, and Crant, 2009). These authors found that, while positivity (Isen, Daubman, and Nowicki, 1987) usually facilitates creative effort, the reverse is true on other occasions (depending upon circumstances). For example, sometimes creativity (or proactivity) is necessary to solve a particularly stressful problem.

The interactive nature of the FLMEW

Ashkanasy (2003; see also Ashkanasy and Dorris, 2017; Ashkanasy and Humphrey, 2011a) stress that processes and emotions at each level interact with each other in a complex fashion. Thus, while theorizing at Level 1 is based in AET and is intended to describe the nature and effects of moment-by-moment emotion in individual employees, it nonetheless incorporates processes at Levels 2 (individual differences) and 3 (interpersonal communication), as well as situational moderators at Levels 4 (groups and teams) and 5 (organizational climate and culture). Thus, Parker at al (2010) showed that proactive states (at Level 1) are a function of individual differences (at Level 2) and contextual variables (at Levels 4 and 5). Similarly, at Level 2, Li, Liang, and Crant (2010) found that the effect of proactivity is also contingent upon the quality of leader–member relationships (at Level 4) and a positive organizational climate (at Level 5). At Level 3, Randloph and Dahling (2013) found that proactive behaviours depended upon trait proactivity (at Level 2) and organizational display rules (at Level 5). Finally in his model explaining how negative emotions (anger and fear) can sometimes lead to proactive behaviour via emotional regulation (at Level 3) Lebel (2017) includes the moderating effects of leader support (at Level 4) and identification with the organization (at Level 5).

Future research

In this chapter, I have sought to outline research on emotions and proactivity in organizations within the framework of Ashkanasy's (2003) FLMEW. Readers would have noticed, however, that while I detail some excellent examples of proactivity research that has considered the effects of emotion at each of the five levels in the model, all said and done, it is really pretty sparse, suggesting that this may be an especially fruitful area for future research.

At Level 1 (within-person), scope remains for researchers to examine proactivity as a phenomenon that, like job satisfaction and performance, is likely to vary from moment to moment, and day to day within the work environment. For example, similar to Minbashian, Wood, and Beckmann (2010), who found that conscientiousness – normally considered a stable personality characteristic – can vary depending on the nature of the task, proactivity might also vary in response to an employees' affective reactions to particular tasks.

At Level 2 (between persons), I focused on proactive personality as an individual difference variable, which researchers have found across many studies relates positively to organizational outcomes and, in particular, acts as a catalyst for positive outcomes (for example, see Chung-Yan and Butler, 2011; Parker and Sprigg, 1999). Like other individual differences, however, proactive personality can have its downsides. For example, Sun and van Emmerik (2015) found that supervisors rate proactive employees negatively if their proactivity is seen to be political. Clearly there is scope for further investigation into the affective consequences of such 'political proactivity'.

The notion of political proactivity might also carry over to Level 3 (interpersonal relationships), in which case it is conceivable that a proactive individual might seek to project a particular (advantageous) emotional expression in order to curry favour with another. In view of Randloph and Dahling's (2013) finding that trait proactive individuals tend to be more eager than others to engage in emotional labour, the idea that this will affect interpersonal relationships in the workplace seems worth pursuing further.

At the team level of analysis (Level 4), one idea that may be worthy of additional research is whether proactivity might be associated with team 'risky shift', whereby team members tend to adopt a more risky position than the team's members would by themselves. While this phenomenon is traditionally cast as a rational response (for example, see Burnstein et al, 1971), more recent evidence (for example, see Lerner et al, 2015) suggests it is quintessentially affective. Given what we know about the relationship between group proactivity and positive affect (compare Fritz and Sonnentag, 2009), it would seem worthwhile to investigate the notion that group proactivity might lead to increased risky behaviour in teams.

Finally, at Level 5 (the organization), I earlier discussed the idea that a PWE is likely to be associated with a 'vigorous organization' (Shirom, 2011) resulting in employees capitalizing on their proactivity to maximize organizational effectiveness. In view of research showing a link between proactivity and entrepreneurship (for example, see Crant, 1996), this sets up the intriguing possibility that a PWE is likely to result in a more entrepreneurial organizational culture though promotion of a proactive organizational climate. Similarly, a high PWE organization can be expected to have greater resilience in the face of difficult environmental conditions, such as were experienced in 2020 during the COVID-19 pandemic.

The notion that proactive behaviour in organizations can be framed across levels of analysis presents some additional intriguing ideas for future research. This is especially so if the dynamic interactive nature of processes with the model are considered. Thus, while Parker and Bindle and their colleagues (Bindl and Parker, 2010; Parker, Bindl, and Strauss, 2010) outline a model of proactive behaviour in individuals (Level 1), teams (Level 4), and the organization (Level 5), there remains scope to study the specific processes of how this occurs with the framework of the FLMEW. One facet in particular that proactivity researchers have yet to explore in detail pertains to Level 3 (perceiving and communicating emotion in interpersonal relationships). While Randolph and Dahling (2013) have made a promising start in this regard, we still need to do more work to understand the nexus of proactivity and interpersonal emotion regulation, especially as they relate to the (relatively recent) notions of co-occurring emotional regulation and interpersonal co-regulation (Troth et al, 2018).

A further possibility for future research would be to test if the findings of To et al (2012; see also To, Fisher, and Ashkanasy, 2015) regarding the personal (Level 2) and situational (Levels 4 and 5) conditions under which employees are inclined to behave proactively. To and his associates studied creative effort. While related to proactivity (for example, see Gong et al, 2012), creative effort is nonetheless a distinct construct, and it will take additional research to determine if the interactions To and his colleagues found would apply to proactive behaviour.

Conclusion

In this chapter, I have endeavoured to map the literature on emotions and proactive behaviour onto Ashkanasy's (2003) five-level model of emotions in the workplace. The model begins at the level of within-person temporal variations in emotions, attitudes, and behaviour; and then proceeds through higher levels of analysis including individual differences, interpersonal communication and perceptions of emotion in relationships, and emotions in groups and teams, to deal ultimately with the organization as a whole. The model is both dynamic and interactive. Emotions, behaviours, and attitudes at each of the five levels can vary moment by moment or day by day and intricately relate to corresponding variables across every level of model.

Across the model, I argue that proactive behaviours tend to be associated with positivity, and especially a positive work environment (PWE, Härtel, 2008). At the same time, however, I acknowledge that proactivity is sometimes required to deal with stressful situations involving time pressure. Over the long haul, however, like creativity in general, proactivity tends to be associated with positive organizational cultures that stem in turn from positive leadership and HRM policies.

References

Ashford, S. J. and Black, J. S. (1996). Proactivity during organizational entry: The role of desire for control. *Journal of Applied Psychology*, 81, 199–214.

Ashford, S. J., Sutcliffe, K. M., and Christianson, M. K. (2009). Leadership, voice, and silence. In J. Greenberg and M. S. Edwards (eds), *Voice and silence in organizations*, Bingley: Emerald Publishing Group, pp 175–201.

Ashforth, B. E. and Humphrey, R. H. (1995). Emotion in the workplace: A reappraisal. *Human Relations*, 48, 97–125.

Ashkanasy, N. M. (2003). Emotions in organizations: a multi-level perspective. In F. Dansereau and F. J. Yammarino (eds), *Research on Multi-level issues*, vol 2, Bingley: Emerald Group Publishing, pp 9–54.

Ashkanasy, N. M. (2007). Organizational climate. In S. R. Clegg and J. R. Bailey (eds), *International Encyclopedia of Organization Studies*, vol 3, Thousand Oaks, CA: Sage, pp. 1028–30.

Ashkanasy, N. M. and Daus, C. S. (2002). Emotion in the workplace: The new challenge for managers. *Academy of Management Perspectives*, 16, 76–86.

Ashkanasy, N. M. and Dorris, A. D. (2017). Emotion in the workplace. *Annual Review of Organizational Psychology and Organizational Behavior*, 4, 67–90.

Ashkanasy, N. M. and Härtel, C. E. (2014). Positive and negative affective climate and culture: The good, the bad, and the ugly. In B. Schneider and K. Barbera (eds), *Oxford Handbook of Organizational Climate and Culture*, New York: Oxford University Press, pp 136–52.

Ashkanasy, N. M., Härtel, C. E. J., and Bialkowski, A. (2020). Affective climate and organization-level emotion management. In L-Q.Yang, R. S.Cropanzano, V. Martinez-Tur, and C. A. Daus (eds), *The Cambridge Handbook of Workplace Affect*, New York: Cambridge University Press, pp 375–85.

Ashkanasy, N. M. and Humphrey, R. H. (2011a). Current emotion research in organizational behavior. *Emotion Review*, 3, 214–24.

Ashkanasy, N. M. and Humphrey, R. H. (2011b). A multi-level view of leadership and emotions: Leading with emotional labor. In A. Bryman, D. Collinson, K. Grint, B. Jackson, and M. Uhl-Bien (eds), *Sage Handbook of Leadership*, London: Sage, pp 363–77.

Ashkanasy, N. M. and Nicholson, G. J. (2003). Climate of fear in organisational settings: Construct definition, measurement and a test of theory. *Australian Journal of Psychology*, 55, 24–9.

Ayoko, O. B. and Härtel, C. E. J. (2002). The role of emotions and emotion management in destructive and productive conflict in culturally heterogeneous workgroups. In N. M. Ashkanasy, W. J. Zerbe, and C. E. J. Härtel (eds), *Managing Emotions in the Workplace*, Armonk New York: M. E Sharpe, pp 77–97.

Barsade, S. G. (2002). The ripple effect: Emotional contagion and its influence on group behavior. *Administrative Science Quarterly*, 47, 644–75.

Bateman, T. S. and Crant, J. M. (1993). The proactive component of organizational behavior: A measure and correlates. *Journal of Organizational Behavior*, 14 103–18.

Baer, M. and Frese, M. (2003). Innovation is not enough: Climates for initiative and psychological safety, process innovations, and firm performance. *Journal of Organizational Behavior*, 24, 45–68.

Bindl, U. K. and Parker, S. K. (2010). Proactive work behavior: Forward-thinking and change-oriented action in organizations In S. Zedeck (ed), *APA Handbook of Industrial and Organizational Psychology*, Washington, DC: American Psychological Association, pp 567–98.

Burnstein, E., Miller, H., Vinocur, A., Katz, S., and Crowley, J. (1971). Risky shift is eminently rational. *Journal of Personality and Social Psychology*, 20, 462–71.

Chiu, C. Y. C., Owens, B. P., and Tesluk, P. E. (2016). Initiating and utilizing shared leadership in teams: The role of leader humility, team proactive personality, and team performance capability. *Journal of Applied Psychology*, 101, 1705–1720.

Chung-Yan, G. A. and Butler, A. M. (2011). Proactive personality in the context of job complexity. *Canadian Journal of Behavioural Science,* 43, 279–86.

Clark, L. A., Watson, D., and Leeka, J. (1989). Diurnal variation in the positive affects. *Motivation and Emotion*, 13, 205–34.

Crant, J. M. (1996). The proactive personality scale as a predictor of entrepreneurial intentions. *Journal of Small Business Management*, 34, 42–9.

Dalal, R. S., Baysinger, M., Brummel, B. J., and LeBreton, J. M. (2012). The relative importance of employee engagement, other job attitudes, and trait affect as predictors of job performance. *Journal of Applied Social Psychology*, 42, E295-E325.

de Rivera, J. (1992). Emotional climate: Social structure and emotional dynamics. *International Review of Studies on Emotions*, 2, 197–218.

Diefendorff, J. M. and Gosserand, R. H. (2003). Understanding the emotional labor process: A control theory perspective. *Journal of Organizational Behavior*, 24, 945–59.

Diefendorff, J. M. and Richard, E. M. (2003). Antecedents and consequences of emotional display rule perceptions. *Journal of Applied Psychology*, 88, 284–94.

Druskat, V. U. and Wolff, S. B. (2001). Group emotional intelligence and its influence on group effectiveness. In C. Cherniss and D. Goleman (eds), *The Emotionally Intelligent Workplace*, San Francisco: Jossey-Bass, pp.132–55.

Dutton, J. E. and Ragins, B. R. (2017). *Exploring Positive Relationships at Work: Building a Theoretical and Research Foundation*. New York: Psychology Press.

Erkutlu, H. (2012). The impact of organizational culture on the relationship between shared leadership and team proactivity. *Team Performance Management,* 18, 102–119.

Fay, D. and Sonnentag, S. (2002). Rethinking the effects of stressors: A longitudinal study on personal initiative. *Journal of Occupational Health Psychology*, 7, 221–34.

Frijda, N. H. (1986). *The Emotions*. New York: Cambridge University Press.

Fritz, C. and Sonnentag, S. (2009). Antecedents of day-level proactive behavior: A look at job stressors and positive affect during the workday. *Journal of Management*, 35, 94–111.

Frost, P. J. (2007). *Toxic Emotions at Work and What You Can Do About Them*. Cambridge, MA: Harvard Business Review Press.

Fujimoto, Y., Härtel, C. E. J., and Panipucci, D. (2005). Emotional experience of individualist-collectivist workgroups: Findings from a study of 14 multinationals located in Australia. In C. E. J. Härtel, W. J. Zerbe and N. M. Ashkanasy (eds), *Emotions in Organizational Behavior*, Mahwah, NJ: Lawrence Erlbaum Associates, Inc., pp 125–60.

George, J. M. (2000). Emotions and leadership: The role of emotional intelligence. *Human Relations*, 53, 1027–55.

Gong, Y., Cheung, S. Y., Wang, M., and Huang, J. C. (2012). Unfolding the proactive process for creativity: Integration of the employee proactivity, information exchange, and psychological safety perspectives. *Journal of Management*, 38, 1611–33.

Gooty, J., Connelly, S., Griffith, J., and Gupta, A. (2010). Leadership, affect and emotions: A state of the science review. *The Leadership Quarterly*, 21, 979–1004.

Grandey, A. A. (2000). Emotional regulation in the workplace: A new way to conceptualize emotional labor. *Journal of Occupational Health Psychology*, 5, 59–100.

Grandey, A. A. (2003). When 'the show must go on': Surface acting and deep acting as determinants of emotional exhaustion and peer-rated service delivery. *Academy of Management Journal*, 46, 86–96.

Härtel, C. E. J. (2008). How to build a healthy emotional culture and avoid a toxic culture. In C. L. Cooper and N. M. Ashkanasy (eds), *Research Companion to Emotion in Organizations*, Cheltenham: Edwin Elgar, pp 575–88.

Härtel, C. E. J. and Ashkanasy, N. M. (2011). Healthy human cultures as positive work environments. In N. M. Ashkanasy, C. E. P. Wilderom, and M. F. Peterson (eds), The *Handbook of Organizational Culture and Climate*, Thousand Oaks, CA: Sage, pp 85–100.

Härtel, C. E. J., and Fujimoto, Y. (2000). Diversity Is not the Problem: Openness to Perceived Dissimilarity Is. *Journal of Management and Organization*, 6, 14–27.

Härtel, C. E. J. and Ganegoda, D. B. (2008). Role of affect and interactional justice in moral leadership. In W. J. Zerbe, C. E. J. Härtel, and N. M. Ashkanasy (eds), *Research on Emotion in Organizations*, vol 4, Bradford: Emerald Group Publishing, pp 155–80.

Härtel, C. E. J. and Page, K. M. (2009). Discrete emotional crossover in the workplace: The role of affect intensity. *Journal of Managerial Psychology*, 24, 237–253.

Hatfield, E., Cacioppo, J. T., and Rapson, R. L. (1993). Emotional contagion. *Current Directions In Psychological Science*, 2, 96–100.

Hochschild, A. R. (1983). *The Managed Heart: Commercialization of Human Feeling*. Berkeley, CA: University of California Press.

Humphrey, R. H. (2002). The many faces of emotional leadership. *The Leadership Quarterly*, 13, 493–504.

Humphrey, R. H., Pollack, J. M., and Hawver, T. (2008). Leading with emotional labor. *Journal of Managerial Psychology*, 23, 151.

Hunt, J. G., Gardner, W. L., and Fischer, D. (2008). Leader emotional displays from near and far: The implications of close versus distant leadership. In R. H. Humphrey (ed), *Affect and Emotion: New Directions in Management Theory and Research* Charlotte, NC: Information Age Publishing, pp 42–65.

Isen, A. M., Daubman, K. A., and Nowicki, G. P. (1987). Positive affect facilitates creative problem solving. *Journal of Personality and Social Psychology*, 52, 1122–31.

Jafri, M. H., Dem, C., and Choden, S. (2016). Emotional intelligence and employee creativity: Moderating role of proactive personality and organizational climate. *Business Perspectives and Research*, 4, 54–66.

James, L. R., Choi, C. C., Ko, C. H. E., McNeil, P. K., Minton, M. K., Wright, M. A., and Kim, K. I. (2008). Organizational and psychological climate: A review of theory and research. *European Journal of Work and Organizational Psychology*, 17, 5–32.

Jordan, P. J., Ashkanasy, N. M., and Härtel, C. E. J. (2002). Emotional intelligence as a moderator of emotional and behavioral reactions to job insecurity. *The Academy of Management Review*, 27, 361–72.

Jordan, P. J., Ashkanasy, N. M., Härtel, C. E. J., and Hooper, G. S. (2002). Workgroup emotional intelligence: Scale development and relationship to team process effectiveness and goal focus. *Human Resource Management Review*, 12, 195–214.

Kim, T. Y., Hon, A. H., and Crant, J. M. (2009). Proactive personality, employee creativity, and newcomer outcomes: A longitudinal study. *Journal of Business and Psychology*, 24, 93–103.

Kimberley, N. and Härtel, C. E. J. (2007). Building a climate of trust during organizational change: The mediating role of justice perceptions and emotion. In C. E. J. Härtel, N. M. Ashkanasy and W. J. Zerbe (eds), *Research on Emotion in Organizations: Functionality, Intentionality and Morality*, Oxford: Elsevier/JAI Press, pp 237–64.

Krzeminska, A., Lim, J., and Härtel, C. E. J. (2018). Psychological capital and occupational stress in emergency services teams: empowering effects of servant leadership and workgroup emotional climate. In L. Petitta, C. E. J. Härtel, N. M. Ashkanasy, and W. Zerbe (eds), *Research on Emotion in Organizations, Volume 14: Individual, Relational, and Contextual Dynamics of Emotions*, Bingley: Emerald Group Publishing, pp 189–215.

Lebel, R. D. (2017). Moving beyond fight and flight: A contingent model of how the emotional regulation of anger and fear sparks proactivity. *Academy of Management Review*, 42, 190–206.

Leavitt, H. J. (2007). Big organizations are unhealthy environments for human beings. *Academy of Management Learning and Education*, 6, 253–263.

LePine, J. A. and Van Dyne, L. (1998). Predicting voice behavior in work groups. *Journal of Applied Psychology*, 83(6), 853–68.

Lerner, J. S., Li, Y., Valdesolo, P., and Kassam, K. S. (2015). Emotion and decision making. *Annual Review of Psychology*, 66, 799–863.

Li, N., Liang, J., and Crant, J. M. (2010). The role of proactive personality in job satisfaction and organizational citizenship behavior: A relational perspective. *Journal of Applied Psychology*, 95, 395–404.

Loi, R., Liu, Y., Lam, L. W., and Xu, A. J. (2016). Buffering emotional job demands: The interplay between proactive personality and team potency. *Journal of Vocational Behavior*, 95, 128–37.

Lopes, P. N., Grewal, D., Kadis, J., Gall, M., and Salovey, P. (2006). Evidence that emotional intelligence is related to job performance and affect and attitudes at work. *Psicothema*, 18 (Supplement), 132–8.

Major, D. A., Turner, J. E., and Fletcher, T. D. (2006). Linking proactive personality and the Big Five to motivation to learn and development activity. *Journal of Applied Psychology*, 91, 927–35.

Martin, J., Knopoff, K., and Beckman, C. (1998). An alternative to bureaucratic impersonality and emotional labor: Bounded emotionality at The Body Shop. *Administrative Science Quarterly*, 43, 429–69.

Mayer, J. D. and Salovey, P. (1997). What is emotional intelligence? In P. Salovey and D. Sluyter (eds), *Emotional Development and Emotional Intelligence: Implications for Educators*, New York: Basic Books, pp 3–31.

Minbashian, A., Wood, R. E., and Beckmann, N. (2010). Task-contingent conscientiousness as a unit of personality at work. *Journal of Applied Psychology*, 95, 793–806.

Morrison, E. W. and Phelps, C. C. (1999). Taking charge at work: Extrarole efforts to initiate workplace change. *Academy of management Journal*, 42, 403–19.

Offermann, L. R., Bailey, J. R., Vasilopoulos, N. L., Seal, C., and Sass, M. (2004). The relative contribution of emotional competence and cognitive ability to individual and team performance. *Human performance*, 17, 219–43.

Parker, S. K., Bindl, U. K., and Strauss, K. (2010). Making things happen: A model of proactive motivation. *Journal of Management*, 36, 827–56.

Parker, S. K. and Sprigg, C. A. (1999). Minimizing strain and maximizing learning: the role of job demands, job control, and proactive personality. *Journal of Applied Psychology*, 84, 925–39.

Parker, S. K., Williams, H. M., and Turner, N. (2006). Modeling the antecedents of proactive behavior at work. *Journal of Applied Psychology*, 91, 636–52.

Petitta, L., Jiang, L., and Härtel, C. E. J. (2017). Emotional contagion and burnout among nurses and doctors: Do joy and anger from different sources of stakeholders matter? (SMI-2016-0125). *Stress and Health, 33*, 358–69.

Pizer, M.K. and Härtel, C. E. J. (2005). For better or for worse: organizational culture and emotions. In C. E. J. Härtel, W. J. Zerbe and N. M. Ashkanasy (eds), *Emotions in Organizational Behavior*, Mahwah, NJ: Lawrence Erlbaum Associates, Inc, pp 342–61.

Randolph, K. L. and Dahling, J. J. (2013). Interactive effects of proactive personality and display rules on emotional labor in organizations. *Journal of Applied Social Psychology, 43*, 2350–9.

Rank, J., Carsten, J. M., Unger, J. M., and Spector, P. E. (2007). Proactive customer service performance: Relationships with individual, task, and leadership variables. *Human Performance, 20*, 363–90.

Schein, E. (1992). *Organizational Culture and Leadership*. San Francisco, CA: Jossey-Bass.

Schneider, B. (2000). The psychological life of organizations. In Ashkanasy, N., Wilderom, C. and Peterson, M. (eds), *The Handbook of Organizational Culture and Climate*, Thousand Oaks, CA: Sage, pp 23–30.

Schneider, B., Ehrhart, M. G., and Macey, W. H. (2011). Organizational climate research: Achievements and the road ahead. In N. M. Ashkanasy, C. E. P. Wilderom, and M. F. Peterson (eds), *The Handbook of Organizational Culture and Climate*, 2nd ed. Thousand Oaks, CA: Sage.

Seibert, S. E., Crant, J. M., and Kraimer, M. L. (1999). Proactive personality and career success. *Journal of Applied Psychology, 84*, 416–27.

Shirom, A. (2011). Vigor as a positive affect at work: Conceptualizing vigor, its relations with related constructs, and its antecedents and consequences. *Review of General Psychology, 15*, 50–64.

Strauss, K., Griffin, M. A., and Rafferty, A. E. (2009). Proactivity directed toward the team and organization: The role of leadership, commitment and role-breadth self-efficacy. *British Journal of Management, 20*, 279–91.

Sun, S. and van Emmerik, H. I. (2015). Are proactive personalities always beneficial? Political skill as a moderator. *Journal of Applied Psychology, 100*, 966–75

Sy, T., Côté, S., and Saavedra, R. (2005). The contagious leader: impact of the leader's mood on the mood of group members, group affective tone, and group processes. *Journal of Applied Psychology, 90*, 295–305.

Thomas, J. P., Whitman, D. S., and Viswesvaran, C. (2010). Employee proactivity in organizations: A comparative meta-analysis of emergent proactive constructs. *Journal of occupational and organizational psychology, 83*, 275–300.

Thompson, J. A. (2005). Proactive personality and job performance: a social capital perspective. *Journal of Applied Psychology, 90*, 1011–1017.

To, M. L., Fisher, C. D., Ashkanasy, N. M., and Rowe, P. A. (2012). Within-person relationships between mood and creativity. *Journal of Applied Psychology*, 97, 519–612.

To, M. L., Fisher, C. D., and Ashkanasy, N. M. (2015). Unleashing angst: Negative mood, learning goal orientation, psychological empowerment, and creative behaviour. *Human Relations*, 68, 1601–22.

Troth, A. C., Lawrence, S. A., Jordan, P. J., and Ashkanasy, N. M. (2018). Interpersonal emotion regulation in the workplace: a conceptual and operational review and future research agenda. *International Journal of Management Reviews*, 20, 523–43.

Virtanen, T. (2000). Commitment and the study of organizational climate and culture. In N. M. Ashkanasy, C. P. M., Wilderom, and M. F. Peterson (eds,), *Handbook of Organizational Culture and Climate*, Thousand Oaks, CA: Sage Publications, pp 339–54.

Watson, D. and Tellegen, A. (1985). Toward a consensual structure of mood. *Psychological Bulletin*, 98, 219–35.

Weiss, H. M., and Cropanzano, R. (1996). Affective Events Theory: A theoretical discussion of the structure, causes and consequences of affective experiences at work. In B. M. Staw and L. L. Cummings (eds), *Research in Organizational Behavior*, vol 18, Oxford: Elsevier Science, pp 1–74.

Williams, H. M., Parker, S. K., and Turner, N. (2010). Proactively performing teams: The role of work design, transformational leadership, and team composition. *Journal of Occupational and Organizational Psychology*, 83, 301–24

Youssef, C. M. and Luthans, F. (2007). Positive organizational behavior in the workplace: The impact of hope, optimism, and resilience. *Journal of Management*, 33, 774–800.

Zaki, J. and Williams, W. C. (2013). Interpersonal emotion regulation. *Emotion*, *13*, 803–10.

4

Affective Events and Proactivity

Sandra Ohly and Laura Venz

Previous research has mainly focused on how positive activated affective states such as work engagement, enthusiasm, and vigour can promote proactive behaviour at work. By combining the theoretical approaches of affective events theory (Weiss and Cropanzano, 1996) and motivation for proactive behaviour (Parker, Bindl, and Strauss, 2010), we broaden this perspective, and discuss additional mechanisms on how affective events can be linked to proactive behaviour via several affective states. In the following, we first provide a short overview of affective events theory before reviewing previous research linking affective events to proactive behaviour. Based on this review, we develop novel ideas on how affective events can foster proactive behaviour, which provide a starting point for future research in this field.

Affective events theory

Affective events theory (AET; Weiss and Cropanzano, 1996) provides a useful framework for understanding the relationship between the work environment, affective reactions and proactive behaviour (Ohly and Schmitt, 2017). AET stipulates that the work environment affects behaviour by making affective work events (defined as something that happens in the workplace) more or less likely. Affective work events cause affective states, which in turn prompt behaviour. Two types of behaviour are differentiated: affect-driven behaviour and judgement-driven behaviour. Although proactive behaviour is not explicitly mentioned, research linking affective states to proactive behaviour (Fritz and Sonnentag, 2009) and theoretical considerations (Lebel,

2017; Parker, Bindl, and Strauss, 2010) support the classification of proactive behaviour as affect-driven using AET nomenclature, and we will follow this line of research in this review by focusing on possible affective mechanisms linking affective events and proactive behaviour. Nevertheless, we will also discuss the possibility of treating proactive behaviour as judgement-driven and explore related mechanisms. Theorizing about affective events, such as in the case of this chapter, has certain advantages: By focusing on discrete events, influences of context, including changes in context as well as bottom-up processes in organizations can be described (Johns, 2017; Morgeson, Mitchell, and Liu, 2015). Moreover, event-level studies, because of their focus on factual information (that is, has an event occurred or not), are advantageous by reducing memory distortion and other kinds of biases inherent in many other types of studies (Hansbrough, Lord, and Schyns, 2015).

Inspired by AET, a number of studies have identified different types of affective events (see Table 4.1). These approaches differ in breadth and focus. For example, some studies examine private events (often under the label of daily hassles), whereas other focus on work events, or on both non-work and work events. Moreover, whereas some studies aim at identifying affective events for specific occupational groups (Kiffin-Petersen, Murphy, and Soutar, 2012), others examine affective events in occupational groups more broadly. Finally, in the classification of events, some studies focus on the expected outcome (Grandey, Tam, and Brauburger, 2002) whereas others classify the events by focusing on their content (for example, successful service encounter). More recently, a taxonomy of affective work events was developed, which aims to be comprehensive and applicable to a broad range of jobs (Ohly and Schmitt, 2014). In this taxonomy, Ohly and Schmitt (2014) differentiate between four types of positive events and seven types of negative events (see Table 4.1). Among the positive events, the cluster *goal attainment, problem solving, task-related success* occurred most frequently, followed by *praise, appreciation, positive feedback*, and *perceived competence in or through social interactions* and *passively experienced externally determined positive experience*. The less frequent positive event cluster, *externally determined positive experiences*, might not occur on a daily basis (for example, receiving a promotion). Among the seven negative events clusters, most resemble previous approaches to workplace stressors. For example, *hindrances in goal attainment, obstacles in completing work tasks, overload* are similar to workplace stressors identified based on action regulation theory (Frese and Zapf, 1994). Based on their pattern of relationship with five discrete affective states (*enthusiastic, angry, worried,*

Table 4.1: Review of taxonomies of affective events

Study	Sample	Assessment of events	Categorizing of events	Resulting categories	Comments
Basch and Fisher, 1998	101 service employees	Employees described an overall of 332 positive and 404 negative events or situations that they had recently experienced at work	Events–emotions matrix	14 categories of positive job events (for example, receiving recognition) and 13 categories of negative job events (for example, personal problems); some are differentiated according to interaction partner (supervisor, colleague, customer)	

Bolger, DeLongis, Kessler, and Schilling, 1989	166 married couples; 42 days; 11,578 diary entries	Checklist of 21 daily (stressful) events based on earlier pilot testing with open response format; included only events that occurred at least 5 per cent of person-days and were associated with distressed daily mood	21 events grouped into ten summary event categories on rational basis and based on their effects on mood	Ten categories:
				• overload at home
				• overload at work
				• family demands
				• other demands
				• transportation problems
				• financial problems
				• interpersonal conflicts or tensions
				  – with one's spouse
				  – with one's child
				  – with a single other person
				  – with multiple other persons on the same day
					Focus on private life; work events might be present in 'other demands' or 'interpersonal conflicts with other person'

(continued)

Table 4.1: Review of taxonomies of affective events (continued)

Study	Sample	Assessment of events	Categorizing of events	Resulting categories	Comments
				Major result: interpersonal conflicts most strongly related to negative mood especially with non-relatives; overload at work related to negative mood	
Conway and Briner, 2002	45 individuals working part or full time; 47 per cent female	Broken promises, exceeded promises	Participants descriptions of broken and exceeded promises were content analyzed and clustered	11 categories of contents: • performance • compensation/rewards • availability of resources • support – social and technical • work outside job description • humane treatment • training • working hours • considerate treatment • recognition of efforts or status • communication	Content categories from Conway's dissertation

Table 4.1: Review of taxonomies of affective events (continued)

Study	Sample	Assessment of events	Categorizing of events	Resulting categories	Comments

Dimotakis, Scott, and Koopman, 2011	71 employees of a public university; average age 42.6 years; 80 per cent female	Daily positive and negative interactions assessed with the 'recent interaction' section of the diary of ambulatory behavioural states; three times each workday; differentiated in interactions with supervisors, coworkers, and clients		Six categories:
				• daily positive and negative interactions
				• differentiated in interactions with
				  – supervisors
				  – coworkers
				  – clients in additional analyses
				• positive interactions related to positive affect
				• negative interactions related to negative affect
					Valence-symmetric relationships; interactive effect of positive and negative affect on job satisfaction

Elfering et al, 2005	23 employees of a Swiss counseling agency; 19 male, four female; average age 43.9 years; 120 events	COMES; 'participants were instructed to document every stressful situation they experienced, both minor and major, for 7 days (5 working days and 2 days off). Situations were shortly described'	'All descriptions were categorized by two judges. The category system … closely resembles the ISTA scales. Inter-rater reliability was κ = .74 (p < .001). Remaining differences between judges were resolved through consensus'	12 categories: • organizational problems 20.8 per cent • coordination problems 11.7 per cent • quantative overload 10.8 per cent • qualitative overload 10.8 per cent • social stressors 8.3 per cent	Both work events and private events were assessed; appraisal of the event as stressful and controllable related to positive mood

(continued)

Table 4.1: Review of taxonomies of affective events (continued)

Study	Sample	Assessment of events	Categorizing of events	Resulting categories	Comments
				• private life 23.3 per cent Events < 5 per cent occurrence: • difficult decisions • unpleasant/challenging tasks • own errors • commuting • work/non-work conflict • others	
Fitness, 2000	175 community residents; 96 female; average age 31.4 years	Interviews about anger-eliciting events	'Responses sorted by the author into categories, according to their thematic similarity'; goal was 'to devise a coding system that would capture the breadth of reposnses as economically as possible' (p 152)	• unjust treatment • immoral behaviour • job incompetence • disrespect • public humiliation by either superior, coworker, or subordinate Major results: frequency of event occurrence differed between supervisors, coworkers, and subordinates	

Table 4.1: Review of taxonomies of affective events (continued)

Study	Sample	Assessment of events	Categorizing of events	Resulting categories	Comments
Grandey, Tam, and Brauburger, 2002	36 working students; majority 18 years old; 44 per cent female; two weeks; 169 events	Instruction 'to record any event that "made you feel strongly while at work" immediately following the event' (p 38)	'Based on the emotion literature review above and an initial random perusal of diary experiences, categories of anger and pride affective events were identified.' The rater received descriptions of each category and training on categorizing with a few sample events. K = .92 for pride events K = .90 for anger events Consensus through discussion	Eight categories: Anger events (42 per cent): Interpersonal-oriented • personal attacks • incivility Performance-oriented • task interference • policy/structure Pride events (26 per cent): External recognition • performance feedback • socioemotional feedback • recognized potential Internal recognition • self-acknowledgement No relationships between types of events and affect reported	Focus on pride and anger as presumably dominant emotions; 22 per cent of events were not categorized; no analyses on event-level (except for relationship with faking)
Gross et al, 2011	76 employees of a government agency; average age 40.6 years; 71 per cent female	Any event that the participant considered straining or pleasant (major or minor); self-observation system COMES	Number of positive or negative events reported in the time span of 6 work days; private events excluded		

(continued)

Table 4.1: Review of taxonomies of affective events (continued)

Study	Sample	Assessment of events	Categorizing of events	Resulting categories	Comments
Hahn, 2000	86 working students; 46 females; 18–54 years old	'Difference, disagreement or incompatibility' with a boss, coworker, subordinate, client/customer, or contrator/supplier during the past 24 h'	Count of days with one or more conflicts	Types of conflicts included: • hostile communication • unreliability • time conflicts • inability to communicate expectations • personal lives interfering with work • client dissatisfaction with services	Major result: individuals with internal locus of control are more reactive in terms of health and anger than individuals with external locus of control
Kiffin-Petersen, Murphy, and Soutar, 2012	276 sales employees; 63 per cent female	Diary study using open-ended questions; participants were asked to recall a specific event and to describe the circumstances surrounding the incident, appraisal, and emotion	Combination of inductive and deductive thematic analysis was used to code the affective events	• best price • conflict-handling • deal-making • everything • giving advice/service • good deed • good news • helping the customer • pleasant customer • problem-solving • providing quotes • receiving a gift • recognition service • regular client • satisfied customer	The four most frequently reported event categories were associated with different emotions

Table 4.1: Review of taxonomies of affective events (continued)

(continued)

Study	Sample	Assessment of events	Categorizing of events	Resulting categories	Comments
Mignonac and Herrbach, 2004	350 managers; 34 per cent female; average age 37 years	Scale containing 19 work events based on research on life events; selection of events unclear; no focus on daily events	Eight positive events: • successfully completed a project or task • received praise from supervisor • received praise form a coworker • went on a vacation • received a raise • improvements in benefits • received a promotion • received an award or acknowledgement of achievement at work • an unpleasant coworker left your work unit Nine negative events: • assigned undesired work or project • a well-liked coworker left your work unit • problems getting along with a supervisor space	Number of positive and negative events experienced in past month weighted for their perceived impact were related to experience of pleasure, comfort, and tiredness in the past week, and to extrinsic satisfaction, intrinsic satisfaction, and affective commitment; weighted count of negative events also related to anxiety and anger; partial support for affect mediating the relationship of events on job attitudes; effect of events on job attitudes partially remain significant	

Table 4.1: Review of taxonomies of affective events (continued)

Study	Sample	Assessment of events	Categorizing of events	Resulting categories	Comments
			• problems getting along with a coworker • personal problems interfered with work • benefits were reduced • denied a promotion • received a negative performance evaluation • denied a raise Two neutral events: • change in work hours or conditions • change in quality of working		
Miner, Glomb, and Hulin, 2005	42 employees of a manufacturing company; average age 40.2 years; 54 per cent female	Six classes of events; goal: 'measuring a broad array of job events'	Positive or negative events related to either work, coworker, or supervisor, self-classified by trained study participants	Major results: hedonic tone was related to reports of positive and negative events of all types, except for positive supervisor events; effect sizes in relation to negative events were three times (work and coworker) to ten times (supervisor) higher than effect sizes for positive events	The base rate of positive events was three times (coworker events) to almost five times (work events) higher than that of negative events; trait hedonic tone moderated the relationship between event occurrence

Table 4.1: Review of taxonomies of affective events (continued)

Study	Sample	Assessment of events	Categorizing of events	Resulting categories	Comments
					and momentary hedonic tone such that individuals who arrived at work in more positive mood reacted less strongly to negative events and more strongly to positive events
Ohly and Schmitt, 2014	218 employees; 42 per cent female	Participants were instructed to note whether they had experienced certain events at work that they evaluated as being positive or negative during the last hours before completing the questionnaire (dichotomous item: yes/no for positive and negative events separately) and to describe the event	Concept-mapping	• goal attainment, problem solving, task-related success • praise, appreciation, positive feedback • perceived competence in or through social interactions • passively experienced, externally determined positive experiences • conflicts and communication problems • technical difficulties, problems with work tools and equipment • hindrances in goal attainment, obstacles in completing work tasks, overload	

(continued)

Table 4.1: Review of taxonomies of affective events (continued)

Study	Sample	Assessment of events	Categorizing of events	Resulting categories	Comments
				• managerial and internal problems, organizational climate • ambiguity, insecurity, loss of control • health problems and private issues • problems in interactions with clients or patients	
Van Eck, Nicolson, and Berkhof, 1998	85 male white-collar workers; average age 42.1 years	Work-related events, negative social interactions, task demands; based on literature review and their relevance and frequency of occurrence in the sample	'Describe any stressful event or situation that may have taken place'	Work: yes – no Social interaction: yes – no Task demand: yes – no Major results: occurrence of event related to negative and positive mood and agitation; type of event unrelated to outcomes when controlling for appraisal of event	Excluded personal-health related items due to confounding with mood outcomes
Zohar, 1997	145 hospital nurses; 22–61 years old	Checklist of 20 daily hassles based on role stress theory: hassle ambiguity, hassle overload, hassle conflict; rated for severity	Events likely to arise from each stressor generated by experienced individuals; merged by judges, criterion-contaminated, and items unrelated to stressors were eliminated	Hassles scales predict emotional exhaustion and depersonalization over and above role conflict, role ambiguity and role overload, and negative affectivity	

Table 4.1: Review of taxonomies of affective events (continued)

Study	Sample	Assessment of events	Categorizing of events	Resulting categories	Comments
Zohar, 1999	41 military parachute trainers; 100 per cent male; 19–23 years old	Hassle severity of occupation-specific events		Hassle severity predicted end of the day mood, fatigue, and subjective workload	
Zohar, Tzischinski, and Epstein, 2003	78 hospital residents; 26–39 years old; 33 per cent female	Goal disruptive events; goal enhancing events; theoretically based on self-regulation, goals and feedback; controlling for socially rewarding interactions (approval, recognition, attention by significant others)	Goal-related events: profession-specific yes–no questions related to the last 15 minutes; based on interviews and debriefings, for example, socially rewarding interactions with supervisors or coworkers	Major results: disruptive events related to negative affect and fatigue; enhancing events related to positive affect; socially rewarding interactions related to positive affect and fatigue but only immediately following the event, not to end of the day measures; some relationships are moderated by workload	Tested the effect of one type of event controlling for other types of events

exhausted, and *feeling at rest*), Ohly and Schmitt concluded that the 11 event clusters are distinguishable. It should be noted, however, that some clusters can be differentiated further. For example, *goal attainment, problem solving, task-related success* could be differentiated into *goal attainment, and task-related success* on the one hand, and *problem solving* on the other hand. We will come back to this issue later. While we believe that this event taxonomy has merit in detailing the proposed relationships of AET, we will discuss below how using other approaches might also shed light on how affective events and proactive behaviour can be linked.

Affective events and proactive behaviour: overview of previous research

In our review of previous research on affective events and proactive behaviours, we refer to Parker, Bindl, and Strauss's (2010) model of proactive motivation. According to the authors, three types of motivation can be distinguished: can-do, reason-to, and energized-to. Can-do motivation 'arises from perceptions of self-efficacy, control, and (low) cost' (p 827), 'energized to motivation refers to activated positive affective states' (p 827) and reason-to motivation refers to questions such as 'why should I engage in this behaviour' and 'what is the value of this behaviour?' Because energized-to motivation refers to activated positive affective states, the link to proactive behaviours is most obvious (see also Ouyang, in this volume), but below we will also refer reason-to and can-do motivation, when appropriate. When possible, we will also differentiate the target of proactive behaviour following previous theorizing (Grant and Ashford, 2008): Self, other people, or the organization (see Figure 4.1).

Effects of Positive Versus Negative Work Events on Affect, Motivation, and Proactive Behaviour

A core distinction within affective events is with regard to their valence: Scholars have differentiated between negative work events and positive ones (for example, (Basch and Fisher, 1998; Casper, Tremmel, and Sonnentag, 2019; Dimotakis, Scott, and Koopman, 2011). When linking affective events to affective outcomes, Ohly and Schmitt (2014) observed valence symmetric and asymmetric relationships. Positive events both enhanced positive affective states and reduced negative affective states. These effects were mostly of equal size, with the exception of the two positive event clusters

Figure 4.1: Guiding framework linking affective events, affect, proactive motivational states and proactive behaviour

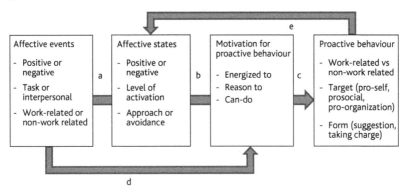

Notes:

Path a: affective events foster specific affective states.

Path b: affective states enhance motivation for proactive behaviour.

Path c: motivation for proactive behaviour makes proactive behaviour more likely.

Path abc (combined): the effect of affective events on proactive behaviour is mediated by affective States and motivation.

Path d: affective events enhance motivation for proactive behaviour directly.

Path e: proactive behaviour leads to specific affective states.

perceived competence in or through social interactions and *passively experienced externally determined positive experience* which reduced *anger* more strongly than they enhanced positive affective states. Two of the negative event clusters showed stronger effects on negative affective states than on positive affective states: *Conflicts and communication problems* more strongly related to anger and *health problems and private issues* to exhaustion.

Given that highly activated affective states might foster proactive action tendencies more strongly (Lebel, 2017; Parker, Bindl, and Strauss, 2010), it is informative which type of event is linked to this type of affect. In the taxonomy development, *goal attainment, problem solving, task-related success* was strongly linked to the positive activated state of *enthusiasm,* and to negative activated states (*anger* and *worried*). In contrast, the second most experienced positive event cluster *praise, appreciation, positive feedback* was linked more strongly to low activated positive affect (*being at rest*) than to *enthusiasm.* Among the negative events, only *conflicts and communication problems* strongly related to the activated state of *anger.*

Activated positive affective states (such as *enthusiasm*) can provide the necessary energy to act on a problem (Parker, Bindl, and Strauss,

2010; see also Ouyang, in this volume), which allows the conclusion that individuals might be more motivated for showing proactive behaviour when experiencing *goal attainment, problem solving, task-related success.* Supporting this argument, a recent study Wang and colleagues (Wang, Zhu et al, 2018) showed that experiencing achievement (and recognition events) is associated with state work engagement (as a positive affective-motivational state), which has been linked to proactive behaviour in prior research (Sonnentag, 2003). Also, negative affective states resulting from negative affective events such as *conflicts* or *goal-disruptive events* might provide the energy to show proactive behaviour, but research so far has been inconclusive (Lebel, 2017; Sonnentag and Starzyk, 2015). Moreover, negative affect can provide information that a situation needs to be changed (Fay and Sonnentag, 2002; Sonnentag and Starzyk, 2015), which is the basis for showing proactive work behaviour that aims at improving the current situation (Strauss and Parker, 2018).

Beyond the energizing effect of activated affective states, there might be specific action tendencies associated with discrete emotions such as fear and anger. Both are highly activated emotions resulting from different appraisal processes (Lebel, 2017), and possibly from different kinds of affective events. Anger is thought to lead to approach (versus avoidance) behaviour, which corresponds to the distinction of prevention- and promotion-oriented proactive behaviour (Spychala and Sonnentag, 2011; Starzyk, Sonnentag, and Albrecht, 2018). The negative event *conflicts and communication problems*, which is strongly linked to anger, might thus lead to more proactive behaviour, and *perceived competence in or through social interactions* and *passively experienced positive events* might reduce the likelihood of proactive behaviour because both are linked to low levels of anger. However, considering that energy to act is not enough to motivate constructive (versus destructive) efforts to deal with a problem, Lebel (2017) proposed that individuals both need a reason to be proactive and need to be convinced that they can do something about the situation. Whereas the reason to be proactive might come from high levels of identification with the organization or from prosocial motivation, support from others might channel the emotional energy of anger into proactive efforts by fostering can-do motivation (Lebel, 2017). Based on this reasoning, one might argue that *conflicts and communication problems* only foster proactive behaviour if these are rare events occurring only with specific colleagues, so that others in the organization can still provide the necessary social support or be the targets of prosocial efforts. In the case of frequent *conflicts and communication problems* with different colleagues, the necessary can-do and reason-to motivation might be lacking for an individual to become proactive and do something about the anger-eliciting situation.

Fear, as another activated negative state, was most pronounced when individuals experienced *ambiguity, loss of control* as an affective event (Ohly and Schmitt, 2014). Lebel argued that the enhanced energy to act through experiencing fear is contingent on the felt responsibility for change (as a reason-to motivation) and social support by others. Thus, not all negative affective events related to fear might spur proactivity. In comparison to fear stemming from internal events within the organization, fear related to outside threats might motivate employees to act prosocially and to voice ideas how to counter the threat when supervisors are seen as open to ideas, which was empirically supported (Lebel, 2016). Contrasting with this perspective, Grant and Ashford (2008) argued that the experience of ambiguous working conditions generally encourages proactive behaviour.

Finally, the individual reaction to negative events might also depend on emotion regulation in that employees respond less strongly to psychological contract breach or even channel their emotions into proactive efforts (Lebel, 2017) when they are able to regulate their negative emotions. These theoretical arguments and empirical findings suggest that contingencies need to be considered in the future when examining proactive behaviour as an outcome of negative affective events.

Effects of task versus interpersonal work events on affect, motivation, and proactive behaviour

Affective work events cannot only be differentiated with regard to their valence, but also with regard to their content in terms of interpersonal versus task-related aspects (Casper, Tremmel, and Sonnentag, 2019). As such, work events can either relate to a work task, such as *goal-attainment, problem solving, task-related success* as an example of a positive task-related work event, or to social encounters at work, such as *conflicts and communication problems* as an example of a negative interpersonal work event, or to both, such as *praise, appreciation, positive feedback* (see Ohly and Schmitt, 2014).

These different event types are likely to foster different appraisal processes (Kiffin-Petersen, Murphy, and Soutar, 2012), which may not only spur energized-to, but also reason-to and can-do motivation. For example, a positive task-related event might foster appraisals of personal mastery (that is fostering self-efficacy) and self-agency (that is fostering control appraisals), whereas a negative interpersonal event might foster appraisal of other-agency (Kiffin-Petersen, Murphy, and Soutar, 2012). Self-efficacy and control appraisals, in turn, represent aspects of can-do motivation (Parker, Bindl, and Strauss, 2010) what might explain at least part of the positive relationships found between positive task-related events, such as feedback (Salanova and Schaufeli, 2008) or job control (Ohly and Fritz, 2010), and proactive work behaviours.

Further, negative interpersonal versus negative task events might be appraised differently in terms of threat, hindrance, or challenge (Searle and Tuckey, 2017). Specifically, negative interpersonal events are more likely to be appraised as threatening, whereas negative task events may be rather appraised as hindering or even challenging. These different forms of appraisal can in turn be linked to different specific emotions (Lazarus, 1991). For instance, negative interpersonal interactions have been linked in particular to threat appraisal (that is evaluation of future harm; Searle and Tuckey, 2017), which mediated the effects on *anger* (Tuckey et al, 2015). This is in line with event-based studies showing negative interpersonal events such as *conflicts and communication problems* (Ohly and Schmitt, 2014) and incivility (Grandey et al, 2002) strongly related to the negative emotion of anger. Anger as a high-activation emotion may not only energize employees to engage in proactive behaviour but may in particular signal a need to change (Lebel, 2017). Put differently, in triggering threat appraisal, negative interpersonal work events might pose a reason-to motivation to engage in proactive work behaviour, for instance to down-regulate anger or frustration (Grant, 2013). Negative task-related events, such as situational constraints (see Table 4.1), on the other hand, are rather related to hindrance appraisal (Searle and Tuckey, 2017). Fay and Sonnentag (2002) suggested that situational constraints initiate thinking about how one may prevent such negative experiences in the future, thus fostering proactive behaviour. Accordingly, situational constraints positively relate to same day proactive behaviour (Fritz and Sonnentag, 2009), in particular issue identification (Sonnentag and Starzyk, 2015). Finally, some negative task-related events, such as time pressure, are even related to challenge appraisal (Ohly and Fritz, 2010), which has in turn been related to positive activation and ultimately proactive behaviour (for example, Binnewies, Sonnentag, and Mojza, 2009). In sum, negative task-related events may not only spur energized-to motivation but also reason-to motivation to engage in proactive work behaviours.

Lastly, interpersonal and task events have also been shown to satisfy or thwart different needs. For example, recognition as one type of event with a stronger social component can be linked to a stronger satisfaction of the need for relatedness, whereas achievement events seem to fulfil the need for competence more strongly (Wang et al, 2018). Given that proactive behaviour is fostered by individuals' feelings of competence (Frese and Fay, 2001; Ohly and Fritz, 2010), it may be that task events are more important than interpersonal events to foster proactive behaviour. Specifically, feelings of competence spur self-efficacy, which is classified as a can-do motivational state in the model of motivation for proactive behaviour (Parker, Bindl, and Strauss, 2010). In addition, experiencing control at work is not only positively related to positive activation (for example, Elfering et al, 2005), but also to autonomy need satisfaction (Van den Broeck et al, 2016), which might enhance control appraisal, another aspect of can-do motivation (Parker, Bindl, and Strauss, 2010). Thus, task-related work events, in particular positive task events, can be linked to proactive behaviour through can-do motivation, not only energized-to motivation. At the same time, however, also lacking competence has been shown to foster proactive work behaviours. Specifically, the experience of low competence might pose a reason-to motivation. For example, task failure (a negative task-related event, see Table 4.1) thwarts competence need satisfaction, which in turn positively predicts proactive behaviour (Fay and Sonnentag, 2012).

In sum, positive task-related events can be linked to higher proactive behaviour through energized-to as well as can-do motivational states. At the same time, also negative task events can be linked to higher proactive behaviour, in particular issue identification (Sonnentag and Starzyk, 2015), voice (Grant, 2013) and taking charge (Fritz and Sonnentag, 2009), through reason-to motivation. Evidence on the role of interpersonal work events for proactive behaviour is less conclusive. Interpersonal work events may evoke particularly strong affective reactions in terms of general positive and negative activation (for example, Dimotakis et al, 2011) as well as anger (Grandey et al., 2002), with anger being particularly prone to be experienced in reaction to negative interpersonal events as compared to negative task events (Venz, Kalde, and Sonnentag, 2014). Hence, potentially, negative interpersonal events may be mainly linked to proactive behaviour through energized-to motivational states. As such, task events might play a larger role in shaping can-do and reason-to motivational states, whereas interpersonal events might play a larger role in shaping energized-to motivational states. Moreover, it might be that task events affect proactive behaviour focussed on one's own task (proactive work behaviour), whereas social events affect proactive behaviour related to another person (for example, proactive helping; Sonnentag and Starzyk, 2015).

Effects of work versus non-work events on affect, motivation, and proactive behaviour

While AET focuses on work events, surely things also happen to employees off work. Non-work events, such as leisure mastery experiences or interpersonal conflict with one's spouse (Table 4.1), might enhance or drain energy in the private life domain, which in turn affects proactive behaviour in this life domain, such as career-related proactive behaviour (Grant and Parker, 2009); for example, studying for a degree part-time). Specifically, when individuals gain energy through experiencing positive events in their private life, or when they share their positive work experiences at home (Ilies, Keeney, and Scott, 2011), proactive behaviour in this life domain gets more likely. In contrast, work-related events might be more important for proactive behaviour in the work domain (for example, Fritz and Sonnentag, 2009). Although plausible, research examining and comparing these life-domain specific effects with regard to proactivity is limited or virtually non-existent.

Research evidence suggests the existence of spill over between life domains, such as for instance documented in a large number of studies on work-to-life conflict and work-to-life enrichment. Research on spill over processes relating work events with private proactive behaviour is rare, though. Some studies have related work experiences to leisure crafting, defined 'as the proactive pursuit and enactment of leisure activities targeted at goal setting, human connection, learning and personal development' (Petrou and Bakker, 2016, p 507). When experiencing overload and low autonomy at work (that is, negative task-related work events) but high autonomy off work (that is, a positive non-work event), employees engage in more leisure crafting. Further, some evidence suggests spill-over effects from the non-work domain to the work domain, which may affect proactive behaviour at work. For example, the event cluster *health problems and private issues*, which relates to the non-work life domain, affects feeling *exhausted* while working (Ohly and Schmitt, 2014). It should be noted however, that it is unclear that this cluster represents an event in the sense of 'something that happens' and is 'bound in time and space'.

One could argue that positive recovery experiences off work (Fritz and Sonnentag, 2005) are closely related to or may even be classified as positive non-work events (for example, experiencing mastery when finishing a piece of art work in an arts class). Several studies have linked such positive non-work experiences to higher at-work proactive behaviour (for example, Sonnentag, 2003). Closer examining this relationship, Ouyang et al (2019) found heightened positive activated affect to mediate the relationship between positive non-work experiences and proactive behaviours at work the next day. Similarly, a good night's sleep has been shown to predict vitality, which then translates into higher proactive behaviour at work (Schmitt, Belschak, and Den Hartog, 2017). In contrast, negative off-job events, such as private hassles, are related to lower on-job proactivity (Fritz and Sonnentag, 2005) and this relationship is due to lower high-activation positive affect (Ouyang et al, 2019). Interestingly, whereas positive off-work experiences may also foster low-activation positive affect, it is only high-activation positive affect that mediates the effects on proactive behaviour at work (Ouyang et al, 2019), indicating that low-activation positive affect does not provide the energetical resources necessary for proactive behaviour. In sum, non-work events seem to have the potential to energize employees, that is, to enhance energized-to motivation, that spills over to the work domain where it translates into proactive behaviour. In addition, off-job experiences such as mastery and control also foster at-job proactive behaviours via role-breath self-efficacy and desire for control, that is via enhanced can-do motivation as well as reason-to motivation (Ouyang et al, 2019).

Further, some research findings suggest that non-work and work events might interact in shaping employee proactivity (Schilpzand, Houston, and Cho, 2018). For instance, Schilpzand, Houston, and Cho (2018) showed empowering leader behaviours, which might be classified a positive work event, to be positively related to next-day's proactive goal-setting and ultimately proactive risk-taking and voice behaviours at work with this relationship being stronger when employees had slept well (indicating a positive non-work experience).

Proactive behaviour as an affective event

So far, we have suggested that affective events have an effect on an employee's energized-to (for example, positive affect), can-do (for example, self-efficacy), and reason-to (for example, anger regulation) motivation, which in turn spark their proactive behaviour. However, engaging in proactive behaviour also has affective and motivational *consequences* (Weigelt et al, 2018; Wolsink et al, 2019; also Zacher, this volume), indicating that an employee's engagement in a specific proactive behaviour may depict an affective event itself (Starzyk,

Sonnentag, and Albrecht, 2018). This reverse effect is depicted as path e in our model (Figure 4.1).

In particular, employees likely evaluate the consequences of their proactive behaviour (Starzyk, Sonnentag, and Albrecht, 2018). As such, showing proactivity might lead to (1) frustration – when evaluated as unpleasant and unsuccessful, (2) threat appraisal – when the employee loses control of the process, or (3) growth – when the proactive behaviour was successful (Bindl, 2019). Hence, proactive behaviour can affect employees via a negative, strain pathway in which proactive behaviour creates negative affective states such as anxiety, and via a positive, energy pathway in which proactive behaviour generates vitality via perceived competence (Cangiano, Parker, and Yeo, 2019). In sum, it seems reasonable that proactive behaviour – when successful – makes people feel good and energized (Wolsink et al, 2019), but that proactive behaviour also bears the danger of several negative consequences. More specifically, for instance, promotion-oriented proactive behaviour may increase task conflict (Spychala and Sonnentag, 2011). Likewise, innovative behaviour, as a type of proactive work behaviour, is related to conflict and worsened coworker relationships (Janssen, 2003). On the other hand, proactive behaviour may also reduce negative events or even generate positive events. For instance, prevention-oriented proactive behaviour, which aims at precluding the recurrence of negative work events, is linked to reduced task conflict (Spychala and Sonnentag, 2011). Proactive networking behaviour is associated with higher social support and positive affect (Baumeler et al, 2018).

Another viewpoint on how proactive behaviour might shape employee affect is from an affect-regulation perspective. As we have outlined before, affective states can motivate proactive behaviour. In terms of anger and other high-activation negative affect, proactive behaviour reactions are likely aimed at down-regulating this negative feeling state (Grant, 2013; Wolsink et al, 2019). Accordingly, speaking up about problems (that is, problem-focused voice) indeed serves down-regulation of negative affect (Starzyk, Sonnentag, and Albrecht, 2018). In sum, successful proactive behaviour can serve an affect-regulation purpose in the sense of up-regulation of positive affective states and down-regulation of negative affective states.

Open questions and future research

Our review of the literature suggests that AET is a useful framework to delineate how affective events are linked to proactive behaviour. Beyond the energizing effect of positive work-related events, there is evidence for effects of specific kinds of events, effects across domains, and on specific kinds of proactive behaviours. Despite this evidence, there are still open research questions. For example, it remains unclear if affective events foster proactive behaviour without affective influences (path d in Figure 4.1). Experienced affect might change the expected valence of an outcome of behaviour (Seo, Feldman Barret, and Bartunek, 2004), but it is also plausible that events might have the same effect without eliciting affective experiences. For example, negative events with coworkers might affect the valence of proactive behaviour intended to benefit the others. More research is needed to study the two-step mediation model (path abc) we proposed.

Moreover, for some specific types of events, for example gratitude events (Fehr et al, 2017), there is little research linking them to proactive behaviour (see Wu and Li, in this volume). In this conjunction, there is not much research on the role of interpersonal work events in relation to proactive behaviour in general; and rarely any research comparing (that is simultaneously testing) task-related and interpersonal events (see Casper, Tremmel, and Sonnentag, 2019; Venz, Kalde, and Sonnentag, 2014, for exceptions). Finally, the boundary conditions (for example, emotion regulation, reason-to) under which the experience of negative events in general, and negative interpersonal events in particular, might spur proactive behaviour need to be explored further. Similarly, research is lacking that examines the interaction of different events, such as between positive and negative or between non-work and work events. Moreover, affective states need to be differentiated by taking a closer look at discrete emotions (for example, anger, fear, enthusiasm, serenity). Similarly, the different targets of proactive behaviour (self, others, and organization) need to be differentiated.

Because affective events are inherently dynamic, diary methods using one or more daily assessments (Bolger, Davis, and Rafaeli, 2003) are suitable to study the relationships proposed in this chapter, in particular when studies use an event-sampling approach (Reis and Gable, 2000), which refers to the assessment of momentary states contingent on the occurrence of predefined events (for example, stressful events; Elfering et al, 2005; anger- and pride-eliciting events; Grandey, Tam, and Brauburger, 2002). This way, a fine-grained picture of how affective events shape affective states, motivation and proactive behaviour can be gained. However, despite this value, the method might pose high demands on study participants when many affective events occur, which is why researchers might want to consider alternative approaches such as interval-contingent assessment (asking at predefined times during the day) or the day reconstruction method (Kahneman et al, 2004). Within the interval-contingent assessment, participants will report their experience in the past few hours, and day reconstruction focuses on the assessment of daily events and activities and associated thoughts and feelings retrospectively, typically at the end of the day. Compared to day reconstruction, interval-contingent assessment yields more daily assessments, which makes it possible to test the mediational sequence we proposed as well as to include work and non-work events. Because of the multiple assessments, potential common source bias in the data is reduced (Podsakoff et al, 2003), and it is possible to test alternative causal effects (for example, proactive behaviour on motivation and affective states).

By reviewing the effects of affective events on proactivity, summarizing the research into an overall framework and discussing avenues for future research we hope to contribute novel insights and provide the basis for more work in this emerging field.

References

Basch, J. and Fisher, C. D. (1998). Affective Events-Emotions matrix: A Classification of Work Events and Associated Emotions, Robina, Australia: Bond University.

Baumeler, F., Johnston, C. S., Hirschi, A., and Spurk, D. (2018). Networking as predictor of work-nonwork enrichment: Mechanisms on the within-and between-person level. *Journal of Vocational Behavior*, 109, 166–77.

Bindl, U. K. (2019). Work-related proactivity through the lens of narrative: investigating emotional journeys in the process of making things happen. *Human Relations*, 72(4), 615–45.

Binnewies, C., Sonnentag, S., and Mojza, E. (2009). Daily performance at work: Feeling recovered in the morning as a predictor of day-level job performance. *Journal of Organizational Behavior*, 30, 67–93.

Bolger, N., Davis, A., and Rafaeli, E. (2003). Diary methods: Capturing life as it is lived. *Annual Review of Psychology*, 54, 579–616.

Bolger, N., DeLongis, A., Kessler, R. C., and Schilling, E. A. (1989). Effects of daily stress on negative mood. *Journal of Personality and Social Psychology*, 57(5), 808–18.

Cangiano, F., Parker, S. K., and Yeo, G. B. (2019). Does daily proactivity affect well-being? The moderating role of punitive supervision. *Journal of Organizational Behavior*, 40(1), 59–72.

Casper, A., Tremmel, S., and Sonnentag, S. (2019). The power of affect: A three-wave panel study on reciprocal relationships between work events and affect at work. *Journal of Occupational and Organizational Psychology*, 92(2), 436–60.

Conway, N., and Briner, R. B. (2002). Full-time versus part-time employees: Understanding the links between work status, the psychological contract, and attitudes. *Journal of Vocational Behavior*, 61(2), 279–301.

Dimotakis, N., Scott, B. A., and Koopman, J. (2011). An experience sampling investigation of workplace interactions, affective states, and employee well-being. *Journal of Organizational Behavior*, 32, 572–88.

Elfering, A., Grebner, S., Semmer, N. K., Kaiser-Freiburghaus, D., Lauper-Del Ponte, S., and Witschi, I. (2005). Chronic job stressors and job control: Effects on event-related coping success and well-being. *Journal of Occupational and Organizational Psychology,* 78, 237–52.

Fay, D. and Sonnentag, S. (2002). Rethinking the effects of stressors: A longitudinal study on personal initiative. *Journal of Occupational Health Psychology,* 7, 221–34.

Fay, D. and Sonnentag, S. (2012). Within-person fluctuations of proactive behavior: How affect and experienced competence regulate work behavior. *Human Performance,* 25, 72–93.

Fehr, R., Fulmer, A., Awtrey, E., and Miller, J. A. (2017). The grateful workplace: A multilevel model of gratitude in organizations. *Academy of Management Review,* 42(2), 361–81.

Fitness, J. (2000). Anger in the workplace: an emotion script approach to anger episodes between workers and their superiors, co-workers and subordinates. *Journal of Organizational Behavior: The International Journal of Industrial, Occupational and Organizational Psychology and Behavior,* 21(2), 147–62.

Frese, M., and Fay, D. (2001). 4. Personal initiative: An active performance concept for work in the 21st century. *Research in Organizational Behavior, 23,* 133–87.

Frese, M. and Zapf, D. (1994). Action as the core of work psychology: A German approach. In H. C. Triandis, M. D. Dunnette and L. M. Hough (eds), *Handbook of Industrial and Organizational Psychology,* 2nd edn, vol 4, Palo Alto, CA: Consulting Psychologist Press, pp 271–340.

Fritz, C. and Sonnentag, S. (2005). Recovery, health, and job performance: Effects of weekend experiences. *Journal of Occupational Health Psychology,* 10, 187–99.

Fritz, C. and Sonnentag, S. (2009). Antecedents of day-level proactive behavior at work: A look at job stressors and positive affect during the workday. *Journal of Management,* 35, 94–111.

Grandey, A. A., Tam, A. P., and Brauburger, A. L. (2002). Affective states and traits in the workplace: Diary and survey data from young workers. *Motivation and Emotion,* 26, 31–55.

Grant, A. M. (2013). Rocking the boat but keeping it steady: The role of emotion regulation in employee voice. *Academy of Management Journal,* 56(6), 1703–23.

Grant, A. M. and Ashford, S. J. (2008). The dynamics of proactivity at work. *Research in Organizational behavior,* 28, 3–34.

Grant, A. M. and Parker, S. K. (2009). 7 redesigning work design theories: The rise of relational and proactive perspectives. *The Academy of Management Annals,* 3(1), 317–75.

Gross, S., Semmer, N. K., Meier, L. L., Kälin, W., Jacobshagen, N., and Tschan, F. (2011). The effect of positive events at work on after-work fatigue: They matter most in face of adversity. *Journal of Applied Psychology,* 96(3), 654–64.

Hahn, S. E. (2000). The effects of locus of control on daily exposure, coping and reactivity to work interpersonal stressors: A diary study. *Personality and Individual Differences,* 29(4), 729–48.

Hansbrough, T. K., Lord, R. G., and Schyns, B. (2015). Reconsidering the accuracy of follower leadership ratings. *The Leadership Quarterly,* 26(2), 220–37.

Ilies, R., Keeney, J., and Scott, B. A. (2011). Work–family interpersonal capitalization: Sharing positive work events at home. *Organizational Behavior and Human Decision Processes,* 114(2), 115–26.

Janssen, O. (2003). Innovative behaviour and job involvement at the price of conflict and less satisfactory relations with co-workers. *Journal of Occupational and Organizational Psychology,* 76, 347–64.

Johns, G. (2017). Reflections on the 2016 decade award: Incorporating context in organizational research. *Academy of Management Review,* 42(4), 577–95.

Kahneman, D., Krueger, A. B., Schkade, D. A., Schwarz, N., and Stone, A. A. (2004). A survey method for characterizing daily life experience: The day reconstruction method. *Science,* 306(5702), 1776–80.

Kiffin-Petersen, S., Murphy, S. A., and Soutar, G. (2012). The problem-solving service worker: Appraisal mechanisms and positive affective experiences during customer interactions. *Human Relations,* 65(9), 1179–206.

Lazarus, R. S. (1991). Progress on a cognitive-motivational-relational theory of emotion. *American Psychologist,* 46(8), 819.

Lebel, R. D. (2016). Overcoming the fear factor: How perceptions of supervisor openness lead employees to speak up when fearing external threat. *organizational behavior and human decision processes,* 135, 10–21.

Lebel, R. D. (2017). Moving beyond fight and flight: A contingent model of how the emotional regulation of anger and fear sparks proactivity. *Academy of Management Review,* 42(2), 190–206.

Mignonac, K., and Herrbach, O. (2004). Linking work events, affective states, and attitudes: An empirical study of managers' emotions. *Journal of Business and Psychology,* 19(2), 221–40.

Miner, A. G., Glomb, T. M., and Hulin, C. (2005). Experience sampling mood and its correlates at work. *Journal of Occupational and Organizational Psychology,* 78(2), 171–93.

Morgeson, F. P., Mitchell, T. R., and Liu, D. (2015). Event system theory: An event-oriented approach to the organizational sciences. *Academy of Management Review,* 40(4), 515–37.

Ohly, S. and Fritz, C. (2010). Work characteristics, challenge appraisal, creativity and proactive behavior: A multi-level study. *Journal of Organizational Behavior,* 31, 543–65.

Ohly, S. and Schmitt, A. (2014). What makes us enthusiastic, angry, feeling at rest or worried? Development and validation of an affective work events taxonomy using concept mapping methodology. *Journal of Business and Psychology.* doi: 10.1007/s10869-013-9328-3.

Ohly, S. and Schmitt, A. (2017). Work design and proactivity. In S. K. Parker and U. K. Bindl (eds), *Proactivity at Work: Making Things Happen in Organizations,* Abingdon: Taylor and Francis, pp 387–410.

Ouyang, K., Cheng, B. H., Lam, W., and Parker, S. K. (2019). Enjoy your evening, be proactive tomorrow: How off-job experiences shape daily proactivity. *Journal of Applied Psychology,* 104, 1003–19.

Parker, S. K., Bindl, U. K., and Strauss, K. (2010). Making things happen: A model of proactive motivation. *Journal of Management,* 36, 827–856.

Petrou, P. and Bakker, A. B. (2016). Crafting one's leisure time in response to high job strain. *Human Relations,* 69(2), 507–29.

Podsakoff, P. M., MacKenzie, S. B., Lee, J.-Y., and Podsakoff, N. P. (2003). Common method biases in behavioral research: A critical review of the literature and recommended remedies. *Journal of Applied Psychology,* 88, 879–903.

Reis, H. T. and Gable, S. L. (2000). Event-sampling and other methods for studying everyday experience. In H. T. Reis and C. M. Judd (eds), *Handbook of Research Methods in Social and Personality Psychology* New York: Cambridge University Press, pp 190–222.

Salanova, M. and Schaufeli, W. B. (2008). A cross-national study of work engagement as a mediator between job resources and proactive behaviour. *The International Journal of Human Resource Management,* 19(1), 116–31.

Schilpzand, P., Houston, L., and Cho, J. (2018). Not too tired to be proactive: Daily empowering leadership spurs next-morning employee proactivity as moderated by nightly sleep quality. *Academy of Management Journal,* 61(6), 2367–87.

Schmitt, A., Belschak, F. D., and Den Hartog, D. N. (2017). Feeling vital after a good night's sleep: The interplay of energetic resources and self-efficacy for daily proactivity. *Journal of Occupational Health Psychology,* 22(4), 443.

Searle, B. J. and Tuckey, M. R. (2017). Differentiating challenge, hindrance, and threat in the stress process. In C. I. Cooper and M. P. Leiter (eds), *The Routledge Companion to Wellbeing at Work,* New York: Routledge, pp 25–36.

Seo, M.-G., Feldman Barret, L., and Bartunek, J. M. (2004). The role of affective experience in work motivation. *Academy of Management Review,* 29, 423–39.

Sonnentag, S. (2003). Recovery, work engagement, and proactive behavior: A new look at the interface between nonwork and work. *Journal of Applied Psychology,* 88, 518–28.

Sonnentag, S. and Starzyk, A. (2015). Perceived prosocial impact, perceived situational constraints, and proactive work behavior: Looking at two distinct affective pathways. *Journal of Organizational Behavior,* 36(6), 806–24.

Spychala, A. and Sonnentag, S. (2011). The dark and the bright sides of proactive work behaviour and situational constraints: Longitudinal relationships with task conflicts. *European Journal of Work and Organizational Psychology,* 20(5), 654–80.

Starzyk, A., Sonnentag, S., and Albrecht, A. G. (2018). The affective relevance of suggestion-focused and problem-focused voice: A diary study on voice in meetings. *Journal of Occupational and Organizational Psychology,* 91(2), 340–61.

Strauss, K. and Parker, S. K. (2018). Intervening to enhance proactivity in organizations: Improving the present or changing the future. *Journal of Management,* 44(3), 1250–78.

Tuckey, M. R., Searle, B., Boyd, C. M., Winefield, A. H., and Winefield, H. R. (2015). Hindrances are not threats: Advancing the multidimensionality of work stress. *Journal of Occupational Health Psychology,* 20(2), 131.

Van den Broeck, A., Ferris, D. L., Chang, C.-H., and Rosen, C. C. (2016). A review of self-determination theory's basic psychological needs at work. *Journal of Management,* 42(5), 1195–229.

Van Eck, M., Nicolson, N. A., and Berkhof, J. (1998). Effects of stressful daily events on mood states: relationship to global perceived stress. *Journal of personality and social psychology,* 75(6), 1572–1.

Venz, L., Kalde, M., and Sonnentag, S. (2014). *Personal Characteristics and the Affective Process at Work: An Experience Sampling Study.* Paper presented at the Academy of Management Proceedings.

Wang, N., Zhu, J., Dormann, C., Song, Z., and Bakker, A. B. (2018). The daily motivators: positive work events, psychological needs satisfaction, and work engagement. *Applied Psychology,* 69, 508–37.

Weigelt, O., Syrek, C. J., Schmitt, A., and Urbach, T. (2018). Finding peace of mind when there still is so much left undone: A diary study on how job stress, competence need satisfaction, and proactive work behavior contribute to work-related rumination during the weekend. *Journal of Occupational Health Psychology,* 24, 373–86.

Weiss, H. M. and Cropanzano, R. (1996). Affective events theory: A theoretical discussion of the structure, causes and consequences of affective experiences at work. *Research in Organizational Behavior,* 18, 1–74.

Wolsink, I., Den Hartog, D. D., Belschak, F. D., and Oosterwijk, S. (2019). Do you feel like being proactive today? Trait-proactivity moderates affective causes and consequences of proactive behavior. *PloS one,* 14(8), e0220172.

Zohar, D. (1997). Predicting burnout with a hassle-based measure of role demands. *Journal of Organizational Behavior,* 18(2), 101–15.

Zohar, D. (1999). When things go wrong: The effect of daily work hassles on effort, exertion and negative mood. *Journal of occupational and organizational psychology,* 72(3), 265–83.

Zohar, D., Tzischinski, O., and Epstein, R. (2003). Effects of energy availability on immediate and delayed emotional reactions to work events. *Journal of Applied Psychology,* 88(6), 1082–93.

5

Exploring Cross-Domain Relations between Emotional Energy and Proactivity

Kan Ouyang

The nature of today's global work environments is competitive, uncertain, and fast-changing. Employee proactive behaviour plays an important role in assuring organizational survival and sustainability in such dynamic work contexts (Bindl and Parker, 2010; Crant, 2000). Proactive behaviour refers to employees' self-initiated and future-oriented behaviours to take control of situations and bring about constructive changes in the workplace (Grant and Ashford, 2008; Parker, Bindl, and Strauss, 2010). Employees can display proactivity through various forms of behaviours, such as expressing constructive work-related ideas or suggestions to supervisors (Morrison, 2011), introducing new procedures to improve work effectiveness (Morrison and Phelps, 1999), seeking feedback from supervisor about work performance (Ashford, Blatt, and Vandewalle, 2003), taking actions to prevent potential work problems (Frese and Fay, 2001), and crafting task or relational boundaries of one's job (Wrzesniewski and Dutton, 2001). Previous studies have shown that employee proactivity leads to beneficial outcomes for individuals and organizations, such as higher performance evaluations, enhanced career success, and better organizational performance (for example, Frese, et al, 2007; Fuller and Marler, 2009; Grant, Parker, and Collins, 2009).

Because of the value of employee proactivity at work, one major stream of research on this topic investigates what factors enhance or undermine proactivity. Prior studies show that individual differences, such as proactive personality (Bateman and Crant, 1993), desire for control (Ashford and Black, 1996), learning goal orientation (Vandewalle et al, 2000), and future work self (Strauss, Griffin, and Parker, 2012), significantly affect proactive behaviour. Additionally, employee proactivity is also influenced by situational factors. Most studies focus on the effects of factors in the work domain, such as work design (Frese, Garst, and Fay, 2007), coworker trust (Parker, Williams, and Turner, 2006), and leadership (Martin, Liao, and Campbell, 2013). Furthermore, Parker, Bindl, and Strauss (2010) united these findings and proposed a model of proactive motivation that three key motivational processes – *can do*, *reason to*, and *energized to* – underlie these effects. *Can do* motivation involves perceptions of capabilities to engage in proactive behaviour (for example, role breadth self-efficacy); *reason to* motivation refers to internal forces that drive employees to act proactively (for example, autonomous motivation); *energized to* motivation recognizes that affective experiences energize individuals and boost their proactivity (for example, activated positive affect).

Unfortunately, little is known about how factors in the non-work domain shape employee proactivity at work. Prior research on work–non-work interface, such as work recovery and work–family conflict, has consistently shown that employees' experiences during off-job time significantly affect their well-being, work attitudes, and work behaviours (for example, Amstad et al, 2011; Demerouti et al, 2009; Ford, Heinen, and Langkamer, 2007; Zhang et al, 2018). Considering the importance of proactivity for employees and organizations, it seems imperative to examine the cross-domain effects of non-work-related factors on proactivity. Moreover, aligning with previous research (Ouyang et al, 2019; Parker, Bindl, and Strauss, 2010), this chapter advocates an affective perspective to understand those cross-domain effects. Thus, this chapter aims to conduct a systematic review of the nonwork antecedents of proactivity at work, illustrate how emotional energy likely links non-work antecedents to proactivity, and discuss the avenues for future research. Such an endeavour helps enrich our knowledge of the antecedents of employee proactivity from both work and non-work domains.

Studies on the relationships between non-work variables and proactivity, still in its infancy, generally examine two categories of non-work factors: one is off-job experiences, or employees' experiences after work (for example, Fritz et al, 2010; Sonnentag, 2003); the other is sleep (Schilpzand, Houston, and Cho, 2018; Schmitt, Belschak, and Den Hartog, 2017). In addition, such non-work-related factors likely influence individuals' affective experiences, which in turn act as energetical activation for employees to engage in proactive behaviour (for example, Ouyang et al, 2019). This perspective of emotional energy could provide insight into understanding the non-work antecedents of proactivity in the workplace. Below, I first define the key concept of employee proactivity to lay the foundation. I then review the empirical findings of the relationships between non-work variables and employee proactivity, as well as presenting emotional energy as one critical underlying process. Future research directions and practical implications for organizations of this research topic are discussed at the end.

Employee proactivity

Employee proactivity has been evinced to be important for employees and organizations to perform well in the work environment of uncertainty and unpredictability (Campbell, 2000; Cangiano and Parker, 2016; Parker, 2000). Although there is no uniform definition for proactivity, scholars have reached agreement on its three core elements: self-initiated, future-focused, and change-oriented (for example, Crant, 2000; Grant and Ashford, 2008; Parker, Wang, and Liao, 2019). Self-initiative denotes that individuals take an active role in initiating proactive behaviour, rather than being requested or directed to behave. In addition, when engaging in proactive behaviour, individuals focus on the future with anticipating potential problems or forthcoming opportunities and acting in advance accordingly. Moreover, the goal of proactivity is to bring about constructive changes and improvements to the organizational environment and/or the individuals within the environment. In line with these fundamental characteristics, in this chapter employee proactivity is defined as employees' self-initiated and future-oriented actions with the aim to constructively change and improve themselves and/or their work environments.

Most studies on proactive behaviour adopt a between-person approach (Bindl and Parker, 2010). While important, such perspective primarily focuses on a relatively static view of the antecedents and outcomes of proactivity. Increasing evidence shows that proactive behaviour varies across days, suggesting intraindividual variability of such behaviour (Fay and Sonnentag, 2012; Ohly and Fritz, 2010; Sonnentag, 2003). Statistically, research of employees' daily proactive behaviour indicates that the within-individual variance of proactivity at the daily level ranges between 40 per cent and 60 per cent (Binnewies, Sonnentag, and Mojza, 2009; Ouyang et al, 2019; Sonnentag, 2003). Using a within-person approach thus helps complement our knowledge of momentary proactive behaviour.

Regarding the operationalization of employee proactivity, on one hand, some scholars focus on examining the general concept of proactivity (for example, Frese et al, 1997; Griffin, Neal, and Parker, 2007). For example, Griffin, Neal, and Parker (2007) investigate employee proactivity that directed towards three different levels: individual-level (for example, initiate better ways of doing one's job), team-level (for example, develop new methods to help one's work unit perform better), and organization-level (for example, propose ways to increase organizational efficiency). The construct of personal initiative is also utilized as an approach to capture employees' generalized proactive tendency at work (for example, 'Whenever there is a chance to get actively involved, I take it' as one sample item; Glaser, Stam, and Takeuchi, 2016; Hong et al, 2015).

On the other hand, studies also focus on specific types of proactive behaviour that are more context-specific, such as taking charge, voice behaviour, issue selling, feedback-seeking, job change negotiation, and career initiative, because employees engage in different forms of proactive behaviour as described above (Crant, 2000; Parker and Collins, 2010). The operationalization of employee proactivity hence involves using proper measures to tap the unique attributes of those self-starting behaviours. In some research contexts, scholars might need to adapt from existing scales or develop new ones to attain more valid and reliable assessment. For example, Lam and Mayer (2014) adapted the voice measure of Van Dyne and LePine's (1998) to fit a customer service context. Parker, Williams, and Turner (2006) developed new measures of proactive idea implementation and proactive problem solving for studying wire makers within a manufacturing organization.

Non-work-domain predictors of employee proactivity

The impact of non-work variables on workplace outcomes has been shown to be fundamental for developing a valid understanding of how people feel and behave at work (for example, Demerouti et al, 2009; Mullins et al, 2014). Nevertheless, our knowledge of the non-work antecedents of employee proactivity is surprisingly limited. This oversight is noteworthy given the important role of non-work factors in shaping workplace outcomes; more importantly, examining non-work-domain variables provides insight into understanding proactive behaviour as a dynamically fluctuating phenomenon, which are demonstrated in the review below. Two types of factors in the non-work domain have received attention, though insufficient, from scholars. In this section, I first review studies that focus on off-job experiences as predictors and then review those that focus on the effect of sleep.

Off-Job experiences and employee proactivity

As one of the first research to examine non-work-domain antecedents of employee proactivity, the study of Sonnentag (2003) focuses on post-work recovery, referring to the process through which individuals mitigate or reverse the negative effects of job demands and stressors and restore the prestressor level of functioning (Craig and Cooper, 1992; Sonnentag and Fritz, 2007). Moreover, this study brings the fluctuation of proactive behaviour to the fore, such that it examines the relationship between post-work recovery on a specific workday and proactive behaviour during the subsequent workday. Data were collected from 147 employees with a paper-and-pencil questionnaire and daily surveys, also paper-and-pencil, over five consecutive workdays. The study found that daily recovery (reported in the morning before starting to work) was positively related to next-day proactive behaviour in the forms of personal initiative and pursuit of learning (reported at the end of workday before leaving the office), and work engagement (also reported at the end of workday) mediated this relationship.

Similarly, Binnewies, Sonnentag, and Mojza (2009) found that feeling recovered in the morning (assessed in the morning before going to work) positively related to daily personal initiative (assessed after work when arriving at home). Job control (assessed in a paper-based general survey) moderated this relationship, such that the relationship was stronger for employees with high levels of job control. The daily surveys of 99 participants over four consecutive workdays were completed through pocket computers.

Instead of looking at general recovery experience, the study of Fritz et al (2010) focuses on one specific recovery experience, that is, psychological detachment from work. It refers to being physically and mentally away from work or work-related thoughts during non-work time (Etzion, Eden, and Lapidot, 1998). With a sample of 107 participants, they found an inverted U-shaped relationship between psychological detachment over the past few weeks and coworker-reported personal initiative. It should be noted that this study used a cross-sectional design.

Examining a variety of off-job experiences, the research of Ouyang et al (2019) highlights the distinct effects of off-job experiences on daily proactive behaviour. 183 participants completed online daily surveys across ten workdays. They reported off-job experiences in the evening before going to bed and proactive behaviour at the end of the workday before leaving the workplace. The findings show that daily off-job mastery (that is, off-job experience that involves learning or challenging opportunities in the non-work domain) and off-job agency (that is, individuals have control over how to spend their off-job time) were positively related to next-day proactivity, daily off-job hassles (that is, extra stressors that occur after work) were negatively related to next-day proactivity, while off-job relaxation (that is, off-job experience that sympathetic activation decreases and little individual effort is involved) and off-job psychological detachment did not significantly affect proactivity. Moreover, the study found that three motivational states, including high-activated positive affect, role breadth self-efficacy, and desire for control, measured in the morning before commencing work mediated those relationships.

Taking a step further, a recent study of Chawla et al (2020) investigates the profiles of daily recovery experiences and their effects on daily proactive behaviour. 207 participants completed two surveys per day for five consecutive workdays, with recovery experiences assessed in the morning before work and proactivity assessed at the end of the workday. The findings suggest that profiles of high levels of all recovery experiences (that is, relaxation, mastery, control, and psychological detachment) have highest levels of proactive behaviour, and profiles of high levels of relaxation, control, and psychological detachment with low levels of mastery have lowest proactivity.

The study of Fritz and Sonnentag (2005) examines weekend experiences and uses a longitudinal design with collecting data over three measurement occasions from 87 employees. Weekend experiences were measured at the end of the weekend (Sunday evening), and personal initiative and pursuit of learning, as indicators of proactivity, were measured at the beginning of the following work week (Monday or Tuesday evening). They found that non-work hassles were negatively associated with both personal initiative and pursuit of learning, and positive work reflection during the weekend (that is, thinking about positive aspects of one's work) was positively associated with pursuit of learning. In addition, social activities during weekend, for example, spending time with others, was not significantly related to proactivity.

Sleep and employee proactivity

There are few studies that investigate the effect of sleep on employee proactive behaviour. Schmitt, Belschak, and Den Hartog (2017) found that sleep quality, not sleep quantity, was positively related to next-day proactivity. This relationship was mediated by next-morning vitality and was significant for employees who reported high rather than low daily self-efficacy. 66 participants answered a general online survey and daily online surveys over seven workdays. Sleep quality and quantity and vitality were measured in the morning before work or when arriving at work, self-efficacy was measured at noon, and daily proactivity was measured in the form of voice behaviour in the afternoon before leaving the office.

The research of Schilpzand and colleagues (2018) examined sleep quality as a driving force for employees to engage in proactive behaviour. The findings suggest that employees' proactive goals at the start of the workday more likely lead to daily proactive behaviours of voice and risk-taking behaviours throughout the workday for those whose sleep quality is better in the previous night. 98 participants completed daily surveys twice per day over a two-week period. Sleep quality and proactive goals were reported in the morning before work, and proactivity was reported in the afternoon before the end of the workday.

Summary

Off-job experiences and sleep quality play significant roles in shaping employees' proactive behaviour at work. This stream of research is basically grounded in resource-related theories, for example, COR theory (Hobfoll, 1989) and self-regulatory resource theory (Baumeister, Muraven, and Tice, 2000), to support for the effects of those non-work-domain predictors, because proactive behaviour is a resource-intensive action (for example, Cangiano and Parker, 2016; Strauss, Parker, and O'Shea, 2017). When employees experience recovery after work or get a good night's sleep, their resources are replenished, providing energy for acting proactively in the workplace. But when employees still think about or continue to work or experience hassles during non-work time, their resources are depleted, which undermines their likelihood of investing resources to proactivity. Moreover, research has begun to exmaine whether resource replenishment per se is sufficient for proactive initiative (Chawla et al, 2020; Ouyang et al, 2019).

Emotional energy as a cross-domain mechanism

As reviewed above, most of the research examines the main effects of non-work factors on employee proactivity. A few studies extend our knowledge by investigating the underlying processes (Ouyang et al, 2019; Schmitt, Belschak, and Den Hartog, 2017; Sonnentag, 2003). Specifically, three mediating variables, namely vitality (Schmitt, Belschak, and Den Hartog, 2017), work engagement (Sonnentag, 2003), and high-activated postive affect (Ouyang et al, 2019), all capture an element of energetic activation of employees to be proactive in the workplace. This is in line with the *energized to* motivation in the model of proactive motivation (Parker, Bindl, and Strauss, 2010). Moreover, research on the work–non-work interface, including recovery (Demerouti et al, 2009), sleep (Mullins et al, 2014), work–family conflict (Amstad et al, 2011), and work–family enrichment (Zhang et al, 2018), has shown significant influence on employees' affective experiences. Further, such affective experiences can spill over from life domain to work domain or cross over from one individual to another (for example, Demerouti, Bakker, and Schaufeli, 2005; Eckenrode and Gore, 1990; Song, Foo, and Uy, 2008; Westman, 2001; Westman, Shadach, and Keinan, 2013). Using an affective perspective thus can deepen our understanding on how non-work-domain functions in terms of shaping employee proactivity at work.

Regarding the relationships between affective experiences and employee proactivity, most studies focus on affect, positive affect in particular, during work (for example, Fritz and Sonnentag, 2009; Ng, Hsu, and Parker, in press; Sonnentag and Starzyk, 2015). The findings show that when experiencing high levels of positive affect at work, employees are energized and engage in proactive behaviour; moreover, studies suggest that high-activated, not low-activated, positive affect matters more for employees being proactive (for example, Bindl et al, 2012; Fay and Sonnentag, 2012; Sonnentag and Starzyk, 2015). There are several theoretical underpinnings that are used to explain the positive affect–proactivity relationship, for example, the broaden-and-build model (Fredrickson, 2001), the affect-as-information theory (Schwarz and Clore, 1983), and the affect-as-resource perspective (Aspinwall, 1998).

Taken together, events and situations during non-work time evoke employees' affective experiencs, which can spill over to the work domain. When employees feel emotionally energized, their approach motivation is likely to be enhanced (for example, Bindl et al, 2012), and their ability to initiate effortful and resource-demanding activities is strengthened (for example, Fritz and Sonnentag, 2009). In addition, such a positive state of feeling good makes them feel secure, thereby encouraging them to adopt a more exploratory strategy with divergent and integrative thinking (Schwarz, 1990). Employees therefore display high levels of proactivity at work. In this sense, an affective perspective is a useful approach for us to link non-work-related factors to employee proactivity.

Future research

I have reviewed the relationships between non-work variables and employee proactivity at work and discussed emotional energy as one critical underlying process. Four main avenues for future research are proposed to extend our knowledge of this issue.

First, prior studies predominantly focus on the main effects of off-job experiences and sleep on employee proactivity. How about other non-work-domain factors? The literature of the work–non-work interface has not been systematically integrated with the proactivity literature. For example, research on work–life balance, work–family conflict, and work–family enrichment are numerous; however, little research explores how these variables influence employees' proactive behaviour at work. As we discussed, scholars could utilize an affective approach to explicate the effects. Based on previous studies on affect at work, researchers could look at affect along two dimensions, valence (that is, positive and negative affect) and activation (that is, high and low activation) (Russell, 1980, 2003). It is also interesting to examine the interplay of positive and negative affect. For instance, profile analysis could be applied to unveil the optimal affective combinations, considering both dimensions of valence and activation, for employees to perform high levels of proactivity. Moreover, a dynamic perspective is encouraged to capture the momentary, fluctuating characteristic of non-work experiences, affect, and proactivity, which enables a more complete view of how non-work variables shape workplace outcome of proactive behaviour.

Second, positive affect is generally regarded as energy-providing for individuals (for example, Ouyang et al, 2019; Parker, Bindl, and Strauss, 2010), but we know little about the role of negative affect. The current findings on negative affect at work and proactivity is mixed, which might suggest a similar pattern for the effects of negative affect during non-work time. On one hand, low-activated negative affect likely broadens attentional focus and prompt divergent thinking, resulting in employees' rumination of what needs to be changed and/or how to change regarding the current situation (for example, Bindl et al, 2012; Martin and Tesser, 1996). On the other hand, high-activated negative affect likely stimulate proactive actions to bring about changes, because such affective state signals that change is needed and also energizes individuals (for example, Sonnentag and Starzyk, 2015). But, high-activated negative affect narrows attentional focus, which might lead the proactive actions to be more difficult to implement (Gable and Harmon-Jones, 2010; Parker, Bindl, and Strauss, 2010). It is thus intriguing and important to examine how negative affect associates nonwork predictors with proactivity, because negative affect triggered by some non-work experiences might result in employees' proactive behaviour at work. In addition, there may be value in examining discrete emotions, as some researchers argue that, in so doing, we are able to focus on the unique characteristics of specific emotions and obtain a more nuanced understanding of the antecedents and outcomes of these emotions (Lebel, 2017; Lindebaum and Jordan, 2012).

Third, employees' affective experiences before work might interact with their work experiences to influence their proactive actions. Current research regarding this issue is scarce and inadequate. Although employees come to work with the state of feeling energized, some work experiences, such as abusive supervision and lack of coworker support (Chiaburu and Harrison, 2008; Michel, Newness, and Duniewicz, 2016), might alleviate or even countervail such benefit. Similarly, employees who feel down before starting to work are likely to be energized under conditions like having an empowering leader (Schilpzand, Houston, and Cho, 2018). Future studies are therefore recommended to explore work-related boundary conditions that moderate the cross-domain effects between non-work-domain factors and proactivity at work.

Finally, little is known about the crossover effect of affective experiences in couples or among family members on proactivity. As aforementioned, emotions and moods can spill over from one domain to another domain and cross over from one person to another (Demerouti, Bakker, and Schaufeli, 2005; Eckenrode and Gore, 1990; Westman, Shadach, and Keinan, 2013). Considering both spillover and crossover effects, emotional contagion likely occurs between employees and their partners or other family members, which in turn affects their work behaviours (Hatfield, Cacioppo, and Rapson, 1994; Song, Foo, and Uy, 2008). For example, a recent study found that when an employee reported less burnout during off-job time, their partner perceived more emotional support from the employee and in turn engaged in more proactive investment to his or her relationships at work (Booth-LeDoux, Matthews, and Wayne, 2019). Relatedly, research findings have shown that work engagement, which is regarded as one type of emotional energy for employees, could transmit between working couples and between colleagues (Bakker and Demerouti, 2009; Bakker and Xanthopoulou, 2009). In this sense, examining emotional contagion in the family and employee proactivity not only extends our knowledge of how work and home domains interconnect regarding proactivity, but also provides insight into the connection between one organization and another.

Practical implications

Practically, this chapter offers some implications for employees and managers. First, current findings have highlighted the importance of non-work factors, such as off-job experiences and sleep, in employee proactivity. Employees, to whom proactivity is important, could deliberately involve themselves in activities, tasks, or experiences that energize individuals and enhance proactivity. For instance, Ouyang et al (2019) suggest that a variety of off-job activities, such as picking up a new hobby, learning a new skill, and determining how to spend the off-job time, could be helpful in providing energy and increasing next-day proactivity. In addition, managers and organizations could also help facilitate such energetic feelings for employees. Workshops or seminars could be provided in organizations to educate employees about the role of non-work-domain experiences, as well as the roles of emotions and moods in proactivity at work. Additionally, employees' work experiences also significantly influence their affect. Managers and organizations could leverage those work-related factors to enhance employee proactivity.

Moreover, it is essential to acknowledge that individuals' affective state is not stable, that is, it swings from hour to hour, day to day. It is not uncommon that employees may have negative experiences during off-job time, such as having arguments with their partner and experiencing a night of poor sleep quality, which influence their affective states before work. As a result, employee proactivity fluctuates as well. Managers should be aware of this phenomenon and have reasonable expectations of employees' proactive behaviour. When employee proactivity increases or diminishes, managers will be more able to respond and guide employees toward proactivity. It is also important that managers pay attention to employees' affective experiences to attain information for predicting their work behaviours and develop countermeasures accordingly.

Conclusion

This chapter offers a systematic review of the effects of non-work-domain predictors of employee proactivity in the workplace. Specifically, most studies focus on sleep quality and off-job experiences and suggest that resource replenishment is crucial for employees to maintain their proactivity. Unfortunately, more research is required to extend our understanding of the effects of other important non-work variables and the underlying processes. The critical importance of emotions and moods has long been acknowledged. Emotional energy could be a useful framework to link the non-work domain to the work domain. As illustrated in the section on Future Research, we have not yet gained a thorough understanding of such cross-domain effects. I hope that this chapter could encourage more scholars and practitioners to explore the non-work predictors of proactivity, touching upon the mechanism of emotional energy, boundary conditions, and other important issues. We therefore will be more prepared to utilize our emotions and moods.

References

Amstad, F. T., Meier, L. L., Fasel, U., Elfering, A., and Semmer, N. K. (2011). A meta-analysis of work-family conflict and various outcomes with a special emphasis on cross-domain versus matching-domain relations. *Journal of Occupational Health Psychology*, 16, 151–69.

Ashford, S. J. and Black, J. S. (1996). Proactivity during organizational entry: The role of desire for control. *Journal of Applied Psychology*, 81, 199–214.

Ashford, S. J., Blatt, R., and Vandewalle, D. (2003). Reflections on the looking glass: A review of research on feedback-seeking behavior in organizations. *Journal of Management*. 29, 773–99.

Aspinwall, L. G. (1998). Rethinking the role of positive affect in self-regulation. *Motivation and Emotion*, 22, 1–32.

Bakker, A. B. and Demerouti, E. (2009). The crossover of work engagement between working couples: A closer look at the role of empathy. *Journal of Managerial Psychology*, 24, 220–36.

Bakker, A. B. and Xanthopoulou, D. (2009). The crossover of daily work engagement: Test of an actor–partner interdependence model. *Journal of Applied Psychology*, 94, 1562–71.

Bateman, T. S. and Crant, J. M. (1993). The proactive component of organizational behavior: A measure and correlates. *Journal of Organizational Behavior*, 14, 103–18.

Baumeister, R. F., Muraven, M., and Tice, D. M. (2000). Ego depletion: A resource model of volition, self-regulation, and controlled processing. *Social Cognition*, 18, 130–50.

Bindl, U. K. and Parker, S. K. (2010). Proactive work behavior: Forward-thinking and change-oriented action in organizations. In S. Zedeck (ed), *APA Handbook of Industrial and Organizational Psychology*, vol 2, Washington, DC: American Psychological Association, pp 567–98.

Bindl, U. K., Parker, S. K., Totterdell, P., and Hagger-Johnson, G. (2012). Fuel of the self-starter: How mood relates to proactive goal regulation. *Journal of Applied Psychology*, 97, 134–50.

Binnewies, C., Sonnentag, S., and Mojza, E. J. (2009). Daily performance at work: Feeling recovered in the morning as a predictor of day-level job performance. *Journal of Organizational Behavior*, 30, 67–93.

Booth-LeDoux, S. M., Matthews, R. A., and Wayne, J. H. (2019). Testing a resource-based spillover-crossover-spillover model: Transmission of social support in dual-earner couples. *Journal of Applied Psychology*. Advance online publication. https://doi.org/10.1037/apl0000460.

Campbell, D. J. (2000). The proactive employee: Managing workplace initiative. *Academy of Management Executive*, 14, 52–66.

Cangiano, F. and Parker, S. K. (2016). Proactivity for mental health and well-being. In S. Clarke, T. M. Probst, F. Guldenmund, and J. Passmore (eds), *The Wiley Blackwell Handbook of the Psychology of Occupational Safety and Workplace Health*, 1st edn, UK: John Wiley and Sons, Ltd, pp 228–50.

Chawla, N., MacGowan, R. L., Gabriel, A. S., and Podsakoff, N. P. (2020). Unplugging or staying connected? Examining the nature, antecedents, and consequences of profiles of daily recovery experiences. *Journal of Applied Psychology*, 105, 19–39.

Chiaburu, D. S., and Harrison, D. A. (2008). Do peers make the place? Conceptual synthesis and meta-analysis of coworker effects on perceptions, attitudes, OCBs, and performance. *Journal of Applied Psychology*, 93, 1082–103.

Craig, A. and Cooper, R. E. (1992). Symptoms of acute and chronic fatigue. In A. P. Smith and D. M. Jones (eds), *Handbook of Human Performance*, vol 3, San Diego, CA: Academic Press, Inc, pp 289–339.

Crant, J. M. (2000). Proactive behavior in organizations. *Journal of Management*, 26, 435–62.

Demerouti, E., Bakker, A., Geurts, S., and Taris, T. (2009). Daily recovery from work-related effort during non-work time. In S. Sonnentag, P. L. Perrrewé, and D. C. Ganster (eds), *Research in Occupational Stress and Well-Being*, vol 7, Oxford: JAI Press, pp 85–123.

Demerouti, E., Bakker, A., and Schaufeli, W. (2005). Spillover and crossover of exhaustion and life satisfaction among dual-earner parents. *Journal of Vocational Behavior*, 67, 266–89.

Eckenrode, J., and Gore, S. (1990). Stress and coping at the boundary of work and family. In J. Eckenrode and S. Gore (eds), *Stress Between Work and Family*, New York: Plenum Press, pp 1–16.

Etzion, D., Eden, D., and Lapidot, Y. (1998). Relief from job stressors and burnout: Reserve service as a respite. *Journal of Applied Psychology*, 83, 577–85.

Fay, D. and Sonnentag, S. (2012). Within-person fluctuations of proactive behavior: How affect and experienced competence regulate work behavior. *Human Performance*, 25, 72–93.

Ford, M. T., Heinen, B. A., and Langkamer, K. L. (2007). Work and family satisfaction and conflict: A meta-analysis of cross-domain relations. *Journal of Applied Psychology*, 92, 57–80.

Fredrickson, B. L. (2001). The role of positive emotions in positive psychology: The broaden-and-build theory of positive emotions. *American Psychologist*, 56, 218–26.

Frese, M. and Fay, D. (2001). Personal initiative (PI): An active performance concept for work in the 21st century. In B. M. Staw and R. M. Sutton (eds), *Research in Organizational Behavior*, vol 23, Amsterdam: Elsevier Science, pp 133–87.

Frese, M., Fay, D., Hilburger, T., Leng, K., and Tag, A. (1997). The concept of personal initiative: Operationalization, reliability and validity in two German samples. *Journal of Occupational and Organizational Psychology*, 70, 139–61.

Frese, M., Garst, H., and Fay, D. (2007). Making things happen: Reciprocal relationships between work characteristics and personal initiative in a four-wave longitudinal structural equation model. *Journal of Applied Psychology*, 92, 1084–102.

Frese, M., Krauss, S. I., Keith, N. K., Escher, S., Grabarkiewicz, R., Luneng, S. T., Heers, C., Unger, J., and Friedrich, C. (2007). Business owners' action planning and its relationship to business success in three African countries. *Journal of Applied Psychology*, 92, 1481–98.

Fritz, C. and Sonnentag, S. (2005). Recovery, health, and job performance: Effects of weekend experiences. *Journal of Occupational Health Psychology*, 10, 187–99.

Fritz, C. and Sonnentag, S. (2009). Antecedents of day-level proactive behavior: A look at job stressors and positive affect during the workday. *Journal of Management*, 35, 94–111.

Fritz, C., Yankelevich, M., Zarubin, A., and Barger, P. (2010). Happy, healthy, and productive: The role of detachment from work during nonwork time. *Journal of Applied Psychology*, 95, 977–83.

Fuller, J. B. and Marler, L. E. (2009). Change driven by nature: A meta-analytic review of the proactive personality literature. *Journal of Vocational Behavior*, 75, 329–45.

Gable, P. and Harmon-Jones, E. (2010). The blues broaden, but the nasty narrows: Attentional consequences of negative affects low and high in motivational intensity. *Psychological Science*, 21, 211–15.

Glaser, L., Stam, W., and Takeuchi, R. (2016). Managing the risks of proactivity: A multilevel study of initiative and performance in the middle management context. *Academy of Management Journal*, 59, 1339–60.

Grant, A. M. and Ashford, S. J. (2008). The dynamics of proactivity at work. *Research in Organizational Behavior*, 28, 3–34.

Grant, A. M., Parker, S., and Collins, C. (2009). Getting credit for proactive behavior: Supervisors reactions depend on what you value and how you feel. *Personnel Psychology*, 62, 31–55.

Griffin, M. A., Neal, A., and Parker, S. K. (2007). A new model of work role performance: Positive behavior in uncertain and interdependent contexts. *Academy of Management Journal*, 50, 327–47.

Hatfield, E., Cacioppo, J., and Rapson, R. L. (1994). *Emotional Contagion*. New York: Cambridge University Press.

Hobfoll, S. E. (1989). Conservation of resources. A new attempt at conceptualizing stress. *American Psychologist*, 44, 513–24.

Hong, Y., Liao, H., Raub, S., and Han, J. H. (2015). What it takes to get proactive: An integrative multilevel model of the antecedents of personal initiative. *Journal of Applied Psychology*, 101, 687–701.

Lam, C. F. and Mayer, D. M. (2014). When do employees speak up for their customers? A model of voice in a customer service context. *Personnel Psychology*, 67, 637–66.

Lebel, R. D. (2017). Moving beyond fight and flight: A contingent model of how the emotional regulation of anger and fear sparks proactivity. *Academy of Management Review*, 42, 190–206.

Lindebaum, D. and Jordan, P. J. (2012). Positive emotions, negative emotions, or utility of discrete emotions? *Journal of Organizational Behavior*, 33, 1027–30.

Martin, L. L. and Tesser, A. (1996). Some ruminative thoughts. In J. R. S. Wyer (ed), *Advances in social cognition*, vol 9, Mahwah, NJ: Erlbaum, pp 1–47.

Martin, S. L., Liao, H., and Campbell, E. M. (2013). Directive versus empowering leadership: A field experiment comparing impacts on task proficiency and proactivity. *Academy of Management Journal*, 56, 1372–95.

Michel, J. S., Newness, K., and Duniewicz, K. (2016). How abusive supervision affects workplace deviance: A moderated-mediation examination of aggressiveness and work-related negative affect. *Journal of Business and Psychology*, 31, 1–22.

Morrison, E. W. (2011). Employee voice behavior: Integration and directions for future research. *Academy of Management Annals*, 5, 373–412.

Morrison, E. W. and Phelps, C. C. (1999). Taking charge at work: Extrarole efforts to initiate workplace change. *Academy of Management Journal*, 42, 403–19.

Mullins, H. M., Cortina, J. M., Drake, C. L., and Dalal, R. S. (2014). Sleepiness at work: A review and framework of how the physiology of sleepiness impacts the workplace. *Journal of Applied Psychology*, 99, 1096–112.

Ng, T. W., Hsu, D. Y., and Parker, S. K. (in press). Received respect and constructive voice: The roles of proactive motivation and perspective taking. *Journal of Management*. https://doi.org/10.1177/0149206319834660.

Ohly, S. and Fritz, C. (2010). Work characteristics, challenge appraisal, creativity, and proactive behavior: A multi-level study. *Journal of Organizational Behavior*, 31, 543–65.

Ouyang, K., Cheng, B. H., Lam, W., and Parker, S. K. (2019). Enjoy your night, stay proactive tomorrow: How off-job experiences shape daily proactivity. *Journal of Applied Psychology*, 104, 1003–19.

Parker, S. K. (2000). From passive to proactive motivation: The importance of flexible role orientations and role breadth self-efficacy. *Applied Psychology: An International Review*, 49, 447–469.

Parker, S. K., Bindl, U. K., and Strauss, K. (2010). Making things happen: A model of proactive motivation. *Journal of Management*, 36, 827–56.

Parker, S. K. and Collins, C. G. (2010). Taking stock: Integrating and differentiating multiple proactive behaviors. *Journal of Management*, 36, 633–62.

Parker, S. K., Wang, Y., and Liao, J. (2019). When is proactivity wise? A review of factors that influence the individual outcomes of proactive behavior. *Annual Review of Organizational Psychology and Organizational Behavior*, 6, 221–48.

Parker, S. K., Williams, H. M., and Turner, N. (2006). Modeling the antecedents of proactive behavior at work. *Journal of Applied Psychology*, 91, 636–52.

Russell, J. A. (1980). A circumplex model of affect. *Journal of Personality and Social Psychology*, 39, 1161–78.

Russell, J. A. (2003). Core affect and the psychological construction of emotion. *Psychological Review*, 110, 145–72.

Schilpzand, P., Houston, L., and Cho, J. (2018). Not too tired to be proactive: Daily empowering leadership spurs next-morning employee proactivity as moderated by nightly sleep quality. *Academy of Management Journal*, 61, 2367–87.

Schmitt, A., Belschak, F. D., and Den Hartog, D. N. (2017). Feeling vital after a good night's sleep: The interplay of energetic resources and self-efficacy for daily proactivity. *Journal of Occupational Health Psychology*, 22, 443–54.

Schwarz, N. (1990). Feelings as information: Informational and motivational functions of affective states. In E. T. Higgins and R. M. Sorrentino (eds), *Handbook of Motivation and Cognition*, vol 2, New York: Guilford, pp 527–61.

Schwarz, N. and Clore, G. L. (1983). Mood, misattribution, and judgments of well-being: Informative and directive functions of affective states. *Journal of Personality and Social Psychology*, 45, 513–23.

Song, Z., Foo, M. D., and Uy, M. A. (2008). Mood spillover and crossover among dual-earner couples: A cell phone event sampling study. *Journal of Applied Psychology*, 93, 443–52.

Sonnentag, S. (2003). Recovery, work engagement, and proactive behavior: A new look at the interface between nonwork and work. *Journal of Applied Psychology*, 88, 518–28.

Sonnentag, S. and Fritz, C. (2007). The Recovery Experience Questionnaire: Development and validation of a measure for assessing recuperation and unwinding from work. *Journal of Occupational Health Psychology*, 12, 204–21.

Sonnentag, S., and Starzyk, A. (2015). Perceived prosocial impact, perceived situational constraints, and proactive work behavior: Looking at two distinct affective pathways. *Journal of Organizational Behavior*, 36, 806–24.

Strauss, K., Griffin, M. A., and Parker, S. K. (2012). Future work selves: How salient hoped-for identities motivate proactive career behaviors. *Journal of Applied Psychology*, 97, 580–98.

Strauss, K., Parker, S. K., and O'Shea, D. (2017). When does proactivity have a cost? Motivation at work moderates the effects of proactive work behavior on employee job strain. *Journal of Vocational Behavior*, 100, 15–26.

Van Dyne L., and LePine J. A. (1998). Helping and voice extra-role behaviors: Evidence of construct and predictive validity. *Academy of Management Journal*, 41, 108–19.

Vandewalle, D., Ganesan, S., Challagalla, G. N., and Brown, S. P. (2000). An integrated model of feedback-seeking behavior: Disposition, context, and cognition. *Journal of Applied Psychology*, 85, 996–1003.

Westman, M. (2001). Stress and strain crossover. *Human Relations*, 54, 717–51.

Westman, M., Shadach, E., and Keinan, G. (2013). The crossover of positive and negative emotions: The role of state empathy. *International Journal of Stress Management*, 20, 116–33.

Wrzesniewski, A. and Dutton, J. E. (2001). Crafting a job: Revisioning employees as active crafters of their work. *Academy of Management Review*. 26, 179–201.

Zhang, Y., Xu, S., Jin, J., and Ford, M. T. (2018). The within and cross domain effects of work-family enrichment: A meta-analysis. *Journal of Vocational Behavior*, 104, 210–27.

6

Job Insecurity and Discretionary Behaviours at Work: A Discrete Emotions Perspective

Emily Guohua Huang, Bingjie Yu, and Cynthia Lee

Worldwide technological and societal changes in the past three decades or so has changed the nature of work dramatically. In such a changing world, job insecurity (JI), referring to perceptions about the threat to the continuity and stability of one's present employment (Shoss, 2017), has become an increasingly prominent focus for both management practitioners and scholars. Numerous studies, including several meta-analyses, have shown its significant impact on employee well-being, attitudes, and performance (Lee, Huang, and Ashford, 2018). Recent JI research calls for more studies on how JI influences employee discretionary behaviours. That is, what would employees do when they perceive JI (Huang et al, 2017; Lee, Huang, and Ashford, 2018)? Given the increasing importance of employee proactive behaviours (such as voice and information-seeking) to organizations in uncertain times, it is crucial for management researchers and practitioners to understand how employees react proactively when they perceive JI and the psychological mechanisms explaining the effects. However, as our review in the next section shows, research on these questions is still very limited and findings are mixed. In this study, we focus on one particular perspective to examine the impact of JI on proactive behaviours – the perspective of discrete emotions. Our goal in this chapter is to develop a conceptual model regarding the relationships among JI, discrete emotions, and discretionary behaviours and to suggest future research directions for this line of research.

JI is a perception of threats to one's employment. One of the key messages we could learn from the JI literature is – people respond to the actual work environment very differently. According to the appraisal theories of emotion (for example, Arnold, 1960; Frijda, 1986; Lazarus, 1968; Roseman, 1979; 1984; Scherer, 1984; Smith and Ellsworth, 1985), people react differently to similar situations based on their appraisals of the situation and these appraisals elicit specific emotions in each person. Each specific emotion has specific behavioural response components (Roseman, 2013) that predict actions. Thus, understanding the different discrete emotions triggered by JI offers us a lens to makes sense of employee behaviours when perceived JI. In the literature, much evidence shows that perceptions of JI generate various negative feelings which in turn affects employee attitudes and behaviours (Huang et al, 2010; 2012; Probst, 2002; 2003). However, there is not much theorization on *what* and *why* specific discrete emotions are associated with JI.

In the emotion literature, efforts have been devoted to categorizing discrete emotions using dimensions such as pleasantness–unpleasantness, arousal–activation, and approach–avoidance (Elliot, Eder, and Harmon-Jones, 2013; Russell, 1980). One dimension that is of particular importance for understanding emotional reactions to JI and its behavioural consequences is to what extent specific emotions may be construed as emerging from, sustaining, and/or impelling approach versus avoidance motivations (Elliot, Eder, and Harmon-Jones, 2013; Roseman, 1994; 2013). While approach-oriented emotions (such as joy and anger) drive people to take actions toward a target, avoidance-oriented emotions (such as fear and contempt) drive people to take actions away from a target. According to the appraisal theories, whether JI may elicit specific approach- or avoidance-oriented emotions depends on how employee perceive the situation. In this research, we theorize JI can elicit four specific negative emotions: anger and frustration, which are approach-oriented, and fear and shame, which are avoidance-oriented. The different emotions in turn determine what behavioural outcomes will be triggered, including positive proactive behaviours such as voice, feedback-, information- and helping-seeking behaviours, as well as negative avoidance behaviours, such as workplace deviant behaviours and turnover. We further propose employee approach/avoidance temperament and employee attributions of JI as conditions that determine the mediating effects of the four discrete emotions.

Job insecurity and employee discretionary behaviours

Proactive behaviours refer to self-initiated and future-focused actions to change oneself or the situation (Parker, Wang, and Liao, 2019). Existing studies have explored the relationships between JI and proactive behaviours. However, the research is still limited, and there are mixed findings. While most studies found that JI hinders proactive behaviours, some scholars found positive or curvilinear relationships.

Negative relationships between JI and a variety of proactive behaviours have been reported. For example, Staufenbiel and König (2010) found that JI, as a hindrance stressor, negatively affects organizational citizenship behaviours (OCBs) via reducing job satisfaction and organizational commitment. De Spiegelaere et al (2014) found that JI hinders innovative work behaviours because it reduces work engagement. Niesen et al (2018) found that JI reduces idea generation of supervisors via psychological contract breach. Based on threat-rigidity theory and broaden-and-build theory, Probst et al (2019) found that JI has a negative effect on creativity via cognitive failures and decreased job-related affective well-being. Based on conservation of resources theory and psychological contract theory, Van Hootegem and De Witte (2019) found that qualitative JI (that is perceptions about the threat to desired job features) has a negative effect on information-seeking and feedback-seeking via decreased occupational self-efficacy and psychological contract breach. Based on self-determination theory, Breevaart et al (2020) found that weekly JI thwarts the fulfillment of psychological needs, thus undermining voice behaviours.

In contrast, positive relationships and non-linear relationships have also been reported. For example, Staufenbiel and König (2010) found that JI, as a challenge stressor, directly motivates employees to engage in OCBs in order to preserve jobs. Viewing proactive behaviours as active job preservation strategies, Shoss (2017) proposed that employees may demonstrate their worth by engaging in noticed and valued behaviours, such as OCBs. Based on social exchange theory and research on personal control, Lam et al (2015) found a U-shaped relationship between JI and OCBs, which was argued as a proactive attempt to preserve jobs. From a job preservation perspective, Yang et al (2019) found that the relationship between JI and taking charge is U-shaped. Buonocore et al (2020) based on activation theory proposed and found an inverted U-shaped relationship between JI and cognitive crafting.

Researchers proposed a number of individual and contextual factors that moderate the relationships between JI and proactive behaviours. For example, Sverke and Hellgren (2001) found that, compared with employees who belong to a trade union, non-affiliated workers engage in more voice when they perceive JI. Berntson, Näswall, and Sverke (2010) found that employability strengthens the negative effect of JI on voice. Schreurs et al (2015) found that JI is mostly a hindrance stressor than a challenge stressor, but the negative effect of JI on voice is weaker for employees with high reward sensitivity. Jiang (2018) found that self-affirmation and work-affirmation buffer the negative effect of JI on creativity. Yang et al (2019) found that job embeddedness attenuates the negative effect of qualitative JI on taking charge. Li, Long, and Er-Yue (2018) proposed and found that for employees who perceive high level of organizational support, JI is negatively related with feedback-seeking according to social exchange theory; when perceived organizational support (POS) is low, JI is positively related with feedback-seeking based on uncertainty reduction theory.

In her review paper, Shoss (2017) summarized four mechanisms by which employees react to JI: stress-related mechanism, social exchange-related mechanism, job-preservation motivation and proactive coping. Our review of the JI-proactive behaviours relationships research seems to suggest that most scholars focus on the stress-related mechanisms (JI as a hindrance stressor) and social exchange-related mechanisms, both of which suggest negative relationships. From the perspective of job preservation motivation, most scholars found positive or curvilinear relationships. That is, JI stimulates the motivation to preserve jobs and avoid potential loss, thus facilitating extra efforts. Shoss (2017) called for more research on the underexplored mechanisms of job preservation and proactive coping. We further advance the perspective of discrete emotions to provide additional theoretical insights on the effects of JI on proactive behaviours.

Although our focus is on proactive behaviours, we also include other behaviours that are at employees' discretion including organizational deviance and voluntary turnover in order to enrich the model and to cover the most commonly studied negative discretionary behaviours. By discretionary behaviours we mean voluntary activities that employees do for themselves or their organizations (Christian, Eisenkraft, and Kapadia, 2015). Turnover or quitting one's job is a voluntary decision to leave the organization for good. Organizational deviance is a type of employee discretionary behaviours that harm the organization and/ or its members (Bennett and Robinson, 2000). While many studies found JI to be positively related to turnover and deviance, our model from the discrete emotions perspective can add to our knowledge about why and under what conditions JI leads to these actions.

Job insecurity and employee discretionary behaviours: a discrete emotions perspective

In the JI literature, although much evidence has been found linking JI to outcomes through emotions (Jiang and Lavaysse, 2018), these studies only tell us that JI leads to a generally negative emotional experience. There is no research on what specific discrete emotions are driven by JI, why and when these emotions are generated. Perhaps the lack of study on how JI generates specific discrete emotions is because JI research has studied affective JI as one particular dimension of JI. It is recognized that the perception of the likelihood of losing one's job or desired features of the job (cognitive JI) is different from the emotional elements of the JI experience, such as being concerned, worried, or anxious about losing the job or job features (affective JI: Huang et al, 2012). Meta-analysis evidence (Jiang and Lavaysse, 2018) has found that affective JI had stronger relations with the majority of outcomes and correlates than did cognitive JI and, in most cases, affective JI mediated the relationships between cognitive JI and its outcomes. While this conceptual clarification has greatly contributed to JI research, we posit that the study of affective JI (AJI) should not preclude research on how cognitive JI leads to specific discrete emotions for the following reasons.

First, research on AJI to date did not clarify what specific emotions should be covered in the construct domain. AJI scales (for example, Huang et al, 2012; Probst, 2003) typically aggregate various kinds of negative emotions (such as worry, fear, anxiety etc; see Table 6.1 for a summary of the existing measures) without explaining why these specific emotions are chosen. While affect is oftentimes used as an umbrella term for emotions, feelings, and mood (Elfenbein, 2007), emotions typically refer to discrete and intense but short-lived experiences that are reactions to specific stimuli and have a range of possible consequences (Frijda, 1993). In emotion research, it is well documented that various discrete emotions do not only differ in the hedonic dimension from positive (pleasant) to negative (unpleasant), but they also differ in many other aspects such as intensity and relevance (refer to for example, Elfenbein, 2007 for a review on different framework). One particular aspect that is of interest to this research is that emotions can be differentiated by whether they elicit approach or avoidance behavioural responses. For example, as Ferris et al (2016) noted, 'experiencing anger results in individuals experiencing approach-oriented action tendencies that facilitate assertion of the self' while 'experiencing anxiety results in individuals experiencing avoidance-oriented action tendencies that facilitate preservation of the self'. Hence, studying the relationship between cognitive JI and each relevant discrete emotion (rather than a generally negative emotional experience as reflected by AJI) can offer a nuanced picture of the JI and behaviour linkage.

Second, there is little research regarding how AJI influences proactive behaviours, perhaps because researchers could only theorize a negative relationship between AJI and proactive behaviours in general, due to the lack of clarity of the emotions involved. Emotion research has clearly demonstrated particular emotions are linked to characteristic patterns of behaviours. There is an increasing number of calls for research linking discrete emotions to organizational behaviours (for example, Ashkanasy and Dorris, 2017). Hence, we believe discrete emotion constitutes a unique perspective to understand the impact of cognitive JI on proactive behaviours.

To our awareness, there is only one study that examined specific discrete emotions as consequences of JI (Reisel et al, 2010) in which the authors studied anger and anxiety as consequences of cognitive JI mediated by job satisfaction. Although their results support a positive impact of JI on the two emotions, unfortunately there is no clear theoretical reason offered for why anger and anxiety were chosen and why job satisfaction mediates the relationships between JI and the two emotions. In this research, we identify specific discrete emotions elicited by a cognitive perception of JI, theorize how these emotions shape different behavioural responses to JI, and explore boundary conditions for these effects. Our overall model is presented in Figure 6.1. We elaborate the proposed relationships below.

Approach-oriented and avoidance-oriented emotions: anger, frustration, fear, and shame

As a critical feature of emotions, motivational direction is used to categorize discrete emotions (Elliot, Eder, and Harmon-Jones, 2013; Roseman, 2013). Approach motivation of emotions refers to 'the impulse to go toward, without specifying the valence of stimuli toward which the impulse is directed, indeed, without the requirement of any evoking stimulus' (Harmon-Jones, Harmon-Jones, and Price, 2013) and avoidance motivation refers to a tendency to avoid stimuli, regardless of the valence of stimuli (Ferris et al, 2016). Traditionally, approach motivation is linked with positive emotions, while avoidance motivation is linked with negative emotions (for example, Russell and Carroll, 1999; Watson et al, 1999). However, more recent research suggested that the emotional valence (positive or negative) and

Figure 6.1: Conceptual model

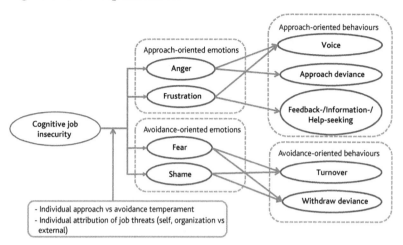

motivational direction as separate features of discrete emotions (for example, Elliot, Eder, and Harmon-Jones, 2013; Ferris et al, 2016). For example, anger is a negative emotion, but it is also approach-oriented (Carver and Harmon-Jones, 2009).

Among the major emotional experiences of JI, we focus on two approach-oriented emotions – anger and frustration, and two avoidance-oriented emotions – fear and shame, for several reasons. First, they are among the mostly included JI-related emotional terms used in the current affective JI measures (Table 6.1). Moreover, they are relatively clearly defined discrete emotions compared with many other emotions used in the JI literature such as the mostly frequently used terms 'concern' or 'worry'. In addition, they are process- instead of result-focused emotions such as depression or strain, which are typically studied as well-being outcomes of JI. Finally, there are relatively clear evidence regarding their approach–avoidance motivation in the literature, which we discuss below.

Among the appraisal theories of emotions, Roseman's (2013) emotion system model provides a framework directly applicable for understanding the approach–avoidance motivation of the discrete emotions we study. According to this model, three fundamental appraisals elicit four types of emotions. Appraisal of whether the situation is consistent versus inconsistent with one's motives is the most fundamental one. Situations perceived as satisfying their motives (that is, high motive consistency) likely elicit contacting emotions (for example, joy, pride, love, hope, etc) that increase the individuals' contact and interaction with the situation. As JI is a perception about threats

Table 6.1: Affective job insecurity measures

Study	Job insecurity construct	Scale (emotion terms *italic*)
Johnson, Messe, and Crano, 1984	Affective	1. The thought of getting fired really *scares* me 2. I am *worried* about the possibility of being fired 3. Working hard would keep me from getting fired 4. If I get fired, I will not know how to tell people 5. If I do good work, my job would be safe 6. I am so *worried* that I would do almost anything to keep my job 7. I am *worried* about the *disgrace* of being fired
Borg and Elizur, 1992	Affective	1. The thought of losing my job *troubles* me 2. The thought of losing my job *worries* me 3. The thought of losing my job *scares* me
Probst, 2003	Job security satisfaction	1. Never been more secure 2. Makes me *tense* 3. *Satisfactory* 4. *Nerve-wracking* 5. Sufficient amount of security 6. Cause for *concern* 7. Acceptable 8. *Discouraging* 9. Inadequate 10. More secure than most in my job or profession 11. *Worrisome* 12. Looks *optimistic* 13. Makes me *anxious* 14. *Upsetting* how little job security I have 15. Excellent amount of security 16. *All right* 17. *Stressful* 18. *Positive* 19. Unacceptably low 20. *Troubling*
Ito and Brotheridge, 2007	Job loss strain	1. I am *concerned* about the possibility of being laid off 2. The possibility of losing my job puts a lot of *strain* on me

Table 6.1: Affective job insecurity measures (continued)

Study	Job insecurity construct	Scale (emotion terms *italic*)
Huang et al, 2010	Affective	1. The lack of job security in this company makes me feel *nervous*
		2. I feel *uneasy* about my chances for remaining with this company
		3. I lose sleep *worrying* about my future with this company
		4. I am *unhappy* with the amount of job security that I have with this company
		5. I am *tense* about maintaining my current job employment status
		6. I am very *unsure* that I can remain employed with this company for as long as I wish
		7. I am *pessimistic* about the job security with this company
		8. I am *troubled* by the thought of losing my job
		9. I am *scared* by the thought of losing my job
		10. I am *worried* that this company will fire me any time

to one's employment or desired job features, it is obviously motive inconsistent (that is, the motive is to keep the job and desired features, but the situation is perceived as inconsistent with this motive – 'I may lose them') and thus not eliciting contacting emotions.

The second appraisal is about control potential. When individuals appraise a situation as low motive consistency and perceive a low chance of reducing the inconsistency (that is, low control potential), distancing emotions (for example, fear, sadness, regret, etc) are likely to occur, which make the individuals move away from the situation. In particular, uncontrollable threats trigger fear. Thus, to the extent that individuals think their JI situation is uncontrollable, they will experience fear (for example, 'I may lose the job and there may be nothing I can do about it').

The third appraisal is about how to contend with motive-inconsistent situations, when one has the potential to do so. The appraisal governing whether to move against or away from the stimulus is instrumental versus intrinsic problem type. When individuals appraise a situation as low motive consistency and they can reduce the inconsistency (that is, high control potential) by changing some attributes of the situation because the inconsistency is merely caused by these attributes (that is, instrumental problem), they tend to experience attack emotions (for example, anger, frustration, guilt, etc), which makes people move against the problematic attributes of the situation. Further, when individuals perceive a clear target responsible for the instrumental problem, anger is experienced, whereas when there is no such target, frustration is experienced. Accordingly, when individuals attribute reasons for JI to the organizationally controllable reasons (for example, unfair procedures of organizational change), they tend to experience anger toward the organization (for example, 'I may lose my job and this is because the organization didn't do things as they should have done'), whereas these attributing to organizational uncontrollable reasons or unknown reasons (for example, industrial changes) tend to experience frustration (for example, 'I may lose my job and this is because the organization doesn't know how to manage the situation').

When individuals appraise a stimulus as low motive-consistency and high control potential, but the stimulus is an intrinsic (instead of instrumental) problem, they experience rejection emotions (for example, shame, disgust, contempt, etc) and are likely to enact the behavioural tendency of moving the stimulus away from the self. Thus, JI could lead to shame if individuals attribute JI as their own responsibility (for example, 'I should have performed better to keep my job but I haven't'). In sum, according to Roseman's model, anger and frustration as attack emotions have an approach-orientation while fear as a distancing emotion and shame as a rejection emotion have a clear avoidance-orientation. The four emotions can all be elicited by cognitive JI under different conditions, which is summarized in Table 6.2. Empirical evidence for the action tendencies associated with these discrete emotions will be reviewed next.

Discrete emotions and discretionary behaviours at work

Behaviours that are at the employees' discretion are different from other behaviours at work such as task performance in that they are not required by the organization and are typically done for personal reasons. Such behaviours are oftentimes more easily shaped by emotions than by cognitions or judgements. We categorize discretionary behaviours using the approach- and avoidance-motivation framework discussed in the above for categorizing emotions, following prior literature (for example, Ferris et al, 2016). Specifically, approach-oriented behaviours involve actions where individuals move toward the situation (for example, fighting for resources when threatened) while avoidance-oriented behaviours involve these where individuals move away from

Table 6.2: Job insecurity and discrete emotions in Roseman's emotion system model

First appraisal – **motive consistency** (that is, satisfying individuals' motives)	Second appraisal – **control potential** (that is, chance of reducing the inconsistency)	Third appraisal	Discrete emotions
High			Contacting emotions (for example, joy, pride, love, hope, etc) likely to enact the behavioural tendency of having more contact and interaction with the situation -*JI does not elicit such emotions*
Low	low		Distancing emotions (for example, fear★, sadness, regret, etc) likely to enact the behavioural tendency of moving away from the situation; uncontrollable threats trigger fear, whereas irrevocable losses make people sad ★*JI elicits fear if the situation is perceived as uncontrollable*
Low	high	Third appraisal – **instrumental problem** (that is, can reduce the inconsistency by changing some attributes of the situation because the inconsistency is merely caused by these attributes)	attack emotions (for example, guilt, anger★, frustration★, etc) likely to enact the behavioural tendency of moving against the problematic attributes of the situation; a clear target responsible for the instrumental problem triggers anger, whereas unclear target make people frustrated ★*JI elicits anger if the situation is perceived as controllable and the organization is perceived as accountable* ★*JI elicits frustration if the situation is perceived as controllable and there is no clear target perceived as accountable*
Low	high	Third appraisal – **intrinsic problem** (that is, some potential to reduce the inconsistency by moving the stimulus away from the self because the stimulus is intrinsically negative)	rejection emotions (for example, shame★, disgust, contempt, etc) likely to enact the behavioural tendency of moving the stimulus away from the self ★*JI elicits shame if the situation is perceived as controllable and as a result of one's own failure*

the situation (for example, fleeing when threatened). Evidence for the links between approach-oriented emotion and approach-oriented behaviours and between avoidance-oriented emotion and avoidance-oriented behaviours can be readily found in the literature. For example, Harmon-Jones (2003) found that anger is positively related with behavioural activation system (BAS), which is sensitive to rewards and causes movement to goals. Ferris et al (2016) found that anger causes approach-oriented counterproductive work behaviours. Similar to anger, frustration is associated with much anticipated effort (Carver, 2006; Smith and Ellsworth, 1985). Harmon-Jones, Harmon-Jones, and Summerell (2017) proposed that frustration belongs to the anger family and drives approach-motivated behaviours.

Neuropsychologists' research found fear is linked to right-prefrontal cortical activity, which is associated with withdrawal motivation (Harmon-Jones and Sigelman, 2001). Experiencing fear means a sense of situational control and a lack of efficacy (Lebel, 2017; Lerner and Keltner, 2001). Fear makes individuals estimate risk pessimistically and avoid risky choices (Lerner and Keltner, 2001). Finally, shame results from a failure to live up to an ego-ideal (Lazarus, 1991) and typically the failure cannot be easily repaired (Lewis, 1992; Poulson, 2000). Although evidence is relatively limited, the prevailing view is that shame makes people take actions to avoid the failure (Gilbert and Andrews, 1998; Tangney and Dearing, 2002; Tracy and Robins, 2004).

In this chapter, we study five approach-oriented behaviours – voice, feedback-, information-, and help-seeking behaviours, and approach deviance, and two avoidance-oriented behaviours – turnover and avoidance deviance. Voice has been used in the management literature to represent the intentional expression of work-related ideas and opinions (Van Dyne, Ang, and Botero, 2003). Feedback-, information-, and help-seeking are viewed as informal learning processes (Emanuel Froehlich et al, 2014; Van Hootegem and De Witte, 2019). Feedback-seeking refers to conscious devotion of effort toward determining the correctness and adequacy of behaviours for attaining valued end states (Ashford and Cummings, 1983); information-seeking refers to a proactive search for non-evaluative information that is acquired via formal or informal sources in organizations (Noe, Tews, and Marand, 2013); and help-seeking refers to the search for others' assistance, information, advice, or support (Hofmann, Lei, and Grant, 2009). Voluntary turnover is a typical form of avoidance by leaving the organization. Organizational deviance (Bennett and Robinson, 2000) can take approach-oriented forms such as violence, theft from coworkers, and damaging company property, or avoidance-oriented forms such as taking unnecessary leave, delaying work, and avoiding others at work. We refer to the former type as approach-oriented workplace deviance and the later as avoidance-oriented workplace deviance following Ferris et al (2016).

We expect a positive link between anger and approach-oriented discretionary behaviours of voice and approach-oriented deviance. As discussed in the above, the experience of anger means individuals perceive their JI situation is dissatisfying, can be changed, and hold the organization as accountable. It motivates individuals to correct negative events or act against the source of blame (Roseman, Wiest, and Swartz, 1994). For example, Lebel (2017) proposed that anger can elicit proactive behaviours, which include speaking up with suggestions. Moreover, anger can even cause attack or harm to others. It has been found to be positively related with deviant or counterproductive work behaviours (Ferris et al, 2016; Rodell and Judge, 2009; Wang et al, 2018).

Proposition 1: cognitive job insecurity is positively related to employee voice and approach-oriented deviance at work via anger.

The experience of frustration means individuals perceive their JI situation is dissatisfying, can be changed, but have no clear target for blame. In such situation, frustration drives employees to speak up ideas and questions (Grant, 2013; Liu and Perrewé, 2005) in order to improve their work situation. In addition, frustrated employees may seek information, feedback, and support (Bindl, 2019) in order to contend with the ambiguous situation. Diefendorff, Richard, and Yang (2008) found that frustration is linked to situational modification strategies, which involves changing the situation, trial to solve problems, and perspective-taking strategies (for example, considering how another person feels). Thus, when perceive JI, employees feeling frustrated tend to have voice, feedback-, information-, and help-seeking behaviours.

Proposition 2: cognitive job insecurity is positively related to employee voice, feedback-seeking, information-seeking, and help-seeking behaviours via frustration.

The action tendencies of fear are avoidance or escape (Lazarus, 1991). Fear causes individual to avoid and generates escape or flight tendencies. In the literature, it has been found that experiencing fear following JI increases turnover intentions (Akgunduz and Eryilmaz, 2018) and it is suggested that fear causes counterproductive withdrawal behaviour

(Gooty, Gavin, and Ashkanasy, 2009) and organizational deviance (Wang et al, 2018).

> *Proposition 3: cognitive job insecurity is positively related to employee turnover and avoidance-oriented deviance at work via fear.*

When shame is experienced as a result of JI, it makes people avoid the situation which is viewed as a personal failure. Poulson (2000) proposed that shame can lead to increased workplace dysfunction and employee turnover. Peng et al (2019) also proposed that shame is associated with turnover intentions. Besides escaping (for example, turnover), shame motivates individuals to deny, hide, and withdraw the shame-inducing situation (Tangney, Stuewig, and Mashek, 2007).

> *Proposition 4: cognitive job insecurity is positively related to employee turnover and avoidance-oriented deviance at work via shame.*

Boundary conditions

Appraisal theories of emotion suggest that cognitive appraisals cause experienced emotions. When individuals perceive JI, their appraisals of the overall situation such as their level of control, reasons for the job threats, should determine which discrete emotions will be experienced. Based on the emotion system model (Roseman, 2013) informing the JI and discrete emotions relationships proposed in the above, we propose two moderators that we deem as fundamental factors affecting the relationships: one individual difference factor – approach–avoidance temperament, and another situational factor – attribution of the job threat.

Individual approach–avoidance temperament

Elliot and Thrash (2002; 2010) suggested that two latent factors account for the shared variance among all personality differences. Approach temperament is defined as a general neurobiological sensitivity to positive (that is, reward) stimuli (present or imagined) that is accompanied by a perceptual vigilance for, an affective reactivity to, and a behavioural predisposition towards such stimuli. Avoidance temperament is defined as a general neurobiological sensitivity to negative (that is, punishment) stimuli (present or imagined) that is accompanied by a perceptual vigilance for, an affective reactivity to, and a behavioural predisposition towards such stimuli. Approach–avoidance temperament is theorized as rudimentary biologically based individual differences that make it distinct from other conceptually related constructs such as promotive and preventive self-regulatory focus, and positive and negative emotionality (Bipp and Demerouti, 2015; Elliot and Thrash, 2010). In other words, approach–avoidance temperament is not affected by external factors like job threats. Due to these features, we adopt it in our examination of the associations between JI and the discrete emotions.

Specifically, we posit that approach temperament weakens the extent that JI would trigger anger, frustration, fear, and shame, while avoidance temperament strengthens the extent that JI would trigger fear and shame. Individual with a high level of approach temperament have a general neurobiological sensitivity to positive instead of negative stimuli. The threat of JI should in general be less impactful on these individuals. For two persons who perceive the same level of job loss likelihood, the one who have a higher level of approach temperament tends to look at the positive side of their job situation and see more possibilities (for example, 'change for a better job', or 'good if I do something new') or put more attention on other aspects of life. Thus, they respond to JI with less negative emotions. In contrast, individual with a high level of avoidance temperament are not only neurophysiologically sensitive to negative stimuli such as loss of job, but they also have a predisposition to move away from such stimuli. JI tends to be more salient in drawing their attention and causes more responses, cognitively, emotionally, as well as behaviourally. Because of the strong natural tendency to see the worse part of the situation, think negatively and ruminate, they are impelled to escape from the situation of JI. The more they try to avoid, the more feelings of fear and shame are produced. However, we do not predict the effect of avoidance temperament on the JI and anger/frustration relationship. On the one hand, high avoidance temperament people may have more anger when faced with JI because they are more sensitive to the negative stimuli of JI than lower avoidance temperament; on the other hand, they may have lower anger and frustration because they avoid direct interaction with the stimuli, thus decreasing chances for triggering the approach-oriented emotions.

Proposition 5: effects of cognitive job insecurity on anger, frustration, fear, and shame are weaker for individuals who have high approach temperament than for these low-approach-temperament individuals.

Proposition 6: effects of cognitive job insecurity on fear and shame are stronger for individuals who have high avoidance temperament than for these low-avoidance-temperament individuals.

Individual attribution of JI: self, organization, and environment

JI can result from not only organizational changes such as downsizing, restructuring, or layoffs as typically described in the literature, but also environmental factors such as industrial restructuring and economic downturn, or individual own reasons such as unsatisfied performance and bad interpersonal relationships. Although these factors oftentimes work together in forming a perception of reasons for JI, individuals' primary attribution of the situation determine how one sees it and thus plays a critical role in shaping the main emotions experienced. Attribution theory (Fiske and Taylor, 1991; Heider, 1958; Kelley, 1967) is among the oldest psychological theories about how individuals make sense of what happens to and around them. One central idea of the attribution theory is that people are like scientists seeking to understand 'why' something happens. Such causal attributions are regarded as the underpinnings for further judgments, emotional reactions, and behaviours. In our case, individuals faced with JI will ask, consciously or unconsciously, 'why does this happen?' and their answers to this question will make a difference in what emotions are generated and, in turn, the behavioural responses. Because JI involves an employment relationship, both the employee and employer are relevant parties that can be attributed as the reason for JI. In addition, individuals may also attribute the threats to the environment external to the organization, such as industrial, technological, or societal reasons.

When employees attribute JI to their own reasons, they will experience more shame that involves intrinsic problems and is felt toward the self (Roseman, 2013). An internal attribution of JI means individuals believe they themselves fail to keep their jobs. Such sense of failure further strengthens the sense of powerlessness and individuals tend to develop more avoidance emotions and behaviours in order to flee from further loss of their self-esteem. However, it is worth to note that an internal attribution is less likely because the JI literature suggests that it is generally a result of various organizational changes and some JI studies use organizational or higher level of changes as proxies or objective indicators of JI (Huang et al, 2012; Jiang and Lavaysse, 2018; Lee, Huang, and Ashford, 2018), which implies an external attribution of JI is more typical. In addition, the 'fundamental attribution error' suggests that individuals tend not to attribute negative outcomes or failures to their own, as a way to protect self-esteem (Heider, 1958), which also explains why an internal attribution of JI is less likely than the other types of attribution.

When employees attribute JI to organizational reasons, we predict that they tend to experience more anger toward the organizations. When employees make attributions that organization is responsible for the threat of the continuity and stability of their present employment, they have a clear target to blame and thus experience anger. When employees attribute JI to external environment reasons that are related to neither themselves nor the organization, they do not have a clear target to blame. In Roseman's emotion system model (2013), when the emotion-eliciting stimulus is caused by circumstances, individuals will experience more emotions felt toward circumstances, such as fear and frustration. Thus, we predict that employees with the attributions of JI to environmental reasons will experience more fear and frustration. Based on the above reasoning, we propose:

> *Proposition 7: individuals who attribute job insecurity to their own reasons tend to experience shame; individuals who attribute job insecurity to organizational reasons tend to experience anger; individuals who attribute job insecurity to environmental reasons or who have no clear attribution tend to experience fear and frustration.*

Discussion

When perceive JI, some employees voice; some seek feedback, information and/or help from others; some do counterproductive things; and others quit. Why? In this chapter, we develop a theory-informed model to answer this question, from the perspective of discrete emotions. Overall, the model suggests moderated mediation effects governing the relationships between JI and the behaviours – JI interacts with individual approach–avoidance temperament and attribution of job threats to determine the experienced emotion(s), which determines whether people would voice, do feedback/information/help-seeking, go deviant, or quit.

This model makes several contributions and is worth further development. First of all, it contributes to the literature of employee proactive reactions to JI. Very limited and mixed findings exist in the literature about the relationships. Most scholars focused on the negative effects of JI on proactive behaviours based on stress-related mechanisms or social exchange-related mechanisms. By exploring the mediating roles of discrete emotions, this study provides a new theoretical perspective to examine the relationships. Based on the appraisal theories of emotion and Roseman's emotion system model in particular, we propose that cognitive JI make employees experience more or less anger, frustration, fear and/or shame, which in turn shapes the behaviours. This is the first step to explore the JI-discrete emotion-workplace behaviours relationships. Using this framework, future research can continue to explore other types of proactive behaviours and the corresponding discrete emotions. For example, employees may contend with JI by job crafting or job-searching behaviours when experiencing frustration; shame may motivate employees to take actions to reduce hindrances, depending on how repairable individuals perceive the situation is.

Second, our proposed model has important implications for the JI research. It informs JI researchers what specific emotions can be generated by JI using the framework of approach–avoidance motivation of emotion. Prior research on affective JI or affective outcomes of JI predominantly focus on the valence dimension of emotion only and thus can only suggest that JI leads to negative (versus positive) emotions. Using the framework of approach–avoidance motivation, we identify anger and frustration as typical approach-oriented emotion responses to JI and fear and shame as typical avoidance-oriented emotion responses to JI. If this model is supported by empirical evidence, future JI research should adopt this approach in order to make more precise predictions about how people respond to JI.

Further, we identify the boundary conditions of the JI discrete emotions relationships. Approach and avoidance temperament as latent factors from trait adjectives, affective dispositions, and the motivational system are fundamental individual difference dimensions that influence appraisals and thus the experienced emotions under the JI situation. We postulate that various individual trait moderators to the JI effects (Lee et al, 2018) found in prior research such as self-esteem and affectivity may be explained by this factor. We examine attributions of job threat (to individual, organizational, or external reasons) as a JI-specific situational factor instead of an individual difference in attributional style, which is likely to be influenced by or has overlaps with individual differences such as approach and avoidance temperament. This particular situational variable is a proximate factor influencing individual responses to JI that potentially captures many other contextual factors. In other words, conditional factors to JI effect found in prior research such as employability and organizational climate (Lee, Huang, and Ashford, 2018) likely work through their influences on how individuals attribute the sources of JI. Moreover, using this model, we can better understand the impact of different environmental features on employee typical emotional and behavioural responses to JI. For example, in the global COVID-19 pandemic, do job-insecure employees typically experience fear and frustration? Future research can examine these ideas.

Finally, this model has implications for the proactivity research. According to Parker, Bindl, and Strauss's (2010) model of the motivational pathways of proactivity, affect energizes people to do proactive behaviours. However, extant research mainly focuses on the cognitive pathways, which were referred to as 'can do' and 'reason to' motivational states in the proactivity literature but the 'energized to' pathway is much less studied. Moreover, the limited research on affect and proactivity is primarily focused on positive affect as energizers. Our model suggests approach-oriented emotions such as anger and frustration (which is typically viewed as 'negative') also energize proactivity such as voice, feedback-seeking, information-seeking, and help-seeking. Thus, further tests and development of the model are also worthwhile in this aspect.

References

Akgunduz, Y. and Eryilmaz, G. (2018). Does turnover intention mediate the effects of job insecurity and co-worker support on social loafing?. *International Journal of Hospitality Management*, 68, 41–9.

Arnold, M. B. (1960). *Emotion and Personality*. New York: Columbia University Press.

Ashford, S. J. and Cummings, L. L. (1983). Feedback as an individual resource: Personal strategies of creating information. *Organizational Behavior and Human Performance*, 32(3), 370–98.

Ashkanasy, N. M. and Dorris, A. D. (2017). Emotions in the workplace. *Annual Review of Organizational Psychology and Organizational Behavior*, 4, 67–90.

Bennett, R. J. and Robinson, S. L. (2000). Development of a measure of workplace deviance. *Journal of Applied Psychology*, 85(3), 349–60.

Berntson, E., Näswall, K., and Sverke, M. (2010). The moderating role of employability in the association between job insecurity and exit, voice, loyalty and neglect. *Economic and Industrial Democracy*, 31(2), 215–30.

Bindl, U. K. (2019). Work-related proactivity through the lens of narrative: investigating emotional journeys in the process of making things happen. *Human Relations*, 72(4), 615–45.

Bipp, T. and Demerouti, E. (2015). Which employees craft their jobs and how? Basic dimensions of personality and employees' job crafting behaviour. *Journal of Occupational and Organizational Psychology*, 88(4), 631–55.

Borg, I. and Elizur, D. (1992). Job insecurity: Correlates, moderators and measurement. *International Journal of Manpower*, 13(2): 13–26.

Breevaart, K., Lopez Bohle, S., Pletzer, J.L., and Muñoz Medina, F. (2020). Voice and silence as immediate consequences of job insecurity. *Career Development International*, 25(2), 204–20.

Buonocore, F., de Gennaro, D., Russo, M., and Salvatore, D. (2020). Cognitive job crafting: A possible response to increasing job insecurity and declining professional prestige. *Human Resource Management Journal*, 30(2), 244–59.

Carver, C. S. (2006). Approach, avoidance, and the self-regulation of affect and action. *Motivation and Emotion*, 30(2), 105–10.

Carver, C. S. and Harmon-Jones, E. (2009). Anger is an approach-related affect: Evidence and implications. *Psychological Bulletin,* 135(2), 183–204.

Christian, M. S., Eisenkraft, N., and Kapadia, C. (2015). Dynamic associations among somatic complaints, human energy, and discretionary behaviors: Experiences with pain fluctuations at work. *Administrative Science Quarterly*, 60(1), 66–102.

De Spiegelaere, S., Van Gyes, G., De Witte, H., Niesen, W., and Van Hootegem, G. (2014). On the relation of job insecurity, job autonomy, innovative work behaviour and the mediating effect of work engagement. *Creativity and Innovation Management*, 23(3), 318–30.

Diefendorff, J. M., Richard, E. M., and Yang, J. (2008). Linking emotion regulation strategies to affective events and negative emotions at work. *Journal of Vocational Behavior, 73*(3), 498–508.

Elfenbein, H. A. (2007). Emotion in organizations: A review and theoretical integration. *The Academy of Management Annals*, 1(1), 315–86.

Elliot, A. J., Eder, A. B., and Harmon-Jones, E. (2013). Approach–avoidance motivation and emotion: Convergence and divergence. *Emotion Review*, 5(3), 308–11.

Elliot, A. J. and Thrash, T. M. (2002). Approach–avoidance motivation in personality: Approach and avoidance temperaments and goals. *Journal of Personality and Social Psychology,* 82(5), 804–18.

Elliot, A. J., and Thrash, T. M. (2010). Approach and avoidance temperament as basic dimensions of personality. *Journal of Personality*, 78(3), 865–906.

Emanuel Froehlich, D., Beausaert, S., Segers, M., and Gerken, M. (2014). Learning to stay employable. *Career Development International*, 19(5), 508–25.

Ferris, D. L., Yan, M., Lim, V. K., Chen, Y., and Fatimah, S. (2016). An approach–avoidance framework of workplace aggression. *Academy of Management Journal*, 59(5), 1777–800.

Fiske, S. T. and Taylor, S. E. (1991). *Social cognition*, (2nd edn. New York: McGraw-Hill.

Frijda, N. H. (1986). *The Emotions*. Cambridge: Cambridge University Press.

Frijda, N. H. (1993). Moods, emotion episodes, and emotions. In M. Lewis and J. M. Haviland (eds), *Handbook of Emotions*, New York, NY: Guilford Press, pp 381–404.

Gilbert, P. and Andrews, B. (eds). (1998). *Shame: Interpersonal Behavior, Psychopathology, and Culture*. Oxford, England: Oxford University Press, pp 78–98.

Gooty, J., Gavin, M., and Ashkanasy, N. M. (2009). Emotions research in OB: The challenges that lie ahead. *Journal of Organizational Behavior: The International Journal of Industrial, Occupational and Organizational Psychology and Behavior*, 30(6), 833–8.

Grant, A. M. (2013). Rocking the boat but keeping it steady: The role of emotion regulation in employee voice. *Academy of Management Journal*, 56(6), 1703–23.

Heider, F. (1958). *The Psychology of Interpersonal Relations*. New York: Wiley.

Harmon-Jones, E. (2003). Anger and the behavioral approach system. *Personality and Individual Differences*, 35(5), 995–1005.

Harmon-Jones, E., Harmon-Jones, C., and Price, T. F. (2013). What is approach motivation?. *Emotion Review*, 5(3), 291–5.

Harmon-Jones, E., Harmon-Jones, C., and Summerell, E. (2017). On the importance of both dimensional and discrete models of emotion. *Behavioral Sciences*, 7(4), 66.

Harmon-Jones, E. and Sigelman, J. (2001). State anger and prefrontal brain activity: Evidence that insult-related relative left-prefrontal activation is associated with experienced anger and aggression. *Journal of Personality and Social Psychology*, 80(5), 797–803.

Hofmann, D. A., Lei, Z., and Grant, A. M. (2009). Seeking help in the shadow of doubt: The sensemaking processes underlying how nurses decide whom to ask for advice. *Journal of Applied Psychology*, 94(5), 1261–74.

Huang, G. H., Lee, C., Ashford, S., Chen, Z., and Ren, X. (2010). Affective job insecurity: A mediator of cognitive job insecurity and employee outcomes relationships. *International Studies of Management and Organization*, 40(1), 20–39.

Huang, G. H., Niu, X., Lee, C., and Ashford, S. J. (2012). Differentiating cognitive and affective job insecurity: Antecedents and outcomes. *Journal of Organizational Behavior*, 33(6), 752–69.

Huang, G. H., Wellman, N., Ashford, S. J., Lee, C., and Wang, L. (2017). Deviance and exit: The organizational costs of job insecurity and moral disengagement. *Journal of Applied Psychology*, 102(1), 26–42.

Ito, J. K. and Brotheridge, C. M. (2007). Exploring the predictors and consequences of job insecurity's components. *Journal of Managerial Psychology*, 22, 40–64.

Jiang, L. (2018). Job insecurity and creativity: The buffering effect of self-affirmation and work-affirmation. *Journal of Applied Social Psychology*, 48(7), 388–97.

Jiang, L. and Lavaysse, L. M. (2018). Cognitive and affective job insecurity: A meta-analysis and a primary study. *Journal of Management*, 44(6), 2307–42.

Johnson, C. D., Messe, L. A., and Crano, W. D. (1984). Predicting job performance of low income workers: The work opinion questionnaire. *Personnel Psychology*, 37, 291–9.

Kelley, H. H. (1967). Attribution theory in social psychology. In D. Levine (ed), *Nebraska Symposium on Motivation*, vol 15, Lincoln: University of Nebraska Press, pp 192–238.

Lam, C. F., Liang, J., Ashford, S. J., and Lee, C. (2015). Job insecurity and organizational citizenship behavior: Exploring curvilinear and moderated relationships. *Journal of Applied Psychology*, 100(2), 499–510.

Lazarus, R. S. (1968). Emotions and adaptation: Conceptual and empirical relations. In W. J. Arnold (ed), *Nebraska Symposium on Motivation*, Lincoln: University of Nebraska Press, pp 175–266.

Lazarus, R. S. (1991). *Emotion and Adaptation*. Oxford University Press on Demand.

Lebel, R. D. (2017). Moving beyond fight and flight: A contingent model of how the emotional regulation of anger and fear sparks proactivity. *Academy of Management Review*, 42(2), 190–206.

Lee, C., Huang, G. H., and Ashford, S. J. (2018). Job insecurity and the changing workplace: Recent developments and the future trends in job insecurity research. *Annual Review of Organizational Psychology and Organizational Behavior*, 5, 335–59.

Lerner, J. S. and Keltner, D. (2001). Fear, anger, and risk. *Journal of Personality and Social Psychology*, 81(1), 146–59.

Lewis, M. (1992). *Shame: The Exposed Self*. New York: The Free Press.

Li, Z., Long, C., and Er-Yue, T. (2018). When does job insecurity lead to feedback-seeking behavior? The counterintuitive moderating role of perceived organizational support. *Current Psychology*, 37(4), 850–61.

Liu, Y. and Perrewe, P. L. (2005). Another look at the role of emotion in the organizational change: A process model. *Human Resource Management Review*, 15(4), 263–80.

Niesen, W., Van Hootegem, A., Handaja, Y., Batistelli, A., and De Witte, H. (2018). Quantitative and qualitative job insecurity and idea generation: The mediating role of psychological contract breach. *Scandinavian Journal of Work and Organizational Psychology*, 3(1), 1–14.

Noe, R. A., Tews, M. J., and Marand, A. D. (2013). Individual differences and informal learning in the workplace. *Journal of Vocational Behavior*, 83(3), 327–35.

Parker, S. K., Bindl, U. K., and Strauss, K. (2010). Making things happen: A model of proactive motivation. *Journal of Management*, 36(4), 827–56.

Parker, S. K., Wang, Y., and Liao, J. (2019). When is proactivity wise? A review of factors that influence the individual outcomes of proactive behavior. *Annual Review of Organizational Psychology and Organizational Behavior*, 6, 221–48.

Peng, A. C. M. , Schaubroeck, J., Chong, S., and Li, Y. (2019). Discrete emotions linking abusive supervision to employee intention and behavior. *Personnel Psychology*, 72(3), 393–419.

Poulson, C. F., II (2000). Shame and work. In N. M. Ashkanasy, W. Zerbe, and C. E. J. Härtel (eds), *Emotions in the Workplace: Research, Theory, and Practice*, Westport, CT: Quorum Books, pp 490–541.

Probst, T. M. (2002). The impact of job insecurity on employee work attitudes, job adaptation, and organizational withdrawal behaviors. In J.M. Brett and F. Drasgow (eds), *The Psychology of Work: Theoretically Based Empirical Research*, Mahwah, NJ: Lawrence Erlbaum, pp 141–68.

Probst, T. M. (2003). Development and validation of the Job Security Index and the Job Security Satisfaction Scale: A classical test theory and IRT approach. *Journal of Occupational and Organizational Psychology*, 76, 451–67.

Probst, T., Chizh, A., Hu, S., Jiang, L., and Austin, C. (2019). Explaining the relationship between job insecurity and creativity: A test of cognitive and affective mediators. *Career Development International*, 25(3), 247–70.

Reisel, W. D., Probst, T. M., Chia, S. L., Maloles, C. M., and König, C. J. (2010). The effects of job insecurity on job satisfaction, organizational citizenship behavior, deviant behavior, and negative emotions of employees. *International Studies of Management and Organization*, 40(1), 74–91.

Rodell, J. B. and Judge, T. A. (2009). Can 'good' stressors spark 'bad' behaviors? The mediating role of emotions in links of challenge and hindrance stressors with citizenship and counterproductive behaviors. *Journal of Applied Psychology*, 94(6), 1438–51.

Roseman, I. J. (1979, September). *Cognitive aspect of emotion and emotional behavior*. Paper presented at the 87th Annual Convention of the American Psychological Association, New York.

Roseman, I. J. (1984). Cognitive determinants of emotions: A structural theory. In P. Shaver (ed), *Review of Personality and social Psychology*, vol 5, Beverly Hills, CA: SAGE, pp 11–36.

Roseman, I. J. (2013). Appraisal in the emotion system: Coherence in strategies for coping. *Emotion Review*, 5(2), 141–9.

Roseman, I. J., Wiest, C., and Swartz, T. S. (1994). Phenomenology, behaviors, and goals differentiate discrete emotions. *Journal of Personality and Social Psychology*, 67(2), 206–21.

Russell, J. A. (1980). A circumplex model of affect. *Journal of Personality and Social Psychology*, 39(6), 1161–78.

Russell, J. A. and Carroll, J. M. (1999). On the bipolarity of positive and negative affect. *Psychological Bulletin*, 125, 3–30.

Scherer, K. R. (1984). On the nature and function of emotions: A component process approach. In K. R. Scherer and P. Ekman (eds), *Approaches to Emotion*, Hillsdale, NJ: Erlbaum, pp 293–317.

Schreurs, B., Guenter, H., Jawahar, I.M., and De Cuyper, N. (2015). Speaking up when feeling job insecure: The moderating role of punishment and reward sensitivity. *Journal of Organizational Change Management*, 28(6), 1107–28.

Shoss, M. K. (2017). Job insecurity: An integrative review and agenda for future research. *Journal of Management*, 43(6), 1911–39.

Smith, C. A. and Ellsworth, P. C. (1985). Patterns of cognitive appraisal in emotion. *Journal of Personality and Social Psychology*, 48(4), 813–38.

Staufenbiel, T. and König, C. J. (2010). A model for the effects of job insecurity on performance, turnover intention, and absenteeism. *Journal of Occupational and Organizational Psychology*, 83(1), 101–17.

Sverke, M. and Hellgren, J. (2001). Exit, voice and loyalty reactions to job insecurity in Sweden: do unionized and non-unionized employees differ?. *British Journal of Industrial Relations*, 39(2), 167–82.

Tangney, J. P. and Dearing, R. L. (2002). *Shame and Guilt*. New York, NY: Guilford Press.

Tangney, J. P., Stuewig, J., and Mashek, D. J. (2007). Moral emotions and moral behavior. *Annual Review of Psychology*, 58, 345–72.

Tracy, J. L. and Robins, R. W. (2004). Putting the self into self-conscious emotions: A theoretical model. *Psychological Inquiry*, 15(2), 103–25.

Van Dyne, L., Ang, S., and Botero, I. C. (2003). Conceptualizing employee silence and employee voice as multidimensional constructs. *Journal of Management Studies*, 40, 1359–92.

Van Hootegem, A. and De Witte, H. (2019). Qualitative job insecurity and informal learning: A longitudinal test of occupational self-efficacy and psychological contract breach as mediators. *International Journal of Environmental Research and Public Health*, 16(10), 1847.

Wang, Y., Peng, K. Z., Mao, Y., and Lan, J. (2018). Development of a Chinese measure on twelve basic emotions and a preliminary test on a two-dimensional model on emotions-job outcome relationship. *Asia Pacific Journal of Management*, 35(2), 529–64.

Watson, D., Wiese, D., Vaidya, J., and Tellegen, A. (1999). The two general activation systems of affect: Structural findings, evolutionary considerations, and psychobiological evidence. *Journal of Personality and Social Psychology*, 76, 820–38.

Yang, Q., Jin, G., Fu, J., and Li, M. (2019). Job insecurity and employees taking charge: The role of global job embeddedness. *Social Behavior and Personality: An International Journal*, 47(4), 1–12.

7

Other-Praising Emotions and Employee Proactivity

Chia-Huei Wu and Chenwei Li

In today's global economy, organizations face complex environments that require rapid responses to changing external environments (Campbell, 2000). To succeed within these increasingly uncertain operating environments, in addition to adapting to changes, employees can proactively respond to challenges (Griffin, Neal, and Parker, 2007) to improve the work environment, such as generating new ideas and finding alternatives to improve work effectiveness, or themselves, such as seeking feedback or career advice to facilitate one's career prospect. Nevertheless, not all employees behave proactively at work. This is the case because being proactive can be demanding and effortful. To be proactive or to make things happen, an individual needs to spend extra time and effort to monitor the environment, identify threats or opportunities, come up with ideas or solutions to make changes and overcome obstacles or resistances. To achieve this, employees need to have enough energy or be energized during the course to support proactive actions.

Positive emotions have been identified as an energizer to boost employees' proactivity (Parker, Bindl, and Strauss, 2010). Firstly, positive emotions broaden one's attention and awareness, leading an individual to see a wide range of behavioural repertoires and promoting curiosity and exploration. As such, positive emotions are likely to influence the selection of proactive goals because it evokes flexible cognitive processes (Fredrickson, 1998, 2001; Isen, 1999) and helps individuals to think ahead and rise to the challenge of pursuing proactive goals. Secondly, positive emotions provide feelings of energy

(Shraga and Shirom, 2009), which helps employees to maintain their engagement and persistence in performing challenging activities (Tsai, Chen, and Liu, 2007). However, there are different positive emotions, such as happy, excited, relaxed, and grateful, among others. Do all positive emotions elevate the levels of proactivity? Proactivity research so far has relied on the affective circumplex model (Russell, 1980) to differentiate emotions into four quadrants – the combinations of high versus low activation and positive versus negative valence. Findings to date in general reveal that high-activated positive emotions play key role energizing employees' proactive activities (for example, Bindl et al, 2012; Warr et al, 2014).

While the affective circumplex model provides a way to differentiate positive emotions into broad categories, the classification is not specific enough to help us understand the function of specific positive emotion in driving an individual's proactive forces (for example, Izard, 2009). Firstly, not all positive emotions have been included in the affective circumplex model. Secondly, the focus on the levels of activation ignores the idiosyncratic meaning of each positive emotion, which should be key to unpack the role of emotions in shaping individual behaviour. As different emotions may be elicited in different contexts, taking the contextual background of a specific emotion into account should be able to help us understand their impact on individual behaviour. As indicated by Bindl (2019), scholars need to investigate how and why affect is critical in the process of engaging in proactivity so as to develop a more differentiated theory on the role of affect for proactivity. In the meantime, proactive behaviour has been mainly studied from a self- or goal-regulatory perspective (Bindl et al, 2012; Parker, Bindl, and Strauss, 2010; Wu et al, 2018), which emphasizes the idea of agency that an individual can bring about change by envisioning goals s/he wants to achieve and striving for such achievement. Nevertheless, employees do not live in a social vacuum. People observe what others do, learning ideas and actions from observing (Bandura, 1971). How vicarious learning, such as observing exemplary others, can inspire employees' proactive behaviour at work via an emotional mechanism, however, has been rarely investigated.

To address the research gap, the aim of this chapter is to discuss how exemplary others can elicit different specific, positive emotions, which, in turn, inspires employees' different proactive behaviour. In this chapter, we focus on four other-praising emotions – gratitude, elevation, admiration, and awe – and suggest that these four emotions can shape different proactive behaviours in the workplace (see Table 7.1 for a summary). We focused on these four other-praising emotions for

Table 7.1: Other-praising emotions and their functions on motivation and proactive behaviour

Other-praising emotions	Definition	Elicited motivations	Elicited proactive behaviour
Gratitude	A moral emotion reflecting a state of being grateful when individuals recognize they have benefited from another's actions (McCullough et al, 2001).	(1) Functions as a 'moral barometer' sensitive to events in which another person provides benefits to the self. (2) Functions as a 'moral motive' and 'moral reinforcer' and makes people act more prosocially (McCullough et al, 2001).	Proactive prosocial behaviour (for example, interpersonal helping and altruism).
Elevation	The emotional response to witnessing acts of virtue or moral beauty, or others' behaviour that exceeds standards of virtue (for example, Algoe and Haidt, 2009; Haidt, 2003).	(1) Emulate the *moral* role model, become a better person (self moral development). (2) Put personal moral values into action and do something good for others (Pohling and Diessner, 2016).	Proactive moral behaviour (for example, moral voice, whistle-blowing behaviour, participation in CSR activities, volunteering).
Admiration	An emotional response to witnessing of extraordinary displays of non-moral excellence such as skill, talent, or achievement by others (Algoe and Haidt, 2009; Haidt, 2003).	(1) Emulate the role model, induce the motivational state of inspiration. (2) Promote individual learning and change, help individuals to develop, grow, and achieve excellence (Schindler et al, 2013).	Proactive learning behaviour (for example, feedback-seeking, mentor-seeking, learning and personal development behaviours and activities).

(continued)

Table 7.1: Other-praising emotions and their functions on motivation and proactive behaviour (continued)

Other-praising emotions	Definition	Elicited motivations	Elicited proactive behaviour
Awe	An emotional response to witnessing of the stimulus (for example, threat, beauty, ability, virtue, supernatural causality) that is *vast* and requires *accommodation* (Haidt, 2003; Keltner and Haidt, 2003)	(1) Experience things that are much larger than the self or the self's ordinary level of experience or frame of reference (Keltner and Haidt, 2003). (2) Adjust mental structures that cannot assimilate a new experience (Keltner and Haidt, 2003). (3) Relate to excellence that is beyond accomplishment and understanding (Schindler et al, 2013). (4) The feeling of being diminished in the presence of something greater than the self, and the motivation to be good to others (Piff et al, 2015; Shiota, Keltner, and Mossman, 2007) – social collective orientation.	Proactive self-transcendent behavior (for example, building social/ group cohesion, proactive socialization into organization).

several reasons. First, other-praising emotions are 'positive emotional responses elicited by exemplary others' (Algoe and Haidt, 2009, p 105). They are different from the well-studied, high-activated positive emotions, such as happiness, that are mainly driven by goal regulations or self-related accomplishment (Algoe and Haidt, 2009). Studying other-praising emotions will help us expand the scope of positive emotions in proactivity literature.

Second, as its name suggests, other-praising emotions are emotions elicited in a relational context. Unpacking how other-praising emotions can shape employees' proactivity will advance the understanding of social influence process in driving employees' proactivity. Studying other-praising emotions and their impact on proactive behaviour will help enrich such understanding because we will be able to identify how others can inspire an individual's proactive behaviour by eliciting specific other-praising emotions.

Third, as different other-praising emotions, such as gratitude, elevation, admiration, and awe, are elicited by different actions from others and induced different motivations (we will elaborate on this shortly), we thus expect that proactive behaviour driven by these emotions can also be different. Proactive behaviour has been largely studied under a 'generalized approach that emphasizes commonalities across different types of proactive behaviour ... to identify core processes and antecedents that facilitate proactivity across multiple domains' (Wu et al, 2018, p 294). However, scholars have started to recognize the differences between proactive behaviours by proposing different classification frameworks (for example, Belschak and Den Hartog, 2010; Griffin, Neal, and Parker, 2007; Parker and Collins, 2010) and unpacking different antecedents and boundary conditions for different forms of proactive behaviour, such as work-unit-oriented proactive behaviour and career-oriented proactive behaviour (Wu et al, 2018). We believe that by studying how different other-praising emotions can drive different forms of proactive behaviour, we are able to differentiate different forms of proactive behaviour.

In brief, we believe that our focus on other-praising emotions will contribute to the discussion of emotion and proactivity in many aspects as we just elaborated. In the following sections, we will firstly introduce four specific other-praising emotions (that is, gratitude, elevation, admiration, and awe) and then specifically elaborate on how each emotion can shape different forms of proactive behaviour in the workplace. We will conclude this chapter by highlighting the value of studying other-praising emotions and providing suggestions for future research.

Other-praising emotions

We now introduce the four other-praising emotions: gratitude, elevation, admiration and awe. These four emotions have been considered as one of families of moral emotions (Haidt, 2003) as they all involve interests or welfare of individuals or the whole society and involve positive evaluations of the perceived target. Specifically, gratitude, elevation and admiration are typical other-praising emotions arising from others' exemplary actions (Algoe and Haidt, 2009; Haidt, 2003) and awe is an emotion arising from perceiving vastness (Keltner and Haidt, 2003), which can be in a social context such as being in the presence of someone with a greater social status. These emotions have not been included in the affective circumplex model and the commonly-used emotion measurements such as the PANAS scale (Watson, Clark, and Tellegen, 1988), giving a good example to show we need to study a wide range of positive emotions. Also, as introduced shortly, these four other-praising emotions are elicited by different elicitors, providing good examples to illustrate how the contextual background of emotions can help us understand the role of emotions in shaping individual behaviour. We now introduce the four emotions specifically.

Gratitude is a moral emotion reflecting a state of being grateful when individuals recognize they have benefited from other's costly, intentional, and voluntary action (McCullough et al, 2001; McCullough, Kimeldorf, and Cohen, 2008). Gratitude thus is an emotional experience elicited by an event (that is, receiving a benefit) and the attributions (that is, other's costly, intentional, and voluntary action) assigned to the event.

Elevation is an emotional response to witnessing acts of virtue or moral beauty, or others' behaviour that exceed standards of virtue (Algoe and Haidt, 2009; Haidt, 2003). It is an emotion that will bring a desire to 'become a better person oneself and to follow the example of the moral exemplar' (Haidt, 2003, p 864), 'put personal moral values into action' and 'do something good for others' (Pohling and Diessner, 2016, p 418). Morally elevated individuals share warm, open feelings in the chest, feel optimistic about humanity, and strive to become more virtuously themselves (Algoe and Haidt, 2009; Haidt, 2003).

Admiration is an emotional response to the witnessing of extraordinary displays of skill, talent, or achievement by others (Algoe and Haidt, 2009; Haidt, 2003). It is 'surprise associated with some pleasure and a sense of approval' (Darwin and Ekman, 1872/1998, p 269) and is an emotion that 'motivates the internalisation and emulation of ideals embodied by an outstanding role model' (Schindler et al, 2013, p 85). To differentiate its difference from elevation, Haidt and his colleagues (Algoe and Haidt, 2009; Haidt, 2003; Haidt and Morris, 2009) define admiration as a response to non-moral excellence. We follow this approach to differentiate elevation and admiration as it helps to differentiate the context how one would respond to the perceived exemplar. However, we are aware of debates on the differentiation between elevation and admiration (Kristjánsson, 2017; Szutta, 2019; Zagzebski, 2017).

Finally, awe is a moral emotional state that 'results when we encounter something vast (usually physically vast, but sometimes small things reveal vast power, genius, or complexity) that cannot be comprehended using existing mental structures' (Haidt and Seder, 2009, p 5). Keltner and Haidt (2003) proposed that the experience of awe has two central elements: perceived vastness – the stimulus surpasses the individuals' boundaries of ordinary experiences; and the need for accommodation – the individuals need to adjust and expand their accustomed mental structures to understand the stimulus.

In the next section, we start elaborating on how these four emotions can elicit different motivations and thus promote different, specific proactive behaviour in the workplace.

Gratitude and proactive prosocial behaviour

As being grateful is evoked by receiving benefits from others (Algoe, Kurtz, and Hilaire, 2016), it usually motivates recipients to contribute to the welfare of the benefactor in turn or other persons. Moral affect theory of gratitude (McCullough et al, 2001) posits that gratitude acts first as a moral barometer, increasing the recipients' sensitivity to the perception that they have been the beneficiaries of another person's actions. Gratitude then serves as a moral motive, motivating the recipients to behave prosocially towards the benefactor and finally as a moral reinforcer, encouraging the benefactor to continue to behave prosocially back to the grateful recipients (and to others) in the future. This theory suggests that gratitude functions to facilitate social exchange between grateful recipients and benefactors through repayment or reciprocation of the benefits. In a meta-analytical study, Ma, Tunney, and Ferguson (2017) found a moderate positive association between gratitude and prosociality. They also indicated that the association is stronger when the prosocial actions were aimed to benefit the benefactors (that is, direct reciprocity) than other parties (that is, indirect reciprocity).

In addition to facilitate reciprocity for social exchange, gratitude helps strengthen a relationship with a responsive interaction partner. As indicated in the find-remind-and-bind theory of gratitude and its related studies (Algoe, 2012; Algoe, Haidt, and Gable, 2008; Algoe and Zhaoyang, 2016), gratitude emotions set the stage for subsequent quality interactions between the grateful recipients and their benefactor, and through repeated interactions, a communal relationship can be established over the long term, contributing to relationship formation and maintenance. Both theories of gratitude suggest that gratitude has a natural dyad of grateful recipients and their benefactor and could be uniquely suited to promote high-quality interpersonal relationships (Algoe et al, 2019).

With this being said, we argue that gratitude emotions draw an individual's attention to intepersonal dynamics and the emotional response, in turn, could motivate the individual to engage in proactive prosocial behaviours such as interpersonal helping and altruistic behaviours in the workplace. Altruism or offering intepersonal help in the workplace (Rioux and Penner, 2001; Smith, Organ, and Near, 1983), which has been studied under the concept of organizational citizenship behaviours, can be regarded as proactive prosocial behaviour (Grant and Ashford, 2008; Grant, Parker, and Collins, 2009). Indivdiuals consiciously choose to engage in these behaviours with the aim of benefitting either specific individuals within an organizational context or an organization itself. Since the experience of gratitude emotions shifts individuals' attention to the well-being of another entity (that is, the benefactor or third party) and a desire to be helpful and cooperative, we expect that grateful persons are more likely to engage in proactive altruistic and helping behaviours in the workplace. Findings from a few studies have lend support for the idea that gratitude can boost an individual's proactivity to benefit others, or proactive prosocial behaviour. For example, grateful employees are more likely to engage in organizational citizenship behaviours (Ford et al, 2018; Spence et al, 2014). Grateful leaders have also been found to demonstrate prosocial leader behaviour toward team members and foster positive, supportive relationships with all those around them (Grant and Gino, 2010; Michie, 2009).

Beyond the invidiual level, the funtion of gratitude on prosocial proactivity can also be extended to the group level. Algoe et al (2019) found that grateful emotional expressions can not only impact the behaviour of the grateful recipients and benefactors, but also influence multiple group members simultaneously. Specifically, they found a third party witnessing effect, in which the third party witnessed to the recipient expressing gratitude toward a benefactor became more helpful and affiliative toward the grateful receipient as well as towards the benefactor in the group. This finding suggests that, in addition to promting one's proative prosocial behaviour, gratitude can spark others' proative prosocial behaviour via a social observation and contagion mechanisms.

Elevation and proactive moral behaviour

Like gratitude, elevation can motivate an individual to engage in prosocial behaviour to demonstrate their virtue or morality (Schnall, Roper, and Fessler, 2010; Thomson et al, 2014; Van de Vyver and Abrams, 2017). Nevertheless, the main trigger as well as the behavioural outcomes of elevation and gratitude emotions can be quite different.

While gratitude is evoked by moral actions that usually benefitted the self, elevation is elicited by moral beauty that was not directed at one's self (Pohling and Diessner, 2016). So unlike gratitude focused more on facilitating interpersonal relationships through reciprocity, elevation is more about the empowerment of exemplar's 'imitably attractive' moral excellence (Zagzebski, 2017) and how an individual can develop similar moral virtues as the moral exemplar. Pohling, Diessner, and Strobel (2018), for example, found that trait moral elevation longitudinally promoted increases of moral identity internalization or overall moral self-concept. Aquino, McFerran, and Laven (2011) found that individuals with high levels of moral identity internalization were more likely than others to experience heightened states of moral elevation emotions. These studies suggest that elevation can play a role in moral identity development, or the development of internal states of goodness or virtues, enhancing one's moral standard and acting moral behaviour proactively. As indicated by Schnall and Roper (2012, p 373) elevation will mainly serve to 'provide a motivational impetus to act on one's moral values' and promote one's moral behaviour, though the elicited moral actions also have prosocial implications. This point is also supported by Thomson and Siegel (2013).

In the work context, we expect that moral elevation can facilitate proactive moral behaviour in different forms. For example, ethical or moral voice, 'the act of speaking out against unethical issues' (Lee et al, 2017, p 48), can be an example of proactive moral behaviour as employees who take a higher moral standard will be more sensitive to unethical issues and raise concerns and suggestions to protect morality at work. Specifically, ethical voice challenges and aims to change existing procedurals, behaviours and policies that are not normatively appropriate (Huang and Paterson, 2017; Lee et al, 2017). It uses moral expressions and provides suggestions that seek to improve ethical decision-making and behaviours before serious unethical problems occur. Moral elevation could play a key role in promoting more ethical voice because it uplifts individuals morally and thus suppresses the effect of immoral desires that might otherwise discourage social responsiveness towards others. Research has shown that individuals with heightened levels of moral identity and courage may be more likely to engage in ethical voice because their moral self-conceptions urge them to behave in a morally consistent way (Chen and Chen, 2018). In this sense, we believe that moral elevation emotions could foster ethical voice among employees.

In contrast to ethical voice that often involves open moral communication directed towards other inside organizational members

(Afsar and Shahjehan, 2018; Huang and Paterson, 2017), whistle-blowing behaviour is considered a type of proactive moral behaviour towards both inside and outside members and involves a whistleblower's rejection of violation in moral dilemmas (Near and Miceli, 1985). Dozier and Miceli (1985) posited that whistle-blowing is a prosocial behaviour intended to benefit others by reporting wrongdoings to parties who can take corrective actions. However, employees who engage in whistle-blowing behaviours may put their positions in danger as whistle-blowing creates discomfort, tension, and opposition from peers or managers who want to sustain established unethical practices shared in the organization. Thus, blowing whistles could involve a complex moral cognitive or emotional process (Miceli et al, 2012). As morally elevated persons are prosocially oriented and always put moral values in check (Algoe and Haidt, 2009), they are more likely to feel the urge to behave ethically in various situations and constantly serve as moral constructive dissenters when they see their managers or peers fail to do so.

From an organizational perspective, we also believe that senior level leaders' moral elevation may prompt companies to engage in corporate social responsibility (CSR) activities. Moral elevation helps leaders become aware of corporate ethical actions, such as holding high ethical operating standards and supporting a local development programme. Engaging in CSR actions is seen as an exemplary display of virtue supporting leaders' own moral goals. Although there is no direct empirical evidence supporting the moral elevation–CSR link, we argue that leaders' moral elevation provides fertile soil for the growth of CSR actions because of its awakening moral standards and virtues. Dedeke (2015) suggested that people could react to moral behaviours done by others in an emotional way. Company CSR activities could be regarded as displays of moral beauty and genuine concern for the welfare of the community, which could evoke feelings of elevation in third-party employees and consumers. Xie, Bagozzi, and Grønhaug (2019), for example, found that company CSR actions trigger feelings of moral elevation among consumers, which leads to consumers' brand advocacy behaviour.

In addition to CSR activities that mainly aim to make contributions outside the organizations, Vianello, Galliani, and Haidt (2010) explored the effects of moral elevation in the workplace and found that an employer's ability to emotionally elevate employees with virtuous behaviour can enhance employee attitudes and help cultivate a healthy organizational culture. This finding suggests that elevation can promote moral-related behaviour and participation within and outside the organization.

Admiration and proactive learning behaviour

Akin to the role-modelling effect (Morgenroth, Ryan, and Peters, 2015), admiration generates a desire for proximity towards the perceived target who demonstrated extraordinary performance. In other words, admiration of an exemplar with great skills, talent, and achievement leads to a conception of oneself as lacking the admired qualities but desiring to possess them, which in turn produces inspiration and emulation. Scholars posited that admiration designates a motivational state that individuals feel that they can potentially be like the exemplar whom they admire and therefore are driven to reach their ideal state as the exemplar (for example, Archer, 2019; Schindler et al, 2013). Individuals who experience admiration emotion are likey to have 'a desire to personally grow'(van de Ven, 2017, p 194). Such desire will then promote one's behaviour to obtain skills, resources, and experiences to achieve the same level of achievement as the exemplar.

Since admiration leads to emulation of excellence presented by exemplars, it motivates individuals to engage in proactive goal-directed learning and development activities in order to reach their self-growth goal. We therefore argue that experiences of admiration can motivate employees to seek more feedback, pursue learning and development in the workplace. Those behaviours can be conceptualized as proactive learning behaviour. In the work context, behaviour such as feedback-seeking (Ashford, Stobbeleir, and Nujella, 2016), proactive career behaviour (that is, career consultation, learning, and skill development) (Claes and Ruiz-Quintanilla, 1998), belong to this category. Feedback-seeking, for example, involves proactive and voluntary actions that employees undertake to obtain evaluations and information (Ashford and Cummings, 1983, 1985; Ashford, Stobbeleir, and Nujella, 2016). Feedback is a valuable resource for individuals because it facilitates their adaption, learning, and performance (Ashford and Cummings, 1983). In addition, employees can actively seek out learning and development opportunities and engage in a series of behaviours to expand their knowledge and skills (for example, Colquitt and Simmering, 1998; Major, Turner, and Fletcher, 2006). These are specific forms of proactive learning behaviour that can be promoted by admiration.

Moreover, Schindler et al (2015; 2013) suggested that admiration could motivate individuals to affiliate with the admired others and to improve (that is, close the gap between their current state and ideal state). It is thus possible that when individuals admire an exemplar who is from a similar work area, they are more likely to seek out the exemplar (or others) and ask the exemplar to be their mentor, who can provide career and job consultation. Mentor-seeking behaviours can also be expanded to general social networks building activities, because employees often build social networks in order to improve work efficiency or their own careers (Ostroff and Kozlowski, 2002). van de Ven (2017) posited that the motivational state aroused by admiration emotion could enable one to focus more on personal long-term goals and to improve in domains valuable to oneself. Therefore, we argue that experiences of admiration at work could motivate general social networks building activities that involve proactively forming interpersonal ties and connections, but with those who can help them to approach the ideal state, for current or future use (for example, Morrison, 2002; Ostroff and Kozlowski, 2002).

Awe and proactive self-transcendent behaviour

Unlike other varieties of positive emotions, awe tends to direct attention away from awareness of the self and towards the surroundings, because excellence of the stimulus is beyond accomplishment and understanding (Shiota, Keltner, and Mossman, 2007). Shiota, Keltner, and Mossman (2007) found that the experience of awe was associated with a sense of the diminished self and the presence of something greater than the self, which leads to a conception of oneself as part of the larger entities such as a community, a culture, or nature. Recently, Bai et al (2017) also found that the small or diminished self served as a central mediator of awe's impacts on various social cognition and behaviour. Like other emotions we have discussed, awe has been related to individuals' engagement in prosocial behaviours such as increased ethical decision-making, generosity, and prosocial values (for example, Piff et al, 2015). But such effect on prosocial behaviours is due to the fact that awe is a collective emotion, one that enables individuals to integrate into broader collectives (Bai et al, 2017; Shiota, Keltner, and Mossman, 2007) and engage in actions that can benefit the collectives.

We argue that given its collective nature, awe can facilitate self-transcendence and promote proactive behaviours reflecting such tendencies, here referring to proactive self-transcendent behaviour. As introduced earlier, awe is elicited when an individual perceives vastness that requests one to adjust and expand her/his perspective to understand the stimulus. Shiota, Keltner, and Mossman (2007, p 945) have clarified that: 'Vastness may be implied by a stimulus, rather than physically inherent in the stimulus ... An individual may be vast in the sense of having great impact on others' lives. What is critical is that the stimulus dramatically expands the observer's usual frame of reference in some dimension or domain.'

Following this, we argue that perceived vastness in the work context can come from different sources such as great organizational prestige, supervisors or colleagues who have extraordinary achievement or social status, or organizational activities (for example, products, business, or CSR) that have a significant impact on the beneficiaries or the society. When an employee feels awe by perceiving vastness in her/his organizational setting, s/he is likely to see her/himself as part of the organization and engage in proactive self-transcendent behaviour to support such self-conception. In line with this, Shiota, Keltner, and Mossman (2007) found that people high in dispositional awe are more likely to emphasize their membership in larger categories – a shift that is vital to the collaboration and cooperation required of social groups (Keltner et al, 2014; Piff et al, 2015).

We suggest that the experiences of awe would likely occur when employees enter their organizations because, at that time, employees, as newcomers, are not familiar with their organizations and people in there and thus are likely to encounter stimulus that could dramatically expand their usual frame of reference. In such context, awe may promote newcomers' proactive self-transcendent behaviour, making them merge into the organization. Following this idea, we expect that awe may facilitate newcomers' proactivity to strengthen their social identity at work. Behaviours such proactively seeking social or group cohesion, actively adapting to new environments, or proactive socialization into organizations (Ashford and Black, 1996; Kammeyer-Mueller and Wanberg, 2003; Kim, Cable, and Kim, 2005; Wanberg and Kammeyer-Mueller, 2000) belong to this category. For newcomers, adjusting to a new job or a new environment can be a daunting task. They not only need to seek task-related information for their new job, but also need to figure out acceptable social behaviours to become functioning members of the organization (for example, Ashford and Black, 1996; Ashforth, Sluss, and Saks, 2007; Kammeyer-Mueller, Livingston, and Liao, 2011). Since experiencing awe enables people to feel more comfortable revising their own mental structure, or acknowledging that currently held mental representations of the environment are not adequate to the occasion (Keltner and Haidt, 2003), awe-prone newcomers or newcomers who are experiencing awe in their first few months of employment could be more proactive in adapting themselves into the new environment by demonstrating more proactive socialization behaviours such as attempting to see things from the bright side, trying to learn more about task/organizational structures, and participating more in social events.

We also speculate that awe can facilitate self-transcendence by promoting behaviours that help individuals to strengthen an identity with their work groups. As groups and teams are ubiquitous in today's work context, work groups or teams could also be an important social identity for employees. We suggest that if the elicitors of awe are at the team level, such as perceiving the vastness of the team leader's or team's work, awe-prone employees in the team are more likely to seek social/group cohesion because they acknowledge that groups are larger than the self and could have a profound impact on their thoughts, feelings, and actions. That is, experiences of awe produce cognitive and behavioural tendencies that enable employees to fold into collaborative groups and teams and engage in collective actions at work.

Conclusion and future research

So far, we have elaborated how the four other-praising emotions could shape employees' proactive behaviour in the workplace. We argue that existing research has not considered how different positive emotions can drive employees' proactive behaviour differently. Focusing on other-praising emotions, and the four emotions specifically, we illustrate that these different emotions can drive different forms of proactive behaviour. This illustration suggests that we need to understand how different positive emotions can boost different forms of proactive behaviour via their unique mechanisms.

In addition, other-praising emotions bring us to recognize the importance of exemplary others in inspiring one's proactivity, which has been rarely discussed in proactivity literature. As we indicated earlier, proactivity has been conventionally viewed from a self-regulation perspective where self-defined goals play a significant role in driving proactivity. Our focus on other-praising emotions bring us to investigate the role of others in facilitating proactivity, highlighting a social learning perspective of proactivity, which should be further examined.

Moreover, we believe that other-praising emotions can expand our perspective to understand the role of positive emotion in shaping proactivity, beyond the energizing perspective that emphasizes the role of high-activated positive emotions, such as excitement and happiness, in triggering and sustaining proactive behaviour in general. For example, as we elaborated on earlier, different other-praising emotions elicit different motives that can trigger different forms of proactive behaviour, suggesting that different positive emotions can also shape the ways or direction of being proactive, beyond energizing. This understanding helps differentiate forms of proactive behaviours, a trend in proactivity literature studies to have a fine-tuned understanding of proactive behaviours.

For future research, firstly, empirical studies should be conducted to examine our speculations. As we reviewed above, several studies have been conducted to examine the role of gratitude in shaping proactive prosocial behaviour in the workplace. However, studies on elevation, admiration, and awe have not been extended to work contexts and linked to proactive behaviours specifically. There are thus opportunities and needs for proactivity researchers to investigate empirically whether these other-praising emotions can promote different forms of proactive behaviour as we proposed. Secondly, we suggest that the investigation should start at the event level so that we can depict clearly how a specific other-praising emotion is elicited in the workplace and whether such emotional experiences can promote specific proactive behaviour afterwards. Although we also can study other-praising emotions at a trait level, such as trait gratitude and trait moral elevation (McCullough, Emmons, and Tsang, 2002; Pohling, Diessner, and Strobel, 2018), which captures dispositional tendencies in experiencing specific other-praising emotions, we believe it is desirable to understand emotional phenomena at the event, intra-individual level, to understand how an other-praising emotional episode evolves and shapes one's actions before moving to the individual level to understand inter-individual differences (see Ashkanasy, in this volume, for the multilevel framework of emotion and Ohly and Venz for the event-level analysis of emotions).

To conclude, we believe investigating how different other-praising emotions can drive proactive behaviours in the workplace should help advance proactivity research by expanding the scope of positive emotions in the literature, the role of exemplary others in inspiring an individual's proactive behaviours at work, and differentitation of proactive behaviours.

References

Afsar, B. and Shahjehan, A. (2018). Linking ethical leadership and moral voice: The effects of moral efficacy, trust in leader, and leader-follower value congruence. *Leadership and Organization Development Journal,* 39(6), 775–93. doi:10.1108/lodj-01-2018-0015.

Algoe, S. B. (2012). Find, remind, and bind: The functions of gratitude in everyday relationships. *Social and Personality Psychology Compass,* 6(6), 455–69. doi:10.1111/j.1751-9004.2012.00439.x.

Algoe, S. B., Dwyer, P. C., Younge, A., and Oveis, C. (2019). A new perspective on the social functions of emotions: Gratitude and the witnessing effect. *Journal of Personality and Social Psychology*. doi:10.1037/pspi0000202.

Algoe, S. B. and Haidt, J. (2009). Witnessing excellence in action: The 'other-praising' emotions of elevation, gratitude, and admiration. *Journal of Positive Psychology*, 4(2), 105–27. doi:10.1080/17439760802650519.

Algoe, S. B., Haidt, J., and Gable, S. L. (2008). Beyond reciprocity: Gratitude and relationships in everyday life. *Emotion*, 8(3), 425–29. doi:10.1037/1528-3542.8.3.425.

Algoe, S. B., Kurtz, L. E., and Hilaire, N. M. (2016). Putting the 'you' in 'thank you': Examining other-praising behavior as the active relational ingredient in expressed gratitude. *Social Psychological and Personality Science*, 7(7), 658–66. doi:10.1177/1948550616651681.

Algoe, S. B. and Zhaoyang, R. (2016). Positive psychology in context: Effects of expressing gratitude in ongoing relationships depend on perceptions of enactor responsiveness. *The Journal of Positive Psychology*, 11(4), 399–415. doi:10.1080/17439760.2015.1117131.

Aquino, K., McFerran, B., and Laven, M. (2011). Moral identity and the experience of moral elevation in response to acts of uncommon goodness. *Journal of Personality and Social Psychology*, 100(4), 703–18. doi:10.1037/a0022540.

Archer, A. (2019). Admiration and motivation. *Emotion Review*, 11(2), 140–50. doi:10.1177/1754073918787235.

Ashford, S. J. and Black, J. S. (1996). Proactivity during organizational entry: The role of desire for control. *Journal of Applied Psychology*, 81(2), 199–214.

Ashford, S. J. and Cummings, L. L. (1983). Feedback as an individual resource: Personal strategies of creating information. *Organizational Behavior and Human Performance*, 32(3), 370–98.

Ashford, S. J. and Cummings, L. L. (1985). Proactive feedback seeking: The instrumental use of the information environment. *Journal of Occupational Psychology*, 58, 67–79.

Ashford, S. J., Stobbeleir, K. D., and Nujella, M. (2016). To seek or not to seek: Is that the only question? Recent developments in feedback-seeking literature. *Annual Review of Organizational Psychology and Organizational Behavior*, 3, 213–39. doi:https://doi.org/10.1146/annurev-orgpsych-041015-062314.

Ashforth, B. E., Sluss, D. M., and Saks, A. M. (2007). Socialization tactics, proactive behavior, and newcomer learning: Integrating socialization models. *Journal Of Vocational Behavior*, 70, 447–62.

Bai, Y., Maruskin, L. A., Chen, S., Gordon, A. M., Stellar, J. E., McNeil, G. D., Peng, K., Keltner, D. (2017). Awe, the diminished self, and collective engagement: Universals and cultural variations in the small self. *Journal of Personality and Social Psychology*, 113(2), 185–209. doi:10.1037/pspa0000087.

Bandura, A. (1971). *Social Learning Theory*. New York: General Learning Press.

Belschak, F. D. and Den Hartog, D. N. (2010). Pro-self, pro-social, and pro-organizational foci of proactive behavior: Differential antecedents and consequences. *Journal of Occupational and Organizational Psychology,* 83, 475–98.

Bindl, U. K. (2019). Work-related proactivity through the lens of narrative: Investigating emotional journeys in the process of making things happen. *Human Relations,* 72(4), 615–45. doi:10.1177/0018726718778086.

Bindl, U. K., Parker, S. K., Totterdell, P., and Hagger-Johnson, G. (2012). Fuel of the self-starter: How mood relates to proactive goal regulation. *Journal of Applied Psychology,* 97, 134–50.

Campbell, D. J. (2000). The proactive employee: Managing workplace initiative. *Academy of Management Executive,* 14(3), 52–66.

Chen, M. and Chen, C. (2018). Dare to speak up: How moral identity relates to ethical voice in the workplace. *Academy of Management Proceedings,* 1, 15478. doi:10.5465/AMBPP.2018.15478abstract.

Claes, R. and Ruiz-Quintanilla, S. A. (1998). Influences of early career experiences, occupational group, and national culture on proactive career behavior. *Journal Of Vocational Behavior,* 52, 357–78.

Colquitt, J. A. and Simmering, M. J. (1998). Conscientiousness, goal orientation, and motivation to learn during the learning process: A longitudinal study. *Journal of Applied Psychology,* 83(4), 654–65. doi:10.1037/0021-9010.83.4.654.

Darwin, C. and Ekman, P. (1872/1998). *The Expression of the Emotions in Man and Animals,* Definitive Edition edn. New York: Oxford University Press.

Dedeke, A. (2015). A Cognitive–Intuitionist model of moral judgment. *Journal of Business Ethics,* 126(3), 437–57. doi:10.1007/s10551-013-1965-y.

Dozier, J. B. and Miceli, M. P. (1985). Potential predictors of whistle-blowing: A prosocial behavior perspective. *Academy of Management Review,* 10(4), 823–36. doi:10.2307/258050.

Ford, M. T., Wang, Y., Jin, J., and Eisenberger, R. (2018). Chronic and episodic anger and gratitude toward the organization: Relationships with organizational and supervisor supportiveness and extrarole behavior. *Journal of Occupational Health Psychology,* 23(2), 175–87. doi:10.1037/ocp0000075.

Fredrickson, B. L. (1998). What good are positive emotions? *Review of General Psychology,* 2(3), 300–19.

Fredrickson, B. L. (2001). The role of positive emotions in positive psychology: The broaden-and-build theory of positive emotions. *American Psychologist,* 56(3), 218–26. doi:http://dx.doi.org/10.1037/0003-066X.56.3.218.

Grant, A. M. and Ashford, S. J. (2008). The dynamics of proactivity at work. *Research in Organizational Behavior,* 28, 3–34.

Grant, A. M. and Gino, F. (2010). A little thanks goes a long way: Explaining why gratitude expressions motivate prosocial behavior. *Journal of Personality and Social Psychology,* 98(6), 946–55. doi:10.1037/a0017935.

Grant, A. M., Parker, S. K., and Collins, C. G. (2009). Getting credit for proactive behavior: Supervisor reactions depend on what you value and how you feel. *Personnel Psychology*, 62, 31–55.

Griffin, M. A., Neal, A., and Parker, S. K. (2007). A new model of work role performance: Positive behavior in uncertain and interdependent contexts. *Academy of Management Journal*, 50, 327–47. doi:http://dx.doi.org/10.5465/AMJ.2007.24634438.

Haidt, J. (2003). The moral emotions. In R. J. Davidson, K. R. Scherer, and H. H. Goldsmith (eds), *Handbook of Affective Sciences*, Oxford: Oxford University Press, pp 852–70.

Haidt, J. and Morris, J. P. (2009). Finding the self in self-transcendent emotions. *Proceedings of the National Academy of Sciences*, 106(19), 7687–8. doi:10.1073/pnas.0903076106.

Haidt, J. and Seder, P. (2009). Admiration and awe. In *Entry for the Oxford Companion to Affective Science*. New York: Oxford University Press, pp 4–5.

Huang, L. and Paterson, T. A. (2017). Group ethical voice: Influence of ethical leadership and impact on ethical performance. *Journal of Management*, 43(4), 1157–84. doi:10.1177/0149206314546195.

Isen, A. M. (1999). On the relationship between affect and creative problem solving. In S. Russ (ed), *Affect, Creative Experience, and Psychological Adjustment*. Philadelphia, PN: Taylor and Francis, pp 3–17.

Izard, C. E. (2009). Emotion theory and research: Highlights, unanswered questions, and emerging issues. *Annual Review of Psychology*, 60(1), 1–25. doi:10.1146/annurev.psych.60.110707.163539.

Kammeyer-Mueller, J. and Wanberg, C. R. (2003). Unwrapping the organizational entry process: Disentangling multiple antecedents and their pathways to adjustment. *Journal of Applied Psychology*, 88(5), 779–94.

Kammeyer-Mueller, J. D., Livingston, B. A., and Liao, H. (2011). Perceived similarity, proactive adjustment, and organizational socialization. *Journal of Vocational Behavior*, 78, 225–36.

Keltner, D. and Haidt, J. (2003). Approaching awe, a moral, spiritual, and aesthetic emotion. *Cognition and Emotion*, 17(2), 297–314. doi:10.1080/02699930302297.

Keltner, D., Kogan, A., Piff, P. K., and Saturn, S. R. (2014). The sociocultural appraisals,values, and emotions (SAVE) framework of prosociality: Core processes from gene to meme. *Annual Review of Psychology*, 65(1), 425–60. doi:10.1146/annurev-psych-010213-115054.

Kim, T.-Y., Cable, D. M., and Kim, S.-P. (2005). Socialization tactics, employee proactivity, and person–organization fit. *Journal of Applied Psychology*, 90(2), 232–41. doi:http://dx.doi.org/10.1037/0021-9010.90.2.232.

Kristjánsson, K. (2017). Emotions targeting moral exemplarity: Making sense of the logical geography of admiration, emulation and elevation. *Theory and Research in Education*, 15(1), 20–37. doi:10.1177/1477878517695679.

Lee, D., Choi, Y., Youn, S., and Chun, J. U. (2017). Ethical leadership and employee moral voice: The mediating role of moral efficacy and the moderating role of leader–follower value congruence. *Journal of Business Ethics,* 141(1), 47–57. doi:10.1007/s10551-015-2689-y.

Ma, L. K., Tunney, R. J., and Ferguson, E. (2017). Does gratitude enhance prosociality? A meta-analytic review. *Psychological Bulletin,* 143(6), 601–635. doi:10.1037/bul0000103.

Major, D. A., Turner, J. E., and Fletcher, T. D. (2006). Linking proactive personality and the Big Five to motivation to learn and development activity. *Journal of Applied Psychology,* 91(4), 927–35.

McCullough, M. E., Emmons, R. A., and Tsang, J.-A. (2002). The grateful disposition: A conceptual and empirical topography. *Journal of Personality and Social Psychology,* 82(1), 112–27. doi:10.1037/0022-3514.82.1.112.

McCullough, M. E., Kilpatrick, S. D., Emmons, R. A., and Larson, D. B. (2001). Is gratitude a moral affect? *Psychological Bulletin,* 127, 249–66. doi:http://dx.doi.org/10.1037/0033-2909.127.2.249.

McCullough, M. E., Kimeldorf, M. B., and Cohen, A. D. (2008). An adaptation for altruism? The social causes, social effects, and social evolution of gratitude. *Current Directions in Psychological Science,* 17(4), 281–5. doi:10.1111/j.1467-8721.2008.00590.x.

Miceli, M. P., Near, J. P., Rehg, M. T., and Van Scotter, J. R. (2012). Predicting employee reactions to perceived organizational wrongdoing: Demoralization, justice, proactive personality, and whistle-blowing. *Human Relations,* 65(8), 923–954. doi:10.1177/0018726712447004.

Michie, S. (2009). Pride and gratitude: How positive emotions influence the prosocial behaviors of organizational leaders. *Journal of Leadership and Organizational Studies,* 15(4), 393–403. doi:10.1177/1548051809333338.

Morgenroth, T., Ryan, M. K., and Peters, K. (2015). The motivational theory of role modeling: How role models influence role aspirants' goals. *Review of General Psychology,* 19, 465–83.

Morrison, E. W. (2002). Newcomers' relationships: The role of social network ties during socialization. *Academy of Management Journal,* 45(6), 1149–60. doi:http://dx.doi.org/10.2307/3069430.

Near, J. P. and Miceli, M. P. (1985). Organizational dissidence: The case of whistle-blowing. *Journal of Business Ethics,* 4(1), 1–16. doi:10.1007/bf00382668.

Ostroff, C. and Kozlowski, S. W. J. (2002). Organizational socialization as a learning process: The role of information acquisition. *Personnel Psychology,* 45(4), 849–74.

Parker, S. K., Bindl, U. K., and Strauss, K. (2010). Making things happen: A model of proactive motivation. *Journal of Management,* 36, 827–56. doi:https://doi.org/10.1177/0149206310363732.

Parker, S. K. and Collins, C. G. (2010). Taking stock: Integrating and differentiating multiple proactive behaviors. *Journal of Management, 36*, 633–62. doi:https://doi.org/10.1177/0149206308321554.

Piff, P. K., Dietze, P., Feinberg, M., Stancato, D. M., and Keltner, D. (2015). Awe, the small self, and prosocial behavior. *Journal of Personality and Social Psychology,* 108(6), 883–99. doi:10.1037/pspi0000018.

Pohling, R. and Diessner, R. (2016). Moral elevation and moral beauty: A review of the empirical literature. *Review of General Psychology,* 20(4), 412–25. doi:10.1037/gpr0000089.

Pohling, R., Diessner, R., and Strobel, A. (2018). The role of gratitude and moral elevation in moral identity development. *International Journal of Behavioral Development,* 42(4), 405–15. doi:10.1177/0165025417727874.

Rioux, S. M. and Penner, L. A. (2001). The causes of organizational citizenship behavior: A motivational analysis. *Journal of Applied Psychology,* 86, 1306–14.

Russell, J. A. (1980). A circumplex model of affect. *Journal of Personality and Social Psychology,* 39, 1161–78

Schindler, I., Paech, J., and Löwenbrück, F. (2015). Linking admiration and adoration to self-expansion: Different ways to enhance one's potential. *Cognition and Emotion,* 29(2), 292–310. doi:10.1080/02699931.2014.903230.

Schindler, I., Zink, V., Windrich, J., and Menninghaus, W. (2013). Admiration and adoration: Their different ways of showing and shaping who we are. *Cognition and Emotion,* 27(1), 85–118. doi:10.1080/02699931.2012.698253.

Schnall, S. and Roper, J. (2012). Elevation puts moral values into action. *Social Psychological and Personality Science,* 3(3), 373–8. doi:10.1177/1948550611423595.

Schnall, S., Roper, J., and Fessler, D. M. T. (2010). Elevation leads to altruistic behavior. *Psychological Science,* 21(3), 315–20. doi:10.1177/0956797609359882.

Shiota, M. N., Keltner, D., and Mossman, A. (2007). The nature of awe: Elicitors, appraisals, and effects on self-concept. *Cognition and Emotion,* 21(5), 944–63. doi:10.1080/02699930600923668.

Shraga, O. and Shirom, A. (2009). The construct validity of vigor and its antecedents: A qualitative study. *Human Relations,* 62, 271–91.

Smith, C. A., Organ, D. W., and Near, J. P. (1983). Organizational citizenship behaviour: Its nature and antecedents. *Journal of Applied Psychology,* 68, 653–63. doi:https://doi.org/10.1037/0021-9010.68.4.653.

Spence, J. R., Brown, D. J., Keeping, L. M., and Lian, H. (2014). Helpful today, but not tomorrow? Feeling grateful as a predictor of daily organizational citizenship behaviors. *Personnel Psychology,* 67(3), 705–38. doi:https://doi.org/10.1111/peps.12051.

Szutta, N. (2019). Exemplarist moral theory – some pros and cons. *Journal of Moral Education,* 48(3), 280–90. doi:10.1080/03057240.2019.1589435.

Thomson, A. L., Nakamura, J., Siegel, J. T., and Csikszentmihalyi, M. (2014). Elevation and mentoring: An experimental assessment of causal relations. *The Journal of Positive Psychology*, 9(5), 402–13. doi:10.1080/17439760.2014.910824.

Thomson, A. L., and Siegel, J. T. (2013). A moral act, elevation, and prosocial behavior: Moderators of morality. *The Journal of Positive Psychology*, 8(1), 50–64. doi:10.1080/17439760.2012.754926.

Tsai, W.-C., Chen, C.-C., and Liu, H.-L. (2007). Test of a model linking employee positive moods and task performance. *Journal of Applied Psychology*, 92, 1570–83.

van de Ven, N. (2017). Envy and admiration: emotion and motivation following upward social comparison. *Cognition and Emotion*, 31(1), 193–200. doi:10.1080/02699931.2015.1087972.

Van de Vyver, J. and Abrams, D. (2017). Is moral elevation an approach-oriented emotion? *The Journal of Positive Psychology*, 12(2), 178–85. doi:10.1080/17439760.2016.1163410.

Vianello, M., Galliani, E. M., and Haidt, J. (2010). Elevation at work: The effects of leaders' moral excellence. *Journal of Positive Psychology*, 5(5), 390–411. doi:10.1080/17439760.2010.516764.

Wanberg, C. R. and Kammeyer-Mueller, J. D. (2000). Predictors and outcomes of proactivity in the socialization process. *Journal of Applied Psychology*, 85(3), 373–85.

Warr, P., Bindl, U. K., Parker, S. K., and Inceoglu, I. (2014). Four-quadrant investigation of job-related affects and behaviours. *European Journal of Work and Organizational Psychology*, 23(3), 342–63. doi:10.1080/1359432x.2012.744449.

Watson, D., Clark, L. A., and Tellegen, A. (1988). Development and validation of brief measures of positive and negative affect: The PANAS scales. *Journal of Personality and Social Psychology*, 54, 1063–70.

Wu, C.-H., Parker, S. K., Wu, L.-Z., and Lee, C. (2018). When and why people engage in different forms of proactive behavior: Interactive effects of self-construals and work characteristics. *Academy of Management Journal*, 61, 293–323. doi:https://doi.org/10.5465/amj.2013.1064.

Xie, C., Bagozzi, R. P., and Grønhaug, K. (2019). The impact of corporate social responsibility on consumer brand advocacy: The role of moral emotions, attitudes, and individual differences. *Journal of Business Research*, 95, 514–30. doi:https://doi.org/10.1016/j.jbusres.2018.07.043.

Zagzebski, L. (2017). *Exemplarist Moral Theory*. Oxford: Oxford University Press.

8

Leader's Anger and Employee Upward Voice

Wu Liu, Fenghao Wang, and Zhenyu Liao

"So why the f★★★ doesn't it do that?!" On a summer day in 2008, Steve Jobs questioned his team angrily when he found out that MobileMe (an online service provided by Apple) did not meet his expectations (Viticci, 2011). Actually, this IT genius and incredible leader often unleashed his incisive temper on those who failed to meet his incredibly high standards and, surprisingly, his teams could often come up with and share great ideas that shook the world eventually. Similarly, in the Oscar-winning movie *Whiplash*, the famed conductor (Mr Fletcher) told his student that, "There are no two words in the English language more harmful than 'good job.'" He felt that it was his responsibility to push people beyond what is expected from them, and he always displayed anger to his students for demanding better performance. In short, anger displayed by the authority seems to motivate members to proactively change the status quo on the way to achieve extraordinary performance. However, we also know that oftentimes, when facing an angry boss, people tend to sweep things under the carpet rather than speaking up (see a recent *Wall Street Journal* article by Shellenbarger, 2012). In this context, anger expressed by the authority figures seems to demotivate members from initiating possible changes and achieving superior performance.

The above anecdotal discussions suggest that leader's anger may have complicated and even seemingly contradictory effects on employee *upward voice*, or employees' expression of constructive work-related ideas to organizational leaders (Morrison, 2011, 2014). In many organizations, employees are uniquely positioned to identify emerging problems and opportunities that can critically influence the effectiveness of work processes and outcomes (Morrison, 2000; Ryan and Oestreich, 1998). In this context, upward voice plays a critical role in linking employees' private knowledge and insights with leaders' organizational influence. Scholars have argued that organizational effectiveness largely depends on members sharing opinions and speaking up with suggestions and concerns (Edmondson, 1999; Erez, LePine, and Elms, 2002; McClean, Detert, and Burris, 2013). Hence, it is not surprising that the antecedents of upward voice are the focus of a growing body of research (see Morrison, 2011, 2014, for a review).

In the leader–member context, employees often fear speaking up to their leaders, because they are concerned about damaging their own image, hurting relationships with leaders, or even being retaliated against (Detert and Edmondson, 2011; Kish-Gephart et al, 2009; Morrison and Milliken, 2000). Meanwhile, prior voice literature has highlighted the important role that leaders play in eliciting voice from subordinates, suggesting critical antecedents such as leader–member exchange relationships (for example, Burris, Detert, and Chiaburu, 2008; Liu, Tangirala, and Ramanujam, 2013; Van Dyne, Kamdar, and Joireman, 2008), ethical leadership styles (Walumbwa and Schaubroeck, 2009) and openness to change (Detert and Burris, 2007; Liu, Zhu, and Yang, 2010).

Although existing voice research is invaluable in demonstrating stable, dyadic-level antecedents of voice for leader–member interactions (see Morrison, 2011, 2014), it has paid limited attention to the effects of leader's emotions on voice. Although some qualitative studies and conceptual discussions have highlighted that employees' own emotions play a critical role (for example, Edwards, Ashkanasy, and Gardner, 2009; Kish-Gephart et al, 2009; Milliken, Morrison, and Hewlin, 2003), we still know little about how leader's emotions affect employee voice (one exception is Liu et al, 2017).

The purpose of this chapter is to review the existing literature on leader emotional expression and employee proactive behaviours, and also to share our experience in the journey of exploring whether and why leader's display of anger influences employee voice. Based on emotion as social information theory (van Kleef, De Dreu, and Manstead, 2010), we differentiate two types of anger: anger towards tasks or task-focused anger, and anger toward employees or person-focused anger. We thought that task-focused anger signals leader's dissatisfaction with tasks or current situation, and it would motivate employees to reflect the status quo, thus leading to upward voice. By contrast, person-focused anger signals leader's dominance and status, and it would threaten employees' self-esteem, thus discouraging voice.

Our initial findings have suggested that it is important to examine voice at the within-individual level and that our hypothesized model makes sense. In the following, we structuralize our experience-sharing in several sections. We will highlight why our exploration is important and meaningful by reviewing the relevant literature, then we will propose our theoretical model, and we will share the empirical work devoted to this project. In the final section, we would like to summarize the lessons and potential future directions to continue this journey.

Leader's emotional expression and employee proactive behaviours

Although quite a few studies have shown that leader's emotional expressions importantly shape employee's affective experiences, attitudes, and behaviours (see a review by Gooty et al, 2010), a systematic investigation starts only after van Kleef and colleagues introduce the Emotion as Social Information (EASI) framework (van Kleef, De Dreu, and Manstead, 2004a). The critical premise of EASI is that an individual's emotion can influence other's affective experience, attitudes, or behaviours in social interactions (Fridlund, 1994; Frijda, 1986; Parkinson, 1996). Integrating previous emotion research (for example, Hatfield, Cacioppo, and Rapson, 1994) and motivated information processing theory (De Dreu and Carnevale, 2003), van Kleef and colleagues have examined the social functions of emotions, mainly in social decision-making settings (for example, negotiation, van Kleef, De Dreu, and Manstead, 2004a; van Kleef et al, 2009; van Kleef, De Dreu, and Manstead, 2010). There are two major routes by which an actor's emotion can influence the target. The emotional contagion route is an unconscious mechanism that the target automatically carries over the emotions expressed by the actor, while the social inferential route describes a cognitive mechanism that the target intentionally interprets the meaning underlying the emotions expressed by the actor.

Recently, scholars have applied the EASI theory to examine how leader emotion influences employee proactive behaviours. Here, we broadly define proactive behaviour as as 'self-initiated, anticipatory action that aims to change and improve the situation or oneself' (Parker and Collins, 2010, p 635). Therefore, besides typical proactive behaviours such as voice, we also include creative and innovative behaviour/performance into this short review. We exclude other studies that use the EASI framework, but examine other behaviours or general performance (for example, Chi and Ho, 2014; van Kleef et al, 2010; van Kleef et al, 2009).

Visser et al (2013) examined how leader emotions (happiness versus sadness) influence employee performance by differentiating creative tasks (tasks that require divergent thinking) from the analytical ones (tasks that require convergent thinking). Based on the emotional contagion logic, they hypothesized that leader happiness would lead to employee happiness, which in turn contributes to creative task performance; while leader sadness would lead to employee sadness, which in turn leads to better analytical task performance. Two experiments with student samples provided supports to these hypotheses.

By contrast, van Kleef, Anastasopoulou, and Nijstad (2010) highlighted the social inferential route when they explored how leader anger influences member creative idea generation. They argued that leader anger would induce more task engagement and thus more creative ideas, but only when the member had high epistemic motivation for interpreting the meaning of leader anger. A laboratory experiment with students lent empirical support to this hypothesis.

One recent study conducted by Liu at al (2017) has highlighted that leader's emotion critically influences employee voice behaviour. Using cell phones to collect interaction data from both managers and their subordinates, the authors obtained 640 interactions from 85 leader–employee dyads in five IT companies in mainland China. They found that leader's positive affect was positively related to employees' voice behaviour for two different reasons. On the one hand, leader's positive affect was contagious to employees (emotional contagion mechanism); and on the other hand, employees were cognitively aware of leader's positive affect (signalling mechanism). Both mechanisms made employees feel psychologically safe, especially when the leader–member exchange relationship was weak. Interestingly, they also found that leader's negative affect was positively related to employees' voice, but neither emotional contagion nor signalling mechanisms explained this effect.

Liu et al's (2017) work highlights the important role of leader's affect in the voice process and also provides insights concerning when employees would choose to speak up to their leaders. With the experience sampling method (ESM) through mobile surveys, they showed that over 60 per cent of the variance of employee voice behaviour actually resided at the within-individual level. This finding confirms the conceptual discussions that employees would choose some episodes to speak up, but not others. It also indicates that it is important to examine voice at the within-individual level.

Moreover, another interesting finding is that both leader's positive emotions and negative emotions were positively related to employee voice. Although it is relatively easy to explain the effects of leader's positive emotions, it is hard to explain the impact of leader's negative emotions. Part of the reason is probably due to the complexity of negative emotions. Indeed, compared with positive emotions (for example, happiness, joy, and enthusiasm), negative emotions (for example, guilt, anger, and sadness) carry richer and more diversified meanings, especially in social interactions (de Rivera et al, 1989; Fredrickson, 1998). For example, when a leader feels guilty toward his or her member, the leader is likely to compensate the member in order to eliminate the guilt feeling. While a leader gets angry towards a member, the leader is likely to punish the member in order to decrease the anger. In other words, different types of negative emotions have distinct or even contradictory implications to social interactions. Therefore, some scholars suggest that it would be more fruitful to examine discrete emotions rather than aggregated affect in the investigation of affective experience in social interactions (van Kleef, De Dreu, and Manstead, 2010).

Anger in social interactions

One important type of discrete emotion explored in this line of research is anger, a discrete emotion associated with a tendency to aggress against a target (a person or a situation, for example, Miron-Spektor et al, 2011; Steinel, van Kleef, and Harinck, 2008; Van Dijk et al, 2008).

Anger signals both frustration from blocked goals and accusation of others' wrongdoing, thus serving important but complicated social functions (Keltner and Haidt, 1999). On the one hand, anger signals dissatisfaction with the current situation, thus calling for situation modification and change. When one is the target of anger expression, people may infer that this person did something wrong and this inference may in turn inform the person's behaviour (for example, apologizing, changing one's conduct, acceding to the other's wishes). Supporting this idea, expressions of anger have been found to elicit greater concessions in negotiations than do expressions of happiness (van Kleef, De Dreu, and Manstead, 2004a). In interactions between leaders and employees, leader's display of anger may increase employee effort and motivation (Van Doorn, van Kleef, and van der Pligt, 2013; van Kleef et al, 2010) as well as team performance (van Kleef, et al, 2009). Just as described at the beginning of the chapter, Steve Jobs' anger seemed to successfully motivated employees at Apple to make innovative achievements.

On the other hand, as anger is also related to accusing and aggressing others, it also signals power and distance (Tiedens, 2001), thus indicating threat and insecurity. As a consequence, anger may elicit a 'prevention orientation', namely a motivation to seek security and avoid pain (Higgins, 1998). Research suggests that observing anger expressions evokes a sense of threat (Miron-Spektor et al, 2011). Not surprisingly, leader's expression of anger has also been found related to low effectiveness (Gaddis, Connelly, and Mumford, 2004; Lewis, 2000) and less coordination among team members (Sy, Côté, and Saavedra, 2005). Just as the other example described at the beginning of the chapter, the anger displayed by the conductor in the movie *Whiplash* hurt some students so badly that those students eventually lost faith in their beloved career.

In short, as anger may signal both situation change and dominance over others, the existing literature of anger seems to suggest contradictory effects of anger, especially in the leader–employee interaction context.

Two types of anger and voice

To unpack the rich meaning of anger in leader–member interactions, we propose to differentiate two types of anger: task-focused anger and person-focused anger. The former emphasizes task performance or status quo as the target of anger, whereas the latter emphasizes the employee as the target of anger. Furthermore, we develop a conceptual model based on the emotion as social information theory (EASI, van Kleef, De Dreu, and Manstead, 2010).

An emotion is defined as a discrete feeling state associated with a particular target, often a person or a situation (Frijda, 1986). In other words, target is a critical component of emotion. It is especially important to consider the target of an emotion in social interactions because it would help to accurately interpret the social information carried with the emotion (Keltner and Haidt, 1999). Supporting this idea, in negotiation settings, Steinel, van Kleef, and Harinck (2008) used computers to manipulate anger with offer (they called 'behaviour-oriented anger') and anger with negotiation partner (they called 'person-oriented anger'). They found that anger with offer elicited more concessions from the other party than anger with person, because anger with offer provided more clear and diagnostic information to the other party than anger with person (van Kleef, De Drue, and

Manstead, 2004a). This finding has also been replicated by Lelieveld et al (2011) in negotiation settings.

Extending these discussions to the context of leader–employee interactions, we argue that these two types of anger exist and have distinct effects on voice. Specially, leader's display of task-focused anger signals leader's dissatisfaction with the current task performance and status quo. It thus calls for situation modification and change. In other words, task-focused anger provides clear and diagnostic information regarding change (Lelieveld et al, 2011; Steinel, van Kleef, and Harinck, 2008), a core purpose of voice (Van Dyne and LePine, 1998). Previous research has suggested that employees are more likely to speak up to their leader to share constructive ideas, opinions, and concerns to change the status quo when their leaders seek such inputs (Tangirala and Ramanujam, 2012). Therefore, we predict that in interaction episodes, leader's display of task-focused anger is positively related to employee voice (H1).

By contrast, the leader's display of person-focused anger signals power, distance, and control over employees (compare, Lemay, Overall, and Clark, 2012; Tiedens, 2001). It may elicit feelings such as fear and threat, as well as prevention-oriented responses of employees (Miron-Spektor et al, 2011). According to the existing voice literature, employees are less likely to speak up when they perceive themselves to be in disadvantaged positions in social hierarchy (Islam and Zyphur, 2005; Liu, Tangirala, Lam, Chen, Jia, and Huang, 2014) or to have low sense of control (Tangirala and Ramanujam, 2008). Therefore, we predict that in interaction episodes, leader's display of person-focused anger is negatively related to employee voice (H2).

In the following, we further propose the mediating mechanisms for these effects.

Leader's display of task-focused anger

We argue that reflection is an important mediator linking leader's display of task-focused anger to employee voice. By definition, reflection refers to a cognitive process in which a person endeavours to increase his or her awareness of personal experiences and therefore his or her ability to learn from them (Anseel, Lievens, and Schollaert, 2009: 23; Gordon and Hullfish, 1961). Leader's display of task-focused anger signals dissatisfaction with the current task performance and status quo, so it motivates employees to analyze current situations and reconsider strategies to make improvements. In a recent experimental research, Van Doorn, van Kleef, and van der Pligt (2013) found that instructor's anger was positively related to students' learning performance. They explained that compared with positive emotions, anger calls for behavioural change. In a similar vein, Miron-Spektor at al (2011) argued and reported that observing anger motivated employees to focus on problems and engage in analytic thinking to make changes. Therefore, leader's display of task-focused anger would lead to employees' reflection.

Employees' reflection, in turn, would lead to voice. One underlying driving force of voice is to reflect upon what is going on, identify gaps with expectation, and make improvements (Morrison and Milliken, 2000). When employees engage in reflection, they are more likely to find space for improvements and thus speak up to leaders. Based on these discussions, we predict that in interaction episodes, employees' reflection mediates the positive relationship between leader's display of task-focused anger and employee voice (H3).

Leader's display of person-focused anger

We argue that self-esteem is an important mediator linking leader's display of person-focused anger to employee voice. Leader's display of person-focused anger may elicit feelings such as fear, threat, and powerlessness (Miron-Spektor et al, 2011). It reminds employees of their low value and dependence on leaders during the interaction. As a result, leader's person-focused anger results in the decrease of employees' self-esteem.

Self-esteem, in turn, would drive employees to speak up (LePine and Van Dyne, 1998). Voice behaviour requires proactive and assertive nonconformance. It is challenging and thus risky because it is often interpreted as trouble-making or rebel (Morrison and Milliken, 2000). Accordingly, self-esteem would encourage voice because it enables employees to stand up to share different opinions and challenge the status quo (Tangirala and Ramanujam, 2012; Van Dyne, Cummings, and McLean Parks, 1995). Supporting this premise in a field study, LePine and Van Dyne (1998) found that employees' self-esteem was positively related to voice in groups. Based on the above discussions, we argue that in interaction episodes, employee self-esteem mediates the negative relationship between leader's display of person-focused anger and employee voice (H4).

Research journey and methodology

Phase 1. Survey instrument development and validation

There were no existing scales to measure the two core independent variables in our study – task-focused anger and person-focused anger.

All existing studies only manipulated them in laboratories (for example, Lelieveld et al, 2011; Steinel, van Kleef, and Harinck, 2008). Therefore, we developed scales to measure them in the field.

First, we carefully reviewed the relevant literature on anger (for example, Azevedo et al, 2010; Lemay, Overall, and Clark, 2012; Tiedens, 2001; Watson and Clark, 1999), and generated ten items for each type of anger (task vs personal) after intensive discussions among co-authors.

Second, we solicited participants with work experience via Wenjuanxing, and asked them to recall and write up a past experience when their direct managers were angry towards them. We then asked them to fill in a survey, including the new anger scale, and measures of abusive supervision (Mitchell and Ambrose, 2007), fear (Watson and Clark, 1999), leader's trait anger (modified from Azevedo et al, 2010), and leader's state anger (modified from Tiedens, 2001). All the survey questions were on five-point Likert scales (1 = 'mostly disagree', and 5 = 'mostly agree'). Our final example was 305 people, with 50.82 per cent female, an average age of 32.13 (SD = 6.67), an average work experience of 8.73 years (SD = 6.42), and an average tenure with the current manager of 3.42 years (SD = 2.77).

Exploratory Factor Analysis (EFA) on the two anger scales revealed that some items had low loadings, or were double-loaded, so we finally chose four items for each anger scale. Specifically, the task-focused anger scale includes the following items: (1) My leader was angry towards me because I did not engage in my work enough; (2) My leader was angry towards me because I did not do well for my assigned task; (3) My leader was angry toward me because my work was not satisfactory; (4) My leader was angry toward me because the task I finished was not up to standard. The person-focused anger scale include the following items: (1) My leader was angry towards me because s/he did not like me as a person; (2) My leader was angry towards me because s/he looked down on me; (3) My leader was angry towards me because s/he hated me; (4) My leader was angry towards me because s/he just wanted to find faults.

We further conducted a series of Confirmatory Factor Analysis (CFA) by including these two new anger scales, abusive supervision, fear, leader's trait anger, and leader's state anger. The CFA results showed that task-focused and person-focused anger were differentiated from each other, and they were also distinguishable from other related constructs, such as fear, abusive supervision, state anger, and trait anger. Table 8.1 shows the descriptive statistics and correlations of these measures.

Table 8.1: Pilot study – means (M), standard deviations (SD), reliabilities, and coefficients

	M	SD	1	2	3	4	5	6
1. Task-focused anger	3.37	1.02	*(.82)*					
2. Person-focused anger	2.16	1.12	-.05	*(.93)*				
3. Fear	3.51	0.83	.49**	.03	*(.86)*			
4. Abusive supervision	2.62	0.96	.08	.69**	.18**	*(.83)*		
5. Leader state anger	3.60	0.83	.14*	.17**	.21**	.31**	*(.84)*	
6. Leader trait anger	3.20	1.04	.01	.44**	.04	.56**	.52**	*(.90)*

Notes: n = 305, the numbers on the diagonal were Cronbach's alphas, *$p < 0.05$
**$p < 0.01$ (two- tailed)

Phase 2. The field study

The second phase of our research is a field study aiming to test our proposed model. We had an opportunity to collect data using the Experience Sampling Method from several construction companies in a northwestern city in China. We invited 56 teams and randomly selected three members from each team to participate in our study.

We tracked participants for 11 working days. On each day, participants filled in mobile surveys twice, once in the morning and the other in the afternoon. In the morning survey, they reported their self-reflection and self-esteem; while in the afternoon survey, they reported leader state anger on that day, task- and person-focused anger, and voice behaviour. To encourage participation, we paid participants 10 RMB (about 1.5 USD) for each mobile survey. Finally, we obtained 656 episodes from 105 members working in 48 teams. Among these 105 members, 21 were female (20 per cent), 95 (90.5 per cent) held a degree from junior college or above, the average age was 31.3 years old.

Measures

We used the same scales as in the Phase 1 study to measure leader state anger, task and person-focused anger. We employed a modified scale from Rosenberg (1965) to measure member's momentary self-esteem. We also modified the scale of systematic reflection scale proposed by Ellis et al (2014) to measure member's momentary self-reflection. Finally, members reported voice behaviour using the scale proposed by Liu et al (2017). Table 8.2 shows the descriptive statistics and correlations of these measures.

Table 8.2: Main study – means (M), standard deviations (SD), reliabilities and correlations

Variables	M	SD	1	2	3	4	5	6
1. Leader anger	2.33	1.22	(.94)					
2. Task-focused anger	2.66	1.51	.33***	(.96)				
3. Person-focused anger	1.98	1.13	.64***	.44***	(.95)			
4. Self-reflection	4.41	1.28	-.21***	-.12**	-.15***	(.95)		
5. Self-esteem	5.40	.90	-.31***	-.22***	-.26***	.37***	(.79)	
6. Voice	4.66	1.26	-.20***	-.05	-.16***	.56***	.39***	(.98)

Notes: n = 656, reliabilities are reported on the diagonal, $*p < 0.05$ $**p < 0.01$ $***p < 0.001$ (two-tailed)

Analysis

The data we collected was nested in nature, with interaction episodes nested within members, and members nested within teams. We thus conducted three-level Hierarchical Linear Modeling (HLM) analysis to check variance partitioning for different variables (see Table 8.3). We found that for all the focal variables, the main variances were at the within-individual and individual levels, rather than at the team level.

Results

We reported HLM results in Table 8.4. Hypothesis 1 predicts that leader task-focused anger would positively lead to employee voice, and Hypothesis 3 argues that such a path is explained by self-reflection. In Model 1, we controlled for employee voice in the previous day and person-focused anger, and we found that leader task-focused anger was negatively but not significantly related to employee voice ($r = -.03$, *n.s.*; Model 1). Therefore, Hypothesis 1 was not supported. In addition, after controlling for self-reflection in previous day and person-focused anger, we found a negative effect of task-focused anger on employee self-reflection ($\gamma = -.05$, $p < .05$; Model 2), and a marginally significant positive effect of self-reflection on voice behaviour ($\gamma = .14$, $p < .10$; Model 4) after controlling for voice in previous day. Results of the mediation test showed a non-significant indirect effect of -.01 (95 per cent CI [-.02, .001]). Therefore, Hypothesis 3 was not supported either.

Hypothesis 2 predicts that leader person-focused anger would lead to employee voice, and Hypothesis 4 argues that such a path is explained by self-esteem. In Model 1, we controlled for employee voice in the previous day and task-focused anger, and we found that leader person-focused anger was positively but not significantly related to employee voice ($\gamma = .03$, *n.s.*; Model 1). Therefore, Hypothesis 2 was not supported. Moreover, after controlling for self-esteem in previous day and task-focused anger, we found a positive but non-significant effect of person-focused anger on self-esteem ($\gamma = .03$, *n.s.*; Model 5), and a significant positive effect of self-esteem on voice behaviour ($\gamma = .13$, $p < .05$; Model 7) after controlling for voice in previous day. Results of the mediation test showed a non-significant indirect effect of -.01 (95 per cent CI [-0.01 0.02]). Therefore, Hypothesis 4 was not supported.

Table 8.3: Parameter estimates and variance components for null models for within-person level variables

Variables	Intercept (g000)	Within-person level variance / percentage	Individual level variance / percentage	Team level variance / percentage
1. Leader anger	2.35***	.67*** / 43.49%	.86*** / 55.73%	.01/ 0.78%
2. Task-focused anger	2.64***	1.07*** / 49.06%	1.04*** / 47.51%	.08 / 3.43%
3. Person-focused anger	2.02***	.47*** / 35.46%	.84*** / 63.19%	.02 / 1.35%
4. Self-reflection	4.49***	.47*** / 29.17%	1.00*** / 62.14%	.14 / 8.69%
5. Self-esteem	5.34***	.28*** / 32.98%	.57*** / 65.74%	.01 / 1.28%
6. Voice	4.69***	.46*** / 29.62%	1.06*** / 68.21%	.03 / 2.18%

Notes: $n = 656$, *$p < 0.05$ **$p < 0.01$ ***$p < 0.001$ (two-tailed)

Table 8.4: Results of the original model testing

	Model 1	Model 2	Model 3	Model 4	Model 5	Model 6	Model 7
Dependent variable	Voice	Self-reflection	Voice	Voice	Self-esteem	Voice	Voice
Control variable							
Self-reflection (T-1)		.15**					
Self-esteem (T-1)					.01		
Voice (T-1)	.05		.03	.03		.04	.04
Independent variable							
Task-focused anger (T-1)	-.03	-.05*		-.02	-.06†		-.02
Person-focused anger (T-1)	.03	.01		.03	.03		.03
Mediators							
Self-reflection (T)			.13†	.14†			
Self-esteem (T)						.13★	.13★

Notes: $n = 656$, †$p < 0.10$ *$p < 0.05$ **$p < 0.01$ ***$p < 0.001$ (two-tailed)

Discussions

It was quite daunting for us to get these results. We thus carefully reviewed each step we followed for identifying the potential reasons. One critical reason we found was that the measures we developed for task- versus person-focused anger were probably employee's attribution toward leader anger rather than leader anger itself. Indeed, the items we created seemed to be not only about leader anger, but also the reasons why the leader is angry. This mistake is perhaps fundamentally rooted in the conceptualization ambiguity for the two types of anger. In experimental and negotiation settings (for example, Lelieveld et al, 2011; Steinel, van Kleef, and Harinck, 2008), it is fairly clear to distinguish the anger toward a negotiation offer from the anger towards a negotiator. However, in work settings where leaders and members usually have past interaction history, the line between task-focused and person-focused is not explicitly clear. A leader displays anger probably because s/he is not satisfied with the task, but the member could interpret leader anger as a personal retaliation for something the member did long time ago. Therefore, member's attribution toward leader anger plays an important role. Whether a leader displays anger is one thing, and how a member attributes the leader anger is another thing. Moreover, these two together would influence how a member responds to leader anger.

Future research

We propose to address the critical limitations of voice research by taking a within-individual approach to examine the effects of leader's display of anger on employee voice. Specially, we propose to differentiate two types of leader's anger. Task-focused anger signals dissatisfaction with the current task performance and situation, thus calling for situation modification and change. We predict that it would be positively associated with voice via employee's reflection. By contrast, person-focused anger signals power and distance over employees (Tiedens, 2001), thus indicating threat and insecurity. We predict that it would be negatively associated with voice via self-esteem. However, our data failed to provide support to these hypotheses. Instead, we found that what we measured was probably anger attribution rather than anger per se.

Despite the findings from our field data, a number of puzzles remain unsettled and future research is needed to further explore the phenomenon. First, it remains debatable if the categorization of task-focused versus person-focused anger is legitimate. Theoretically, our study is focused on leader anger episodes, which may vary in time; that is, we concentrate on within-individual variances of leader anger. Therefore, one assumption we made was that each leader anger episode is different to the extent by which it is task-focused or person-focused. Indeed, we did find considerable variances in our measure of person-focused leader anger, but this might be due to a lack of construct validity. One possibility (as mentioned before) is that the measure captured employee attribution of leader anger, rather than leader anger per se. Another possibility might be that the task-focused anger scale reflected anger triggered by employees (that is 'me'), while the person-focused anger scale covered anger elicited due to leaders (that is 'him or her'). In either case, future research shall revalidate the scale. For example, it might be helpful to change the scale anchors from agreement to frequency.

Second, although we found some support to the hypothesized negative effect of person-focused anger attribution on voice behaviour, we failed to obtain evidence supporting the positive effect of leader anger on employee proactivity. Thus, future research might endeavour to explore whether, why, and when leader anger may evoke employee proactivity. One possible direction might be affective mechanisms; that is, employees engage in proactive behaviours following leader anger because they experience certain affective feelings that motivate them to fix the status quo. Such possibility has been discussed both theoretically (van Kleef, 2009) and practically (Liu et al, 2017). It is also possible to consider boundary conditions of such effects. As Liu et al (2017) demonstrated, employees' reliance on leader emotions as social information may weaken when they have satisfactory relationships. It is therefore legitimate to propose certain boundary conditions for this effect.

Third, because our data was collected solely from China, the generalizability of our conclusion remains questionable in other cultural contexts. Indeed, cross-cultural research has documented culturally divergent emotion perceptions and different functions of expressions (Fang, van Kleef, and Sauter, 2019; Kitayama et al, 2015). Therefore, our current finding may not be generalizable to Western culture. Among various cultural dimensions, power distance might play a particularly critical role, because it shapes how employees view their relationships with leaders (which are oftentimes power-asymmetric). As a consequence, power distance might alter employee responses toward leader anger. Future research is welcome in exploring the generalizability of our predictions.

Another reflection from this project is about the EASI framework. One important contingency factor in the EASI model is whether the social situation is corporative or competitive (van Kleef, De Dreu, and Manstead, 2010). It is argued that the actor's emotion is more likely to lead to affective reactions when the situation is corporative, whereas more to inferential reactions when the situation is competitive. In addition, they also discussed two broad strategies contingent upon whether the situation is corporative or competitive – moving against or moving towards. In the leader–member interaction context, is the situation corporative or competitive? Some would argue that leader–member exchange (LMX) probably can help to make a distinction and should be considered (for example, Liu et al, 2017). True. One potential direction for us to pursue is to take LMX into consideration. However, anger, as a strong social signal with implication to the social interaction, may itself define whether the situation is corporative or competitive, despite the past history of interaction partners (for example, Ballinger and Rockmann, 2010). For example, despite high LMX between a leader and a member, a furious storm unleashed by a leader may immediately change the member's view of the interactional context, thus reacting accordingly in emotion and behaviour. Therefore, it is indeed a complicated problem to resolve in the future.

The core of the strategic inference route in the EASI model is how targets interpret actors' emotional expression, and for sure it is not a knee-jerk reflex even after we take epistemic and social motivations into consideration. van Kleef and colleagues have provided a powerful framework, but not details for each discrete emotion. One potentially helpful framework in the emotion literature is the appraisal-tendency framework proposed by Lerner and Keltner (2000). It categorized different discrete emotions based on cognitive dimensions and discussed how each emotion may arouse a cognitive tendency to appraise future events. In the future, scholars may transfer the appraisal-tendency framework into the social interaction contexts, so that we could better understand how exactly an expression of a discrete emotion, such as anger, would influence the target's social inference in specific ways.

References

Anseel, F., Lievens, F., and Schollaert, E. (2009). Reflection as a strategy to enhance task performance after feedback. *Organizational Behavior and Human Decision Processes*, 110, 23–35.

Avolio, B. J., Bass, B. M., and Jung, D. I. (1999). Re-examining the components of transformational and transactional leadership using the multifactor leadership questionnaire, *Journal of Occupational and Organizational Psychology*. 72, 441–62.

Azevedo, F. B. D., Wang, Y. P., Goulart, A. C., Lotufo, P. A., and Benseñor, I. M. (2010). Application of the Spielberger's State-Trait Anger Expression Inventory in clinical patients. *Arquivos de neuro-psiquiatria,* 68(2), 231–4.

Ballinger, G. A. and Rockmann, K. W. (2010). Chutes versus ladders: Anchoring events and a punctuated-equilibrium perspective on social exchange relationships. *Academy of Management Review,* 35, 373–91.

Bolger, N., Davis, A., and Rafaeli, E. (2003). Diary methods: Capturing life as it is lived. *Annual Review of Psychology,* 54, 579–616.

Brockner, J. (1988). *Self-Esteem at Work: Research, Theory, and Practice.* Lexington, MA: Lexington Books.

Burris, E.R., Detert, J.R., and Chiaburu, D.S. (2008). Quitting before leaving: The mediating effect of psychological attachment and detachment on voice. *Journal of Applied Psychology,* 93, 912–22.

Chatman, J.A. and Flynn, F.J. (2005). Full-cycle organizational psychology research. *Organization Science,* 16, 434–47.

Chi, N.W. and Ho, T.R. (2014). Understanding when leader negative emotional expression enhances follower performance: The moderating roles of follower personality traits and perceived leader power. *Human Relations,* 67, 1051–72.

De Dreu, C. K. W. and Carnevale, P. J. D. (2003). Motivational bases of information processing and strategy in conflict and negotiation. In M. P. Zanna (ed), *Advances in Experimental Social Psychology,* vol 35, New York: Academic Press, pp 235–91.

de Jong, B.A. and Elfring, T. (2010). How does trust affect the performance of ongoing teams? The mediating role of reflexivity, monitoring, and effort. *Academy of Management Journal,* 53, 535–49.

de Rivera, J., Possel, L., Verette, J. A., and Weiner, B. (1989). Distinguishing elation, gladness, and joy. *Journal of Personality and Social Psychology,* 57, 1015–23.

Detert, J.R. and Burris, E.R. (2007). Leadership behavior and employee voice: Is the door really open? *Academy of Management Journal,* 50, 869–84.

Detert, J.R. and Edmondson, A.C. (2011). Implicit voice theories: Taken-for-granted rules of self-censorship at work. *Academy of Management Journal,* 54, 461–88.

Detert, J.R. and Treviño, L.K. (2010). Speaking up to higher ups: How supervisor and skip-level leaders influence employee voice. *Organization Science,* 21, 241–70.

Dorfman, P. W. and Howell, J. P. (1988). Dimensions of national culture and effective leadership in patterns. *Advances in International Comparative Management,* 3, 127–50.

Dutton, J. E., Ashford, S. J., Wierba, E.E., O'Neill, R., and Hayes, E. (1997). Reading the wind: How middle managers assess the context for issue selling to top managers. *Strategic Management Journal,* 15, 407–25.

Edmondson, A.C. (1999). Psychological safety and learning behavior in work teams. *Administrative Science Quarterly,* 44, 350–83.

Edwards, M.S., Ashkanasy, N.M., and Gardner, J. (2009). Deciding to speak up or remain silent following observed wrongdoing: The role of discrete emotions and climate of silence. In J. Greenberg and M. Edwards (eds), *Voice and Silence in Organizations*, Bingley: Emerald, pp 83–110.

Ellis, S., Carette, B., Anseel, F., and Lievens, F. (2014). Systematic reflection implications for learning from failures and successes. *Current Directions in Psychological Science*, 23(1), 67–72.

Erez, A. and Isen, A.M. (2002). The influence of positive affect on the components of expectancy motivation. *Journal of Applied Psychology*, 87, 1055–67.

Fang, X., van Kleef, G. A., and Sauter, D. A. (2019). Revisiting cultural differences in emotion perception between Easterners and Westerners: Chinese perceivers are accurate, but see additional non-intended emotions in negative facial expressions. *Journal of Experimental Social Psychology*, 82, 152–9.

Fredrickson, B. L. (1998). What good are positive emotions? *Review of General Psychology*, 2: 300–19.

Fridlund, A. J. (1994). *Human Facial Expression: An Evolutionary View*. San Diego, CA: Academic Press.

Frijda, N. H. (1986). *The Emotions*. New York: Cambridge University Press.

Gaddis, B., Connelly, S., and Mumford, M. D. (2004). Failure feedback as an affective event: Influences of leader affect on subordinate attitudes and performance. *Leadership Quarterly*, 15, 663–86.

Glomb, T. M. (2002). Workplace anger and aggression: Informing conceptual models with data from specific encounters. *Journal of Occupational Health Psychology*, 7, 20–36.

Grant, A. M. and Ashford, S. J. (2008). The dynamics of proactivity at work. In B. M. Staw and A. Brief (eds), *Research in Organizational Behavior*, vol 28, Greenwich, CT: JAI Press, pp 3–34.

Gordon, H. and Hullfish, S. P. H. (1961). *Reflective Thinking: The Method of Education*. New York: Dodd, Mead and Co.

Gooty, J., Connelly, S., Griffith, J., and Gupta, A. (2010). Leadership, affect and emotions: A state of the science review. *The Leadership Quarterly*, 21(6), 979–1004.

Hatfield, E., Cacioppo, J. T., and Rapson, R. L. (1994). *Emotional Contagion*. New York: Cambridge University Press.

Higgins, E. T. (1998). Promotion and prevention: Regulatory focus as a motivational principle. In M. P. Zanna (ed), *Advances in Experimental Social Psychology*, vol 30, New York, NY: Academic Press, pp 1–46.

Hofstede, G. H. (1980). *Culture's Consequences: International Differences in Work-Related Values*. Beverly Hills, CA: Sage.

Inness, M., LeBlanc, M. M., and Barling, J. (2008). Psychosocial predictors of supervisor-, peer-, subordinate-, and service-provider-targeted aggression. *Journal of Applied Psychology*, 93, 1401–11.

Islam, G. and Zyphur, M.J. (2005). Power, voice, and hierarchy: Exploring the antecedents of speaking up in groups. *Group Dynamics: Theory, Research, and Practice*, 9, 93–103.

Kitayama, S., Park, J., Boylan, J. M., Miyamoto, Y., Levine, C. S., Markus, H. R., Karasawa, M., Coe, C. L., Kawakami, N., Love, G. D., and Ryff, C. D. (2015). Expression of anger and ill health in two cultures: An examination of inflammation and cardiovascular risk. *Psychological Science*, 26(2), 211–20.

Lelieveld, G.-J., Van Dijk, E., Van Beest, I., Steinel, W., and van Kleef, G. A. (2011). Disappointed in you, angry about your offer: Distinct negative emotions induce concessions via different mechanisms. *Journal of Experimental Social Psychology*, 47, 635–41.

Lewis, K. M. (2000). When leaders display emotion: how followers respond to negative emotional expression of male and female leaders. *Journal of Organizational Behavior*, 21, 221–34.

Lemay, E. P., Jr., Overall, N. C., and Clark, M. S. (2012, 17 September). Experiences and interpersonal consequences of hurt feelings and anger. *Journal of Personality and Social Psychology*. Advance online publication. doi: 10.1037/a0030064.

LePine, J.A. and Van Dyne, L. (1998). Predicting voice behavior in work groups. *Journal of Applied Psychology*, 83, 853–68.

Lerner, J. S. and Keltner, D. (2000). Beyond valence: Toward a model of emotion-specific influences on judgement and choice. *Cognition and Emotion*, 14(4), 473–93.

Liu, W., Gong, Y., and Liu, J. (2014). When do firms reap more benefits from top management team OCB? A managerial discretion perspective. *Journal of Applied Psychology*, 99, 523–34.

Liu, W., Song, Z.L., Li, X., and Liao, Z.Y. (2017). Why and when leader's positive emotion promotes employee voice behavior. *Academy of Management Journal*, 60(1), 238–63.

Li, H. and Townsend, L. (2008). Mobile research in marketing: Design and implementation issues. *International Journal of Mobile Marketing*, 3, 32–40.

Liu, W., Tangirala, S., and Ramanujam, R. (2013). The relational antecedents of voice targeted at different leaders. *Journal of Applied Psychology*, 98, 841–51.

Liu, W., Tangirala, S., Lam, W., Chen, Z., Jia, R., Xu Huang. (2015). When and why peers' positive mood influences team members' voice behavior. *Journal of Applied Psychology*, 100(3), 976–89.

Liu, W., Zhu, R., and Yang, Y. (2010). I warn you because i like you: Voice behavior, employee identifications, and transformational leadership. *Leadership Quarterly*, 21, 189–202.

Jones, S.C. (1973). Self- and interpersonal evaluations. *Psychological Bulletin*, 79, 185–99.

Keltner, D. and Haidt, J. (1999). Social functions of emotions at four levels of analysis. *Cognition and Emotion*, 13, 505–21.

Kish-Gephart, J.J., Detert, J.R., Treviño, L.K., and Edmondson, A.C. (2009). Silenced by fear: The nature, sources and consequences of fear at work. *Research in Organizational Behavior*, 29, 163–93.

Kruglanski, A. W. and Webster, D. M. (1996). Motivated closing of the mind: 'Seizing' and 'freezing'. *Psychological Review*, 103, 263–83.

McClean, E., Detert, J. R., and Burris, E. R. (2013). When does voice lead to exit? It depends on leadership. *Academy of Management Journal*, 56, 525–48.

Milliken, F.J., Morrison, E.W., and Hewlin, P.F. (2003). An exploratory study of employee silence: Issues that employees don't communicate upward and why. *Journal of Management Studies*, 40, 1453–76.

Miron-Spektor, E., Efrat-Treister, D., Rafaeli, A., and Schwarz-Cohen, O. (2011). Others' anger makes people work harder not smarter: The effect of observing anger and sarcasm on creative and analytic thinking. *Journal of Applied Psychology*, 96, 1065–75.

Mitchell, M. S. and Ambrose, M. L. (2007). Abusive supervision and workplace deviance and the moderating effects of negative reciprocity beliefs. *Journal of Applied Psychology*, 92(4), 1159–68.

Morrison, E.W. (2011). Employee voice behavior: integration and directions for future research. *Academy of Management Annals*, 5, 373–412.

Morrison, E.W. (2014). Employee voice and silence. *Annual Review of Organizational Psychology and Organizational Behavior*, vol 1: 173–97.

Morrison, E.W. and Milliken, F.J. (2000). Organizational silence: A barrier to change and development in a pluralistic world. *Academy of Management Review*, 25, 706–25.

Parker, S.K. and Collins, C.G. (2010). Taking stock: Integrating and differentiating multiple proactive behaviors. *Journal of Management*, 36, 633–62.

Parkinson, B. (1996). Emotions are social. *British Journal of Psychology*, 87, 663–83.

Podsakoff, P.M., MacKenzie, S.B., Lee, J.Y., and Podsakoff, N.P. (2003). Common method biases in behavioral research: A critical review of the literature and recommended remedies. *Journal of Applied Psychology*, 88, 879–903.

Rosenberg, M. (1965). *Society and the Adolescent Self-Image*. Princeton, NJ: Princeton University Press.

Ryan, K. D., and Oestreich, D. K. (1998). *Driving Fear Out of the Workplace: Creating the High Trust, High Performance Organization*, 2nd edn. San Francisco, CA: Jossey-Bass.

Seibert, S.E., Crant, J.M., and Kraimer, M.L. (1999). Proactive personality and career success. *Journal of Applied Psychology*, 84, 416–27.

Shellenbarger, S. (2012). When the boss is a screamer. *The Wall Street Journal*. Retrieved from www.wsj.com/articles/SB10000872396390444477240457758 9302193682244

Song, Z., Foo, M., and Uy, M. (2008). The spillover and crossover of moods among dual-earner couples: An event sampling cell phone study. *Journal of Applied Psychology*, 93, 443–52.

Song, Z., Foo, M., Uy, M., and Sun, S. (2011). Unraveling the daily stress crossover between the unemployed and their employed spouses. *Journal of Applied Psychology*, 96, 151–68.

Steinel, W., van Kleef, G. A., and Harinck, F. (2008). Are you talking to me? Separating the people from the problem when expressing emotions in negotiation. *Journal of Experimental Social Psychology*, 44, 362–9.

Sy, T., Côté, S., and Saavedra, R. (2005). The contagious leader: Impact of the leader's mood on the mood of group members, group affective tone, and group processes. *Journal of Applied Psychology*, 90, 295–305.

Tangirala, S., and Ramanujam, R. (2008). Employee silence on critical work issues: The cross-level effects of procedural justice climate. *Personal Psychology*, 61, 37–68.

Tangirala, S. and Ramanujam, R. (2012). Ask and you shall hear (But not always): An examination of the relationship between manager consultation and employee voice. *Personnel Psychology*, 65, 251–82.

Tiedens, L. Z. (2001). Anger and advancement versus sadness and subjugation: The effect of negative emotion expressions on social status conferral. *Journal of Personality and Social Psychology*, 80, 86–94.

van Dijk, E., van Kleef, G. A., Steinel, W., and van Beest, I. (2008). A social functional approach to emotions in bargaining: When communicating anger pays and when it backfires. *Journal of Personality and Social Psychology,* 94, 600–14.

Van Doorn, E. A., van Kleef, G. A., and van der Pligt, J. (2013, 23 December). How instructors' emotional expressions shape students' learning performance: The roles of anger, happiness, and regulatory focus. *Journal of Experimental Psychology: General*. Advance online publication. doi: 10.1037/a0035226.

Van Dyne, L., Cummings, L. L., and McLean Parks, J. (1995). Extra-role behaviors: In pursuit of construct and definitional clarity (a bridge over muddied waters). In L. L. Cummings and B. M. Staw (eds), *Research in organizational behavior*, vol 17, Greenwich, CT: JAI Press, pp 215–85.

Van Dyne, L. and Lepine, J.A. (1998). Helping and voice extra-role behaviors: Evidence of construct and predictive validity. *Academy of Management Journal*, 41, 108–19.

Van Dyne, L., Kamdar, D., and Joireman, J. (2008). In-role perceptions buffer the negative impact of low LMX on helping and enhance the positive impact of high LMX on voice. *Journal of Applied Psychology*, 93, 1195–207.

van Kleef, G.A., Anastasopoulou, C., and Nijstad, B.A. (2010) Can expressions of anger enhance creativity? A test of the emotions as social information (EASI) model. *Journal of Experimental Social Psychology*, 46, 1042–8.

van Kleef, G. A. and Côté, S. (2007). Expressing anger in conflict: When it helps and when it hurts. *Journal of Applied Psychology*, 92, 1557–69.

van Kleef, G. A., De Dreu, C. K. W., and Manstead, A. S. R. (2004a). The interpersonal effects of anger and happiness in negotiations. *Journal of Personality and Social Psychology*, 86, 57–76.

van Kleef, G. A., De Dreu, C. K. W., and Manstead, A. S. R. (2004b). The interpersonal effects of emotions in negotiations: A motivated information processing approach. *Journal of Personality and Social Psychology*, 87, 510–28.

van Kleef, G. A., De Dreu, C. K. W., and Manstead, A. S. R. (2010). An interpersonal approach to emotion in social decision making: The emotions as social information model. *Advances in Experimental Social Psychology*, 42: 45–96.

van Kleef, G. A., Homan, A. C., Beersma, B., and Van Knippenberg, D. (2010). On angry leaders and agreeable followers: How leaders' emotions and followers' personalities shape motivation and team performance. *Psychological Science*, 21, 1827–34.

van Kleef, G.A., Homan, A.C., Beersma, B., van Knippenberg, D.,van Knippenberg, B., and Damen, F. (2009). Searing sentiment or cold calculation? The effects of leader emotional displays on team performance depend on follower epistemic motivation. *Academy of Management Journal*, 52, 562–80.

Viticci, F. (2011). 'Inside Apple' reveals Steve Jobs anecdotes, Apple's little known facts. *MacStories*. Retrieved from www.macstories.net/news/inside-apple-reveals-steve-jobs-anecdotes-apples-little-known-facts/

Visser, V.A., van Knippenberg, D., van Kleef, G.A., and Wisse, B. (2013). How leader displays of happiness and sadness influence follower performance: Emotional contagion and creative versus analytical performance. *Leadership Quarterly*, 24, 172–88.

Walumbwa, F.O. and Schaubroeck, J. (2009). Leader personality traits and employee voice behavior: Mediating roles of ethical leadership and work group psychological safety. *Journal of Applied Psychology*, 94, 1275–86.

Watson, D., Clark, L.A., and Tellegen, A. (1988). Development and validation of brief measures of positive and negative affect: The PANAS scales. *Journal of Personality and Social Psychology*, 54, 1063–70.

Watson, D. and Clark, L. A. (1999). *The PANAS-X: Manual for the Positive and Negative Affect Schedule-Expanded Form*. Ames: The University of Iowa.

West, M. A. (2000). Reflexivity, revolution and innovation in work teams. In M. M. Beyerlein, D.A. Johnson and S.T. Beyerlein (eds), *Product Development Teams*, vol 5, Stamford, CT: JAI Press, pp 1–29.

Wheeler, L. and Reis, H.T. (1991). Self-recording of everyday life events: origins, types and uses. *Journal of Personality*, 59, 339–54.

Wong, C. S. and Law, K. S. (2002). The effects of leader and follower emotional intelligence on performance and attitude: An exploratory study. *Leadership Quarterly*, 13, 243–74.

9

Affect and Proactivity in Teams

Hector P. Madrid and Malcolm Patterson

The relationship between affect and proactivity is established at the employee level of analysis. Individuals' positive and negative moods have the potential to drive proactive problem prevention, voice behaviour, and taking charge due to information processing and motivational processes (Cangiano, Bindl, and Parker, 2017). In addition, the relationship between affect and proactivity can also operate at the team level of analysis through interpersonal mechanisms and social integration processes; however, theory and empirical research about how team affect is related to team proactivity is still underdeveloped. This is a sensitive limitation in the proactivity literature because in today's organizations teamwork is an essential form of organizing work, due to the complexities of tasks that cannot be executed by individual employees. Also, teamwork helps ensure rapid responses to environmental demands, facilitates creativity and innovation and increases the likelihood of achieving high quality outcomes. Therefore, teamwork contributes to the effectiveness of organizations and even their survival. Thus, to further develop the affect and proactivity literature, in this chapter we survey and discuss emergent research on affect at the group level of analysis and how and when the effects of group affect on proactivity are likely to happen. Accordingly, in the first section, we present the team effectiveness model in which team level affect and proactivity occur, together with describing the psychological processes that explain their reciprocal relationships. Then, we present and discuss the theory and evidence about the etiology of affect and proactivity in the context of teamwork.

Team effectiveness model

Research on teamwork has proposed and largely validated that team effectiveness is described by a process model in which teams' achievement of their goals is given by their inputs, mediators, and outputs (Gladstein, 1984; Ilgen et al, 2005; Mathieu et al, 2019; McGrath, 1964). Team inputs refer to the set of individual and organizational resources available for the operation of the team. Examples of those resources are the skills, knowledge, and dispositions of team members, together with the financial, material, and technological means to perform the relevant tasks (Mathieu et al, 2008). Team mediators, categorized in terms of behavioural processes and emergent states, are the means by which resources are translated into results in the team (Ilgen et al, 2005). Behavioural processes are the collection of interpersonal behaviours performed among team members to use the resources available in the execution of tasks, such as goal specification, coordination, monitoring, collaboration, and conflict management (Marks, Mathieu, and Zaccaro, 2001). In turn, emergent properties are team-level psychological states resulting from social interaction among team members, expressed in, for example, cohesion, trust, psychological safety, or, on the negative side, interpersonal conflict (Mathieu et al, 2019). Team emergent states also influence, or feedback, behavioural processes, such that, for instance, trust facilitates collaboration, while conflict reduces coordination (compare, Ilgen et al, 2005). Regarding team outputs, they are the results of the use of the team inputs, through team mediators, manifested in the quantity and quality of work done, adaptation, innovation, and team members' attitudes, such as job satisfaction and commitment (Burke et al, 2006; Campion, Medsker, and Higgs, 1993; West, 2002).

In this structural representation, proactive behaviour with interpersonal meaning and implications, such as voice and innovation behaviour, is a type of team behavioural process (Figure 9.1) (Harris and Kirkman, 2017; Williams, Parker, and Turner, 2010). Voice behaviour is the active proposal of ideas to solve problems, improve procedures, and take advantage of new opportunities in the work environment, which is only possible in an interpersonal forum where these ideas are communicated (Morrison, 2014). Teams are an example of this interpersonal context, in which team member voice behaviour is the active exchange of ideas among team members to foster team effectiveness (Lepine and Dyne Van, 1998; Morrison, Wheeler-Smith, and Kamdar, 2011). Innovation behaviour corresponds to the exploration, experimentation, testing, and implementation of new

Figure 9.1: Team effectiveness model applied to team proactivity and affect

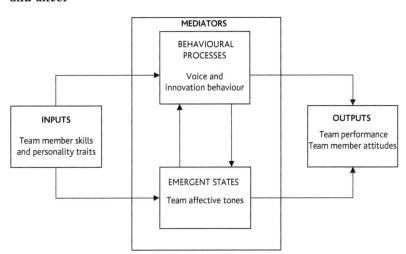

and useful ideas (Kanter, 1988). Translated into the team context, innovation emerges as a collective behavioural process directed to solve problems and make changes based on the development of new strategies and solutions (De Dreu and West, 2001).

Affect is also part of the team mediators and represents a form of emergent states (Figure 9.1). In this context, team members' affective experience has been conceptualized as team affective tones, which are shared and consistent affective states experienced by team members as a whole (George, 1996). Mirroring conceptualizations of affect at the individual level, examples of positive and negative team affective tones are the collective states of enthusiasm, comfort, anxiety, and disappointment, respectively, which represent the mood of teams (Warr et al, 2014).

Applying the model of team effectiveness to team-level proactivity and affect, conceptualizes both constructs as derived from the input resources of the team (Collins et al, 2013; Harris and Kirkman, 2017). For instance, team composition in terms of personality traits of team members should play a role here, such that, for example, the proactive and openness to experience dispositions of team members may explain the extent to which voice and innovation behaviour unfold within the team (Hammond et al, 2011; Thomas, Whitman, and Viswesvaran, 2010; Zare and Flinchbaugh, 2019). In parallel, affective dispositions embedded in team members' extraversion and neuroticism traits may be one of the sources of positive and negative affective tones (Collins et al, 2013).

Continuing the process model of team effectiveness, team-level proactivity and team affective tones influence each other (compare, Ilgen et al, 2005). The first intuitive causality effect stems from affective tones towards behavioural processes. In this case, shared positive and negative feelings infuse and motivate, for example, the suggestion and experimentation of (novel) ideas (Madrid, Niven, and Vasquez, 2019). In contrast, these behavioural processes should also have an effect on team affective tones because voice and innovation behaviour may result in team member feelings of shared enthusiasm or worry.

Finally, team member voice, innovation behaviour and team affective tones contribute to team outputs. The proposal and exchange of new ideas, as well as their experimentation, promises to improve the quality of the work carried out by the team (King and Anderson, 1990). Also, these forms of proactivity may benefit better adaptation to changes unfolding in the environment, the production of novel procedures, products, and services, and also a better sense of team member satisfaction when voice and innovation behaviour deliver positive results (Morrison, 2014; Shipton et al, 2006). Affective tones should facilitate, or inhibit, these behavioural processes, influencing also team performance.

Hence, team proactivity and affect are central components of team effectiveness. Thus, the understanding of their etiology and how they operate and influence each other is highly valuable for teamwork management.

Affective tones and proactivity

The effects of team affective tones on team proactivity

At the employee level of analysis, affective states are well-known for influencing individual proactivity (Cangiano, Bindl, and Parker, 2017). Positive moods expressed in enthusiasm, joy, and inspiration drive proactive problem identification, voice, and taking charge, together with the generation, promotion, and implementation of novel ideas (Bindl et al, 2012; Madrid and Patterson, 2019; Madrid et al, 2014; Warr et al, 2014). On the other hand, employees' negative affect has mixed effects on proactivity and innovation. In general, states composed of anxiety, worry, and nervousness are not directly related to proactive and innovation behaviour because those effects seem to be context-dependent (Madrid and Patterson, 2018; Madrid et al, 2014). In the case of voice behaviour, negative moods have the potential of increasing the likelihood of suggesting ideas to make changes in the work environment when the tasks to be executed imply high complexity, expressed in the need to solve difficult problems, manage uncertainty, and use expert knowledge (Madrid, Patterson, and Leiva, 2015). In the case of innovation, indirect evidence, observed in research on the related construct of employee creativity, indicates that negative moods could increase the generation and use of novel ideas when the work environment provides social support (George and Zhou, 2007).

One set of psychological mechanisms explaining the influences of affect on proactive and innovation behaviour focuses on information processing (Bindl et al, 2012; Madrid and Patterson, 2018). The latter denotes the function played by perception, memory, and attention, together with how information gathered from the environment is processed.

Positive moods lead to positive priming of perception and memory, such that perception is directed to positive conditions in the environment when individuals experience positive feelings, while recalled memories are about satisfactory and rewarding past experiences related to the tasks being performed (Isen, 1984; Isen et al, 1978). The same feelings expand attentional focus; therefore, more information to solve the problems is available, and this information is processed using flexible and divergent thinking, such that, for example, multiple possible ideas are explored in order to solve problems (Fredrickson, 2001). On the other hand, negative moods prime perception and memory by directing cognition to negative and unsatisfactory conditions in the environment and past experiences (Fredrickson, 2004; Schwarz and Skurnik, 2003). As part of the same affective experience, attention is narrow, and information processing is convergent and analytic, leading to the exploitation of well-established knowledge available in the environment (George and Zhou, 2007; Nijstad et al, 2010).

Motivation is the other mechanism that has been proposed as mediating the effects of employee affect on proactivity (Seo, Barrett, and Bartunek, 2004). Moods involve not only differences in pleasure, but also degrees of activation and energy expenditure (Russell, 1980). As such, high-activated positive feelings, such as enthusiasm and joy, but not those low in arousal, like comfort and calm, drive proactive and innovative behaviour, because they provide the willingness to engage in problem-solving (Madrid and Patterson, 2019; Madrid et al, 2014).

The same rationale applies to high-activated negative versus low-activated negative moods (for example, anxiety versus disappointment) because the former provides the energy to approach and engage in social exchange, such as coordination and collaboration, whereas the latter leads to withdrawal behavioural tendencies (Warr et al, 2014).

Information processing and motivational mechanisms are intrapersonal psychological processes; thereby, they are primarily suitable for explaining affect, cognition, and behaviour at the individual level of analysis. In contrast, the psychological processes involved in the effects of team-level affect on proactivity should be those with interpersonal meaning.

Accordingly, the influences of team affective tones on social cognition and behaviour in groups occur through processes of social integration. The latter is an umbrella construct, which contains emergent states and behavioural processes with interpersonal meaning, such as cohesion, trust, psychological safety, collaboration, and conflict (Knight and Eisenkraft, 2014).

Cohesion, trust, and psychological safety are team emergent states. Cohesion is the sense of collective identity among team members. When cohesion is strong, team members are more likely keen to work together, enhancing continuity and viability of the team over time (Beal et al, 2003). Trust is the state built among team members denoting attributions of good intentions in the social exchange. Team members are willing to take risks, such as sharing information and delegating responsibilities to others, in teams where trust is present (Costa, 2003; De Jong and Elfring, 2010; De Jong, Dirks, and Gillespie, 2015; Sheppard and Sherman, 1998). Psychological safety is a similar construct to trust, but whereas trust describes the extent to which the benefit of the doubt is given to others, psychological safety describes the extent that others give the benefit of the doubt to you (Edmondson and Lei, 2014). Accordingly, psychological safety is the collective sense that makes team members feel they can be themselves; their capabilities are acknowledged and respected, and their voice is heard (Edmondson, 1999). Therefore, strong team psychological safety leads to active participation and engagement in teamwork (Frazier et al, 2017).

In turn, collaboration and conflict are behavioural processes. Collaboration involves the collective execution of tasks and mutual social support among team members (Beersma et al, 2003; Tjosvold, 1984). Social support is expressed in instrumental and emotional assistance (Drach-Zahavy, 2004; Ganster, Fusilier, and Mayes, 1986). In the first case, team members share knowledge and experiences with each other to solve problems and improve performance. Whereas, emotional support is expressed in concern about the emotional needs of the other team members and the provision of advice when it is appropriate. In contrast, conflict is the team members' perception of incompatibility about their interests, viewpoints, and way of interacting (Jehn and Bendersky, 2003). More specifically, task conflict is disagreement about the content of the work to be carried out within the team; process conflict refers to discrepancies about the procedures and methods utilized to perform the team's tasks, while relationship conflict involves disagreements among team members based on their work-related values, interests, and motivations (Behfar et al, 2011; Beitler, Scherer, and Zapf, 2018; DeChurch, Mesmer-Magnus, and Doty, 2013; Guenter et al, 2016). As might be expected, in general, all forms of conflict exert negative effects on teamwork (De Dreu and Weingart, 2003; De Wit, Greer, and Jehn, 2012), except task conflict that might increase team performance under certain contextual conditions, such as when psychological safety is strong within the team (Bradley et al, 2012).

Team affective tones exert influences on social integration, which in turn should shape team proactivity (compare, Knight and Eisenkraft, 2015). When the tone of the team is positive, expressed in the experience of enthusiasm, joy, excitement and inspiration, trust and psychological safety increase, while collaboration ripples throughout the team (Barsade, 2002; Frazier et al, 2017). These effects are likely because the expansive cognition embedded in positive feelings may open perspectives about the problems teams need to manage and enhance team members flexibility in seeing the viewpoints of others. As a result, social integration, stemming from the positive affective tone, should be conducive to greater performance of voice and innovation behaviour. Both voice and innovation are risky behaviours because they promote change, challenge the status quo, and often face resistance; thus, social integration contributes to these behaviours because trust and psychological safety relieve the sense of risk (Costa, 2003; Edmondson and Lei, 2014). Furthermore, suggesting, and experimenting with, ideas only makes sense in a forum of collaboration, which, as described above, emanates from team positive affective tones.

The relationship between negative affective tone entails more complexity. Shared negative feelings only dampen social integration when the source of them pertain to the internal, but not external, team environment (Knight and Eisenkraft, 2015). As such, if negative affective tones emerge due to adverse internal events, such as the experience of errors or failures, or poor previous performance, these affective tones could stifle the sense of cohesion, trust, and safety, limiting collaboration and even increasing the chance of conflict. These effects may emerge because negative feelings narrow cognition, reducing perspective-taking of others' viewpoints, together with boosting irritability and impulsivity, leading to higher levels of emotional conflict (Greer and Jehn, 2007). These states and actions are dysfunctional to team voice and innovation behaviour, because lack of social integration may invoke withdrawal behavioural tendencies, suppressing the suggestion and examination of novel ideas.

The effects of team behavioral processes on team affective tones

According to the model of team effectiveness, affect is thought to have a reciprocal relationship with behavioural processes and other emergent states, where affects not only effect behavioural processes and states, but the latter may also be the reciprocal cause of shared affect among team members (Ilgen et al, 2005; Mathieu et al, 2019).

The states of cohesion, trust, and psychological safety are likely to shape team affective tones. The rationale for this relationship derives from the affect-as-information hypothesis, which proposes that affective states are built from information about the characteristics of the environment (Clore, Gaspar, and Garvin, 2001; Martin and Stoner, 1996; Schwarz and Clore, 1983). As such, for example, positive moods are constructed due to the presence of rewarding conditions in the immediate environment, whereas negative moods emerge from the presence of threats (Watson, 2000; Watson et al, 1999). The extrapolation of these principles to the interpersonal realm has led to the theory of emotion-as-social information (van Kleef, 2009; van Kleef, Homan, and Cheshin, 2012). According to this framework, in the social domain, affect conveys information about the interpersonal attitudes, motivations, and intentions of individuals participating in the social interaction. Thus, positive feelings emerge when there are perceptions that the others are concerned with the quality of social exchange and well-being of others (Madrid, Niven, and Vasquez, 2019). In contrast, negative feelings arise from perceptions signalling that interaction partners are not interested in the quality of the relationship or if they are perceived as having negative attitudes toward the social exchange. As a result, it may be the case that the states of cohesion, trust, and psychological safety, together with collaboration expressed in interpersonal facilitation and social support, would increase the construction of positive affective tones because they involve affiliation meaning. In contrast, the lack of social integration exhibited in task, process, and relationship conflict should participate in the emergence of team negative affective tones due to the experience of weak bonding.

A Note on Affect Dispersion and Diversity

Thus far, we have based our review on the assumption that affective tones are homogenous states that represent the emotional experience of each team member. However, not all teams are defined by strong shared affective states because, inevitably, team members will differ in the level of the feeling they experience. For example, while in some teams all team members could tend towards feeling the same level of enthusiasm, in others there may be considerably more variation in the strength of enthusiasm experienced by team members. The construct of team affect dispersion (or diversity) has been coined to capture this phenomenon (Barsade and Gibson, 2012; Barsade and Knight, 2015; Collins et al, 2013). In teams, when affective tones are low in dispersion, all team members are prone to feel the shared feelings with the same intensity, which informs about a 'strong' affective tone. In contrast, team affective tones are 'weak' when the level of feelings experienced is high in dispersion, which implies that team members differ in the level of feelings experienced, such that in some cases, the affective state is weak, in others moderate, and in others strong.

The implications of affective tones' dispersion remain relatively unexplored; however, initial insights propose two possible alternatives. Based on the categorization–elaboration model of group diversity (Van Knippenberg, De Dreu, and Homan, 2004), affective dispersion could be understood as a form of diversity within teams, namely, the presence of diverse degrees of affective experience among team members. The elaboration hypothesis indicates that high dispersion might have benefits for team effectiveness because affective dispersion would lead to a broader array of cognitive processes that increases intra and interpersonal flexibility and, thereby, better performance, expressed in, for example, creativity and innovation (George and King, 2007). However, the categorization hypothesis stresses that diversity is an expression of existing sub-groups within the group, which increases the likelihood of tension and conflict due to incompatibilities in viewpoints (Van Knippenberg, De Dreu, and Homan, 2004). Thus, dispersed affective tones, either positive or negative, may have negative consequences for behavioural processes such as team voice and innovation behaviour, due to the possible underlying conflict in this affective configuration.

The etiology of team affective tones

The construction of group-level affect is associated with an array of etiological factors and processes (Kelly and Barsade, 2001). The essential variable participating in the emergence of team affective tones is the composition of the team in terms of the individual differences of its members; thus, affective-laden team members' personality traits influence the likelihood of building positive or negative shared affective states (Barsade and Gibson, 1998; Collins et al, 2013). For example, the mean-level of team members' extroversion is linked to the mean-level of positive affective tones, due to the temperamental and affective components of this personality trait (for example, enthusiasm, joy, inspiration) (Eysenck, 1974; Lucas and Baird, 2004; Wilt and Revelle, 2009). In contrast, the composition based on the mean-level of neuroticism among team members, which is a trait conveying negative affective tendencies (for example, anxiety, tension, worry) (Watson and Clark, 1992; Widiger, 2009), contributes to the emergence of the mean-level of negative affective tones. The same applies to trait affect, which refers to the stable tendencies to experience positive or negative feelings over time, such as activation and excitement or anger and fear, respectively (Watson, 2000; Watson et al, 1999). In this case, team composition based on team members' positive or negative trait affect explains why the team is characterized by positive or negative affective tones, respectively (Collins et al, 2013). Therefore, the extent of team members' extraversion and neuroticism or positive and negative traits affect determines, in part, the kind of group affective states experienced within the team.

The translation of compositional team conditions into group-level states occurs through processes of affect convergence (Kelly and Barsade, 2001). Emotional contagion is one of these mechanisms, which is the transference to interaction partners of an individual's feelings, who catch this affective experience (Elfenbein, 2014). Thus, a team member who is feeling excited may spread this mood among the other team members, whereas another team member experiencing nervousness may propagate this feeling, making other team members feel nervous. Emotional contagion is mostly unconscious, occurring due to the mimicry of facial expression and non-verbal communication that human beings tend to perform from the behaviour of others (Hatfield, Cacioppo, and Rapson, 1992). Adopting a facial expression that reflects the facial expression of another leads to catching the mood of the latter. Emotional contagion is particularly likely from individuals with salience within teams, as is the case of team leaders, formally defined as influential individuals who concentrate power and resources. Supporting this assertion, leaders' affective dispositions embedded in affective laden personality traits (for example, extraversion and neuroticism), together with their concomitant moods, are often caught by their followers, which might unfold in affective tones if the followers work together (Sy and Choi, 2013).

Recently, another psychological process, called affective presence, has been proposed as an etiological factor of shared affect in groups. Affective presence is an individual's tendency to consistently elicit the same feelings among interaction partners, independent of affective personality traits and contagion (Eisenkraft and Elfenbein, 2010). Thus, an individual could tend to provoke enthusiasm among interaction partners (positive affective presence), although s/he is feeling tense in his/her interpersonal realm, while another individual could tend to produce nervousness in others (negative affective presence), even when he or she is feeling enthusiastic. Although the roots of affective presence are not still well understood, the application of this construct to the teamwork setting has shown that team members reliably describe their team leaders in terms of positive or negative affective presence (Madrid et al, 2016). Furthermore, this research has also established that affective presence is correlated to team affective tones and concomitant interpersonal processes such as team information sharing, interpersonal facilitation, innovation, and service performance (Jiang et al, 2018; Madrid, Totterdell, and Niven, 2016; Madrid et al, 2018). Thus, affective presence is emerging as a complementary process to emotional contagion for explaining why and how group affect is formed in teams.

Team affect also is derived from deliberate and intentional influences of team members. In this context, emotion has a social and communicative component, such that individuals may enact emotion expression behaviour to demonstrate their feelings and communicate their attitudes, motivations and intentions towards the social exchange with other team members, influencing, therefore, the others' affect, cognition and behaviour (van Kleef, 2009). For example, the expression of enthusiasm communicates positive attitudes toward the relationship with others and also affiliative intentions, which leads to positive affective reactions among interaction partners (van Kleef, Homan, and Cheshin, 2012). In contrast, the expression of anger demonstrates indifference towards the affiliation processes, which is often conducive to negative affective experiences among group members (van Knippenberg and van Kleef, 2016). Another form of intentional affective influence occurs due to deliberate interpersonal emotion regulation (Troth et al, 2018). This refers to active behaviours oriented to change, provoke, or modulate affective states in others, in order to improve or worsen the affective experience of interaction partners (Niven, Totterdell, and Holman, 2009; Zaki and Williams, 2013). In the first case, individuals, for example, behave to reduce negative feelings in others, such as those associated with distress like anxiety, tension, and worry. This effect is achieved by modifying the situations that provoke negative affect, helping to deploy attention and cognitively reappraise affect-eliciting events, and supporting the expression of negative feelings (Gross and Thompson, 2007). On the other hand, individuals also enact behaviours to worsen the affect of the other, such as using destructive criticizing, being unresponsive or giving the cold-shoulder (Niven et al, 2011). Both emotion expression and interpersonal emotion regulation behaviours can be enacted by any member of the group; however, as discussed above, these behaviours are particularly influential when performed by salient individuals. Supporting this assumption, studies have shown that leaders' emotional expression and emotion regulation contribute to building affective experiences of group members in the context of teams (Little, Gooty, and Williams, 2016; Madrid, Niven, and Vasquez, 2019; van Knippenberg and van Kleef, 2016).

At the contextual level, team task characteristics also influence the group affective states shared among its members (Collins et al, 2013). Thus, mirroring the effects of task characteristics at the job level, when team members have to collectively manage tasks involving skill variety, complexity, challenges, and social meaning, an enthusiastic shared affective tone is likely to emerge (compare, Christian, Garza, and Slaughter, 2011; Hackman and Oldham, 1976). In contrast, shared stressful conditions, such as ambiguity, heavy workloads, and tight deadlines, increase the likelihood of an anxious affective tone (compare, Karasek, 1979; Wall et al, 1996). Furthermore, events derived from environmental characteristics and social behaviour in the teamwork setting are linked to the emergence of affective tones as well. Accordingly, collective events influencing all team members, for example, goal attainment, performance recognition, and positive feedback, spark the collective sense of pride, whereas events involving, for instance, errors, communication problems, and interpersonal conflict, elicit the shared experience of frustration (Basch and Fisher, 1998; Ohly and Schmitt, 2015). All the above contextual conditions are particularly influential when teamwork involves greater interdependency, which is the extent to which team members depend on the work of each other, so that task performance requires tight coordination to implement working procedures and attain the team's common goals (Courtright et al, 2015). As such, the greater the interdependence, the stronger should be the effects of task characteristics and affective events on the shared affective experiences of team members.

Finally, organizational culture also operates in the construction of group affect. In this scenario, affective culture is defined as group norms that dictate the appropriateness of experiencing and expressing positive or negative feelings (Barsade and Gibson, 2012; Barsade and Knight, 2015). Thus, some cultures reward the expression of positive feelings, such as enthusiasm, joy, and happiness, which should unfold into positive affective tones, whereas in other cultural settings, like those characterized by aggressive assertiveness, the expression of negative feelings is not curbed, it is accepted and even encouraged (Javidan et al, 2006), which should increase the emergence of negative affective tones. In general, the construct of affective culture has been defined at the organizational level of analysis; however, displays rules could also operate at closer environments, such as those described by the social context within teams.

Conclusion

In this chapter, we argued and discussed the possible relationships between affect and proactivity in teams. Accordingly, based on the proposals of the process models of teamwork, affective tones and team proactive behaviours are emergent states and behavioural processes respectively, that facilitate and contribute to team performance and building job attitudes of their members. Given their relevance, we surveyed and discussed theory and evidence about how affective tones, conductive to proactivity, emerge within teams. This review revealed that etiological factors participating in the construction of team-level affect are those associated with the composition of individual differences, task characteristics, affective-laden events, and the intentional influence of team members. Ultimately, understanding the relationship between affect and proactivity at the team level is valuable for promoting intervention of teamwork processes in organizations and increasing the possibility of functional team outcomes.

References

Barsade, S. G. (2002). The ripple effect: Emotional contagion and its influence on group behavior. *Administrative Science Quarterly*, 47(4), 644–75. http://dx.doi.org/10.2307/3094912.

Barsade, S. G. and Gibson, D. E. (1998). Group emotion: A view from top and bottom. *Research on Managing Groups and Teams,* 1, 81–102.

Barsade, S. G. and Gibson, D. E. (2012). Group affect: Its influence on individual and group outcomes. *Current Directions in Psychological Science*, 2(2), 119–23. https://doi.org/10.1177/0963721412438352.

Barsade, S. G. and Knight, A. P. (2015). Group affect. *Annual Review of Organizational Psychology and Organizational Behavior*, 2(1), 21–46. http://dx.doi.org/10.1146/annurev-orgpsych-032414-111316.

Basch, J. and Fisher, C. D. (1998). Affective events-emotions matrix: A classification of work events and associated emotions. *School of Business Discussion Papers*, 65.

Beal, D. J., Cohen, R. R., Burke, M. J., and McLendon, C. L. (2003). Cohesion and performance in groups: A Meta-analytic clarification of construct relations. *Journal of Applied Psychology*, 88(6), 989–1004. https://doi.org/10.1037/0021-9010.88.6.989.

Beersma, B., Hollenbeck, J. R., Humphrey, S. E., Moon, H., Conlon, D. E., and Ilgen, D. R. (2003). Cooperation, competition, and team performance: Toward a contingency approach. *Academy of Management Journal*, 46(5), 572–90. https://doi.org/10.2307/30040650.

Behfar, K. J., Mannix, E. A., Peterson, R. S., and Trochim, W. M. (2011). Conflict in small groups: The meaning and consequences of process conflict. *Small Group Research*, 42(2), 127–76. https://doi.org/10.1177/1046496410389194.

Beitler, L. A., Scherer, S., and Zapf, D. (2018). Interpersonal conflict at work: Age and emotional competence differences in conflict management. *Organizational Psychology Review*, 8(4), 195–227. https://doi.org/10.1177/2041386618808346.

Bindl, U., Parker, S. K., Totterdell, P., and Hagger-Johnson, G. (2012). Fuel of the self-starter: How mood relates to proactive goal regulation. *Journal of Applied Psychology*, 97(1), 134–50. http://dx.doi.org/10.1037/a0024368.

Bradley, B. H., Postlethwaite, B. E., Klotz, A. C., Hamdani, M. R., and Brown, K. G. (2012). Reaping the benefits of task conflict in teams: The critical role of team psychological safety climate. *Journal of Applied Psychology*, 97(1), 151–8. https://doi.org/10.1037/a0024200.

Burke, C. S., Stagl, K. C., Salas, E., Pierce, L., and Kendall, D. (2006). Understanding team adaptation: A conceptual analysis and model. *Journal of Applied Psychology*, 91, 1189–207. http://dx.doi.org/10.1037/0021-9010.91.6.1189.

Campion, M. A., Medsker, G. J., and Higgs, A. C. (1993). Relations between work group characteristics and effectiveness: Implications for designing effective work groups. *Personnel Psychology*, 46, 823–50. http://dx.doi.org/10.1111/j.1744-6570.1993.tb01571.x.

Cangiano, F., Bindl, U. K., and Parker, S. K. (2017). The hot side of proactivity: Exploring and affect-based perspective of proactivity in organizations. In S. K. Parker and U. K. Bindl (eds), *Proactivity at Work: Making Things Happen in Organizations*, New York Routledge.

Christian, M. S., Garza, A. S., and Slaughter, J. E. (2011). Work engagement: A quantitative review and test of its relations with task and contextual performance. *Personnel Psychology*, 64(1), 89–136. https://doi.org/10.1111/j.1744-6570.2010.01203.x.

Clore, G. L., Gaspar, K., and Garvin, E. (2001). Affect as information. In J. P. Forgas (ed), *Handbook of Affect and Social Cognition*, Mahwah, NJ: Erlbaum, pp 121–44.

Collins, A. L., Lawrence, S. A., Troth, A. C., and Jordan, P. J. (2013). Group affective tone: A review and future research directions. *Journal of Organizational Behavior*, 34, S43– S62. https://doi.org/10.1002/job.1887.

Costa, A. C. (2003). Work team trust and effectiveness. *Personnel Review*, 32(5), 605–22. https://doi.org/10.1108/00483480310488360.

Courtright, S. H., Thurgood, G. R., Stewart, G. L., and Pierotti, A. J. (2015). Structural interdependence in teams: An integrative framework and meta-analysis. *Journal of Applied Psychology*, 100(6), 1825–46. https://doi.org/10.1037/apl0000027.

De Dreu, C. K. W. and Weingart, L. R. (2003). Task versus relationship conflict, team performance, and team member satisfaction: A meta-analysis. *Journal of Applied Psychology*, 88(4), 741–9. http://dx.doi.org/10.1037/0021-9010.88.4.741.

De Dreu, C. K. W. and West, M. A. (2001). Minority dissent and team innovation: The importance of participation in decision making. *Journal of Applied Psychology*, 86(6), 1191–201. http://dx.doi.org/10.1037/0021-9010.86.6.1191.

De Jong, B. A. and Elfring, T. (2010). How does trust affect the performance of ongoing teams? The mediating role of reflexivity, monitoring, and effort. *Academy of Management Journal*, 53(3), 535549. http://dx.doi.org/10.5465/amj.2010.51468649.

De Jong, B., Dirks, K., and Gillespie, N. (2015). Trust and team performance: A meta-analysis of main effects, contingencies, and qualifiers. *75th Annual Meeting of the Academy of Management, AOM 2015*, 101(8), 744–9. https://doi.org/10.5465/AMBPP.2015.234.

De Wit, F. R. C., Greer, L. L., and Jehn, K. A. (2012). The paradox of intragroup conflict: A meta-analysis. *Journal of Applied Psychology*, 97(2), 360–90. https://doi.org/10.1037/a0024844.

DeChurch, L. A., Mesmer-Magnus, J. R., and Doty, D. (2013). Moving beyond relationship and task conflict: Toward a process-state perspective. *Journal of Applied Psychology*, 98(4), 559–78. https://doi.org/10.1037/a0032896.

Drach-Zahavy, A. (2004). Toward a multidimensional construct of social support: Implications of provider's self-reliance and request characteristics. *Journal of Applied Social Psychology*, 34(7), 1395–420. http://dx.doi.org/10.1111/j.1559-1816.2004.tb02012.x.

Edmondson, A. C. (1999). Psychological safety and learning behavior in work teams. *Administrative Science Quarterly*, 44, 350–83. http://dx.doi.org/10.2307/2666999.

Edmondson, A. C. and Lei, Z. (2014). Psychological safety: The history, renaissance, and future of an interpersonal construct. *Annual Review of Organizational Psychology and Organizational Behavior*, 1(1), 23–43. https://doi.org/10.1146/annurev-orgpsych-031413-091305.

Eisenkraft, N. and Elfenbein, H. A. (2010). The way You make me feel: Evidence for individual differences in affective presence. *Psychological Science*, 21(4), 505–510. https://doi.org/10.1177/0956797610364117.

Elfenbein, H. A. (2014). The many faces of emotional contagion: An affective process theory of affective linkage. *Organizational Psychology Review*, 4(4), 326–62. https://doi.org/10.1177/2041386614542889.

Eysenck, H. J. (1974). *Eysenck on Extraversion*, New York: Halsted Press.

Frazier, M. L., Fainshmidt, S., Klinger, R. L., Pezeshkan, A., and Vracheva, V. (2017). Psychological safety: A meta-analytic review and extension. *Personnel Psychology*, 70(1), 113–65. https://doi.org/10.1111/peps.12183.

Fredrickson, B. L. (2001). The role of positive emotions in positive psychology: The broaden-and-build theory of positive emotions. *American Psychologist*, 56, 218–26. http://dx.doi.org/10.1037/0003-066X.56.3.218.

Fredrickson, B. L. (2004). The broaden-and-build theory of positive emotions. *Philosophical Transactions of the Royal Society of London Series B-Biological Sciences*, 359(1449), 1367–77. https://doi.org/10.1098/rstb.2004.1512.

Ganster, D. C., Fusilier, M. R., and Mayes, B. T. (1986). Role of social support in the experience of stress at work. *Journal of Applied Psychology*, 71(1), 102–10. https://doi.org/10.1037//0021-9010.71.1.102.

George, J. M. (1996). Group afective tone. In M. A. West (ed), *Handbook of Work Group Psychology*, Chichester:Wiley and Sons.

George, J. M. and King, E. B. (2007). Potential pitfalls of affect convergence in teams: Functions and dysfunctions of group affective tone. In E. A. Mannix, M. A. Neale, and C. P. Anderson (eds), *Research on Managing Groups and Teams: Affect and Groups*, Bingley: Elsevier.

George, J. M. and Zhou, J. (2007). Dual tuning in a supportive context: Joint contributions of positive mood, negative mood, and supervisory behaviors to employee creativity. *Academy of Management Journal*, 50, 605–22. http://dx.doi.org/10.5465/amj.2007.25525934.

Gladstein, D. L. (1984). Groups in context – A model of task group effectiveness. *Administrative Science Quarterly*, 29(4), 499–517. http://dx.doi.org/10.2307/2392936.

Greer, L. L. and Jehn, K. (2007). The pivotal role of negative affect in understanding the effects of process conflict on group performance. In E. Mannix, M. Neale, and C. Anderson (eds), *Affect and Groups*, Oxford: Emerald Group Publishing Limited, pp 21–43.

Gross, J. J. and Thompson, R. (2007). Emotion regulation: Conceptual foundations. In J. J. Gross (ed), *Handbook of Emotion Regulation*, New York: Guilford, pp 3–24.

Guenter, H., van Emmerik, H., Schreurs, B., Kuypers, T., van Iterson, A., and Notelaers, G. (2016). When task conflict becomes personal: The impact of perceived team performance. *Small Group Research*, 47(5), 569–604. https://doi.org/10.1177/1046496416667816.

Hackman, J. R. and Oldham, G. R. (1976). Motivation through the design of work: Test of a theory. *Organizational Behavior and Human Performance*, 16(2), 250–79. http://dx.doi.org/10.1016/0030-5073(76)90016-7.

Hammond, M. M., Neff, N. L., Farr, J. L., Schwall, A. R., and Zhao, X. Y. (2011). Predictors of individual-level Innovation at work: A meta-analysis. *Psychology of Aesthetics Creativity and the Arts*, 5(1), 90–105. https://doi.org/10.1037/a0018556.

Harris, T. B. and Kirkman, B. L. (2017). Teams and proactivity. In S. K. Parker and U. K. Bindl (eds), *Proactivity at Work: Making Things Happen in Organizations*, New York Routledge, pp 530–58.

Hatfield, E., Cacioppo, J. T., and Rapson, R. L. (1992). Primitive emotional contagion. In M. S. Clark (ed), *Emotion and Social Behavior. Review of Personality and Social Psychology*, vol 14, Thousand Oaks, CA Sage, pp 151–77.

Hatfield, E., Cacioppo, J. T., and Rapson, R. L. (1993). Emotional contagion. *Current Directions in Psychological Science*, 3, 96–9. http://dx.doi.org/10.1017/CBO9780511819568.008.

Ilgen, D. R., Hollenbeck, J. R., Johnson, M., and Jundt, D. (2005). Teams in organizations: From input-process-output models to IMOI models. *Annual Review of Psychology*, 56, 517–43. http://dx.doi.org/10.1146/annurev.psych.56.091103.070250.

Isen, A. M. (1984). Toward understanding the role of affect in cognition. In R. S. Wyer and T. K. Srull (eds), *Handbook of Social Cognition*, New York: Erlbaum, pp 174–236.

Isen, A. M., Shalker, T. E., Clark, M., and Karp, L. (1978). Affect, accessibility of material in memory, and behavior-cognitive loop. *Journal of Personality and Social Psychology*, 36(1), 1–12. https://doi.org/10.1037//0022-3514.36.1.1.

Javidan, M., House, R., Dorfman, P., Hanges, P., and Sully de Luque, M. (2006). Conceptualizing and measuring cultures and their consequences: A comparative review of GLOBE's and Hofstede's approaches. *Journal of International Business Studies*, 37(6), 897–914. http://dx.doi.org/10.1057/palgrave.jibs.8400234.

Jehn, K. A. and Bendersky, C. (2003). Intragroup conflict in organizations: A contingency perspective on the conflict-outcome relationship. *Research in Organizational Behavior*, 25(03), 187–242. https://doi.org/10.1016/S0191-3085(03)25005-X.

Jiang, J., Gu, H., Dong, Y., and Tu, X. (2018). The better I feel, the better I can do: The role of leaders' positive affective presence. *International Journal of Hospitality Management*, 78, 251–60. http://dx.doi.org/10.1016/j.ijhm.2018.09.007.

Kanter, R. M. (1988). When a thousand flowers bloom – Structural, collective, and social conditions for innovation in organization. *Research in Organizational Behavior*, 10, 169–211. http://dx.doi.org/10.1016/B978-0-7506-9749-1.50010-7.

Karasek, R. A. (1979). Job demands, job decision latitude, and mental strain – Implications for job redesign. *Administrative Science Quarterly*, 24(2), 285–308. http://dx.doi.org/10.2307/2392498.

Kelly, J. R. and Barsade, S. G. (2001). Mood and emotions in small groups and work teams. *Organizational Behavior and Human Decision Processes*, 86(1), 99–130. http://dx.doi.org/10.1006/obhd.2001.2974.

King, N. and Anderson, N. R. (1990). Innovation in working groups. In M. A. West and J. M. Farr (eds), *Innovation and Creativity at Work*, London: Wiley, pp 81–100.

Knight, A. P. and Eisenkraft, N. (2015). Positive is usually good, negative is not always bad: The effects of group affect on social integration and task performance. *Journal of Applied Psychology*, 100(4), 1214–27. https://doi.org/10.1037/apl0000006.

Lepine, J. A. and Dyne Van, L. (1998). Predicting voice behavior in work groups. *Journal of Applied Psychology*, 83, 853–68. http://dx.doi.org/10.1037/0021-9010.83.6.853.

Little, L. M., Gooty, J., and Williams, M. (2016). The role of leader emotion management in leader–member exchange and follower outcomes. *The Leadership Quarterly*, 27(1), 85–97. http://dx.doi.org/10.1016/j.leaqua.2015.08.007.

Lucas, R. E. and Baird, B. M. (2004). Extraversion and emotional reactivity. *Journal of Personality and Social Psychology*, 86(3), 473–85. https://doi.org/10.1037/0022-3514.86.3.473.

Madrid, H. P., Niven, K., and Vasquez, C. A. (2019). Leader interpersonal emotion regulation and innovation in teams. *Journal of Occupational and Organizational Psychology*. https://doi.org/10.1111/joop.12292.

Madrid, H. P. and Patterson, M. G. (2018). Affect and creativity. In R. Reiter-Palmon and J. C. Kaufmann (eds), *Individual Creativity in the Workplace*, New York: Elsevier.

Madrid, H. P. and Patterson, M. G. (2019). How and for whom time control matter for innovation? The role of positive affect and problem-solving demands. *Applied Psychology*, 0(0), 1–27. https://doi.org/10.1111/apps.12194.

Madrid, H. P., Patterson, M. G., Birdi, K. S., Leiva, P. I., and Kausel, E. E. (2014). The role of weekly high-activated positive mood, context, and personality in innovative work behavior: A multilevel and interactional model. *Journal of Organizational Behavior*, 35(2), 234–56. https://doi.org/10.1002/job.1867.

Madrid, H. P., Patterson, M. G., and Leiva, P. I. (2015). Negative core affect and employee silence: How differences in activation, cognitive rumination, and problem-solving demands matter. *Journal of Applied Psychology*, 100(6), 1887–1898. https://doi.org/10.1037/a0039380.

Madrid, H. P., Totterdell, P., and Niven, K. (2016). Does leader-affective presence influence communication of creative ideas within work teams? *Emotion*, 16(6). https://doi.org/10.1037/emo0000183.

Madrid, H. P., Totterdell, P., Niven, K., and Barros, E. (2016). Leader affective presence and innovation in teams. *Journal of Applied Psychology*, 101(5). https://doi.org/10.1037/apl0000078.

Madrid, H. P., Totterdell, P., Niven, K., and Vasquez, C. A. (2018). Investigating a process model for leader affective presence, interpersonal emotion regulation, and interpersonal behaviour in teams. *European Journal of Work and Organizational Psychology*, 27(5), 642–56. https://doi.org/10.1080/1359432X.2018.1505719.

Marks, M. A., Mathieu, J. E., and Zaccaro, S. J. (2001). A temporally based framework and taxonomy of team processes. *Academy of Management Review*, 26(3), 356–76. http://dx.doi.org/10.5465/amr.2001.4845785.

Martin, L. L. and Stoner, P. (1996). Mood as input: What we think about how we feel determines how we think. In L. L. Martin and A. Tesser (eds), *Striving and Feeling: Interactions Among Goals, Affect, and Self-Regulation*, Mahwah, NJ Erlbaum, pp 279–301.

Mathieu, J. E., Gallagher, P. T., Domingo, M. A., and Klock, E. A. (2019). Embracing complexity: Reviewing the past decade of team effectiveness research. *Annual Review of Organizational Psychology and Organizational Behavior*, 6(1), 17–46. https://doi.org/10.1146/annurev-orgpsych-012218-015106.

Mathieu, J. E., Maynard, M. T., Rapp, T., and Gilson, L. (2008). Team effectiveness 1997–2007: A review of recent advancements and a glimpse into the future. *Journal of Management*, 34, 410–76. https://doi.org/10.1177/0149206308316061.

McGrath, J. E. (1964). *Social Psychology: A Brief Introduction*. New York Holt, Rhinehart and Winston.

Morrison, E. W. (2014). Employee voice and silence. *Annual Review of Organizational Psychology and Organizational Behavior*, 1(1), 173–97. https://doi.org/10.1146/annurev-orgpsych-031413-091328.

Morrison, E. W., Wheeler-Smith, S. L., and Kamdar, D. (2011). Speaking up in groups: A cross-level study of group voice climate and voice. *Journal of Applied Psychology*, 96(1), 183–91. https://doi.org/10.1037/a0020744.

Nijstad, B. A., De Dreu, C. K. W., Rietzschel, E. F., and Baas, M. (2010). The dual pathway to creativity model: Creative ideation as a function of flexibility and persistence. *European Review of Social Psychology*, 21, 34–77. https://doi.org/10.1080/10463281003765323.

Niven, K., Totterdell, P., and Holman, D. (2009). A classification of controlled interpersonal affect regulation strategies. *Emotion*, 9(4), 498. https://doi.org/10.1037/a0015962.

Niven, K., Totterdell, P., Stride, C., and Holman, D. (2011). Emotion regulation of others and self (EROS): The development and validation of a new individual difference measure. *Current Psychology*, 30(53–73). http://dx.doi.org/10.1007/s12144-011-9099-9.

Ohly, S. and Schmitt, A. (2015). What makes us enthusiastic, angry, feeling at rest or worried? Development and validation of an affective work events taxonomy using concept mapping methodology. *Journal of Business and Psychology*, 30(1), 15–35. https://doi.org/10.1007/s10869-013-9328-3.

Russell, J. A. (1980). A circumplex model of affect. *Journal of Personality and Social Psychology*, 39(6), 1161–78. https://doi.org/10.1037/h0077714.

Schwarz, N. and Clore, G. L. (1983). Mood, misattribution, and judgments of well-being – Informative and directive functions of affective states. *Journal of Personality and Social Psychology*, 45(3), 513–23. http://dx.doi.org/10.1037/0022-3514.45.3.513.

Schwarz, N. and Skurnik, I. (2003). Feeling and thinking: Implications for problem solving. In J. E. Davidson and R. J. Sternberg (eds), *The Psychology of Problem Solving*, Cambridge: Cambridge University Press, pp 263– 90.

Seo, M. G., Barrett, L. F., and Bartunek, J. M. (2004). The role of affective experience in work motivation. *Academy of Management Review*, 29(3), 423–439. http://dx.doi.org/10.5465/amr.2004.13670972.

Sheppard, B. H. and Sherman, D. M. (1998). The grammars of trust: A model and general implications. *Academy of Management Review*, 23(3), 422–37. http://dx.doi.org/10.5465/amr.1998.926619.

Shipton, H. J., West, M. A., Parkes, C. L., Dawson, J. F., and Patterson, M. G. (2006). When promoting positive feelings pays: Aggregate job satisfaction, work design features, and innovation in manufacturing organizations. *European Journal of Work and Organizational Psychology*, 15(4), 404–30. http://dx.doi.org/10.1080/13594320600908153.

Sy, T. and Choi, J. N. (2013). Contagious leaders and followers: Exploring multi-stage mood contagion in a leader activation and member propagation (LAMP) model. *Organizational Behavior and Human Decision Processes*, 122(2), 127–40.

Thomas, J. P., Whitman, D. S., and Viswesvaran, C. (2010). Employee proactivity in organizations: A comparative meta-analysis of emergent proactive constructs. *Journal of Occupational and Organizational Psychology*, 83(2), 275–300. https://doi.org/10.1348/096317910x502359.

Tjosvold, D. (1984). Cooperation theory and organizations. *Human Relations*, 37(9), 743–67. http://dx.doi.org/10.1177/001872678403700903.

Troth, A. C., Lawrence, S. A., Jordan, P. J., and Ashkanasy, N. M. (2018). Interpersonal emotion regulation in the workplace: A conceptual and operational review and future research agenda. *International Journal of Management Reviews*, 20(2), 523–43. https://doi.org/10.1111/ijmr.12144.

van Kleef, G. A. (2009). How emotions regulate social life: The emotions as social information (EASI) model. *Current Directions in Psychological Science*, 18(3), 184–8. http://dx.doi.org/10.1111/j.1467-8721.2009.01633.x.

van Kleef, G. A., Homan, A., and Cheshin, A. (2012). Emotional influence at work: Take it EASI. *Organizational Psychology Review*, 2(4), 311–39. https://doi.org/10.1177/2041386612454911.

Van Knippenberg, D., De Dreu, C. K. W., and Homan, A. C. (2004). Work group diversity and group performance: An integrative model and research agenda. *Journal of Applied Psychology*, 89(6), 1008–22. https://doi.org/10.1037/0021-9010.89.6.1008.

Van Knippenberg, D. and van Kleef, G. A. (2016). Leadership and affect: Moving the hearts and minds of followers. *Academy of Management Annals*, 10(1), 799–840. https://doi.org/10.1080/19416520.2016.1160515.

Wall, T. D., Jackson, P. R., Mullarkey, S., and Parker, S. K. (1996). The demands-control model of job strain: A more specific test. *Journal of Occupational and Organizational Psychology*, 69, 153–66. http://dx.doi.org/10.1111/j.2044-8325.1996.tb00607.x.

Warr, P. B., Bindl, U., Parker, S. K., and Inceoglu, I. (2014). Job-related affects and behaviors: Activation as well as valence. *European Journal of Work and Organizational Psychology*, 23(3), 342–63. https://doi.org/dx.doi.org/10.1080/1359432X.2012.744449.

Watson, D. (2000). *Mood and Temperament*. New York Guilford Press.

Watson, D. and Clark, L. A. (1992). On traits and temperament – General and specific factors of emotional experience and their relation to the 5-factor model. *Journal of Personality*, 60(2), 441–76. https://doi.org/10.1111/j.1467–6494.1992.tb00980.x.

Watson, D., Wiese, D., Vaidya, J., and Tellegen, A. (1999). The two general activation systems of affect: Structural findings, evolutionary considerations, and psychobiological evidence. *Journal of Personality and Social Psychology*, 76(5), 820–38. https://doi.org/10.1037/0022-3514.76.5.820.

West, M. A. (2002). Sparkling fountains or stagnant ponds: An integrative model of creativity and innovation implementation in work groups. *Applied Psychology: An International Review*, 51, 3355–87. http://dx.doi.org/10.1111/1464-0597.00951.

Widiger, T. A. (2009). Neuroticism. In M. Leary and R. Hoyle (eds), *Handbook of Individual Differences in Social Behavior*, New York:The Guilford Press.

Williams, H. M., Parker, S. K., and Turner, N. (2010). Proactively performing teams: The role of work design, transformational leadership, and team composition. *Journal of Occupational and Organizational Psychology*, 83(2), 301–24. https://doi.org/10.1348/096317910X502494.

Wilt, J. and Revelle, W. (2009). Extraversion. In M. Leary and R. Hoyle (eds), *Handbook of Individual Differences in Social Behavior*, New York: The Guilford Press.

Zaki, J. and Williams, W. C. (2013). Interpersonal emotion regulation. 13(5), 803–10. https://doi.org/10.1037/a0033839.

Zare, M. and Flinchbaugh, C. (2019). Voice, creativity, and big five personality traits: A meta-analysis. *Human Performance*, 32(1), 30–51. https://doi.org/10.1080/08959285.2018.1550782.

10

The Dual Pathway Model of Group Affective Tone on Team Creativity: The Role of Team Task Complexity and Supportive Context

Nai-Wen Chi

Proactivity refers to a set of self-starting, action-oriented behaviours aimed at taking initiative in improving the current circumstances or creating new situations (Crant, 2000; Unsworth and Parker, 2003). Being proactive in teams is critical since proactivity can help the team members to master change in complex and uncertain work environments (Griffin, Neal, and Parker, 2007; Wu and Wang, 2015). Within the components of proactivity, the self-starting facet is closely related to creativity, since it involves identifying problems and generating novel solutions (Unsworth and Parker, 2003). In addition, generating creative ideas is essential for successful and positive changes in the organization (Parker and Collins, 2010). Thus, this chapter focuses on the question of how to promote team creativity to make the teams more proactive by discussing the role of group affective tone.

Team creativity refers to the production of novel and useful ideas concerning products, services, processes, and procedures by a team of employees working together (Shin and Zhou, 2007). Similar to the research interests in how individual positive/negative moods influence individual creativity (George, 2011; George and Zhou, 2007; Zhou and Hoever, 2014), team researchers also attempted to clarify how shared affective states among team members influence team creativity (for example, Chi, 2019; Kim and Shin, 2015; Shin, Kim, and Lee, 2019; Tsai, Chi, Grandey, and Fung, 2012). Group affective tone, which refers to 'consistent or homogeneous affective reactions within a group' (George, 1990, p 108), is composed of two important dimensions: positive group affective tone (PGAT) and negative group affective tone (NGAT). In teams with PGAT, members consistently experience positive affective states such as excitement and enthusiasm. On the other hand, members consistently feel negative affective states such as distress, anxiety, and hostility in teams with NGAT. Recent studies have shown that PGAT and NGAT are independent dimensions and can influence group-level outcomes in unique ways (Chi and Huang, 2014; Collins, Lawrence, Troth, and Jordan, 2013; Knight and Eisenkraft, 2015; Paulsen, Klonek, Schneider, and Kauffeld, 2016). However, as shown in Table 10.1, the relationships between PGAT/ NGAT and team creativity are mixed and divergent. Therefore, the questions regarding whether, how, and when PGAT/NGAT influence team creativity remained unanswered (Barsade and Knight, 2015; Collins et al, 2013).

This chapter aims to contribute to the GAT and creativity literature in several ways. First, this chapter provides an overview of the theoretical foundations, research designs, and current findings on the GAT–team creativity link. Second, integrating the divergent results about the PGAT/NGAT–team creativity relationship, this chapter proposes a dual pathway model that highlights the potential mechanisms and boundary conditions of GAT on team creativity. Specifically, PGAT increases team creativity via facilitating promotion-focused actions (that is, team members' actions that aim to pursue positive outcomes, such as taking risks, and exploring new possibilities and information; Shin, 2014), whereas NGAT leads to team creativity by fostering prevention-focused actions (that is, team members' actions that aim to avoid problems and failure, such as critically identifying potential problems and reviewing the possible solutions; George and King, 2007). Furthermore, the strengths of the two paths depend on the interplay between two contextual factors: team task complexity (that is, simple/routine tasks versus complex/uncertain tasks; De Dreu and Weingart, 2003) and team supportive context (that is, support from the organization, the supervisor, or the other members that can facilitate the team functions, such as supervisor or member support, or team-based reward system).

Finally, this chapter provides avenues for future studies on GAT by offering conceptual and methodological suggestions to improve GAT research, including: (1) considering the roles of dynamic and

Table 10.1: Review of empirical evidence regarding the GAT–team creativity relationship

Article	Types of team	Timeframe of GAT	Creative outcomes	Rating sources	GAT–creativity relationship	Moderators and findings	Mediators and findings
Tsai et al (2012, JOB)	68 R & D teams	past one week	Team creativity (M = 4.46, SD = 0.65)	Team leaders	PGAT: r = .09 (M = 3.10, SD = 0.4) NGAT: r = -.19 (M = 1.60, SD = 0.37)	*Team trust* attenuates the positive relationship between PGAT and team creativity. However, when PGAT is low whereas team trust is high, NGAT is positively related to team creativity	N/A
Chi (2019)	122 R & D teams	past two weeks	Team creativity (M = 3.49, SD = 0.78)	Team leaders	PGAT: r = .48 (M = 2.98, SD = 0.43)	*Supervisory support* attenuates the positive relationship between PGAT and information exchange, and team creativity	Team information exchange
Chi and Chen (2014)	47 R & D teams	past one week	Team innovation (M = 5.49, SD = 0.92)	Team leaders	PGAT: r = .30 (M = 2.84, SD = 0.72) NGAT: r = .03 (M = 1.77, SD = 0.56)	The relationship between NGAT and team innovation becomes positive when *reward for innovation* is high; however, this relationship became negative when *reward for innovation* is low	N/A

(continued)

Table 10.1: Review of empirical evidence regarding the GAT–team creativity relationship (continued)

Article	Types of team	Timeframe of GAT	Creative outcomes	Rating sources	GAT–creativity relationship	Moderators and findings	Mediators and findings
Shin, Kim, and Lee (2019, JCB)	116 work teams with different functions: strategy and planning, managerial support, finance, accounting, and auditing, and sales and marketing	past one week	Team creative outcomes (M = 3.47, SD = 0.56)	Team leaders	PGAT: r = .28 (M = 3.30, SD = 0.42)	*Transformational leadership* strengthens the positive relationship between PGAT and team reflexivity	Team reflexivity
Kim and Shin (2015, APJM)	97 work teams with different functions: planning/strategy/operations, human resource management, sales, finance/accounting, and R & D	past one week	Team creativity (M = 3.52, SD = 0.51)	Team leaders	PGAT: r = .40 (M = 3.30, SD = 0.57)	N/A	Team collective efficacy
Shin (2014, SGR)	98 work teams with different functions: planning and strategy, sales, human resource management and development, R & D, finance and accounting, and marketing	past one week	Team creativity (M = 3.40, SD = 0.61)	Team leaders	PGAT: r = .40 (M = 3.32, SD = 0.41) NGAT: r = –.24 (M = 2.14, SD = 0.43)	N/A	Team reflexivity, team promotion focus: PGAT is positively related to team reflexivity and promotion focus, which in turn increases team creativity. NGAT is unrelated to team prevention focus

Table 10.1: Review of empirical evidence regarding the GAT–team creativity relationship (continued)

Article	Types of team	Timeframe of GAT	Creative outcomes	Rating sources	GAT–creativity relationship	Moderators and findings	Mediators and findings
Jones and Kelly (2009, GD)	80 student teams and 120 individuals	manipulating GAT by watching movies	Slogan-generation tasks	Two research assistants	Groups in negative moods generated more creative slogans than individuals in negative moods	N/A	Time spent on the tasks
Grawitch, Munz, and Kramer (2003, GD)	57 student teams	manipulating GAT by imaginary tasks	Team creativity/ assessed using 'Real Estate Appraisal Sheet'	Two independent raters	Groups with positive moods are more creative than groups with neutral and negative moods	N/A	Task focus
Rhee (2006)	72 student teams	manipulating GAT by recalling and writing tasks	Team creativity/ assessed using 'space survival' tasks	Two independent raters	PGAT: r = -.02	N/A	Broadening-and-building interactions

Figure 10.1: Conceptual framework

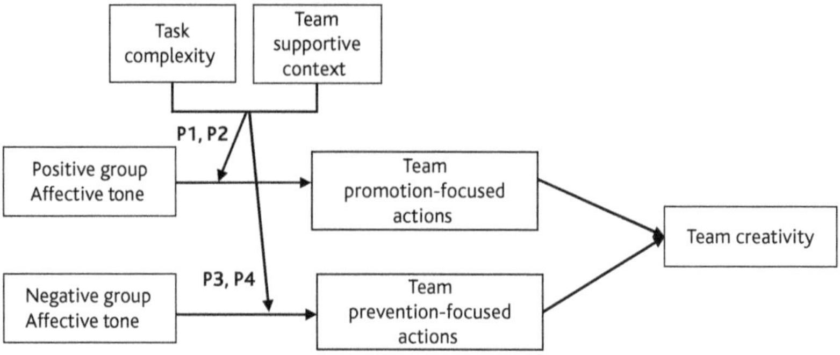

fluctuations in GAT and employing the experience sampling design to explore how within-team fluctuations in GAT influence team processes and creativity; (2) exploring how affective diversity in team members' affective traits and states influence team creativity; and (3) investigating how team members' personality traits influence the effects of PGAT/NGAT on team creativity via different pathways. The conceptual model is presented in Figure 10.1.

Positive group affective tone and team creativity

As Barsade and Knight (2015) noted, the theorizing behind the GAT–team creativity relationship has been grounded in theories at the individual level. For example, previous studies have used affect-as-information theory (Schwarz and Clore, 2003) to explain the relationship between PGAT and creativity. These studies contend that individuals' information processing is guided by their current mood states: positive moods signal a safe situation, in which 'good progress has been made and more effort may not be needed' (George, 2011). Specifically, positive moods signal a safe and unproblematic situation, which leads individuals to feel relatively unconstrained and promotes a top-down, less effortful and heuristic information processing (Baas, De Dreu, and Nijstad, 2008; George and Zhou, 2007). These facilitate more expansive and divergent thinking as well as playfulness, leading individuals to take risks and to explore new possibilities (Clore, Gasper, and Garvin, 2001; Schwarz, 2012). At the team level, when members collectively experience positive moods within teams, the aforementioned functions of positive moods can help members to make new connections between relevant information and propose novel ideas during team interactions (George and King, 2007). Supporting the prediction of the affect-as-information perspective, Grawitch, Munz, and Kramer (2003) conducted a laboratory study and found that teams with PGAT generated more original ideas than teams in neutral moods. In the organizational settings, Tsai et al (2012) found that PGAT increases team creativity, but only when team trust is low.

Second, several researchers used the broaden-and-build theory of positive emotions (Fredrickson, 1998, 2001) to explain the association between PGAT and team creativity (for example, Kim and Shin, 2015; Rhee, 2006; Shin, 2014; Shin, Kim, and Lee, 2019). The broaden-and-build theory suggests that positive emotions broaden individual thought-action repertoires and scope of attention, which facilitates divergent thinking and leads individuals to explore new possibilities. These in turn help individuals to build enduring resources to cope with difficult situations (Fredrickson, 1998, 2001). In general, both theoretical perspectives suggest that PGAT broadens members' focus and thinking (Schwarz, 2012) as well as enhances members' cognitive flexibility, enabling them to process information in a more flexible and integrative way (Bless and Fiedler, 2006; Schwarz, 2012), which leads members to generate more useful and novel ideas. In support of the broaden-and-build perspective, Rhee's (2006) laboratory study indicated that PGAT increases team creativity via enhancing broadening-and-building interactions (for example, building on ideas, morale-building communication). In the organizational context, Shin (2014) found that PGAT is positively related to team reflexivity (that is, team members collectively reflect on and communicate about the teams' objectives and processes; West, 1996) and team promotion focus (that is, members' collective motivations to approach positive outcomes; Rietzschel, 2011), which in turn facilitate team creativity. Similarly, in a survey-based study of 97 work teams, Kim and Shin (2015) suggested that PGAT leads to higher team creativity via enhancing collective efficacy (that is, members' shared beliefs in the team's capacity to achieve team goals). Finally, Chi (2019) found that PGAT promotes higher team creativity by increasing the degree to which team members share and exchange work-related knowledge and information (that is, team information exchange; Gong et al, 2013).

Although the review reveals that PGAT benefits team creativity by facilitating promotion-focused actions (for example, team reflexivity and team information exchange) and states (for example, team promotion focus and collective efficacy), only a few studies have explored the boundary conditions of the PGAT–team creativity linkage, and their results are mixed and divergent (see Table 10.1). First, some studies find that PGAT is unrelated or negatively related to team creativity when the context is supportive. For example, Tsai et al (2012) found that PGAT is negatively related to team creativity when team trust is high. Similarly, Chi (2019) proposed the substituting perspective to explain the PGAT–team creativity association. In this view, supervisory support may substitute for the beneficial effects of PGAT in team creativity: PGAT is unrelated to team creativity when supervisory support is high, whereas PGAT becomes salient for team creativity when supervisory support is absent. Using 122 R & D teams as the research sample, the results were consistent with the substituting perspective. Interestingly, using 121 teams with diversified team tasks, Shin, Kim, and Lee (2019) found a completely different pattern: a high level of transformational leadership pronounces the positive indirect effects of PGAT on team creativity and change-oriented citizenship behaviours via team reflexivity. As a result, it remains unclear whether contextual factors (especially, a supportive context) strengthen or weaken the relationship between PGAT and team creativity.

In addition, although team researchers have highlighted the importance of team task characteristics on team processes and outcomes (for example, Campbell, 1988; McGrath, 1984), previous studies have yet explicitly focused on how task characteristics influences the effectiveness of PGAT on team creativity (George and King, 2007). According to the single-reality and group centrism perspectives, George and King (2007) theorized that PGAT might lead to the development of a single-shared reality that promotes overconfidence or group centrism problems in the real teams with complex tasks and equivocal information (for example, R & D teams). Similarly, Kelly and Spoor (2007) proposed that the effects of PGAT on team processes and consequences will be different based on the team task type (that is, creativity, friendship, decision-making, and sports team). Though PGAT leads to positive interpersonal consequences, such as increased agreement and cohesion as well as better communication among members, participants also believe that PGAT can distract members from their tasks and reduce careful information processing, especially for task-oriented teams (that is, creativity and decision-making teams). Using the construction management teams as the research sample, Wu and Wang (2015) found that task variety moderates the association between PGAT and team proactivity. The aforementioned evidence highlights the importance of considering how team task types may moderate the PGAT–team creativity relationship.

Overall, this review of the current literature suggests that PGAT is generally good for team creativity. However, whether a supportive team context can enhance or attenuate the beneficial effect of PGAT on team creativity is not clear. Furthermore, studies have rarely explicitly tested the contingent effect of team tasks on the association between PGAT and team creativity. In the next section, I will briefly review the current progress regarding the evidence for the effects of NGAT.

Negative group affective tone and team creativity

Similar to the literature in PGAT, scholars have theorized how NGAT influences team creative outcomes based on theories at the individual-level (Barsade and Knight, 2015). However, there are different theoretical expectations for the NGAT–team creativity relationship. On the one hand, grounded in the affect-as-information theory, several researchers have suggested that NGAT signals a problematic and dangerous situation in which greater effort is needed to identify and solve potential problems, thereby leading to a more systematic information processing style (Kooij-de Bode, van Knippenberg, and van Ginkel, 2010). The detail-oriented information processing activated by NGAT helps team members to critically review and evaluate the information at hand, which might increase the elaboration of task-related information in teams (George and King, 2007). When team members thoroughly consider and elaborate task-related knowledge and information, team members are able to propose the ideas with higher quality and usefulness (Hoever, Zhou, and van Knippenberg, 2018).

On the other hand, building on the individual-level threat–rigidity hypothesis, Rhee (2007) theorized that NGAT limits the range of possible reactions by team members and leads them to focus on specific actions and narrow their thought–action repertoires. The threat–rigidity hypothesis suggests that external threats and/or pressure would lead team members to seek consensus to respond to such dangerous situations efficiently (Staw, Sandelands, and Dutton, 1981). Hence, team members narrow the scope of their attention and restrict the amount of information processed, leading them to ignore divergent information, resulting in rigid responses (Gladstein and Reilly, 1985). Rhee (2007) further theorized that such restricted and rigid responses trigger members' outcome-based interactions, including monitoring each member's behaviours to meet the deadline and rejecting others' ideas. These all hamper team creativity.

Unlike the PGAT literature, the empirical findings for the NGAT–team creativity relationship are highly divergent and mixed. Employing a survey-based research design, Tsai et al (2012) found that NGAT is negatively related to team creativity in R & D teams. Using 98 work teams as the research sample, Shin (2014) also indicated that NGAT was negatively associated with team creativity and that team prevention focus did not explain this association. Using experiments to induce members' emotions, Jones and Kelly (2009) reported that NGAT leads members to show dissatisfaction with the current situation and strive for better ideas, thereby generating more creative ideas (for example, slogans). However, Grawitch, Munz, and Kramer (2003) found that NGAT has no effect on team creativity in their experiments. Finally, focusing on team members' mean-level of negative affectivity, Kooij-de Bode, Van Knippenberg, and Van Ginkel (2010) found that teams with NGAT (a high mean level of negative affectivity) can make better decisions when information was distributed within teams.

The inconsistent findings on the relationship between NGAT and team creativity may suggest the existence of moderators. For example, Tsai et al (2012) found a complex three-way interaction among PGAT, NGAT, and team trust on team creativity. They found that NGAT can increase team creativity, but only when PGAT is low and team trust is high. This finding seems to suggest that NGAT may increase team creativity in a supportive team context (for example, team trust), but more theoretical and empirical work is needed to support this contention. However, as shown in Table 10.1, only a few studies have examined boundary conditions of the relationship between NGAT and team creativity.

Second, although George and King (2007) argued that PGAT may have potential negative consequences for teams with complex team tasks, they also theorized that NGAT may be helpful in mitigating single-shared reality and group centrism in such teams. These, in turn, promote minority dissent and realistic fact-driven consideration of potential problems. However, they also noted that NGAT is not always beneficial for all types of teams, suggesting that team type may serve as the boundary condition. Supporting this assertion, Higgs, Plewnia, and Ploch (2005) found that diversified teams (members often experience NGAT; Philips and Lount, 2007) can produce better team outcomes for complex team tasks. Kelly and Spoor (2007) proposed that the benefits of NGAT, such as systematic and detailed-oriented information processing, are more important for task-oriented teams (for example, creativity, problem-solving, and decision-making). Although participants in their study believe that NGAT can produce negative interpersonal consequences (for example, increased disagreement or conflicts), they also indicated that NGAT facilitates active task behaviours and produces greater attention to detail in task-oriented groups.

Overall, this review of the current literature on NGAT suggests that NGAT is not always harmful to team creativity. The effects of NGAT on team creativity may depend on the team supportive context as well as the team task type. It is plausible that NGAT promotes more creative ideas, especially for teams with supportive context and complex tasks.

A dual pathway model

To address identified unanswered questions, I propose a dual pathway model to integrate the mechanisms and boundary conditions for the effects of PGAT and NGAT on team creativity as well as providing a more balanced view regarding the effects of PGAT and NGAT. Specifically, I propose that PGAT increases team creativity via the promotion-focused pathway, whereas NGAT leads to team creativity through the prevention-focused pathway. Importantly, the strengths of the two pathways depend on the team supportive context and team task complexity. In the following sections, I will elaborate on this model first, then develop several empirically testable propositions, which may be the focus of future studies.

Promotion-focused pathway: The moderating roles of task complexity and the team supportive context

As mentioned earlier, the mood-as-information and broaden-and-build theory suggest that PGAT signals a safe and playful situation, which promotes a less effortful information-processing as well as broadens members' thought–action repertoires and scope of attention (George, 2011; Rhee, 2007). These elements enhance team members' shared beliefs and collective motivations to achieve desirable outcomes (Kim and Shin, 2015; Shin, 2014) and lead team members to communicate about the team's goals and share task-related information to pursue positive consequences (Chi, 2019; Shin, Kim, and Lee, 2019). These promotion-focused states and actions, in turn, boost team creativity (Gong et al, 2013; Shin, 2014). Building on these findings, I further theorize that the strength of this promotion-focused pathway depends on the interplay between task complexity and the team supportive context.

Task complexity refers to the predictability of team tasks (De Dreu and Weingart, 2003), which may influence the complexity of team working methods as well as the requirements of information-processing. For teams with less complex tasks (for example, functional planning, services and sales, or manufacturing teams), members engage in simple and routine tasks, such as routine discussion and planning, routine execution decisions, services with standardized procedures, and standardized tasks in production and manufacturing (De Dreu and Weingart, 2003). For teams with complex tasks (for example, R & D teams), members perform more uncertain, difficult, and dynamic tasks, such as designing a new product, creating a brand new system, and non-routine production tasks (George and King, 2007). As noted by George and King (2007), for teams working on complex tasks, members have to collect diverse information and consider alternative views in order to deal with difficult and uncertain tasks. Hence, team members will have to employ more extensive, critical, and substantive processing strategies when performing these types of team tasks (Forgas, 1995). Thus, the information-processing strategies required for the complex team tasks are not congruent with the information-processing promoted by PGAT, which might attenuate the beneficial effect of PGAT.

Furthermore, the effect of PGAT on team creativity via a promotion-focused pathway when teams face complex task will be further influenced by the team supportive context. Tsai et al (2012) have proposed that PGAT with a supportive team context might lead to the development of a single shared reality and formation of group centrism (that is, members strive to maintain the coherence and agreement within teams). Specifically, PGAT informs team members that everything is well and the current situation and safe, enhancing teams' sense of optimism (Gibson and Earley, 2007). This effect will be exacerbated in a supportive team context (for example, members are confident with other members' abilities or believe that the supervisors will fully support their teams), leading team members to move towards consensus within teams, conservatism, rejection of divergent ideas, and resistance to change (Kruglanski et al, 2006). These tendencies are inconsistent with the information-processing required for complex tasks, which may prevent members from engaging in creative processes, thus harming overall team creativity (Tsai et al, 2012). Although no known studies have directly tested this proposition, I can find some initial evidence from recent studies. For example, using 68 R & D teams as a research sample (that is, teams with complex tasks), Tsai et al (2012) found that PGAT with a supportive team context (that is, high team trust) reduces team creativity. Similarly, by collecting data from 122 R & D teams (again, teams with complex tasks), Chi (2019) indicated that PGAT reduces team creativity via inhibiting team information exchange, when supervisor support is high. Based on the above, the following is proposed:

Proposition 1: for teams with complex tasks, the positive effect of PGAT on team creativity via the promotion-focused pathway will be attenuated when teams are more supportive.

Yet, PGAT can be beneficial for creativity in teams with both simple tasks and a supportive team context. Simple and routine tasks represent a relatively familiar and certain team environment, which places minimum cognitive demands on team members (Zhang and Kwan, 2018). When the team tasks are simple, certain, and typical (for example, routine planning and design in logistics and routine execution tasks in production and manufacturing; De Dreu and Weingart, 2003), team members need only to develop routines to specify the standardized procedures (Zhang and Kwan, 2018). Thus, team members are more likely to take actions based on these procedures (Zhang and Kwan, 2018) and employ heuristic processing, which produces the responses with the least amount of effort (Forgas and George, 2001). Hence, the less systematic and effortful information-processing promoted by PGAT will be more efficient for teams with simple team tasks, and the supportive context may further enhance this effect since team members are confident in themselves and/or believe that their leaders will fully support the team's actions. Shin, Kim, and Lee (2019) collected data regarding PGAT and team creativity from 116 work teams with less complex team tasks, including managerial support (33.6 per cent), planning (27.6 per cent), finance/accounting (13.8 per cent), and sales and marketing (19.8 per cent). Supporting our proposition, they found that the positive indirect effect of PGAT on team creativity via team reflexivity was more pronounced in a supportive team context (that is, high levels of transformational leadership). Based on the aforementioned theoretical perspectives and empirical evidence, the following is proposed

Proposition 2: for teams with simple tasks, the positive effect of PGAT on team creativity via the promotion-focused pathway will be strengthened when teams are more supportive.

Prevention-focused pathway: The moderating roles of task complexity and the team supportive context

Based on the review above, NGAT may narrow team members' thought–action repertoires and range of attention due to the threat–rigidity perspective (Staw, Sandelands, and Dutton, 1981), leading members to focus on task-related actions such as planning, monitoring, and critical evaluations (Rhee, 2007). Although these actions help to complete the team tasks, they also restrict the exploration of divergent and creative ideas. However, based on the mood-as-information perspective (Schwarz and Clore, 2003), George and King (2007) suggested that NGAT alerts the team members to identify potential problems regarding the current situations and activates a detailed-oriented information-processing to critically review the information at hands. Such systematic information-processing also increases team creativity via improving the usefulness of ideas (Hoever, Zhou, and Knippenberg, 2018). Although the two perspectives have divergent predictions regarding the relationship between NGAT and team creativity, both perspectives suggest that NGAT leads team members to take action to prevent problematic situations from occurring (that is, prevention-focused pathway), such as expressing concerns about current issues or identifying factors that may cause the team to fail to accomplish its tasks. To reconcile the conflicting predictions of the two perspectives, I further theorize how team task complexity and supportive context jointly influence the effect of NGAT on team creativity.

When team members perform complex and unusual tasks, they need to engage in substantive information-processing to interpret ambiguous information and understand the current situation (Forgas, 1995; Forgas and George, 2001). The careful, detailed-oriented, and systematic information-processing triggered by NGAT is particularly useful for complex team tasks, since NGAT leads team members to carefully analyze ambiguous and atypical information and identify potential problems (George and King, 2007). However, the mere existence of NGAT is insufficient to enhance team creativity because of a lack of motivation and clear direction in performing complex tasks. Baas, De Dreu, and Nijstad (2008) noted that negative moods increase individual effort in creative tasks only when tasks are perceived as serious/important and performance and extrinsic rewards are emphasized. Similarly, George and Zhou (2002) also theorized that negative moods can promote creativity when the context is perceived as supporting and rewarding creativity. Applying these arguments to team settings, when the team tasks are complex and team members perceive their team context as supporting and rewarding creativity, the prevention-focused actions (that is, carefully review and analyze the information to come up with useful solutions) activated by NGAT will be further strengthened since team members are encouraged and rewarded to pursue creative thoughts to fulfill complex team tasks.

Based on the sample of 47 R & D teams (again, teams with complex tasks), Chi and Chen (2014) indicated that NGAT increases team innovation when members' perceived rewards for innovation were high, whereas this relationship became negative when perceived rewards for innovation were low. These findings are consistent with our argument that a supportive context (for example, rewards for innovation) is essential for teams with NGAT to boost creativity when performing complex tasks. Hence, I propose the following proposition:

> *Proposition 3: for teams with complex tasks, NGAT will have a stronger positive effect on team creativity via the prevention-focused pathway when teams are more supportive.*

By contrast, NGAT might have no effect or even a negative effect on team creativity for teams with simple tasks. Simple team tasks are relatively familiar, certain, and typical, which require a less systematic and effortful information-processing (Forgas and George, 2001). For simple team tasks, it is not necessary to carefully review and elaborate task-related information since the tasks are routine and the external environment is certain (Zhang and Kwan, 2018). Therefore, the careful and detailed-oriented information-processing triggered by NGAT is incongruent with the requirements of simple team tasks, thereby inhibiting the benefits of NGAT on identifying potential problems and proposing better solutions. Furthermore, when performing simple team tasks in a certain environment (for example, laboratory settings without external threats or time pressure), NGAT may lead members to focus their activities on intragroup relationships rather than tasks (Grawitch, Munz, and Kramer, 2003), since the tasks only place minimum cognitive demands on team members (Zhang and Kwan, 2018). Similarly, Kelly and Spoor (2007) found that participants believe that the prevention-focused actions triggered by NGAT (for example, showing disagreement, overly criticizing others' ideas and thoughts) may produce negative interpersonal consequences in creativity groups within laboratory settings.

As noted earlier, the prevention-focused actions activated by NGAT may impair interpersonal processes rather than improve tasked-related processes when the team tasks are simple (Grawitch, Munz, and Kramer, 2003; Kelly and Spoor, 2007). The aforementioned detrimental effects of NGAT on team creativity might be further exacerbated when the team context is *less* supportive. When the team context is less supportive (for example, team members do not trust each other, there is a lack of support from others), the prevention-focused actions promoted by NGAT (for example, monitoring, critically reviewing, displaying disagreement) are more likely to create tension and conflicts among team members since the members do not trust each other. These, in turn, hamper team creativity (Rhee, 2007). Based on the above, the final proposition is proposed:

> *Proposition 4: for a team with simple tasks, NGAT will have a negative effect on team creativity via the prevention-focused pathway, when teams are less supportive.*

Theoretical extension and emerging areas in the GAT-creativity field

Although this chapter has identified unanswered questions in the GAT–team creativity field and offered several testable propositions, several emerging areas that help to advance our understanding in the GAT literature are further discussed in this section.

How dynamics and fluctuation of group affective tone influence team creativity

By definition, GAT is viewed as the composition of team members' affective 'states' (George, 1990; Collins et al, 2013) and group affect researchers have made clear distinction between state and trait group affect (for example, Barsade et al, 2000; van Knippenberg, Kooij-de Bode, and van Ginkel, 2010). However, as I summarized in Table 10.1, most research in the GAT-creativity field has measured PGAT or NGAT at a single time point or using a timeframe (for example, past one week or two weeks) that falls between the state/trait affect. Although I fully understand the difficulty of collecting team-level data across multiple time points, this one-shot approach fails to capture the dynamic changes and fluctuations in GAT (Collins et al, 2013). Since positive or negative events (for example, making good progress in team tasks or receiving negative feedback from the team managers) may occur at any point within team interactions and the generation of creative ideas is an ongoing process, it is more appropriate to measure GAT and team creative processes by employing the event-contingent experience sampling method (that is, asking team members to report key events in their team interactions and provide ratings after the occurrence of events; Beal, 2015).

To my knowledge, only one study has employed the experience sampling method to capture how the fluctuations and dynamic changes in PGAT/NGAT influence team performance outcomes over time, that of Paulsen et al (2016). By collecting data from 34 software engineering project teams over 14 weeks, Paulsen et al (2016) found that weekly PGAT is positively related to and weekly NGAT is negatively related to weekly progress in team performance. Interestingly, these weekly GAT–performance relationships became stronger in the second half of the project (when the deadline of the project is approaching). A study of military teams preparing for a prestigious competition, conducted by Knight (2015), found that PGAT in the second half of the project leads to a decline in exploratory searching activities, which improves subsequent team performance. By contrast, NGAT at the midpoint sustains team members' exploratory efforts over the second half of the project, thereby hindering subsequent team performance. Although Knight (2015) did not actually employ the experience sampling design, he did collect data regarding PGAT, NGAT, and team exploratory searching three times and incorporated the role of time into his theoretical model. The aforementioned pair of studies provide excellent examples of capturing the dynamics and fluctuations of GAT. I highly recommend that future researchers employ the event-contingent experience sampling method to test how PGAT and NGAT influence team promotion- and prevention-focused actions and creative outcomes over time and explore how the context influences the effects of PGAT and NGAT over time.

How affective diversity in group affective tone influences team creativity

Although George (1990, 1996) conceptualized GAT as homogenous and consistent affective states among team members, another line of group affect research has focused on how affective diversity or divergence influences team performance outcomes (for example, Barsade et al, 2000; Kaplan, LaPort, and Waller, 2013). Using 62 top management teams as the research sample, Barsade et al (2000) found that team members' diversity in trait positive affectivity was positively related to team conflicts and negatively related to team cooperation. However, team members' diversity in trait negative affectivity had no effect on team processes. In a field study of nuclear power plant crews, Kaplan, LaPort, and Waller (2013) also reported that team members' diversity in trait positive affectivity reduced team effectiveness via increasing negative emotions during team interactions (that is, the crisis simulation). Overall, the findings of previous field studies appear to suggest that less affective diversity (or affective homogeneity) is beneficial for team functions.

Although both studies have focused on the diversity in affective 'traits' rather than 'states', George and King (2007) have theorized that diversity in members' affective states (that is, affective heterogeneity) can facilitate creative outcomes by fully exploiting the diverse knowledge, experience, and information-processing within teams. George and King (2007) proposed that diversity in members' affective states differs from diversity in affective traits in several ways. First, diversity in affective states is determined by both contextual factors and affective traits. Second, contextual factors might influence affective states, but not affective traits. Hence, team members' affective diversity in traits or states may have differing implications for team creativity. Recently, Emich and Vincent (2020) have tested how affective diversity in team members' moods influences team creativity. By conducting three laboratory studies involving 427 student teams, Emich and Vincent (2020) found that affective homogeneity in promotion-focused positive moods (for example, happiness) or negative moods (for example, anger) increases team creativity, whereas affective homogeneity in prevention-focused negative moods (for example, tension, fear) reduces team creativity. In looking at affective heterogeneity, they found that when team members experience both activated promotion-focused moods and deactivated moods, members with activated promotion-focused moods dominate the creative process. Emich and Vincent's (2020) results clearly show the complicated patterns shaping association between affective heterogeneity/homogeneity and team creativity. To further address this issue, I encourage future researchers to incorporate both affective heterogeneity/homogeneity into our theoretical model, and employ different conceptualizations (for example, mean, SD, or rwg values of group affective tone) to examine whether affective heterogeneity/homogeneity triggers team creativity via promotion-focused or prevention-focused pathways.

How team members' personality traits influence the effects of group affective tone on team creativity

So far I have reviewed and theorized how contextual factors such as team tasks and supportive context influence the effects of PGAT and NGAT on team creativity. However, no known studies have attempted to investigate how team members' personality traits influence the effects of PGAT or NGAT on team creativity. It is surprising, since team members' personality traits may influence their interpretations of, as well as their reactions to, PGAT or NGAT (Chi and Huang, 2014; Ilies, Wagner, and Morgeson, 2007). Although PGAT facilitates team creativity via triggering promotion-focused actions (for example, information-sharing and exchanging), team members with high levels of emotional skills (for example, managing others' emotions) are able to reap the benefits of PGAT while avoiding the downsides of PGAT (for example, lack of attention to the task, overconfidence) (Collins et al, 2016).

NGAT, by contrast, serves as a negative feedback regarding insufficiency in goal progress and a problematic situation on its own (George and King, 2007). Therefore, how team members respond to negative signals may depend on their personality traits related to goal-related self-regulation. For example, researchers have indicated that learning-oriented individuals (that is, individual tendency to develop competence and acquire new skills; Dweck, 1999) tend to seek out challenges and to persist in difficult situations (Alexander and van Knippenberg, 2014). In addition, they view the risk of failure as opportunities for learning rather than threats. Therefore, team members' average level in learning and developing new skills (that is, team learning goal orientation; TLGO) may influence team members' interpretation as well as reactions to the signals conveyed by NGAT. Overall, it will be fruitful for future researchers to integrate different facets of members' personality traits into our model based on various theoretical perspectives, and investigate how these traits change the strength of the effects of PGAT and NGAT on team creativity via promotion- or prevention-focused pathways.

References

Alexander, L. and Van Knippenberg, D. (2014). Teams in pursuit of radical innovation: A goal orientation perspective. *Academy of Management Review*, 39(4), 423–38.

Baas, M., De Dreu, C. K. W., and Nijstad, B. A. (2008). A meta-analysis of 25 years of mood-creativity research: Hedonic tone, activation, or regulatory focus? *Psychological Bulletin*, 134(6), 779–806.

Barsade, S. G. (2002). The ripple effect: Emotional contagion and its influence on group behavior. *Administrative Science Quarterly*, 47, 644–75.

Barsade, S. G., Ward, A. J., Turner, J. D.F., and Sonnenfeld, J. A. (2000). To your heart's content: A model of affective diversity in top management teams. *Administrative Science Quarterly*, 45, 802–36.

Barsade, S. and Knight, A. P. (2015). Group affect. *Annual Review of Organizational Psychology and Organizational Behavior*, 2, 21–46.

Beal, D. J. (2015). ESM 2.0: State of the art and future potential of experience sampling methods in organizational research. *Annual Review of Organizational Psychology and Organizational Behavior*, 2, 383–407.

Bless, H. and Fiedler, K. (2006). Mood and the regulation of information processing and behavior. In J. P. Forgas (ed), *Affect in Social Thinking and Behavior*, New York: Psychology Press, pp 65–84.

Campbell, D. J. (1988). Task complexity: A review and analysis, *Academy of Management Review*, 13(1), 40–52.

Chi, N. W. (2019). Is support always good? Exploring whether supervisory support enhances or attenuates the beneficial effect of positive group affective tone on team and individual creativity. *Research on Emotion in Organizations*, 15, 133–57.

Chi, N. W. and Chen, L. (2014). Can negative group affective tone facilitate team innovation? Exploring the moderating roles of innovation rewards and team promotion focus. *Unpublished Manuscript*.

Chi, N. W. and Huang, J. C. (2014). Mechanisms linking transformational leadership and team performance: The mediating roles of team goal orientation and group affective tone. *Group and Organization Management*, 39, 300–25.

Chi, N. W., Chung, Y. Y., and Tsai, W. C. (2011). How do happy leaders enhance team performance? The mediating roles of transformational leadership, group affective tone and team processes. *Journal of Applied Social Psychology*, 41, 1421–54.

Clore, G. L., Gasper, K., and Garvin, E. (2001). Affect as information. In J. P. Forgas (ed), *Handbook of Affect and Social Cognition*, Mahwah, NJ: Lawrence Erlbaum Associates Publishers, pp 121–44.

Collins, A. L., Jordan, P. J., Lawrence, S. A., and Troth, A. C. (2016). Positive affective tone and team performance: The moderating role of collective emotional skills. *Cognition and Emotion*, 30(1), 167–82.

Collins, A. L., Lawrence, S. A., Troth, A. C., and Jordan, P. J. (2013). Group affective tone: A review and future research directions. *Journal of Organizational Behavior*, 34, 43–62.

Crant, J. M. (2000). Proactive behavior in organizations. *Journal of Management*, 26, 435–62.

De Dreu, C. K. W., and Weingart, L. R. (2003). A contingency theory of task conflict and performance in groups and organizational teams. In M. A. West, D. Tjosvold, and K. G. Smith (eds), *International Handbook of Organizational Teamwork and Cooperative Working*, Chichester: John Wiley and Sons, Ltd, pp 151–66.

Dweck, C. S. (1999). *Self-theories: Their role in motivation, personality, and development.* Ann Arbor, MI: Psychology Press.

Emich, K. J. and Vincent, L. C. (2020). Shifting focus: The influence of affective diversity on team creativity. *Organizational Behavior and Human Decision Processes*, 156, 24–37.

Forgas, J. P. (1995). Mood and judgment: The affect infusion model (AIM). *Psychological Bulletin,* 117(1), 39–66.

Forgas, J. P. and George, J. M. (2001). Affective influences on judgments and behavior in organizations: An information processing perspective. *Organizational Behavior and Human Decision Processes,* 86(1), 3–34.

Fredrickson, B. L. (1998). What good are positive emotions? *Review of General Psychology,* 2(3), 300–19.

Fredrickson, B. L. (2001). The role of positive emotions in positive psychology: The broaden-and-build theory of positive emotions. *American Psychologist,* 56(3), 218–26.

Gamero, N., González-Romá, V., and Peiró, J. M. (2008). The influence of intra-team conflict on work teams' affective climate: A longitudinal study. *Journal of Occupational and Organizational Psychology,* 81(1), 47–69.

George, J. M. (1990). Personality, affect, and behavior in groups. *Journal of Applied Psychology,* 75, 107–16.

George, J. M. (1995). Leader positive mood and group performance: The case of customer service. *Journal of Applied Social Psychology,* 25, 778–94.

George, J. M. (1996). Group affective tone. In M. A. West (ed), *Handbook of Work Group Psychology*, Chichester: Wiley, pp 77–93.

George, J. M. (2011). Dual tuning: A minimum condition for understanding affect in organizations? *Organizational Psychology Review,* 1(2), 147–64.

George, J. M. and King, E. B. (2007). Potential pitfalls of affect convergence in teams: Functions and dysfunctions of group affective tone. In E. A. Mannix, M. A. Neale, and C. P. Anderson (eds), *Research on Managing Groups and Teams*, vol 10, Greenwich, CT: JAI Press, pp 97–124.

George, J. M. and Zhou, J. (2002). Understanding when bad moods foster creativity and good ones don't: The role of context and clarity of feelings. *Journal of Applied Psychology,* 87, 687–97.

George, J. M. and Zhou, J. (2007). Dual tuning in a supportive context: Joint contributions of positive mood, negative mood, and supervisory behaviors to employee creativity. *Academy of Management Journal,* 50, 605–22.

Gibson, C. B. and Earley, P. C. (2007). Collective cognition in action: Accumulation interaction, examination, and accommodation in the development and operation of group efficacy beliefs in the workplace. *The Academy of Management Review,* 32(2), 438–58.

Gladstein, D. L. and Reilly, N. P. (1985). Group decision making under threat: The Tycoon game. *Academy of Management Journal,* 28(3), 613–27.

Gong, Y., Kim, T. Y., Zhu, J., and Lee, D. R. (2013). A multilevel model of team goal orientation, information exchange, and creativity. *Academy of Management Journal,* 56, 827–51.

Grawitch, M. J., Munz, D. C., and Kramer, T. J. (2003). Effects of member mood states on creative performance in temporary workgroups. *Group Dynamics: Theory, Research, and Practice, 7,* 41–54.

Griffin, M. A., Neal, A., and Parker, S. K. (2007). A new model of work role performance: Positive behavior in uncertain and interdependent contexts. *Academy of Management Journal,* 5: 327–47.

Higgs, M., Plewnia, U., and Ploch, J. (2005). Influence of team composition and task complexity on team performance. *Team Performance Management,* 11, 227–50.

Hoever, I. J., Zhou, J., and van Knippenberg, D. (2018). Different strokes for different teams: The contingent effects of positive and negative feedback on the creativity of informationally homogeneous and diverse teams. *Academy of Management Journal,* 61(6), 2159–81.

Ilies, R., Wagner, D. T., and Morgeson, F. P. (2007). Explaining affective linkages in teams: Individual differences in susceptibility to contagion and individualism-collectivism. *Journal of Applied Psychology,* 92(4), 1140–8.

Jones, E. E. and Kelly, J. R. (2009). No pain, no gains: Negative mood leads to process gains in idea-generation groups. *Group Dynamics: Theory, Research, and Practice,* 13(2), 75–88.

Kaplan, S., LaPort, K., and Waller, M. J. (2013). The role of positive affectivity in team effectiveness during crises. *Journal of Organizational Behavior,* 34(4), 473–91.

Kelly, J. R. and Spoor, J. R. (2007). Naïve theories about the effects of mood in groups: A preliminary investigation. *Group Processes and Intergroup Relations,* 10, 203–22.

Kim, M. and Shin, Y. (2015). Collective efficacy as a mediator between cooperative group norms and group positive affect and team creativity. *Asia Pacific Journal of Management,* 32(3), 693–716.

Knight, A. P. and Eisenkraft, N. (2015). Positive is usually good, negative is not always bad: The effects of group affect on social integration and task performance. *Journal of Applied Psychology,* 100, 1214–27.

Kooij-de Bode, H. J., Van Knippenberg, D., and Van Ginkel, W. P. (2010). Good effects of bad feelings: Negative affectivity and team decision-making. *British Journal of Management,* 21, 375–92.

Kruglanski, A. W., Pierro, A., Mannetti, L., and De Grada, E. (2006). Groups as epistemic providers: Need for closure and the unfolding of group-centrism. *Psychological Review,* 113(1), 84–100.

McGrath, J. E. (1984). *Groups: Interaction and performance.* Englewood Cliffs, NJ: Prentice Hall.

Parker, S. K. and Collins, C. G. (2010). Taking stock: Integrating and differentiating multiple proactive behaviors. *Journal of Management,* 36(3), 633–62.

Paulsen, H. F. K., Klonek, F. E., Schneider, K., and Kauffeld, S. (2016). Group affective tone and team performance: A week-level study in project teams. *Frontiers in Communication,* 1 (November), 1–10.

Phillips, K. W. and Lount, R. B. (2007). The affective consequences of diversity and homogeneity in groups. In E. A. Mannix, M. A. Neale, and C. P. Anderson (eds), *Research on Managing Groups and Teams*, vol 10, Greenwich, CT: JAI Press, pp 1–20.

Rhee, S. Y. (2006). Shared emotions and group effectiveness: The role of broadening-and-building interactions. In K. M. Weaver (ed), *Proceedings of the Sixty-Fifth Annual Meeting of the Academy of Management*, Briar Cliff, NY: Academy of Management, pp B1–B6.

Rhee, S. Y. (2007). Group emotions and group outcomes: The role of group-member interactions. In E. A. Mannix, M. A. Neale, and C. P. Anderson (eds), *Research on Managing Groups and Teams*. vol 10, Greenwich, CT: JAI Press, pp 65–96.

Rietzschel, E. F. (2011). Collective regulatory focus predicts specific aspects of team innovation. *Group Processes and Intergroup Relations,* 14(3), 337–45.

Schwarz, N. (2012). Feelings-as-information theory. In P. A. M. Van Lange, A. W. Kruglanski, and E. T. Higgins (eds), *Handbook of Theories of Social Psychology*, Thousand Oaks, CA: Sage Publications Ltd, pp 289–308.

Schwarz, N. and Clore, G. L. (2003). Mood as information. Psychological Inquiry, 14, 296–303.

Shin, S. J. and Zhou, J. (2007). When is educational specialization heterogeneity related to creativity in research and development teams? Transformational leadership as a moderator. *Journal of Applied Psychology,* 92, 1709–21.

Shin, Y. (2014). Positive group affect and team creativity: Mediation of team reflexivity and promotion focus. *Small Group Research,* 45(3), 337–64.

Shin, Y., Kim, M., and Lee, S. H. (2019). Positive group affective tone and team creative performance and change-oriented organizational citizenship behavior: A moderated mediation model. *Journal of Creative Behavior,* 53, 52–68.

Staw, B. M., Sandelands, L. E., and Dutton, J. E. (1981). Threat-rigidity effects in organizational behavior: A multilevel analysis. *Administrative Science Quarterly,* 26(4), 501–24.

Sy, T., Cote, S., and Saavedra, R. (2005). The contagious leader: Impact of the leader's mood on the mood of group members, group affective tone, and group processes. *Journal of Applied Psychology,* 90, 295–305.

Tsai, W. C., Chi, N. W., Grandey, A. A., and Fung, S. C. (2012). Exploring boundary conditions of the relationship between positive group affective tone and team creativity: Negative group affective tone and team trust as moderators. *Journal of Organizational Behavior,* 33, 638–56.

Unsworth, K, L. and Parker, S, K. (2003) Proactivity and innovation: promoting a new workforce for the new workplace. In D. Holman, T. D. Wall, C. W. Clegg, P. Sparrow, and A. Howard (eds) *The New Workplace: A Guide to the Human Impact of Modern Work Practices*, Chichester: Wiley, pp 175–96.

West, M. A. (1996). Reflexivity and work group effectiveness: A conceptual integration. In M. A. West (ed), *Handbook of Work Group Psychology*, Chichester: John Wiley, pp 555–79.

Wu, C.-H. and Wang, Z. (2015). How transformational leadership shapes team proactivity: The mediating role of positive affective tone and the moderating role of team task variety. *Group Dynamics: Theory, Research, and Practice*, 19, 137–51.

Zhang, X. and Kwan, H. K. (2018). Team learning goal orientation and innovation: Roles of transactive memory system and task interdependence. *GSL Journal of Business Management and Administration Affairs*, 1, 109–19.

Zhou, J. and Hoever, I. J. (2014). Research on workplace creativity: A review and redirection. *Annual Review of Organizational Psychology and Organizational Behavior*, 1, 333–59.

PART III

The Emotional Consequences
of Proactivity

11

Proactivity and Well-Being: Initiating Changes to Fuel Life Energy

Shunhong Ji, Zhijun Chen, and Francesco Cangiano

To cope with increasing uncertainty and complexity, organizations have adopted more flexible structures and managerial styles, encouraging their workforces to display proactive behaviours at work (Grant and Ashford, 2008; Liu et al, 2019; Parker, Williams, and Turner, 2006; Belschak and Den Hartog, 2011). These proactive behaviours, ranging from taking charge, voice and innovative behaviour to job crafting and issue selling, pertain to employees' self-initiated actions aiming to bring about improvements in the workplace (Frese and Fay, 2001; Griffin, Neal, and Parker, 2007; Parker and Collins, 2010). Due to their overall relevance to organizational competence and success, during the last decade organizational scholars have devoted much attention to identifying factors motivating employee proactive behaviours (see Cai et al, 2019; Parker, Williams and Turner, 2006; Parker, Bindl, and Strauss 2010 for reviews).

One conclusion from previous studies and these integrative reviews is that individual motivational states play an important role in driving various proactive behaviours, which can be further categorized into three groups as 'can do', 'reason to', and 'energized to' states (Parker, Bindl, and Strauss, 2010). While 'can do' refers to one's perceived capability in being proactive, 'reason to' captures individual perception of their obligation and duties to become proactive. Meanwhile, 'energized to' pertains to affective antecedents and processes driving individual proactive behaviour. In the current literature, 'can do' and 'reason to' mechanisms have received significant attention, whereas 'energized to' states such as affective experiences and emotions remain still somewhat underrepresented in the literature (Cai et al, 2019; Cangiano, Bindl, and Parekr, 2017). Furthermore, the majority of studies linking affective experiences with individual proactivity tended to focus on affect and emotions as antecedents of proactive behaviour, rather than as outcomes (Cai et al, 2019).

As an extension to the current literature, we propose well-being – an individual mental state that includes emotional and affective experiences (Linley and Joseph, 2004; Ryan and Deci, 2001), as important outcomes of individual proactive behaviour. Although little research has investigated the well-being consequences of proactive behaviour, it is a significant outcome for its effects on dealing with psychological stress and mental health in the workplace (Griffin, and Clarke, 2011). After reviewing this line of investigation, we find a considerable space for further theorizing this important relationship. Besides, and perhaps most importantly, highlights on well-being consequences would enrich our understanding about how to obtain sustainable proactivity over a longer period (Cangiano, Parker, and Yeo, 2019).

By initiating this theoretical shift, we aim to address three challenges the proactivity literature is facing. First, the proactivity-affective experience relationship is not well understood. Given its change-oriented nature, affect is naturally involved and plays an important role when an employee displays proactive behaviour at work (Bindl, 2018). Moreover, the proactive journey often involves multiple stages (Parker, Bindl, and Strauss, 2010; Perry-Smith and Mannuchi, 2017) such that initial engagement in proactivity can shape subsequent affect (Fay and Hüttges, 2017). As such, affect and emotions not only reflect personal experience and cognition in the process, but also transmit influences due to initial proactivity and link them with later proactive endeavours. Therefore, it is theoretically valuable to delineate why and how proactive behaviour shapes individual affective experience and well-being outcomes.

Second and relatedly, preliminary findings about how proactivity leads to affective experiences are largely mixed and inconclusive (Thomas, Whitman, and Viswesvaran, 2011; Tornau and Frese, 2013). On the one hand, some studies find proactivity leads to positive affect, by drawing on a need satisfaction rationale (for example, Bakker and Oerlemans, 2019; Singh, Ragins, and Tharenou, 2009). On the other hand, findings from a few other studies have shown an opposite pattern, suggesting that proactivity depletes employees' social-psychological resources (for example, Hagger et al, 2010). These controversial findings suggest a finely nuanced understanding of the emotional journey in the self-starting process. For instance, effort spared to sort out the theoretical framework to depict a comprehensive picture and distinguish the difference in research mechanisms or pathways will contribute beneficial insights to the fields of management and organizational behaviour.

Last but not least, there is still considerable space for further theorizing the proactivity–affect relationship, which is currently explained largely by the need satisfaction perspective and the resource depletion argument mentioned above. Though both perspectives have received empirical support, more recent advancement in the proactivity literature suggests after initial proactivity employees can experience other affective feelings (Bindl, 2018). These affective feelings differ from those predicted by the need satisfaction perspective or the resource depletion argument not only in terms of types of motivation, which focus on how proactive behaviours and their consequences are aligned with individual goals and purposes, but also with regard to purposes of motivation, which focus on how these alignments occur for distinctive purposes (Kanfer, Frese, and Johnson, 2017).

Consequently, our theorization of the proactivity–affect/well-being relationship aims to extend the proactivity literature by enriching current understanding of this important association. Our conceptual journey starts with a scientific mapping of the current literature to identify major themes and perspectives adopted in this line of investigation and their key findings. Then, we focus on the two established frameworks, namely the need satisfaction framework and the resource depletion rationale. Building on our analysis, we further discuss alternative pathways via which proactive behaviours may lead to affective outcomes, followed by a discussion about future research directions.

A quantitative review and scientific mapping

To make sense of this important research domain, we searched the Web of Science for empirical journal articles published in the fields of management, business, and applied psychology with keywords related to proactivity and well-being. First, we utilized an approach adopted by Cai et al (2019) to select keywords concerning proactive behaviour, including generic terms (for example, proactivity, proactive behaviour, self-initiated, personal initiative, and change-oriented citizenship) and distinct types of proactive behaviour (for example, taking charge, voice, issue-selling, and feedback-seeking). Meanwhile, in terms of the connotation, well-being is an individual mental state that includes emotional experiences and cognitive functioning (Ryan and Deci, 2001) and has been asserted as the core of positive psychology (Linley and Joseph, 2012). Thus, we searched well-being and life satisfaction using a broad set of search terms such as well-being, affectivity, emotion, and mood.

Combing both domains of research, we identified approximately 116 papers published between 2009 and 2019. After several rounds of literature retrieval, we then narrowed our list by checking whether the study was considered in a targeted organizational behaviour and context, and excluded ten papers. Among them, there were six papers discussing proactive emotion regulation (that is, how to manage emotional responses proactively) rather than investigating the role of proactive behaviour on individual experiences and well-being, and one study analyzed the seeking source profile and feedback-processing in safety management instead of feedback-seeking behaviour. At the same time, not in line with our content, two studies focused on impact of supervisor's voice endorsement on employees' job satisfaction and stress, and one study examined two mediating pathways, in which self-initiated and emotion acted as mutually independent mediators and existed no interaction. Moreover, we further removed five conceptual review articles and 45 papers that purely focus on how affective experiences shape individual engagement into proactive behaviours. Eventually, we settled on 56 relevant papers.

Next, we conducted a bibliographic analysis on these studies using a well-established technique of scientific mapping (for example, Parker, Morgeson, and Johns, 2017) to create visual representations of the key topics and connections among these topics. More specifically, we used a VOS (visualization of similarities) program, which has the advantage of generating better representations of the underlying data than alternative approaches, to calculate the relevance of terms and keywords and measured their co-occurrence tendency (with 627 links and total links strength of 998). These calculations became the input for our further analysis and visual mapping.

From this procedure, we identified four unique clusters of research topics in this field with each cluster representing strongly associated terms that pertain to a specific topic. Figure 11.1 is a graphic illustration of this mapping. As shown in Figure 11.1, the first cluster (red), labelled 'self-efficacy' and 'job satisfaction', reflects research largely rooted in the self-determination theory, which focuses on how proactive behaviour is

Figure 11.1: Scientific mapping of the relevant research

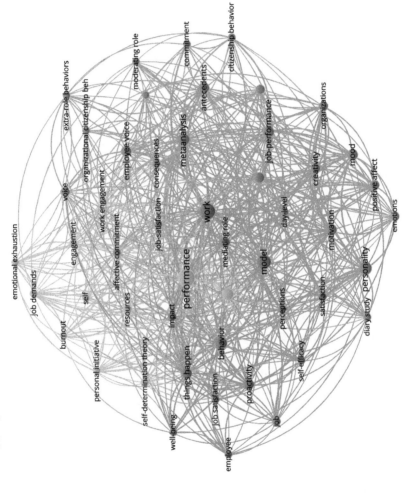

associated with enhanced self-confidence and well-being. The second cluster (yellow), labelled 'resources and emotional exhaustion', maps on to the resource-depletion argument and consider personal resource conservation or burnout as typical outcomes. Meanwhile, the third cluster (blue), labelled 'types of affects and emotions', refers to research focusing on different affective experiences and highlighting more diary studies to grasp them. The final cluster (green), labelled 'well-being and its evolution', focuses on the antecedents, moderators, and consequences of this process. What distinguishes this cluster from the others is its special emphasis on well-being outcomes of proactivity from a longer time frame and a dynamic perspective. Building on these findings, we then organize our review based on the major theoretical frameworks underpinning the existing literature.

A developmental perspective/pathway

Is proactivity beneficial to employee well-being? Some researchers believe so because proactive behaviours such as proactive information-seeking, voice, and network-building are positively associated with supervisory rating of job performance as supervisors may regard proactive employees as more creative and innovative (Binnewies, Ohly, and Sonnentag, 2007). Meanwhile, supervisory rating of job performance is positively related to compensational benefits like level of salary, which in turn enhances employee well-being and life satisfaction (Diener and Oishi, 2000; Ervasti and Venetoklis, 2010; Judge and Locke, 1993; Pittau, Zelli, and Gelman, 2010). In this sense, we can expect proactive behaviour to be positively related to individual well-being and life satisfaction.

Then, rooted in the self-determination theory (Deci and Ryan, 2002), fulfillment of basic and innate psychological needs (that is, competence, autonomy, and relatedness) is vital for human well-being. A few researchers, as shown in Cluster 1 of Table 11.1, have provided a direct explanation by contending that being proactive can satisfy these fundamental needs and lead to several positive feelings. According to the need-based theories (for example, need hierarchy theory, multiple discrepancy theory, and the self-concordance model), people have a fundamental need to develop reliable and mutually supportive relationships with others at work (Mellor et al, 2008). Meanwhile, proactive endeavours such as seeking information and feedback at work can help individuals build up high quality social relationships (Belschak and Den Hartog, 2011). Indeed, prior research has found that proactivity is positively associated with interpersonal support and fosters job satisfaction (Ashforth, Sluss, and Saks, 2007), life satisfaction (Lucas, Dyrenforth, and Diener, 2008), and mental health and well-being (Mack et al, 2017).

Focusing on individual need for power and status, other researchers also suggest that personal initiatives lead to better career development (Eby, Butts, and Lockwood, 2003) and career success (Seibert, Kraimer, and Crant, 2001), and more promotion at work (Blickle, Witzki, and Schneider, 2009), which in turn foster individual well-being and life satisfaction (Redman and Snape, 2006). This expectation is based upon a positive connection between promotion and life satisfaction (Todd et al, 2009). In other words, proactive employees will report higher life satisfaction due to their intrinsic and extrinsic career success. Meanwhile, prior research also shows this prediction is contingent on factors such as individual income and job characteristics such that moderators should be taken into account (Erdogan et al, 2012) and more longitudinal studies could be employed to reveal the mechanism (Ohly, Sonnentag, and Niessen, 2010).

At the same time, some studies have argued that, due to its change-focused nature, proactive endeavours lead to challenging opportunities such that individuals will have more positive evaluation of personal competence and sense of mastery (Strauss and Parker, 2014). In other words, by being proactive and engaging in challenging activities, people perceive that they have achieved more and better goals, leading to higher satisfaction and more positive evaluation of personal well-being (Greguras and Diefendorff, 2010). Focusing on one's need for achievement, this line of investigation predicts that the positive relationships between personal proactivity and affective outcome are mediated by individual self-evaluation such as personal competence (Rochlen, Good, and Carver, 2009). In addition, one may also have a stronger sense of control that can increase well-being and life satisfaction (Gadermann and Zumbo, 2007).

In sum, based on a developmental pathway, researchers appreciate the positive role of intrinsic and extrinsic elements owing to one's proactive behaviour. Along with this line, they propose that individuals tend to experience a higher level of well-being and life satisfaction resulting from the fulfillment of their basic needs when they engage in personal initiatives.

A resource depletion perspective/pathway

While the developmental perspective describes benefits of proactive behaviours and positive implications upon individual well-being, other researchers have explored the 'dark side' of this relationship and suggested that being proactive may actually hurt individual well-being (Bolino, Valcea, and Harvey, 2010). This stream of research argues that proactivity consumes personal energy and valuable resources, also because of its change-focused nature (Grant and Ashford, 2008). In accounting for such influences, these studies often draw on the conservation of resources (CoR) theory (Halbesleben and Bowler, 2007; Hobfoll, 1989, 2002;) as an overarching framework, which is based on the supposition that people strive to retain, protect, and build resources and that what is threatening to them is the potential or actual loss of these valued resources.

Based on this theory, some scholars speculated that being proactive consumes critical resources for the reason that proactivity is recognized as a goal-regulation process and each stage demands self-regulatory resource when the focal employees envision, plan for, enact, and reflect upon the implications of their proactive behaviour (Bindl et al, 2012; Bindl, 2018). These regulatory resources are limited, and become depleted when exerted in the process (Baumeister et al, 1998). Moreover, employees cannot focus enough on achieving task-related goals and lead to worse task performance when they are proactive actors at work. Even if they want to maintain their task performance, this will also require focal employees to take extra efforts and conduct more self-regulation, which would use up more resources and energy, and increase the ego-depletion (Hagger et al, 2010). According to the strength model of self-control (Hagger et al, 2010), depletion of individual regulatory resources is negatively related to mental health and well-being (Hülsheger and Schewe, 2011). As such, engagement in proactive behaviour may potentially worsen employee mental health and personal well-being (Fay and Hüttges, 2017).

A different perspective pays attention to the interpersonal nature of proactivity. Although behaving proactively may enhance feelings of relatedness at work (Strauss and Parker, 2014), challenging the status quo could potentially spark tension with colleagues and supervisors (Bolino, Valcea, and Harvey, 2010). Scholars who considered such interpersonally risky nature of proactivity argue that proactive behaviour challenges rules and practices endorsed by the social system of the work environment, by increasing uncertainties and ambiguities (Bolino, Valcea, and Harvey, 2010; Katz and Kahn, 1978). Similarly, proactive endeavours create challenges to task coordination and accomplishment of collective goals because the collaborated nature of teamwork requires every member to adjust and adapt their behaviours based on actions of other teammates (Axtell, Holman, and Wall, 2011). Therefore, team members, especially those who are challenged or even hurt, would react negatively to other members' proactive behaviours (Grant, Parker, and Collins, 2009) and report task and relationship conflicts (Spychala and Sonnentag, 2011). Eventually, proactive members will begin to feel a pressure and start to worry about potential consequences of their proactivity (Schmidt et al, 2014), which will backfire on their well-being and satisfaction. Some of these considerations were corroborated by Fay and Hüttges (2017), who showed that daily proactivity was positively related to daily salivary cortisol levels, which reflect feelings of anxiety, depression, or irritability.

Overall, a key assumption of this perspective is the cost associated with proactivity. Consequently, it identifies individual proactivity as a resource depleting endeavour and a potential source of tension and stress. Under these circumstances, people taking personal initiative are likely to necessitate a greater exertion of resources and experience tension at work, thus resulting in poorer well-being outcomes.

Moderators and dynamic spirals

To reconcile the seemingly inconsistent findings from the two perspectives previously discussed, some scholars proposed to examine the factors that shape the relationship between proactivity and affect (Cangiano, Bindl and Parker, 2017; Cangiano, Parker, and Yeo, 2019). In this section we summarize key research findings regarding how individual and situational contingencies influence the affective consequences of proactive behaviour.

Individual level factors

Although being proactive is by definition self-initiated and self-directed, it is not necessarily a voluntary effort fueled by intrinsic reasons (Strauss, Parker, and O'Shea, 2017). In fact, proactivity may also be performed for extrinsic reasons, for example to gain other's approval or avoid criticism when staff are expected to be proactive and take personal initiative (Bolino, Valcea, and Harvey, 2010). In these circumstances, proactivity is more likely to require significant regulatory effort, which may lead to negative affective experiences. This idea is corroborated by various studies. For instance, Pingel, Fay, and Urbach (2019) showed that externally motivated proactive behaviour was positively associated with feelings of irritability and rumination two weeks later. In a similar vein, Strauss, Parker, and O'Shea (2017) found that supervisor-rated proactive behaviour was associated with greater job strain when employees reported low levels of autonomous motivation and high controlled motivation. Thus, there is increasing evidence that motivation significantly shapes the affective outcomes of proactivity: high controlled motivation seems to exacerbate the resource-consuming nature of this behaviour. In contrast, autonomously regulated proactivity appears to buffer against these negative consequences (Cangiano and Parker, 2016). It is also worth noting that some of the potential risks associated with proactive behaviour may be offset by intrinsic rewards. For example, temporarily enhanced levels of stress and rumination to overcome barriers to implementing an idea may be counterbalanced by the sense of accomplishment ensuing from achieving a meaningful goal.

Less attention has been directed towards the role of personal dispositions. Cangiano and Parker (2016) speculated that employees with a weaker disposition to behave proactively may necessitate greater regulatory effort to override personal tendencies (Baumeister, 2002), which may render occasional proactivity more stressful for employees. Additionally, passive and reactive employees are less likely to find intrinsic enjoyment in the proactive process compared to workers with a personal tendency towards proactivity (Cangiano, Bindl, and Parker, 2017). However, to our knowledge, no studies have so far investigated the moderating role of proactive personality in shaping the affective consequences of proactivity. Similarly, there has been little discussion around how the Big Five personality traits may influence the proactivity–affect outcomes relationship. For instance, scholars have argued that neurotic individuals may be better creative problem solvers compared to those low in neuroticism due to their tendency to dwell on problems to a greater extent (Perkins et al, 2015). However, this natural disposition may exacerbate some of the negative affective outcomes of proactive efforts. Neuroticism may accentuate the stressful consequences of proactivity by magnifying the likelihood of ruminative thoughts and anxiety, especially in working environments characterized by low psychological safety.

Situational contingencies

Aside from individual factors, scholars have recognized that affective consequences of proactivity are also contingent on features of the social/situational environment. In particular, these features are related to organizational provision of support and resources and also are associated with how other colleagues respond to these proactive behaviours. For instance, proactive efforts are not always warmly welcomed by colleagues and supervisors (Crant, 2000). Instead, being proactive may expose employees to criticism, rejection, and reprimands, all of which may threaten their self-concept and lead to negative affective experiences (Bolino, Valcea, and Harvey, 2010). For this reason, leader behaviours, perceptions, and expectations play an important role in shaping employees' display of proactive behaviour (Scott and Bruce, 1994; Wu and Parker, 2017) and its affective outcomes including personal well-being (Inceoglu et al, 2018). Some of these ideas were empirically supported in a diary study by Cangiano, Parker, and Yeo (2019) who showed that daily proactivity was associated with greater anxiety after work among employees with supervisors intolerant of mistakes and prone to blaming.

Another important moderating factor is perceived organizational support (POS), which describes how individual employees perceive their organization as caring and fostering their well-being (Eisenberger et al, 2001). Employees who feel supported are more likely to be proactive (Caesens et al, 2016a) and report better well-being (Caesens, Stinglhamber, and Ohana, 2016b). Feeling respected and admired by coworkers and supervisors may enhance the positive consequences of proactivity by boosting perceptions of competence and self-esteem (Blader and Yu, 2017). Drawing upon the control-process theory on affect (Carver and Scheier, 1990), Zacher et al (2019) reported that employees who showed personal initiative and, at the same time, felt supported and valued by their organization were more likely to report improvements in positive mood and lower negative mood six months later, consistent with the idea that perceptions of organizational support influence the affective consequences of proactivity.

Dynamic spirals

In addition to moderating effects, new perspectives emerged from recent studies focusing on the dynamic relationship between proactivity and individual emotional experiences/affective consequences. These perspectives are derived from the broaden-and-build theory of positive emotions (Fredrickson, 2001) and focus on the dynamic nature of proactivity (Cangiano, Bindl, and Parker, 2017). According to this theory, which aims to explain how and why positive emotions promote human flourishing, experiencing positive affect encourages people to broaden their awareness and engage in more exploratory action. Over time, this process helps to build new resources and skills that result in greater well-being and resilience, in a positive upward spiral (Fredrickson, 2001). Within this framework, scholars speculated that the self-determined nature of proactivity energizes individuals and fuels further proactive behaviour by broadening employees' control over their surrounding environment and their ability to deal with future challenges (Parker et al, 2013). Nonetheless, a positive spiral may not always occur. When proactivity fails to yield the desired outcomes (for example, causing instead criticism, rejection, or neglect from others), employees may experience a range of negative affective outcomes (Lindsley, Brass, and Thomas, 1995), thus discouraging future proactive efforts. Over time, these negative consequences may accumulate and generate negative spirals, where employees become gradually more passive and complacent in their role in an attempt to minimize further losses (Pingel, Fay, and Urbach, 2019).

Alternative pathways

Although moderators and dynamic spirals help account for inconsistent predictions, they are still rooted in the developmental perspective and the resource-depletion perspective. As such, there is a question whether these perspectives can be integrated or further extended. In response, a few scholars have proposed alternative theorizations to delineate the proactivity–affective experience relationship. For instance, according to Cangiano, Parker, and Yeo (2019), daily proactive behaviours shape individual well-being through two distinct pathways (that is, proactivity enhanced vitality via perceived competence as an energy-generating pathway and decreased detachment from work at bed time through higher anxiety as a strain pathway).

Different from the integrated perspective above, Bindl (2018) disentangled the emotional journey individuals take through the lens of narratives in a qualitative study. She used three narratives, including proactivity as frustration, threat and growth, to explain how negative emotions might be salient in the proactive journey. Her model also associates these negative emotions with different stages of proactivity, ranging from issue identification, implementation and reflection, to predict how these negative emotions further explain individual engagement into proactive behaviour in the future. Together, these theorizations unpack the proactive process as distinct stages and associate each stage with unique forms of affective experience, which has provided richer understanding of this phenomenon beyond those focusing on moderators and dynamic spirals.

What to study next?

Building on recent attempts to disentangle and integrate these perspectives (for example, Cai et al, 2019; Cangiano, Bindl, and Parker, 2019), we wish to highlight several possible directions for future research within this line of investigation. Overall, we recommend future studies to focus on four major issues.

Further unpack the proactive journey

Proactivity is a process that includes the generation of a proactive goal and then striving for goal achievement (Parker, Bindl, and Strauss, 2010). Thus, the proactive journey might involve different types of proactive behaviours in combination (Perry-Smith and Mannucci 2017), which might be associated with dissimilar affective experience and emotional outcomes. In this regard, with a longitudinal design, Fritz and Sonnentag (2009) showed a positive relationship between taking charge and daily moods as well as affective states. Meanwhile, Lam, Spreitzer, and Fritz (2014) reported a curvilinear (inverted U-shape) relationship between voice behaviour and affective states. Although this finding is based on a cross-sectional design that does not account for temporal dynamics, it suggests that the affective consequences of proactivity might not generalize across distinct types of proactive behaviours.

In other words, whether the developmental perspective, the resource-depletion perspective or the dynamic spirals play a bigger role depends also on the nature of the proactive behaviour (Liu et al, 2019). What makes this issue more complicated is the fact there are multiple forms of proactive behaviours (Parker and Collins, 2010) that can be categorized into dissimilar factors (Griffin, Neal, and Parker, 2007). Future research can either examine the proactivity–affective experience relationship by examining specific types of proactive behaviour to take into account their unique nature. What would make this investigation more interesting is to take into account the effect of other types of behaviours including adaptive and affiliative behaviours. For the same reason, we recommend future research to look into profiles of individual proactive behaviour and unpack the affective outcomes of these profiles.

Examine differential mediating mechanisms

Based on our summary, it is obvious that different proactive behaviours are related to dissimilar affective experiences or outcomes such as moods and emotions. As such, it is reasonable to expect that these relationships are transmitted via distinct mediating mechanisms, especially because emotions are more intense than moods and affective states. The first question we observe after reviewing the current literature is, between momentary emotional feeling and long-term affective perception, whether the same proactive behaviour takes its effect through the same mediating pathways. At the same time, future research can also examine at what stage and for what reason individual behavioural routines and habits will strengthen or mitigate the influences of proactive behaviour upon individual well-being and life satisfaction (Mensmann and Frese, 2019).

Second, it is theoretically interesting if future studies can explore whether proactive behaviour leads to affective experience through multiple mediating mechanisms at the same time, though some of them might be contradictory toward each other in nature. For instance, employee voice behaviour would result in a positive affect by the realization of individual prosocial motivation and self-impression management. If so, maybe studies focusing on the moderators and dynamic spirals can help make these pathways distinct. These issues are related not only to the intensity of the specific affective experience but also the time frame of the phenomenon. This is of special significance when the dependent variable is related to employees' career-related outcomes (Greguras and Diefendorff, 2010). Meanwhile, we wonder whether being proactive can simultaneously generate both positive and negative affective experiences (Cangiano, Parker, and Yeo, 2019). If so, future research can draw on new perspectives to explore the relations between these two affects. For instance, more examination ought to be carried out on whether it is a functional, ambivalent link or dynamic model.

Welcome methodological changes

Although earlier studies adopted predominantly a cross-sectional methodology, our scientific mapping of previous studies highlights an increasing number of investigations featuring longitudinal designs. This trend is encouraging because it allows a deeper understanding of the dynamics affecting the well-being consequences of proactivity (see Figure 11.2). We also think it is valuable to study proactive behaviour as episodic events and link it with several different spirals, which would

Figure 11.2: Co-occurrence in all keywords of diary study in proactivity–affect research

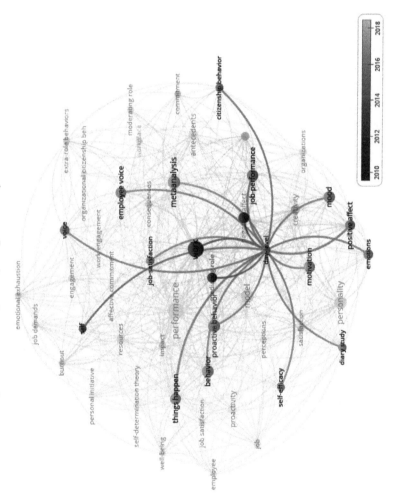

then require the researchers to make multiple records through dissimilar methods at the same time. In this manner, subsequent studies can also examine how different emotional regulation tactics and strategies are used throughout the proactive journey, to provide insights about how momentary emotional outcomes can gradually pave the way for long-term well-being and life satisfaction.

Consider contextual differences

Another domain noteworthy of future attention is to theorize various contextual influences during the proactive journey, with national culture as an exemplary choice (Liu et al, 2019). At first, cross-cultural research on well-being have shown that constituents of well-being are tailored by the culture (Oishi and Diener, 2001) and highlighted the impact of evaluation and explanation of affects, self-cognition, and dispositions on subjective well-being resulted from cultural differences (Wirtz et al, 2010; Cheng, Cheung, and Montasem, 2014). Second, even though researchers have started to explore how proactive behaviours might be linked with individual affect and emotions in different manners across the globe, a direct cross-cultural comparison is still unavailable, with Smale et al (2019) as an exemption. In their study, Smale et al (2019) found national culture moderated the effect of proactive behaviour on individual evaluation of their financial success and work–life balance, both of which will be further related to individual well-being and life satisfaction. In addition to national culture, features such as the abundance of valuable resources, organizational structure, team interdependence, and characteristics of the social network are all potential factors for consideration. We thus recommend future research to explore contextual differences in the proactivity–affective experience relationship.

Conclusion

During the past two decades, both proactivity and individual well-being have become buzzwords in organizational behaviour research. Meanwhile, an increasing number of studies have tried to link them together. In the current literature, the majority of these studies focus on emotions and affect as predictors of individual proactive behaviour instead of the other way around. After conducting a quantitative review, we believe it is worthwhile to explore how being proactive shapes individual affective experience. In order to achieve this purpose, we first conducted a scientific mapping of prior research to identify four key themes/domains. Then, we summarized two major perspectives explaining the positive and negative effect from proactivity to individual affective experience, respectively. Next, we turned our attention to endeavours trying to reconcile this dispute, by focusing on studies examining moderators and dynamic spirals. In addition, we looked into studies that explore alternative explanations. Together, we provided a systematic integration of this line of investigation, which then highlights four future directions for subsequent research. We hope these suggestions put forward in the chapter can provide useful means for advancing future research.

References

Ashforth, B. E., Sluss, D. M., and Saks, A. M. (2007). Socialization tactics, proactive behavior, and newcomer learning: Integrating socialization models. *Journal of Vocational Behavior,* 70(3), 447–62.

Axtell, C., Holman, D., and Wall, T. (2011). Promoting innovation: a change study. *Journal of Occupational and Organizational Psychology,* 79(3), 509–16.

Bakker, A.B. and Oerlemans, W.G.M. (2019). Daily job crafting and momentary work engagement: A self-determination and self-regulation perspective. *Journal of Vocational Behavior,* 112(6), 417–30.

Baumeister, R. E., Bratslavsky, E., Muraven, M., and Tice, D. M. (1998). Ego depletion: Is the active self a limited resource? *Journal of Personality and Social Psychology,* 74(5), 1252–65.

Baumeister, R. F. (2002). Ego depletion and self-control failure: An energy model of the self's executive function. *Self and Identity,* 1(2), 129–36.

Belschak, F. D. and Den Hartog, D. N. (2011). Pro-self, prosocial, and pro-organizational foci of proactive behavior: differential antecedents and consequences. *Journal of Occupational and Organizational Psychology,* 83(2), 475–98.

Bindl, U. K., Parker, S. K., Totterdell, P., and Hagger-Johnson, G. (2012). Fuel of the self-starter: How mood relates to proactive goal regulation. *Journal of Applied Psychology,* 97(1), 134–50.

Bindl, U. K. (2018). Work-related proactivity through the lens of narrative: investigating emotional journeys in the process of making things happen. *Human Relations,* 72(4), 615–45.

Binnewies, C., Ohly, S., and Sonnentag, S. (2007). Taking personal initiative and communicating about ideas: what is important for the creative process and for idea creativity?. *European Journal of Work and Organizational Psychology,* 16(4), 432–55.

Blader, S. L. and Yu, S. (2017). Are status and respect different or two sides of the same coin? *Academy of Management Annals,* 11(2), 800–24.

Blickle, G., Witzki, A., and Schneider, P. B. (2009). Self-initiated mentoring and career success: a predictive field study. *Journal of Vocational Behavior,* 74(1), 94–101.

Bolino, M., Valcea, S., and Harvey, J. (2010). Employee, manage thyself: The potentially negative implications of expecting employees to behave proactively. *Journal of Occupational and Organizational Psychology*, 83(2), 325–45.

Caesens, G., Marique, G., Hanin, D., and Stinglhamber, F. (2016a). The relationship between perceived organizational support and proactive behaviour directed towards the organization. *European Journal of Work and Organizational Psychology*, 25(3), 398–411.

Caesens, G., Stinglhamber, F., and Ohana, M. (2016b). Perceived organizational support and well-being: a weekly study. *Journal of Managerial Psychology*, 31(7), 1214–30.

Cai, Z., Parker, S. K., Chen, Z., and Lam, W. (2019). How does the social context fuel the proactive fire? A multi-level review and theoretical synthesis. *Journal of Organizational Behavior*, 40(2): 209–30.

Cangiano, F., Bindl, U. K., and Parker, S. K. (2017). The 'hot' side of proactivity: exploring an affect-based perspective on proactivity in organizations. In Sharon K. Parker, and Uta K. Bindl (eds), *Proactivity at Work: Making Things Happen in Organizations*, New York: Routledge, pp 355–84.

Cangiano, F. and Parker, S. K. (2016). Proactivity for mental health and well-being. In S. Clarke, T. M. Probst, F. Guldenmund, and J. Passmore (eds), *The Wiley Blackwell Handbook of the Psychology of Occupational Safety and Workplace Health*, Chicester, UK: John Wiley and Sons, pp 228–50.

Cangiano, F., Parker, S. K., and Yeo, G. B. (2019). Does daily proactivity affect well-being? The moderating role of punitive supervision. *Journal of Organizational Behavior*, 40(1), 59–72.

Carver, C. S. and Scheier, M. F. (1990). Origins and functions of positive and negative affect: A control-process view. *Psychological Review*, 97(1), 19–35.

Cheng, C., Cheung, M., and Montasem, A. (2014). Explaining differences in subjective well-being across 33 nations using multilevel models: universal personality, cultural relativity, and national income. *Journal of Personality*, 84(1), 46–58.

Crant, J. (2000). Proactive behavior in organizations. *Journal of Management*, 26(3), 435–62.

Deci, E. L. and Ryan, R. M. (2002). *Handbook of Self-Determination Research*. Rochester: The University of Rochester Press.

Diener, E. and Oishi, S. (2000). Money and happiness: income and subjective well-being across nations. In E. Diener and E. M. Suh (eds), *Culture and Subjective Well-Being*, Cambridge, MA: MIT Press.

Eby, L. T., Butts, M., and Lockwood, A. (2003). Predictors of success in the era of the boundaryless career. *Journal of Organizational Behavior*, 24(6), 689–708.

Eisenberger, R., Armeli, S., Rexwinkel, B., Lynch, P. D., and Rhoades, L. (2001). Reciprocation of perceived organizational support. *Journal of Applied Psychology*, 86(1), 42–51.

Erdogan, B., Bauer, T. N., Truxillo, D. M., and Mansfield, L. R. (2012). Whistle while you work: a review of the life satisfaction literature. *Journal of Management*, 38(4), 1038–83.

Ervasti, H. and Venetoklis, T. (2010). Unemployment and subjective well-being: an empirical test of deprivation theory, incentive paradigm and financial strain approach. *Acta Sociologica*, 53(2), 119–39.

Fay, D., and Hüttges, A. (2017). Drawbacks of proactivity: effects of daily proactivity on daily salivary cortisol and subjective well-being. *Journal of Occupational Health Psychology*, 22(4), 429–42.

Fredrickson, B. L. (2001). The role of positive emotions in positive psychology. the broaden-and-build theory of positive emotions. *American Psychologist*, 56(3), 218–26.

Frese, M. and Fay, D. (2001). Personal initiative (PI): An active performance concept for work in the 21st century. In B. M. Staw, and R. M. Sutton (eds), *Research in Organizational Behavior*, vol 2, Amsterdam: Elsevier Science, pp 133–87.

Fritz, C. and Sonnentag, S. (2009). Antecedents of day-level proactive behavior: A look at job stressors and positive affect during the workday. *Journal of Management*, 35(1), 94–111.

Gadermann, A. M. and Zumbo, B. D. (2007). Investigating the intra-individual variability and trajectories of subjective well-being. *Social Indicators Research*, 81(1): 1–33.

Grant, A. M. and Ashford, S. J. (2008). The dynamics of proactivity at work. *Research in Organizational Behavior*, 28, 3–34.

Grant, A. M., Parker, S., and Collins, C. (2009). Getting credit for proactive behavior: supervisor reactions depend on what you value and how you feel. *Personnel Psychology*, 62(1), 31–55.

Greguras, G. J. and Diefendorff, J. M. (2010). Why does proactive personality predict employee life satisfaction and work behaviors? a field investigation of the mediating role of the self-concordance model. *Personnel Psychology*, 63(3), 539–560.

Griffin, M. A. and Clarke, S. (2011). Stress and well-being at work. In S. Zedeck (eds), *APA Handbook of Industrial and Organizational Psychology. Maintaining, Expanding, and Contracting the Organization*, vol 3, Washington DC: American Psychological Association, pp 359–97.

Griffin, M. A., Neal, A., and Parker, S. K. (2007). A new model of work role performance: Positive behavior in uncertain and interdependent contexts. *Academy of Management Journal*, 50(2), 327–47.

Hagger, M., Wood, C., Stiff, C., and Chatzisarantis, N. (2010). Ego depletion and the strength model of self-control: A meta-analysis. *Psychological Bulletin*, 136(4), 495–525.

Halbesleben, J. R. B. and Bowler, W. M. (2007). Emotional exhaustion and job performance: The mediating role of motivation. *Journal of Applied Psychology,* 92(1), 93–106.

Hobfoll, S. E. (1989). Conservation of resources. A new attempt at conceptualizing stress. *American Psychologist,* 44(3), 513–24.

Hobfoll, S. E. (2002). Social and psychological resources and adaptation. *Review of General Psychology,* 6(4), 307–24.

Hülsheger, Ute R. and Schewe, A. F. (2011). On the costs and benefits of emotional labor: a meta-analysis of three decades of research. *Journal of Occupational Health Psychology,* 16(3), 361–89.

Inceoglu, I., Thomas, G., Chu, C., Plans, D., and Gerbasi, A. (2018). Leadership behavior and employee well-being: an integrated review and a future research agenda. *The Leadership Quarterly,* 29(1), 179–202.

Judge, T. A. and Locke, E. A. (1993). Effect of dysfunctional thought processes on subjective well-being and job satisfaction. *Journal of Applied Psychology,* 78(3), 475–90.

Kanfer, R., Frese, M., and Johnson, R. E. (2017). Motivation related to work: A century of progress. *Journal of Applied Psychology,* 102(3): 338–55.

Katz, D. and Kahn, R. L. (1978). *The Social Psychology of Organizations,* 2nd edn. New York: Wiley.

Lam, C. F., Spreitzer, G., and Fritz, C. (2014). Too much of a good thing: Curvilinear effect of positive affect on proactive behaviors. *Journal of Organizational Behavior,* 35(4), 530–46.

Lindsley, D. H., Brass, D. J., and Thomas, J. B. (1995). Efficacy–performance spirals: A multilevel perspective. *Academy of Management Review,* 20, 645–78.

Linley, P.A., and Joseph, S. (2004) Applied positive psychology: A new perspective for professional practice. In P. A. Linley and S. Joseph (eds), *Positive Psychology in Practice,* Hoboken, NJ: John Wiley & Sons, pp 3–12.

Liu, W., Tangirala, S., Lee, C., and Parker, S. K. (2019). New directions for exploring the consequences of proactive behaviors: Introduction to the special issue. *Journal of Organizational Behavior,* 40(1), 1–4.

Lucas, R. E., Dyrenforth, P. S., and Diener, E. (2008). Four myths about subjective well-being. *Social and Personality Psychology Compass,* 2(5), 2001–15.

Mack, D. E., Gunnell, K. E., Wilson, P. M., and Wierts, C. (2017). Well-being in group-based exercise classes: Do psychological need fulfillment and interpersonal supports matter?. *Applied Research in Quality of Life,* 12(1), 89–102.

Mellor, D., Stokes, M., Firth, L., Hayashi, Y., and Cummins, R. (2008). Need for belonging, relationship satisfaction, loneliness, and life satisfaction. *Personality and Individual Differences,* 45(3), 213–18.

Mensmann, M. and Frese, M. (2019). Who stays proactive after entrepreneurship training? Need for cognition, personal initiative maintenance, and well-being. *Journal of Organizational Behavior,* 40, 20–37.

Ohly, S., Sonnentag, S., Niessen, C., and Zapf, D. (2010). Diary studies in organizational research: An introduction and some practical recommendations. *Journal of Personnel Psychology*, 9(2), 79–93.

Oishi, S. and Diener, E. (2001). Goals, culture, and subjective well-being. *Personality & Social Psychology Bulletin*, 27(12), 93–108.

Parker, S. K., Bindl, U. K., and Strauss, K. (2010). Making things happen: a model of proactive motivation. *Journal of Management,* 36(4), 827–56.

Parker, S. K. and Collins, C. G. (2010). Taking stock: Integrating and differentiating multiple proactive behaviors. *Journal of Management*, 36(3), 633–62.

Parker, S. K., Johnson, A., Collins, C., and Nguyen, H. (2013). Making the most of structural support: Moderating influence of employees' clarity and negative affect. *Academy of Management Journal*, 56(3), 867–92.

Parker, S. K., Morgeson, F. P., and Johns, G. (2017). One hundred years of work design research: looking back and looking forward. *Journal of Applied Psychology,* 102(3), 403–20.

Parker, S. K., Williams, H. M., and Turner, N. (2006). Modeling the antecedents of proactive behavior at work. *Journal of Applied Psychology,* 91(3), 636–52.

Perkins, A. M., Arnone, D., Smallwood, J., and Mobbs, D. (2015). Thinking too much: Self-generated thought as the engine of neuroticism. *Trends in cognitive sciences*, 19(9), 492–8.

Perry-Smith, J. E. and Mannucci, P. V. (2017). From creativity to innovation: The social network drivers of the four phases of the idea journey. *Academy of Management Review*, 42(1), 53–79.

Pingel, R., Fay, D., and Urbach, T. (2019). A resources perspective on when and how proactive work behaviour leads to employee withdrawal. *Journal of Occupational and Organizational Psychology*, 92(2), 410–35.

Pittau, M. G., Zelli, R., and Gelman, A. (2010). Economic disparities and life satisfaction in European regions. *Social Indicators Research,* 96(2), 339–61.

Redman, T. and Snape, E. (2006). The consequences of perceived age discrimination amongst older police officers: Is social support a buffer? *British Journal of Management,* 17(2), 167–75.

Rochlen, A. B., Good, G. E., and Carver, T. A. (2009). Predictors of gender-related barriers, work, and life satisfaction among men in nursing. *Psychology of Men and Masculinity,* 10(1), 44–56.

Ryan, R. M. and Deci, E. L. (2001). On happiness and human potentials: a review of research on hedonic and eudaimonic well-being. *Annual Review of Psychology,* 52(1), 141–66.

Schmidt, S., Roesler, U., Kusserow, T., and Rau, R. (2014). Uncertainty in the workplace: examining role ambiguity and role conflict, and their link to depression-a meta-analysis. *European Journal of Work and Organizational Psychology,* 23(1), 91–106.

Scott, S. G. and Bruce, R. A. (1994). Determinants of innovative behavior: A path model of individual innovation in the workplace. *Academy of Management Journal,* 37(3), 580–607.

Seibert, S. E., Kraimer, M. L., and Crant, J. M. (2001). What do proactive people do? A longitudinal model linking proactive personality and career success. *Personnel Psychology,* 54(4), 845–74.

Singh, R., Ragins, B. R., and Tharenou, P. (2009). Who gets a mentor? A longitudinal assessment of the rising star hypothesis. *Journal of Vocational Behavior,* 74(1), 11–17.

Smale, A., Bagdadli, S., Cotton, R., Dello Russo, S., Dickmann, M., Dysvik, A., Gianecchini, M., Kaše, R., Lazarova, M., Reichel, A., Rozo, P., Verbruggen, M. (2019). Proactive career behaviors and subjective career success: The moderating role of national culture. *Journal of Organizational Behavior,* 40(1), 105–122.

Spychala, A. and Sonnentag, S. (2011). The dark and the bright sides of proactive work behaviour and situational constraints: Longitudinal relationships with task conflicts. *European Journal of Work and Organizational Psychology,* 20(5), 654–80.

Strauss, K. and Parker, S. K. (2014). Effective and sustained proactivity in the workplace: A self-determination theory perspective. In M. Gagne (ed), *The Oxford Handbook of Work Engagement, Motivation, and Self-Determination Theory.* New York: Oxford University Press.

Strauss, K., Parker, S. K., and O'Shea, D. (2017). When does proactivity have a cost? Motivation at work moderates the effects of proactive work behavior on employee job strain. *Journal of Vocational Behavior,* 100(6), 15–26.

Thomas, J. P., Whitman, D. S., and Viswesvaran, C. (2011). Employee proactivity in organizations: A comparative meta-analysis of emergent proactive constructs. *Journal of Occupational and Organizational Psychology,* 83(2), 275–300.

Todd, S. Y., Harris, K. J., Harris, R. B., and Wheeler, A. R. (2009). Career success implications of political skill. *The Journal of Social Psychology,* 149(3), 279–304.

Tornau, K. and Frese, M. (2013). Construct clean-up in proactivity research: A meta-analysis on the nomological net of work-related proactivity concepts and their incremental validities. *Applied Psychology,* 62(1), 44–96.

Wirtz, D., Chiu, C., Diener, E., and Oishi, S. (2010). What constitutes a good life? Cultural differences in the role of positive and negative affect in subjective well-being. *Journal of Personality,* 77(4), 1167–96.

Wu, C. H. and Parker, S. K. (2017). The role of leader support in facilitating proactive work behavior: A perspective from attachment theory. *Journal of Management,* 43(4), 1025–49.

Zacher, H., Schmitt, A., Jimmieson, N. L., and Rudolph, C. W. (2019). Dynamic effects of personal initiative on engagement and exhaustion: The role of mood, autonomy, and support. *Journal of Organizational Behavior,* 40(1), 38–58.

12

Affective Consequences of Proactivity

Hannes Zacher

Proactive behaviour in the work context involves self-initiated and future-oriented actions or goal-directed behaviours that employees show with the aim to create positive change in the self (for example, learning a new skill) or the work environment (for example, implementing a more efficient process; Grant and Ashford, 2008; Parker and Collins, 2010). Employees with a more proactive personality have a relatively stable tendency to engage in such proactive behaviours (Bateman and Crant, 1993; Crant, 1995). Meta-analyses show that individuals differences in proactive personality and behaviour are generally positively related to performance outcomes, even when controlling for the Big Five personality traits (Fuller and Marler, 2009; Thomas, Whitman, and Viswesvaran, 2010; Tornau and Frese, 2013). Moreover, proactivity is positively related to career success (Seibert, Crant, and Kraimer, 1999; Seibert, Kraimer, and Crant, 2001), favourable outcomes of the job search process (Brown et al, 2006), and business growth (Campos et al, 2017). Accordingly, numerous studies have attempted to uncover the individual and contextual predictors of proactive behaviour, including personality, beliefs, and affect, as well as job design and leader behaviour (for reviews, see Bindl and Parker, 2011; Parker and Bindl, 2017).

With regard to affect, it is now well-established that high-activated positive affect predicts proactive behaviour, including employees' proactive goal-setting, planning, goal implementation, and feedback-seeking (Bindl and Parker, 2012), as well as voice behaviour (that is, speaking up in teams; Wang et al, 2019). In terms of the motivational antecedents of proactivity, positive affect belongs to the 'energized to' category, whereas self-beliefs and self-determination belong to the 'can do' and 'reason to' categories, respectively (Parker, Bindl, and Strauss, 2010). A number of daily diary studies have shown that positive affective states are positively related to proactive behaviour on the same workday, as well as the following workday, even when job stressors are taken into account (Fay and Sonnentag, 2012; Fritz and Sonnentag, 2009). Another set of studies found that high-activated positive mood positively predicted proactive goal regulation (Bindl et al, 2012).

Moreover, some research suggests that both positive and negative affect can contribute to proactive behaviour (Den Hartog and Belschak, 2007; Sonnentag and Starzyk, 2015). Theoretical work has argued that intense negative emotions, such as anger and fear, can motivate proactive behaviour by signalling a need for change of current circumstances (Lebel, 2017). Empirical research has shown that supervisors react more positively to employee proactive behaviours in performance evaluations when employees express low levels of negative affect (Grant, Parker, and Collins, 2009). In addition, empirical findings suggest that emotional regulation is important to voice constructively and effectively (Grant, 2013). Researchers have further argued and shown that the link between positive affect and proactive behaviour may be characterized by a curvilinear pattern, such that proactive behaviour is highest when employees experience moderate levels of positive affect, as compared to low and high positive affect (Lam, Spreitzer, and Fritz, 2014).

In contrast, much less theoretical and empirical research has focused on the psychological consequences of proactivity at work, including positive and negative affective states that employees may experience *after* engaging in proactive behaviour. Accordingly, the goal of this chapter is to address the potential affective consequences of proactive personality and behaviour. In the following sections, I first briefly introduce the notion of employee affect, including emotions, moods, and trait affectivity. Second, I describe a conceptual model on the proximal consequences of (change in) proactive personality and behaviour (that is, positive changes in the self and/or work environment), more distal psychological consequences (that is, changes in resources, need satisfaction, goal progress), and, eventually, different affective consequences. I also outline the role of potential boundary conditions of the effects of proactivity on affective consequences, including individual and contextual demands, resources, and barriers, as well as individual differences in trait affectivity. Third, I describe differences between a within-person perspective (that is, change in proactive behaviour and affective experiences over time) and a between-person perspective (that is, individual differences in proactive behaviour and affective experiences). Fourth, I review existing empirical studies that have examined affective consequences of different forms of proactivity. Finally, I conclude the chapter with several suggestions for future research.

Affective experiences at work

Affective experiences or states can be broadly differentiated in rather short-lived and intense emotions (for example, momentary feelings of joy or anger) and longer-lasting and less differentiated moods (Barsade and Gibson, 2007; Brief and Weiss, 2002). Emotions and moods can be pleasant or unpleasant, high- or low-activated states (Watson, Clark, and Tellegen, 1988). The resulting 'affect circumplex' (that is, emotions and moods presented along two orthogonal valence and activation dimensions) includes high-activated positive experiences such as enthusiasm and excitement, low-activated positive experiences such as feeling calm and relaxed, high-activated negative experiences such as anger and fear, as well as low-activated negative experiences such as sadness and feeling hopeless (Warr et al, 2014).

In contrast to more dynamic emotions and moods, employees' trait affectivity reflects their relatively stable tendencies to experience positive or negative emotions and moods more or less frequently in their (work) lives. These dispositions are closely related to the personality characteristics extraversion and neuroticism, respectively (Rusting and Larsen, 1997). Research has demonstrated that affective experiences are associated with occupational well-being (for example, work engagement and emotional exhaustion; Zacher et al, 2019) as well as job performance (Beal et al, 2005; Cole, Walter, and Bruch, 2008). Thus, affective experiences may mediate effects of proactivity on important outcomes.

Conceptual model of affective consequences of proactive behaviour

The conceptual model to structure the literature review and discussion in this chapter is presented in Figure 12.1. In a nutshell, the model starts with effects of change, or individual differences, in proactive personality and behaviour on positive changes in the self and/or the work context. The strengths of these effects is proposed to be moderated by individual and contextual demands (for example,

Figure 12.1: Conceptual model

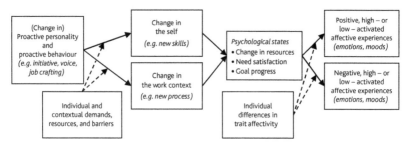

time pressure, personal goals), resources (for example, energy, job autonomy), and barriers (for example, health problems, organizational constraints). Positive changes in the self and/or the work context, in turn, are expected to influence different psychological states. In this chapter, I particularly focus on employees' perceptions of changes in resources, need satisfaction, and goal progress. The extent to which employees experience these psychological states should, subsequently, give rise to positive or negative, high- or low-activated affective experiences. In the following, I will outline the propositions of the model in further detail.

Effects of individual differences and change in proactive personality and behaviour

I first propose that, consistent with a common definition of proactivity (Grant and Ashford, 2008), individual differences and changes in proactive personality and proactive behaviour should generally result in positive changes either in the self or in the work environment (Figure 12.1). Employees with a more proactive personality and those who frequently show proactive behaviour intend to create change through their actions. However, whether or not changes in the self or the environment actually occur likely depends on a number of individual and contextual boundary conditions (see next section). For example, a more proactive personality has been shown to be associated with learning (Bertolino, Truxillo, and Fraccaroli, 2011; Parker and Sprigg, 1999), changes in job characteristics (Li et al, 2014), job search intensity and success (Brown et al, 2006; Zacher, 2013), and career success (Seibert, Kraimer, and Crant, 2001).

Consequences of an employee showing high levels of personal initiative, a broad form of proactive work behaviour that is self-starting and aims to overcome barriers (Frese and Fay, 2001), may be that the employee acquires new knowledge or skills, or that a work procedure is improved before problems occur. Another form of proactive behaviour, employee voice (Morrison, 2014), could lead to changes in employees' social status (Weiss and Morrison, 2018) or improvements in how team members communicate with each other about work-related issues (LePine and Van Dyne, 1998; Van Dyne and LePine, 1998). Proactive job crafting behaviours (for example, asking one's supervisor for feedback or more challenging projects) can lead to actual increases in challenging job demands, structural and social job resources (for example, greater autonomy and support), as well as to a decrease in hindering job demands (Rudolph et al, 2017; Tims and Bakker, 2010). Finally, engaging in proactive feedback-seeking behaviour might lead to a reduction in feelings of uncertainty about one's performance and, subsequently, changes in work performance (Anseel et al, 2015).

Boundary conditions of effects of proactivity

The effectiveness of proactive personality and behaviour in inducing changes to the self and to the work environment likely depends on a number of boundary conditions, including individual and contextual demands, resources, and hindrances (see Hirschi, Shockley, and Zacher, 2019; ten Brummelhuis and Bakker, 2012). In particular, if individuals' self-set work goals (for example, unrealistic or too difficult goals) or contextually set work demands (for example, time pressure, heavy workload) are too high, it is less likely that proactive employees will successfully create positive changes in the self or work environment. In contrast, lower or moderate goals and demands should increase the likelihood of positive changes. It is also important that proactive employees possess sufficient individual resources (for example, health, energy) and contextual resources (for example, job autonomy, social support) to be able to implement changes in the self or work environment. Finally, if there are hindrances or barriers in the self (for example, lack of abilities, illness) or in the work environment (for example, organizational constraints), it is also less likely that proactive tendencies and concrete behaviours manifest in meaningful changes in the self or work environment. A number of empirical studies have demonstrated interactive effects of proactive personality and behaviour with other individual and contextual factors on more or less distal workplace outcomes (for example, Cunningham and De La Rosa, 2008; Ng and Feldman, 2012; Schmitt, Den Hartog, and Belschak, 2015). However, research has so far neglected examining whether actual changes in the self and the work environment mediate these associations between proactivity and work outcomes.

Psychological states resulting from changes in the self and the work environment

Changes in the self and the work environment, in turn, are conceptualized to result in a number of different psychological states (see Figure 12.1). I will focus on three such states in the following: employees' perceptions of changes in resources, satisfaction of basic needs, and goal progress. First, researchers have suggested that proactive behaviour can deplete or generate employees' personal resources (Belschak, Hartog, and Fay, 2010; Bolino, Valcea, and Harvey, 2010; Cangiano and Parker, 2016). Personal resources can be defined as anything that is valued by individuals, including material belongings, personal characteristics, and supportive relationships (Hobfoll, 1989; Hobfoll et al, 2018). In particular, Bolino et al have argued that proactive behaviours (and other active states and behaviours of employees, such as organizational citizenship behaviour and work engagement) consume employees' physical, mental, and emotional energy resources due to regulatory demands (Bolino et al, 2015; Bolino and Turnley, 2005; Halbesleben, Harvey, and Bolino, 2009). Moreover, these researchers suggested that proactivity can drain employees' resources due to negative feedback and resistance from others, including supervisors and colleagues (Bolino, Turnley, and Anderson, 2017; Bolino, Valcea, and Harvey, 2010). Thus, proactive behaviour can be a source of job strain, as it may lead to energy depletion, conflicts, and frustration.

Other scholars have supplemented this rather negative focus on resource depletion with a more positive focus on resource generation. Specifically, Cangiano and Parker (2016) argued that proactive behaviour may also have the potential to generate personal resources, including self-efficacy and positive affect, via a 'motivation pathway'. Accordingly, in their model on the health and well-being consequences of proactivity, these researchers argued that individual and contextual boundary conditions (for example, feedback, intrinsic motivation) determine whether proactive employees follow the resource-depletion of motivation pathway.

A second relevant psychological state following from proactive behaviour is the satisfaction of important psychological needs, such as the needs for autonomy, competence, and relatedness postulated by self-determination theory (Gagné and Deci, 2005; Ryan and Deci, 2000). In particular, Strauss et al have argued that employees who engage in proactivity may be more likely to meet these needs, particularly if they are intrinsically motivated (Strauss and Parker, 2014; Strauss, Parker, and O'Shea, 2017). In terms of the need for autonomy, research has indeed shown that proactive personality and proactive behaviour can increase employees' control orientations as well as job autonomy (Frese, Garst, and Fay, 2007; Li et al, 2014; Zacher et al, 2019). For instance, based on action regulation theory (Hacker, 2003; Zacher and Frese, 2018), Zacher et al (2019) argued and showed that change in personal initiative across six months is positively associated with a change in job autonomy across a subsequent six-months period. Similarly, theorizing on job crafting suggests that employees' proactive attempts to better align their job characteristics with their own abilities and needs leads to increased need satisfaction and higher meaning at work (Bakker, 2010; Wrzesniewski and Dutton, 2001). Moreover, engaging in voice behaviour and feedback-seeking may also fulfill employees' needs for autonomy, competence, and relatedness by suggesting improvements and by influencing others and the work environment in positive ways (Strauss and Parker, 2014).

Finally, positive changes in the self and the work environment could signal to proactive employees that they are making progress toward their valued personal and work-related goals. Perceived goal progress is an important dimension of the self-regulatory goal-striving process (Johnson and Howe, 2013). From a control theory perspective, proactive behaviour involves an active, deliberate action regulation process that can be linked to the experience of intense self-focused emotions, such as pride, contentment, and guilt (Bindl and Parker, 2012; Carver and Scheier, 1990). In particular, Carver and Scheier's (1990) control-process theory on affect provides a useful framework to explain the affective consequences of proactivity, because it focuses on the self-regulation of behaviour and the emergence of affective experiences. The theory extends control theory, which suggests that people monitor their behaviour and potentially change it to reduce discrepancies between their goals and the current state (Carver and Scheier, 1982). The focus of this primary feedback system is on action control.

To explain the emergence of affective experiences, Carver and Scheier (1990) introduced a second, higher-order feedback system ('meta-monitoring') that senses and evaluates discrepancies between expected and actual rates of goal progress in the first feedback system. Specifically, the second system compares the rate of discrepancy reduction in the action control system with an acceptable or desired reference value for progress. The outcome of this comparison leads to changes in affective experiences (Carver and Scheier, 1990). When employees perceive that they are making adequate progress in goal pursuit, positive affect increases and negative affect decreases. In contrast, when employees perceive that they are not making sufficient progress, negative affect increases and positive affect decreases (Carver and Scheier, 1990). For instance, based on these arguments of the control-process theory on affect, Zacher et al (2019) found that change in personal initiative across six months negatively predicted change in positive mood across the following six months. Moreover, change in personal initiative positively predicted change in negative mood when perceived organizational support was low, but not when such perceived support was high. They argued that perceived support is a psychological resource that can mitigate the resource-depleting effect (that is, increase in negative mood) of proactive behaviour (see also Cangiano and Parker, 2016).

The role of trait affectivity

Finally, the conceptual model (Figure 12.1) suggests that employees' trait affectivity moderates the effects of psychological states on subsequent affective experiences. Based on trait activation theory (Tett and Guterman, 2000; Tett, Simonet, Walser, and Brown, 2013), I argue that employees with high levels of either positive or negative trait affectivity are likely to react more strongly to certain trait-relevant psychological states. For example, employees with high levels of positive affectivity (similar to extraversion) may experience stronger affective consequences if their proactive engagement involves interacting with other people at work and, thus, generates social resources and fulfills needs for relatedness. For example, these employees might experience higher levels of positive affect after engaging in the job crafting dimension of 'increasing social resources' at work (Tims and Bakker, 2010). In contrast, employees with high negative affectivity (similar to neuroticism) may be more likely to experience strong affective consequences if their proactive engagement involves preventing problems and mistakes. Accordingly, these employees may experience higher levels of positive affect after engaging in prohibitive (as compared to promotive) voice behaviour (Liang, Farh, and Farh, 2012). Similarly, they should react more strongly to proactive engagement in the job crafting dimension 'decreasing hindering job demands', which has also been categorized as avoidance job crafting (as opposed to approach job crafting) (Bruning and Campion, 2019; Zhang and Parker, 2019).

Between-person differences and within-person change in proactivity and affect

The conceptual model (Figure 12.1) distinguishes between within-person changes and between-person differences in proactive personality and proactive behaviour. Research taking a between-person perspective typically focuses on the extent to which employees differ in their general, average, or stable levels of (work) behaviour. Accordingly, studies using between-person designs (for example, cross-sectional survey studies) aim to explain variability between employees. In contrast, research adopting a within-person perspective focuses on the extent to which employee behaviour fluctuates or changes over different periods of time, such as hours, days, weeks, months, or years. Over the past few decades, researchers in organizational psychology and management have increasingly adopted within-person longitudinal designs to investigate variability and change in different forms of employee behaviour (Zacher and Rudolph, 2020), including task performance (Chi, Chang, and Huang, 2015), organizational citizenship behaviour (Dalal et al, 2009), and innovative behaviour (Zacher and Wilden, 2014).

It is important to distinguish within-person variability in proactivity from within-person change in proactivity. While both rely on intensive longitudinal designs and measurement, within-person studies that focus on intraindividual variability (for example, many daily diary studies) are not able to draw conclusions about intraindividual change over time. In contrast, within-person studies that focus on intraindividual change can describe how and possibly explain why proactivity changes within employees over a certain period of time. Moreover, examining within-person effects of change in one variable (for example, proactive behaviour) on changes in other variables (for example, positive mood) allows stronger conclusions regarding causality than studies that focus on between- or within-person variability (Wang et al, 2017; Zacher and Rudolph, 2020).

While proactive personality is defined as a relatively stable tendency to create change in the work environment (Bateman and Crant, 1993), lifespan developmental scholars have argued that even personality traits are not 'set like plaster', but can change throughout the life course and up until old age (Roberts, Walton, and Viechtbauer, 2006; Srivastava et al, 2003). According to the neo-socioanalytic model of personality development and related frameworks, these changes are due to adaptation processes of individuals to their (work) environment and associated demands (Nye and Roberts, 2019; Woods et al, 2019). For instance, researchers have shown that change in employees' personality is influenced by characteristics of their occupations across 15 years (Wille and De Fruyt, 2014). With regard to proactive personality, researchers have demonstrated positive reciprocal effects with work characteristics, particularly job demands and job autonomy, across a time period of three years (Li et al, 2014). The affective consequences of a longer-term change in proactive personality, however, have so far not been explored empirically.

In contrast to proactive personality, changes in proactive behaviours are more likely across relatively shorter time intervals, such as hours, days, weeks, and months. Nevertheless, proactivity researchers have neglected dynamic effects of proactive behaviour (for exceptions, Fay and Sonnentag, 2002; Frese, Garst, and Fay, 2007). However, with a growing interest in the more dynamic affective and well-being consequences of proactivity, it becomes increasingly important to focus on change in proactive behaviour over time. For instance, a recent study on affective and well-being consequences of change in proactive behaviour over a time period of six months has shown that change in personal initiative can impact on subsequent changes in positive and negative moods, above and beyond variance explained by initial individual differences in personal initiative (Zacher et al, 2019). Moreover, change in personal initiative had a negative indirect effect on change in emotional engagement, and a positive indirect effect on change in emotional exhaustion through changes in positive and negative moods. A similar idea in this context suggests that the combination of employees' more stable level of proactive personality and their more dynamic level of proactive behaviour plays a role for affective and well-being consequences of this behaviour (Cangiano, Bindl, and Parker, 2017). Specifically, employees with lower levels of proactive personality might react more negatively after engaging in proactive behaviour because they have to invest more effort into this behaviour.

Literature review

Conceptual approaches to affective consequences of proactivity

This chapter is not the first to conceptually discuss affective consequences of proactivity.

Strauss and Parker (2014), drawing mainly on self-determination theory (Ryan and Deci, 2000), argued that proactive behaviour, as well as the motivations underlying this behaviour (for example, intrinsic versus extrinsic motivation), can impact on employee affect and well-being. As core underlying mechanisms, these researchers proposed a sense of ownership and involvement of the self, as well as the satisfaction of important psychological needs. To further advance research on the well-being consequences of proactive behaviour, Cangiano and Parker (2016) proposed that proactive behaviour can influence employee affect and occupational well-being outcomes via a resource-generation pathway (based on self-determination theory; Gagné and Deci, 2005) and via a resource-depletion pathway (based on conservation of resources theory; Hobfoll, 1989), and that the strength of these effects depends on multiple individual and contextual factors. They argued that 'proactivity is likely to affect mental health and well-being in multiple ways, and that moderating variables and mediating processes need to be considered' (p 229). Proactive employees should be more likely to follow the resource-generation pathway toward well-being when they feel supported and are intrinsically motivated to engage in proactive behaviour, whereas they are more likely to follow the resource-depletion pathway toward job strain when they do not feel supported and are extrinsically motivated (Cangiano and Parker, 2016).

In another book chapter, Cangiano, Bindl, and Parker (2017) suggested that proactive behaviour is not only influenced by affective experiences (for example, Bindl et al, 2012), but that proactive behaviour also can have important consequences for these experiences. In particular, the researchers argued that proactive behaviour can generate 'flow experiences' (that is, enjoyable states of consciousness in which people become fully immersed in challenging, but not overwhelming, activities; Csikszentmihalyi, 1997). At the same time, Cangiano, Bindl, and Parker (2017) argued that proactivity may also give rise to negative affect, due to increased stress and anxiety about evaluations and criticism of one's behaviour by supervisors and peers.

Finally, Parker et al have focused on affective and well-being consequences of proactivity in the context of their research on 'wise proactivity', that is, proactive efforts that consider the appropriateness of the behaviour and its fit with the self and environment (Parker and Liao, 2016; Parker, Wang, and Liao, 2019). In a review of 95 studies on individual-level outcomes of proactivity, these researchers showed that strategic considerations (for example, situational judgment), social considerations (for example, supportive relationships at work), and self-regulatory considerations (for example, learning orientation) determine whether proactivity is more or less effective for individuals (Parker, Wang, and Liao, 2019). It is likely that effective proactivity will, in turn, lead to increased positive and decreased negative affect (Carver and Scheier, 1990; Zacher et al, 2019).

Empirical studies on affective consequences of proactive personality

Employees with a more proactive personality have the tendency to be active rather than passive, to affect positive change in their environment, and to be relatively less constrained by situational forces than employees with a less proactive personality (Bateman and Crant, 1993). While no quantitative review of associations between proactive personality and affective states exists, a meta-analysis of cross-sectional studies found that proactive personality is negatively related to indicators of the burnout syndrome, including emotional exhaustion, depersonalization, and reduced feelings of personal accomplishment (Alarcon, Eschleman, and Bowling, 2009). The researchers argue that proactive employees self-select into work environments that they can change for the better and leave work environments that do not offer such opportunities for control. Consistently, researchers have suggested that a more proactive personality may be particularly beneficial in terms of well-being when employees have high levels of personal control over stressors they face at work (Cunningham and De La Rosa, 2008). Indeed, a recent study showed that coping in the form of positive reinterpretation mediated the link between proactive personality and strain among victims of workplace bullying (Park and DeFrank, 2018).

A number of primary studies have examined direct associations between proactive personality and affective states. First, a study found that positive and negative affect mediated the positive relationship between proactive personality and innovative behaviour (Li et al, 2017). Proactive personality was positively related to positive affect and negatively related to negative affect. Second, a similar study found that positive affect and work engagement serially mediated the positive relationship between proactive personality and innovative behaviour (Kong and Li, 2018). Again, proactive personality was positively related to positive affect. Finally, a set of two studies found that job reflective learning and activated positive affective states serially mediated the relationship between proactive personality and employee creativity (Li et al, 2019). Specifically, learning from successes influenced joviality, whereas learning from failures led to attentiveness.

Several studies have examined interactive effects of proactive personality with other variables on affective experiences as outcomes. First, a study found that the combination of high job demands and low job control only predicted strain among employees with a more (versus less) proactive personality (Parker and Sprigg, 1999). Second, a more recent study found that high levels of negative affect strengthened the positive indirect effects of proactive personality on task performance and affective commitment via job engagement (Haynie, Flynn, and Mauldin, 2017). Third, a study showed that a more proactive personality buffered the positive relationships of two role stressors (that is, role ambiguity and role conflict) with negative affect (Zhang, Crant, and Weng, 2019). Finally, another recent study showed that a more proactive personality weakened the positive effect of hostile customer relations on workers' mental health symptoms (Mazzetti et al, 2019).

In summary, there is evidence that individual differences in proactive personality are positively associated with positive affect and well-being, and negatively associated with negative affect and strain. While some studies suggest that a more proactive personality supports employees in coping with occupational stressors and, subsequently, reduces strain, overall there is currently mixed evidence whether a more proactive personality buffers or boosts the effects of unfavourable work conditions (for example, high demands, low control) on employee strain.

Empirical studies on affective consequences of proactive behaviour

A relatively larger number of studies has investigated relationships between different forms of proactive behaviour and employee well-being outcomes; most of these studies have focused on between-person differences in proactive behaviour and well-being outcomes and not on within-person changes in these constructs. These studies can be broadly classified into studies that demonstrated beneficial effects of proactive behaviour on affective outcomes, detrimental effects on affective outcomes, and both positive and negative effects (that is, dual-pathway studies).

Beneficial effects of proactive behaviour

Consistent with most studies on proactive personality, several studies found positive relationships of proactive behaviour with well-being and negative relationships with strain, including cross-sectional, diary, and experimental studies. First, a cross-sectional study showed that employees' proactive coping behaviour was positively related to positive affect (Greenglass and Fiksenbaum, 2009). Another cross-sectional study of older employees found a positive relationship between proactive behaviour and positive affect which, in turn, was related to a later anticipated retirement age (Claes and Van Loo, 2011). Similarly, a study reported a positive relationship between personal initiative and occupational well-being, and a negative relationship with emotional exhaustion (Wang and Li, 2015).

Another cross-sectional study with teachers showed that proactive behaviour was positively related to affective well-being outcomes, including job satisfaction and commitment (Ghitulescu, 2018). In addition, collaborative behaviour buffered the negative link of proactive behaviour with experienced conflict. Based on an extended job demand–control model, a set of two studies found that employees' voice behaviour and their perceived ability to manage personal resources buffered the effects of perceived abusive supervision on various negative affective and behavioural reactions, including dissatisfaction, emotional exhaustion, and turnover intentions (Frieder, Hochwarter, and DeOrtentiis, 2015).

Second, based on affective events theory (Weiss and Cropanzano, 1996), a daily diary study showed that problem-focused voice in meetings was related to lower negative affect at the end of the next workday (Starzyk, Sonnentag, and Albrecht, 2018). Contrary to expectations, suggestion-focused voice was not related to positive affect at the end of the next workday. Based on control theory, a weekly diary study showed that proactive behaviour during the work week buffered the negative effects of unfinished tasks at the end of the week on competence need satisfaction and rumination on the weekend (Weigelt et al, 2019).

Third, a quasi-experimental field study with 39 employees showed that a job-crafting intervention decreased negative affect and increased self-efficacy and job resources (Van den Heuvel, Demerouti, and Peeters, 2015). Another randomized controlled field experiment with entrepreneurs showed that the need for cognition positively predicted the maintenance of personal initiative following a training (Mensmann and Frese, 2019). In contrast to expectations, personal initiative maintenance had no effects on general and professional affective well-being outcomes.

Finally, in an experimental study, the researchers manipulated affect (positive, negative, and neutral), and measured proactive personality, proactive behaviour in a team interactions task, as well as affective experiences and physiological activation (Wolsink et al, 2019). The study results showed that positive affect reduced proactive behaviour among participants with a more proactive personality, whereas negative affect increased proactive behaviour among participants with a less proactive and more passive–reactive personality. In addition, participants with a more proactive personality experienced increased positive affect after showing proactive behaviour, whereas more passive–reactive participants experienced reduced negative affect after showing proactive behaviour (Wolsink et al, 2019).

Detrimental effects of proactive behaviour

Other studies in this area have found negative effects of proactive work behaviours on affective and well-being outcomes, including cross-sectional, diary, and longitudinal studies. First, a cross-sectional study by Bolino and Turnley (2005) investigated links between 'individual initiative', a dimension of organizational citizenship behaviour, and occupational well-being outcomes. Individual initiative involves working compulsively above and beyond expectations to complete work tasks. The researchers found that higher partner-rated individual initiative was related to higher self-rated role overload, job stress, and work–family conflict.

Second, a daily diary study across three workdays showed that daily personal initiative was positively related to daily cortisol output, an indicator of strain. In contrast to expectations, a test of the hypothesized association between daily personal initiative and fatigue in the evening did not meet conventional levels of statistical significance, and work overload and negative affect did not emerge as mediators (Fay and Hüttges, 2017). The researchers argued that employees' resources (for example, time, energy) are limited and they need to invest additional effort to maintain task performance and show initiative, which should lead to strain.

Third, a two-wave survey study across two weeks examined employee motivations as moderators of the association between proactive behaviour and job strain (Strauss, Parker, and O'Shea, 2017). The researchers hypothesized that when employees experience pressure and coercion at work (that is, high controlled motivation), and this cannot be compensated by high levels of autonomous motivation, proactive behaviour is likely to lead to job strain due to resource depletion. Results showed that supervisor ratings of employee proactive behaviour were positively associated with employee job strain when controlled motivation was high and, at the same time, autonomous motivation was low. Under all other conditions, proactive behaviour was unrelated to job strain. Strauss, Parker, and O'Shea (2017) concluded that proactive behaviour only leads to strain when employees experience pressure and obligation without experiencing autonomous motivation.

Consistent with the study by Strauss, Parker, and O'Shea (2017), a recent longitudinal study with three measurement waves found that proactivity can have costs, especially if it is externally motivated (Pingel, Fay, and Urbach, 2019). Specifically, based on conservation of resources theory, the researchers found that proactive behaviour was positively associated with emotional and cognitive strain. Emotional strain, in turn, was positively related to employee withdrawal. Moreover, external motivation for proactivity strengthened the effects of proactive behaviour on strain.

Dual-pathway effects of proactive behaviour

Consistent with the dual pathway model of proactivity and well-being (Cangiano and Parker, 2016), a third set of recent studies has shown that proactive behaviour can be a double-edged sword at work, as it leads to both favourable and unfavourable employee outcomes. First, a qualitative study examined the 'emotional journeys' that employees go through when engaging in proactive behaviour (Bindl, 2019). Results suggested three narratives associated with these journeys, including a 'proactivity-as-frustration' narrative (that is, proactive behaviour as a generally unpleasant action), a 'proactivity-as-threat' narrative (that is, proactive behaviour that derailed at the beginning due to fear), and a 'proactivity-as-growth' narrative (that is, proactive behaviour that is first associated with negative affect and later with positive affect and sustained motivation).

Second, based on self-determination theory and the stressor-detachment model, a daily diary study found empirical support for an 'energy-generating pathway', in which daily proactive behaviour is positively associated with perceived competence and, in turn, feelings of vitality at the end of the work day (Cangiano, Parker, and Yeo, 2019). Moreover, the researchers found that, when perceived punitive supervision is high (that is, supervisors are perceived as prone to blaming employees for their mistakes), a 'strain pathway' exists, in which daily proactive behaviour is positively associated with anxiety at the end of the workday which, in turn, is negatively related to detachment from work at bedtime.

Third, another within-person, longer-term longitudinal study investigated effects of change in personal initiative over six months on changes in emotional engagement and exhaustion over the following six months (Zacher et al, 2019). Based on the control-process theory on affect, the researchers hypothesized that changes in positive and negative mood mediate these effects conditional upon employees' level of perceived organizational support. Moreover, based on action regulation theory, they assumed that change in job autonomy also acts as a mediator. Results of the study showed that change in personal initiative negatively predicted change in positive mood and, when perceived organizational support was low, positively predicted change in negative mood. In addition, consistent with previous studies on effects of proactivity on work characteristics (Frese, Garst, and Fay, 2007; Li et al, 2014), change in personal initiative positively predicted change in job autonomy. Change in personal initiative had a negative indirect effect on change in emotional engagement, and a positive indirect effect on change in emotional exhaustion through changes in positive and negative mood, but not through change in job autonomy. The researchers also tested a reverse causal model (that is, effects of change in occupational well-being on change in personal initiative through changes in affect and job autonomy), which did not yield significant indirect effects.

Suggestions for future research

The goal of this chapter was to address the hitherto rather neglected topic of affective consequences of proactivity. To this end, I presented a conceptual model on the affective consequences of (change in) proactive personality and behaviour, and I reviewed existing theoretical and empirical work on the topic. Now, I will outline suggestion for future research.

Future research on the affective consequences of proactivity could use the conceptual model presented in this chapter (Figure 12.1) to examine why and when individual differences and change in proactivity lead to positive and negative affective and well-being outcomes. First, more experimental and longitudinal work is needed on the mechanisms that translate (change in) proactivity into (change in) affective experiences. In particular, future studies should examine whether or not proactive behaviour leads to the intended positive changes in the self and the environment. While these intended changes are mentioned in definitions of proactivity (Grant and Ashford, 2008), proactive behaviour may not always yield the intended outcomes. In addition, more research is needed on the relative importance of different psychological states, including perceived changes in resources, need satisfaction, and goal progress, in mediating effects of proactivity on affective outcomes. Previous research has theorized on these mechanisms (for example, Strauss, Parker, and O'Shea, 2017; Zacher et al, 2019), but not explicitly addressed and compared them.

Second, the conceptual model suggests that individual and contextual demands, resources, and barriers, as well as individual differences in trait affectivity, moderate the processes leading from proactivity to affective outcomes. A few studies have examined single moderators of association of proactivity with well-being and strain, such as motivation (Strauss, Parker, and O'Shea, 2017), punitive supervision (Cangiano, Parker, and Yeo, 2019), and perceived organizational support (Zacher et al., 2019). A crucial next step is to compare the relative importance of these boundary conditions to develop a more specific yet parsimonious model of the outcomes of proactivity.

Third, there is a broad range or proactivity constructs (for example, personal initiative, voice, job-crafting, feedback-seeking), as well as various affective and well-being outcomes (for example, high- and low-activated positive and negative affect, emotional engagement and exhaustion) that can be considered in future studies. It remains to be investigated whether the mechanisms and boundary conditions suggested by the conceptual model apply to all of these proactivity constructs and outcomes or only to specific ones. Importantly, future research should examine which types of proactive behaviour are most beneficial and which are most detrimental to employees' positive affective experiences and well-being – both in the short term and in the long run.

Finally, with regard to study designs, the literature review in this chapter suggests that more studies on within-person changes in proactivity and affect across different time intervals are needed. The few existing studies on the affective consequences of proactivity have used cross-sectional, diary, longitudinal, and experimental methods. Nevertheless, the vast majority of these studies have focus on between- or within-person variability, not change. Thus, future work should assess proactivity and affective outcomes (as well as potential mechanisms and boundary conditions) across multiple time points to better understand how change in proactivity is associated with previous, concurrent, or subsequent changes in affective experiences and occupational health and well-being outcomes (for example, Zacher et al, 2019).

Conclusion

The number of between- and within-person studies on the affective and well-being consequences of proactivity has increased over the last few years, and the empirical evidence suggests that proactive personality and behaviour can have both beneficial and detrimental effects on affective experiences and well-being. Future research should focus on the mechanisms and boundary conditions of these effects to better understand why proactivity constitutes a double-edged sword in terms of affective and well-being outcomes in the work context. In particular, more research is needed that focuses on change (instead of variability) in these constructs.

References

Alarcon, G., Eschleman, K. J., and Bowling, N. A. (2009). Relationships between personality variables and burnout: A meta-analysis. *Work & Stress,* 23(3), 244–63. doi:10.1080/02678370903282600.

Anseel, F., Beatty, A. S., Shen, W., Lievens, F., and Sackett, P. R. (2015). How are we doing after 30 years? A meta-analytic review of the antecedents and outcomes of feedback-seeking behavior. *Journal of Management,* 41(1), 318–48. doi:10.1177/0149206313484521.

Bakker, A. B. (2010). Engagement and 'job crafting': Engaged employees create their own great place to work. In S. L. Albrecht (ed), *Handbook of Employee Engagement: Perspectives, Issues, Research and Practice,* Cheltenham: Edward Elgar, pp 229–44.

Barsade, S. G. and Gibson, D. E. (2007). Why does affect matter in organizations? *Academy of Management Perspectives,* 21(1), 36–59. doi:10.5465/AMP.2007.24286163.

Bateman, T. S. and Crant, J. M. (1993). The proactive component of organizational behavior: A measure and correlates. *Journal of Organizational Behavior,* 14, 103–118. doi:10.1002/job.4030140202.

Beal, D. J., Weiss, H. M., Barros, E., and MacDermid, S. M. (2005). An episodic process model of affective influences on performance. *Journal of Applied Psychology,* 90(6), 1054–68. doi:10.1037/0021-9010.90.6.1054.

Belschak, F. D., Hartog, D. N., and Fay, D. (2010). Exploring positive, negative and context-dependent aspects of proactive behaviours at work. *Journal of Occupational and Organizational Psychology,* 83(2), 267–73. doi:10.1348/096317910X501143.

Bertolino, M., Truxillo, D. M., and Fraccaroli, F. (2011). Age as moderator of the relationship of proactive personality with training motivation, perceived career development from training, and training behavioral intentions. *Journal of Organizational Behavior,* 32(2), 248–63. doi:10.1002/job.670.

Bindl, U. K. (2019). Work-related proactivity through the lens of narrative: Investigating emotional journeys in the process of making things happen. *Human Relations,* 72(4), 615–645. doi:10.1177/0018726718778086.

Bindl, U. K. and Parker, S. K. (2011). Proactive work behavior: Forward-thinking and change-oriented action in organizations. In S. Zedeck (ed), *APA Handbook of Industrial and Organizational Psychology,* vol 2, Washington, DC: American Psychological Association, pp 567–98.

Bindl, U. K. and Parker, S. K. (2012). Affect and employee proactivity: A goal-regulatory perspective. In N. Ashkanasy, C. Härtel, and W. Zerbe (eds), *Experiencing and Managing Emotions in the Workplace,* Bingley: Emerald, pp 225–54.

Bindl, U. K., Parker, S. K., Totterdell, P., and Hagger-Johnson, G. (2012). Fuel of the self-starter: How mood relates to proactive goal regulation. *Journal of Applied Psychology,* 97(1), 34–150. doi:10.1037/a0024368.

Bolino, M. C., Hsiung, H. H., Harvey, J., and LePine, J. A. (2015). 'Well, I'm tired of tryin'!' Organizational citizenship behavior and citizenship fatigue. *Journal of Applied Psychology,* 100(1), 56–74. doi:10.1037/a0037583.

Bolino, M. C. and Turnley, W. H. (2005). The personal costs of citizenship behavior: The relationship between individual initiative and role overload, job stress, and work-family conflict. *Journal of Applied Psychology,* 90(4), 740. doi:10.1037/0021-9010.90.4.740.

Bolino, M. C., Turnley, W. H., and Anderson, H. J. (2017). The dark side of proactive behavior: When being proactive may hurt oneself, others, or the organization. In S. K. Parker and U. K. Bindl (eds), *Proactivity at Work: Making Things Happen in Organizations,* New York: Taylor & Francis.

Bolino, M. C., Valcea, S., and Harvey, J. (2010). Employee, manage thyself: The potentially negative implications of expecting employees to behave proactively. *Journal of Occupational and Organizational Psychology,* 83(2), 325–45. doi:10.1348/096317910X493134.

Brief, A. P. and Weiss, H. M. (2002). Organizational behavior: Affect in the workplace. *Annual Review of Psychology,* 53, 279–307. doi:10.1146/annurev. psych.53.100901.135156.

Brown, D. J., Cober, R. T., Kane, K., Levy, P. E., and Shalhoop, J. (2006). Proactive personality and the successful job search: A field investigation with college graduates. *Journal of Applied Psychology,* 91(3), 717–27.

Bruning, P. F., and Campion, M. A. (2019). Exploring job crafting: Diagnosing and responding to the ways employees adjust their jobs. *Business Horizons,* 62(5), 625–35. doi:10.1016/j.bushor.2019.05.003.

Campos, F., Frese, M., Goldstein, M., Iacovone, L., Johnson, H. C., McKenzie, D., and Mensmann, M. (2017). Teaching personal initiative beats traditional training in boosting small business in West Africa. *Science,* 357(6357), 1287–90. doi:10.1126/science.aan5329.

Cangiano, F., Bindl, U. K., and Parker, S. K. (2017). The 'hot' side of proactivity: Exploring an affect-based perspective on proactivity in organizations. In S. K. Parker and U. K. Bindl (eds), *Proactivity at Work: Making Things Happen in Organizations,* New York: Taylor & Francis, pp 355–84.

Cangiano, F. and Parker, S. K. (2016). Proactivity for mental health and well-being. In S. Clarke, T. M. Probst, F. Guldenmund, and J. Passmore (eds), *The Wiley Blackwell Handbook of the Psychology of Occupational Safety and Workplace Health,* London: Wiley, pp 228–50.

Cangiano, F., Parker, S. K., and Yeo, G. B. (2019). Does daily proactivity affect well-being? The moderating role of punitive supervision. *Journal of Organizational Behavior,* 40(1), 59–72. doi:10.1002/job.2321.

Carver, C. S. and Scheier, M. F. (1982). Control theory: A useful conceptual framework for personality-social, clinical, and health psychology. *Psychological Bulletin*, 92, 111–35. doi:10.1037/0033-2909.92.1.111.

Carver, C. S. and Scheier, M. F. (1990). Origins and functions of positive and negative affect: A control-process view. *Psychological Review*, 97(1), 19–35. doi:10.1037/0033-295X.97.1.19.

Chi, N. W., Chang, H. T., and Huang, H. L. (2015). Can personality traits and daily positive mood buffer the harmful effects of daily negative mood on task performance and service sabotage? A self-control perspective. *Organizational Behavior and Human Decision Processes*, 131, 1–15. doi:10.1016/j.obhdp.2015.07.005.

Claes, R. and Van Loo, K. (2011). Relationships of proactive behaviour with job-related affective well-being and anticipated retirement age: An exploration among older employees in Belgium. *European Journal of Ageing*, 8, 233–41. doi:10.1007/s10433-011-0203-7.

Cole, M. S., Walter, F., and Bruch, H. (2008). Affective mechanisms linking dysfunctional behavior to performance in work teams: A moderated nediation study. *Journal of Applied Psychology*, 93(5), 945–58.

Crant, J. M. (1995). The proactive personality scale and objective job performance among real estate agents. *Journal of Applied Psychology*, 80(4), 532–7. doi:10.1037/0021-9010.80.4.532.

Csikszentmihalyi, M. (1997). *Finding Flow: The Psychology of Engagement with Everyday Life*. New York: Basic Books.

Cunningham, C. J. L. and De La Rosa, G. M. (2008). The interactive effects of proactive personality and work-family interference on well-being. *Journal of Occupational Health Psychology*, 13(3), 271–82. doi:10.1037/1076-8998.13.3.271.

Dalal, R. S., Lam, H., Weiss, H. M., Welch, E. R., and Hulin, C. L. (2009). A within-person approach to work behavior and performance: Concurrent and lagged citizenship-counterproductivity associations, and dynamic relationships with affect and overall job performance. *Academy of Management Journal*, 52, 1051–66. doi:10.5465/AMJ.2009.44636148.

Den Hartog, D. N. and Belschak, F. D. (2007). Personal initiative, commitment and affect at work. *Journal of Occupational and Organizational Psychology*, 80(4), 601–22. doi:10.1348/096317906X171442.

Fay, D. and Hüttges, A. (2017). Drawbacks of proactivity: Effects of daily proactivity on daily salivary cortisol and subjective well-being. *Journal of Occupational Health Psychology*, 22(4), 429–42. doi:10.1037/ocp0000042.

Fay, D. and Sonnentag, S. (2002). Rethinking the effects of stressors: A longitudinal study on personal initiative. *Journal of Occupational Health Psychology*, 7, 221–34. doi:10.1037/1076-8998.7.3.221.

Fay, D. and Sonnentag, S. (2012). Within-person fluctuations of proactive behavior: How affect and experienced competence regulate work behavior. *Human Performance,* 25(1), 72–93. doi:10.1080/08959285.2011.631647.

Frese, M. and Fay, D. (2001). Personal initiative: An active performance concept for work in the 21st century. *Research in Organizational Behavior,* 23, 133–187. doi:10.1016/S0191-3085(01)23005–6.

Frese, M., Garst, H., and Fay, D. (2007). Making things happen: Reciprocal relationships between work characteristics and personal initiative in a four-wave longitudinal structural equation model. *Journal of Applied Psychology,* 92, 1084–102. doi:10.1037/0021-9010.92.4.1084.

Frieder, R. E., Hochwarter, W. A., and DeOrtentiis, P. S. (2015). Attenuating the negative effects of abusive supervision: The role of proactive voice behavior and resource management ability. *The Leadership Quarterly,* 26(5), 821–37. doi:10.1016/j.leaqua.2015.06.001.

Fritz, C. and Sonnentag, S. (2009). Antecedents of day-level proactive behavior: A look at job stressors and positive affect during the workday. *Journal of Management,* 35(1), 94–111. doi:10.1177/0149206307308911.

Fuller, J. B. and Marler, L. E. (2009). Change driven by nature: A meta-analytic review of the proactive personality literature. *Journal of Vocational Behavior,* 75(3), 329–45. doi:10.1016/j.jvb.2009.05.008.

Gagné, M. and Deci, E. L. (2005). Self-determination theory and work motivation. *Journal of Organizational Behavior,* 26(4), 331–62. doi:10.1002/job.322.

Ghitulescu, B. E. (2018). Psychosocial effects of proactivity: The interplay between proactive and collaborative behavior. *Personnel Review,* 47(2), 294–318. doi:10.1108/PR-08-2016-0209.

Grant, A. M. (2013). Rocking the boat but keeping it steady: The role of emotion regulation in employee voice. *Academy of Management Journal,* 56(6), 1703–23. doi:10.5465/amj.2011.0035.

Grant, A. M. and Ashford, S. J. (2008). The dynamics of proactivity at work. *Research in Organizational Behavior,* 28, 3–34. doi:10.1016/j.riob.2008.04.002.

Grant, A. M., Parker, S., and Collins, C. (2009). Getting credit for proactive behavior: Supervisor reactions depend on what you value and how you feel. *Personnel Psychology,* 62(1), 31–55. doi:10.1111/j.1744-6570.2008.01128.x.

Greenglass, E. R. and Fiksenbaum, L. (2009). Proactive coping, positive affect, and well-being: Testing for mediation using path analysis. *European Psychologist,* 14(1), 29–39. doi:10.1027/1016-9040.14.1.29.

Hacker, W. (2003). Action regulation theory: A practical tool for the design of modern work processes? *European Journal of Work and Organizational Psychology,* 12, 105–30. doi:10.1080/13594320344000075.

Halbesleben, J. R. B., Harvey, J., and Bolino, M. C. (2009). Too engaged? A conservation of resources view of the relationship between work engagement and work interference with family. *Journal of Applied Psychology,* 94(6), 1452–1465. doi:10.1037/a0017595.

Haynie, J. J., Flynn, C. B., and Mauldin, S. (2017). Proactive personality, core self-evaluations, and engagement: The role of negative emotions. *Management Decision,* 55(2), 450–63. doi:10.1108/MD-07-2016-0464.

Hirschi, A., Shockley, K. M., and Zacher, H. (2019). Achieving work-family balance: An action regulation model. *Academy of Management Review,* 44(1), 150–71. doi:10.5465/amr.2016.0409.

Hobfoll, S. E. (1989). Conservation of resources: A new attempt at conceptualizing stress. *American Psychologist,* 44(3), 513–24. doi:10.1037/0003-066X.44.3.513.

Hobfoll, S. E., Halbesleben, J., Neveu, J.-P., and Westman, M. (2018). Conservation of resources in the organizational context: The reality of resources and their consequences. *Annual Review of Organizational Psychology and Organizational Behavior,* 5, 103–28. doi:10.1146/annurev-orgpsych-032117-104640.

Johnson, R. E. and Howe, M. (2013). The importance of velocity, or why speed may matter more than distance. *Organizational Psychology Review,* 3, 62–85.

Kong, Y. and Li, M. (2018). Proactive personality and innovative behavior: The mediating roles of job-related affect and work engagement. *Social Behavior and Personality: An International Journal,* 46(3), 431–46. doi:10.2224/sbp.6618.

Lam, C. F., Spreitzer, G., and Fritz, C. (2014). Too much of a good thing: Curvilinear effect of positive affect on proactive behaviors. *Journal of Organizational Behavior,* 35(4), 530–46. doi:10.1002/job.1906.

Lebel, R. D. (2017). Moving beyond fight and flight: A contingent model of how the emotional regulation of anger and fear sparks proactivity. *Academy of Management Review,* 42(2), 190–206. doi:10.5465/amr.2014.0368.

LePine, J. A. and Van Dyne, L. (1998). Predicting voice behavior in work groups. *Journal of Applied Psychology,* 83(6), 853–68. doi:10.1037/0021-9010.83.6.853.

Li, F., Chen, T., Chen, Y. F. N., Bai, Y., and Crant, J. M. (2019). Proactive yet reflective? Materializing proactive personality into creativity through job reflective learning and activated positive affective states. *Personnel Psychology.* doi:10.1111/peps.12370.

Li, M., Liu, Y., Liu, L., and Wang, Z. (2017). Proactive personality and innovative work behavior: The mediating effects of affective states and creative self-efficacy in teachers. *Current Psychology,* 36(4), 697–706. doi:10.1007/s12144-016-9457-8.

Li, W.-D., Fay, D., Frese, M., Harms, P. D., and Gao, X. Y. (2014). Reciprocal relationship between proactive personality and work characteristics: A latent change score approach. *Journal of Applied Psychology,* 99(5), 948–65. doi:10.1037/a0036169.

Liang, J., Farh, C. I., and Farh, J. L. (2012). Psychological antecedents of promotive and prohibitive voice: A two-wave examination. *Academy of Management Journal,* 55(1), 71–92. doi:10.5465/amj.2010.0176.

Mazzetti, G., Simbula, S., Panari, C., Guglielmi, D., and Paolucci, A. (2019). 'Woulda, coulda, shoulda': Workers' proactivity in the association between emotional demands and mental health. *International Journal of Environmental Research and Public Health,* 16(18), 3309. doi:10.3390/ijerph16183309.

Mensmann, M. and Frese, M. (2019). Who stays proactive after entrepreneurship training? Need for cognition, personal initiative maintenance, and well-being. *Journal of Organizational Behavior,* 40(1), 20–37. doi:10.1002/job.2333.

Morrison, E. W. (2014). Employee voice and silence. *Annual Review of Organizational Psychology and Organizational Behavior,* 1(1), 173–97. doi:10.1146/annurev-orgpsych-031413-091328.

Ng, T. W. H. and Feldman, D. C. (2012). Age and innovation-related behavior: The joint moderating effects of supervisor undermining and proactive personality. *Journal of Organizational Behavior,* 34(5), 583–606. doi:10.1002/job.1802.

Nye, C. and Roberts, B. W. (2019). A neo-socioanalytic model of personality development. In B. B. Baltes, C. W. Rudolph, and H. Zacher (eds), *Work Across the Lifespan,* London: Academic Press, pp 47–79.

Park, J. H. and DeFrank, R. S. (2018). The role of proactive personality in the stressor–strain model. *International Journal of Stress Management,* 25(1), 44–59. doi:10.1037/str0000048.

Parker, S. K. and Bindl, U. K. (2017). *Proactivity at Work: Making Things Happen in Organizations.* New York: Routledge.

Parker, S. K., Bindl, U. K., and Strauss, K. (2010). Making things happen: A model of proactive motivation. *Journal of Management,* 36(4), 827–56. doi:10.1177/0149206310363732.

Parker, S. K. and Collins, C. G. (2010). Taking stock: Integrating and differentiating multiple proactive behaviors. *Journal of Management,* 36(3), 633–62. doi:10.1177/0149206308321554.

Parker, S. K. and Liao, J. (2016). Wise proactivity: How to be proactive and wise in building your career. *Organizational Dynamics,* 3(45), 217–27. doi:10.1016/j.orgdyn.2016.07.007.

Parker, S. K. and Sprigg, C. A. (1999). Minimizing strain and maximizing learning: The role of job demands, job control, and proactive personality. *Journal of Applied Psychology,* 84(6), 925–39. doi:10.1037/0021-9010.84.6.925.

Parker, S. K., Wang, Y., and Liao, J. (2019). When is proactivity wise? A review of factors that influence the individual outcomes of proactive behavior. *Annual Review of Organizational Psychology and Organizational Behavior,* 6, 221–248. doi:10.1146/annurev-orgpsych-012218-015302.

Peng, Z. and Wu, C. (eds) (2020) *Emotion and Proactivity.* Bristol: Bristol University Press.

Pingel, R., Fay, D., and Urbach, T. (2019). A resources perspective on when and how proactive work behaviour leads to employee withdrawal. *Journal of Occupational and Organizational Psychology*, 92(2), 410–35. doi:10.1111/joop.12254.

Roberts, B. W., Walton, K. E., and Viechtbauer, W. (2006). Patterns of mean-level change in personality traits across the life course: A meta-analysis of longitudinal studies. *Psychological Bulletin*, 132(1), 1–25. doi:10.1037/0033-2909.132.1.1.

Rudolph, C. W., Katz, I. M., Lavigne, K. N., and Zacher, H. (2017). Job crafting: A meta-analysis of relationships with individual differences, job characteristics, and work outcomes. *Journal of Vocational Behavior*, 102, 112–38. doi:10.1016/j.jvb.2017.05.008.

Rusting, C. L. and Larsen, R. J. (1997). Extraversion, neuroticism, and susceptibility to positive and negative affect: A test of two theoretical models. *Personality and Individual Differences*, 22(5), 607–12.

Ryan, R. M. and Deci, E. L. (2000). Self-determination theory and the facilitation of intrinsic motivation, social development, and well-being. *American Psychologist*, 55(1), 68–78. doi:10.1037/0003-066X.55.1.68.

Schmitt, A., Den Hartog, D. N., and Belschak, F. D. (2015). Is outcome responsibility at work emotionally exhausting? Investigating employee proactivity as a moderator. *Journal of Occupational Health Psychology*, 20(4), 491–500. doi:10.1037/a0039011.

Seibert, S. E., Crant, J. M., and Kraimer, M. L. (1999). Proactive personality and career success. *Journal of Applied Psychology*, 84, 416–27.

Seibert, S. E., Kraimer, M. L., and Crant, J. M. (2001). What do proactive people do? A longitudinal model linking proactive personality and career success. *Personnel Psychology*, 54(4), 845–74. doi:10.1111/j.1744–6570.2001.tb00234.x.

Sonnentag, S. and Starzyk, A. (2015). Perceived prosocial impact, perceived situational constraints, and proactive work behavior: Looking at two distinct affective pathways. *Journal of Organizational Behavior*, 36(6), 806–24. doi:10.1002/job.2005.

Srivastava, S., John, O. P., Gosling, S. D., and Potter, J. (2003). Development of personality in early and middle adulthood: Set like plaster or persistent change? *Journal of Personality and Social Psychology*, 84(5), 1041–53. doi:10.1037/0022-3514.84.5.1041.

Starzyk, A., Sonnentag, S., and Albrecht, A. G. (2018). The affective relevance of suggestion-focused and problem-focused voice: A diary study on voice in meetings. *Journal of Occupational and Organizational Psychology*, 91(2), 340–61. doi:10.1111/joop.12199.

Strauss, K., and Parker, S. K. (2014). Effective and sustained proactivity in the workplace: A self-determination theory perspective. In M. Gagné (ed), *The Oxford Handbook of Work Engagement, Motivation, and Self-Determination Theory*, Oxford: Oxford University Press, pp 50–72.

Strauss, K., Parker, S. K., and O'Shea, D. (2017). When does proactivity have a cost? Motivation at work moderates the effects of proactive work behavior on employee job strain. *Journal of Vocational Behavior,* 100, 15–26. doi:10.1016/j.jvb.2017.02.001.

ten Brummelhuis, L. L. and Bakker, A. B. (2012). A resource perspective on the work-home interface: The Work–Home Resources Model. *American Psychologist,* 67(7), 545–56. doi:10.1037/a0027974.

Tett, R. P. and Guterman, H. A. (2000). Situation trait relevance, trait expression, and cross-situational consistency: Testing a principle of trait activation. *Journal of Research in Personality,* 34(4), 397–423. doi:10.1006/jrpe.2000.2292.

Tett, R. P., Simonet, D. V., Walser, B., and Brown, C. (2013). Trait activation theory: Applications, developments, and implications for person–workplace fit. In N. D. Christiansen and R. P. Tett (eds), *Handbook of Personality at Work,* New York: Routledge, pp 71–100.

Thomas, J. P., Whitman, D. S., and Viswesvaran, C. (2010). Employee proactivity in organizations: A comparative meta-analysis of emerging proactive constructs. *Journal of Occupational and Organizational Psychology,* 83, 275–300. doi:10.1348/096317910X502359.

Tims, M. and Bakker, A. B. (2010). Job crafting: Towards a new model of individual job redesign. *South African Journal of Industrial Psychology,* 36, 1–9. doi:10.4102/sajip.v36i2.841.

Tornau, K. and Frese, M. (2013). Construct clean-up in proactivity research: A meta-analysis on the nomological net of work-related proactivity concepts and their incremental validities. *Applied Psychology: An International Review,* 62, 44–96. doi:10.1111/j.1464-0597.2012.00514.x.

Van den Heuvel, M., Demerouti, E., and Peeters, M. C. W. (2015). The job crafting intervention: Effects on job resources, self-efficacy, and affective well-being. *Journal of Occupational and Organizational Psychology,* 88(3), 511–32. doi:10.1111/joop.12128.

Van Dyne, L. and LePine, J. A. (1998). Helping and voice extra-role behaviors: Evidence of construct and predictive validity. *Academy of Management Journal,* 41(1), 108–19. doi:10.5465/256902.

Wang, H. and Li, J. (2015). How trait curiosity influences psychological well-being and emotional exhaustion: The mediating role of personal initiative. *Personality and Individual Differences,* 75, 135–40. doi:10.1016/j.paid.2014.11.020.

Wang, M., Beal, D. J., Chan, D., Newman, D. A., Vancouver, J. B., and Vandenberg, R. J. (2017). Longitudinal research: A panel discussion on conceptual issues, research design, and statistical techniques. *Work, Aging and Retirement,* 3(1), 1–24. doi:10.1093/workar/waw033.

Wang, Z., Xu, S., Sun, Y., and Liu, Y. (2019). Transformational leadership and employee voice: An affective perspective. *Frontiers of Business Research in China,* 13(1), 2. doi:10.1186/s11782-019-0049-y.

Warr, P., Bindl, U. K., Parker, S. K., and Inceoglu, I. (2014). Four-quadrant investigation of job-related affects and behaviours. *European Journal of Work and Organizational Psychology*, 23(3), 342–63. doi:10.1080/1359432X.2012.744449.

Watson, D., Clark, L. A., and Tellegen, A. (1988). Development and validation of brief measures of positive and negative affect: The PANAS scales. *Journal of Personality and Social Psychology*, 54, 1063–70. doi:10.1037/0022-3514.54.6.1063.

Weigelt, O., Syrek, C. J., Schmitt, A., and Urbach, T. (2019). Finding peace of mind when there still is so much left undone – A diary study on how job stress, competence need satisfaction, and proactive work behavior contribute to work-related rumination during the weekend. *Journal of Occupational Health Psychology*, 24(3), 373–86. doi:10.1037/ocp0000117.

Weiss, H. M. and Cropanzano, R. (1996). Affective Events Theory: A theoretical discussion of the structure, causes and consequences of affective experiences at work. In B. M. Staw and L. L. Cummings (eds), *Research in Organizational Behavior*, Greenwich, CT: JAI Press, pp 1–74.

Weiss, M. and Morrison, E. W. (2018). Speaking up and moving up: How voice can enhance employees' social status. *Journal of Organizational Behavior*. doi:10.1002/job.2262.

Wille, B. and De Fruyt, F. (2014). Vocations as a source of identity: Reciprocal relations between Big Five personality traits and RIASEC characteristics over 15 years. *Journal of Applied Psychology*, 99(2), 262–81. doi:10.1037/a0034917.

Wolsink, I., Den Hartog, D. D., Belschak, F. D., and Oosterwijk, S. (2019). Do you feel like being proactive today? Trait-proactivity moderates affective causes and consequences of proactive behavior. *PLoS ONE*, 14(8), e0220172. doi:10.1371/journal.pone.0220172.

Woods, S. A., Wille, B., Wu, C. H., Lievens, F., and De Fruyt, F. (2019). The influence of work on personality trait development: The demands-affordances TrAnsactional (DATA) model, an integrative review, and research agenda. *Journal of Vocational Behavior*, 110, 258–71. doi:10.1016/j.jvb.2018.11.010.

Wrzesniewski, A. and Dutton, J. E. (2001). Crafting a job: Revisioning employees as active crafters of their work. *Academy of Management Review*, 26(2), 179–201. doi:10.5465/AMR.2001.4378011.

Zacher, H. (2013). Older job seekers' job search intensity: The interplay of proactive personality, age, and occupational future time perspective. *Ageing & Society*, 33(7), 1139–66. doi:10.1017/S0144686X12000451.

Zacher, H. and Frese, M. (2018). Action regulation theory: Foundations, current knowledge, and future directions. In D. S. Ones, N. R. Anderson, C. Viswesvaran, and H. K. Sinangil (eds), *The SAGE Handbook of Industrial, Work and Organizational Psychology*, 2nd edn, vol 2: Organizational psychology, Thousand Oaks, CA: Sage, pp 80–102.

Zacher, H. and Rudolph, C. W. (2020). How a dynamic way of thinking can challenge existing knowledge in organizational behavior. In Y. J.-L. Griep, S. D. Hansen, T. Vantilborgh, and J. Hofmans (eds), *Handbook on the Temporal Dynamics of Organizational Behavior*. Cheltenham: Edward Elgar.

Zacher, H., Schmitt, A., Jimmieson, N. L., and Rudolph, C. W. (2019). Dynamic effects of personal initiative on engagement and exhaustion: The role of mood, autonomy, and support. *Journal of Organizational Behavior,* 40(1), 38–58. doi:10.1002/job.2277.

Zacher, H. and Wilden, R. G. (2014). A daily diary study on ambidextrous leadership and self-reported employee innovation. *Journal of Occupational and Organizational Psychology,* 87(4), 813–20. doi:10.1111/joop.12070.

Zhang, F., and Parker, S. K. (2019). Reorienting job crafting research: A hierarchical structure of job crafting concepts and integrative review. *Journal of Organizational Behavior,* 40(2), 126–46. doi:10.1002/job.2332.

Zhang, Y., Crant, J. M., and Weng, Q. D. (2019). Role stressors and counterproductive work behavior: The role of negative affect and proactive personality. *International Journal of Selection and Assessment,* 27(3), 267–79. doi:10.1111/ijsa.12255.

Conclusions and Future Directions

Chia-Huei Wu and Kelly Z. Peng

The collection of chapters in this book is aimed to offer comprehensive reviews on studies of emotion and proactivity, disseminate new thinking to advance the understanding of the emotional process of proactivity, and provide suggestions for future research. There is a consensus that emotion and proactivity is a topic that should be further studied by all authors of this book, which is elaborated in Chapter 1 (Peng, Li, and Bindl), especially based on the quantitative review of the literature. All our authors have collectively indicated research avenues for exploration with several in consents. Grounding on these, this chapter provides an integrative review of all the chapters and outlines the agreed future research avenues from this edited book.

An integrative review

The chapters in this book have collectively extended our understanding of the subject on emotion and proactivity. To offer an overview of how all the chapters have extended the understanding of the subject, we use Figure 13.1 to indicate the links between work across chapters. As indicated, in almost all chapters, the 'energized to' process or the energy perspective proposed by Parker, Bindl, and Strauss (2010) is the seminal and influential work to understand the role of emotion in proactivity research. In brief, they propose that emotion, positive emotion in particular, will bring energy to employees to initiate and foster their actions to make changes at work. We used the dash-line triangle in the figure to represent their work.

Peng, Li, and Bindl, (Chapter 1) have done a systematic review of the literature from both a quantitative and qualitative perspective. The findings based on the quantitative review indicate that emotions began

Figure 13.1: An overview of chapters in this book

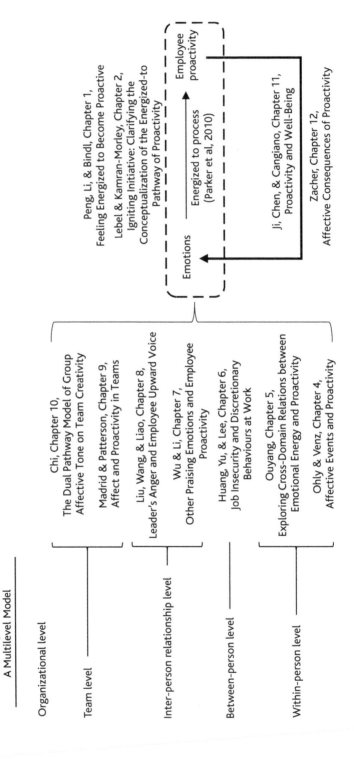

to receive attention from proactivity researchers in the last two decades. However, the knowledge is dispersed and limited. Findings based on the qualitative review show that the positive and negative affect shows effects on proactivity differently, yet negative affect is still inconclusive no matter as antecedents or consequences of proactivity. Both the quantitative and qualitative reviews show that discrete emotions and the proactivity link is an under-investigated topic. More importantly, the chapter concludes that there are two major theoretical perspectives: energy perspective – affective experiences, especially positive ones, serve as energy/resource to be proactive at work; and information perspective – emotions convey differential social cues to self and others to inform proactive behaviour differently. Such a theoretical summary would facilitate and guide the future research, and the latter one will benefit the research of discrete emotion and proactivity particularly.

Lebel and Kamran-Morley (Chapter 2) propose to focus on how discrete emotions may impact proactivity. By doing this, scholars will be able to look into the role of specific emotions in facilitating or impeding employees' proactivity. Their chapter thus extends Parker, Bindl, and Strauss's (2010) work by expanding the scope of emotion discussed in the proactivity literature and highlighting that there could be alternative motivational processes other than the energizing process, that emotions can shape employees' proactivity. The chapter also suggests proactivity scholars focusing on contingent, rather than main, effects to better understand when discrete emotional states impact proactivity.

Next, Ashkanasy (Chapter 3) offers a multilevel model perspective in studying emotions, providing a framework to pin down the level of analysis of which scholars should be mindful when they study emotion and proactivity in the workplace. As Parker, Bindl, and Strauss (2010) did not address the level of analysis in their work, Ashkanasy's chapter extends the discussion on emotion and proactivity by highlighting the importance to look into the concepts and functions of emotion in different levels of context. As shown in the figure, he proposed five levels of analysis of emotions: (1) within person temporal variation in emotions; (2) between-person individual differences in experiencing and expressing emotions; (3) perception and communication of emotions in interpersonal relationships; (4) emotions in groups and teams; and (5) emotional culture and culture at the organizational level of analysis. His chapter helps enrich studies on emotion and proactivity in the workplace because emotional phenomena at different levels are different in their nature (for example, individual's positive feeling versus positive group affective tone) and processes (for example, individual emotional reactions versus social contagion among a group of people). Therefore, Ashkanasy's chapter further extends the scope of studies on emotion and proactivity by directing researchers' attention to investigate the contexts. The value of the multilevel framework can be demonstrated when we map Chapter 4 to Chapter 10 onto different levels, as shown in Figure 13.1.

Ohly and Venz's (Chapter 4) work on event analysis offers an approach to study emotion and proactivity at the within-person level, as individuals have different emotional reactions in responding to different work events, which shape their proactive actions consequently. In this chapter, Ohly and Venz have reviewed and indicated how specific work events can engender specific emotional reactions, which then have implications for employees' proactive behaviour. As such, their chapter not only offers an approach for a within-person analysis but also indicates work events shape employees' emotion and proactivity. So far, work events analysis has been rarely used to understand employees' emotion and proactivity. Ohly and Venz's chapter offers an excellent example, showing how we can use the approach to enrich our knowledge about employees' emotion and proactivity.

Ouyang (Chapter 5) offers a review on emotion and proactivity from a cross-domain (for example, work and family) perspective, a different angle to understand emotion and proactivity at the within-person level. Her chapter indicates that an individual's proactivity at work is not only shaped by events or experiences at work but also shaped by activities and experiences in other life domains. Such an angle extends the contexts of studying emotion and proactivity beyond workplace and highlights that we cannot ignore an individual's life context when we seek to understand his/her emotional experiences and work behaviours. In the meantime, the recognition of cross-domain influence highlights that managers or organizations will need to pay attention to the role of work–family or work–life balance policies and practices in promoting employees' well-being and proactivity.

Next, in Chapter 6, Huang, Yu, and Lee focus on how job insecurity can induce different emotions and consequently proactive actions. We consider their chapter as an example to study emotion and proactivity at the between-person level, as they suggest that those experiencing higher levels of job insecurity, comparing to those experiencing higher levels of job insecurity, are more likely to experience approach-oriented emotions such as anger, and avoidance-oriented emotions such as fear. Approach-oriented emotions will then drive employees to behave proactively to cope with the negative situations, such as voice or feedback-seeking. In contrast, avoidance-oriented emotions will lead individuals to withdraw their effort and have a higher intention to leave. This chapter thus suggests that job insecurity can elicit different emotions and different reactions across individuals in responding to such an unfavourable situation.

Moving towards the interpersonal relationship level, Wu and Li's chapter (Chapter 7) focuses on other praising emotions, namely gratitude, elevation, admiration, and awe, engendered when an individual observes behaviours or achievement of exemplary others. Their focus brings our attention to investigate positive emotions in an interpersonal interaction context. Their analysis of the four emotions also indicates that these different emotions provide different reasons for an individual to behave proactively, highlighting that positive emotions not only fuel energy for one to be proactive but also implies reasons (such as motivating to help others, seeking to improve oneself) that direct one's proactive actions. As discussed in the chapter, Wu and Li suggest that the four other praising emotions (that is, gratitude, elevation, admiration, and awe) can drive different forms of proactive behaviour (that is, proactive prosocial behaviour, proactive moral behaviour, proactive learning behaviour, proactive self-transcendent behaviour, respectively). Their work extends Parker, Bindl, and Strauss's (2010) work by discussing specific forms of positive emotions in an inter-person interaction context, elucidating different motivational mechanisms that positive emotions can drive one's proactive behaviour as well as identifying different forms of proactive behaviours.

Liu, Wang, and Liao's chapter (Chapter 8) also focuses on the interpersonal relationship level, but in the leader–follower interaction context specifically. They review studies on leader emotional expression and employee proactive behaviours and present a study aiming to unpack how leaders' anger can drive employees' voice. The function of anger, the function in social interactions, and how it is functional or dysfunctional in speaking up are elaborated on, and echo the call for more research in discrete emotions and proactivity across chapters in this book. Although their hypotheses were not supported in the presented empirical study, the study addressed the critical limitations of voice research by taking a within-individual approach to examine the interpersonal effects of leader's display of anger on employee voice. Furthermore, the reflections on the research journey suggest future research of emotion and proactivity, especially concerning anger and voice in the relational context.

We then have two chapters discussing emotion and proactivity at the team level. Madrid and Patterson (Chapter 9) provide an overview of emotion and proactivity in teams, which has not been properly discussed in the literature. Drawing on a team effectiveness model, they offer a framework to pin down the role of team (or group) affective tone and team proactivity as team processes in explaining the link between team input and team outcomes. They then focus on the relationships between team affective tone and team proactivity by indicating that team affective tone and team proactivity can shape each other. Their chapter thus not only offers an overview of studies on team emotion and team proactivity, but provides a concise framework to facilitate the future research at team level.

Next, Chi's chapter (Chapter 10) further zooms into group affective tone and team creativity, a specific form of team proactivity focusing on generating new ideas. In his chapter, Chi reviews studies on group affective tone and team creativity and proposes a conceptual model to extend the previous work. His conceptual model recognizes the complexity of group positive and negative affective tone in driving team creativity by elucidating how team's task complexity and team's supportive context can shape the effect of the two group affective tones on team regulatory actions (promotion versus prevention actions). These two chapters (Chapter 9 and 10) together indicate how we can extend research on emotion and proactivity at the team level. Comparing to the amount of studies at the individual level, more studies are needed to enrich our understanding of emotion and proactivity at the team level.

Echoing the call in Chapter 3 by Ashkanasy, Chapters 4 to 10, altogether, demonstrate the showcase how we can study emotion and proactivity at different levels . Nevertheless, what has not been covered in this book is the analysis of emotion and proactivity at the organizational level. To our knowledge, such an analysis has not been discussed in the literature. We hope that this edited book together with Ashkanasy's chapter can draw scholar's attention to the discussion at the organizational level and spark future research accordingly.

The final two chapters, Chapter 11 and Chapter 12, focus on the impact of proactivity on individual emotional experiences and well-being. While the majority of proactivity research has only considered proactivity as the behavioural outcomes shaped by emotions, recent studies have started looking into the impact of proactivity on individual's emotional experiences (Liu, Tangirala, Lee, and Parker, 2019). In Chapter 11, Ji, Chen, and Cangiano offer an overview on proactivity and well-being with a bibliographic analysis. They identified four clusters (that is, efficacy and job satisfaction; resources and emotional exhaustion; types of affects and emotions; well-being and its evolution) and review theoretical perspectives behind each cluster of research and offer directions for future research. Their chapter makes a significant contribution by pinning down research areas and directions on the subject of proactivity and well-being. In Chapter 12, Zacher provides a conceptual model to depict how proactivity can affect one's emotional experiences. The conceptual model incorporates the function of proactivity in driving changes in oneself or the environment, which then result in different psychological states, such as goal achievement or need satisfaction, and thus emotional experiences. In addition to proposing the process, the model also considers individual and situational factors that can facilitate or impede the process. Zacher's work can thus guide future research to unpack the impact of proactivity on individual affective consequences.

Altogether, the collected chapters offer a comprehensive review on emotion and proactivity from different angles and levels of analysis,in turn, provide insights for how we can extend the current research to enrich our understanding on the relationship between emotion and proactivity in various contexts.

Four research avenues

The chapters in this book have offered various ways to advance studies on emotion and proactivity. Here we take a holistic view and summarize four research avenue for future studies. The first research avenue, as emphasized collectively in the chapters in Parts I and II of this book, is to advance our knowledge regarding the function of specific emotions on proactivity. Instead of focusing on clusters of emotions, such as positive or negative in valence of emotion, future studies are encouraged to analyze discrete emotions or specific affective experiences. The focus on specific emotions will enrich the scope of emotions discussed in the proactivity literature. In addition, the focus on specific emotions can help us pin down the context with specific contingency factors, and identify the motivational process associated with the specific functions of the certain emotion in shaping specific forms of proactive actions.

The second research avenue is to explore the motivational functions of emotions on proactivity. Studies so far has mainly drawn on Parker, Bindl and Strauss's work (2010) to consider emotion as a source of energy to sustain proactivity. However, the energy perspective is not fine-grained enough to depict how emotions can fuel proactivity (see Lebel and Kamran-Morley, Chapter 2) and is neither broad enough to enrich analyses of contexts. Other than energy, emotion can also function as social information for self and other (see Peng, Li, and Bindl, Chapter 1). This perspective is founded in the functional perspective of discrete emotion. Together with the above research call, as such, it is time to unpack different motivational functions or mechanisms to depict how specific emotions can facilitate or undermine proactivity.

The third research avenue is to bring a multilevel perspective to study the relationship between emotion and proactivity. Ashkanasy (Chapter 3) has offered a multilevel framework to delineate how we can understand emotional phenomena at different levels in organizations and how such framework can be applied to study proactivity. This multilevel framework highlights the importance to take contexts into account when we study emotion and proactivity. As we illustrated in the previous section, our collected chapters have demonstrated how we can use a multilevel lens as guidance to investigate emotion and proactivity at different levels of phenomena. In addition to understanding phenomena at a specific level, future studies are encouraged to unpack the multilevel dynamics in emotions and proactivity by investigating cross-level influence between emotion and proactivity.

The fourth research avenue is to unpack how proactivity can shape emotional experiences in turns and to further understand the longitudinal dynamics between emotion and proactivity. The proactivity literature so far mainly considers how to promote proactivity and only pays attention to consequences of proactivity in recent years (see Liu et al, 2019, for a special issue on new directions for exploring the consequences of proactive behaviours). Unpacking how one's proactive actions can influence her/his emotions not only help us understand how proactivity can bring and twist with one's emotional experiences but also how proactivity can affect an individual's well-being and social interactions with others due to the resulting emotions.

To conclude, this edited book indicates the need to investigate the links between emotion and proactivity and provides directions for future research. The four key research directions summarized above suggest that it is time to expand perspectives while digging into specific emotions to unpack the multilevel and longitudinal dynamics of emotion and proactivity.

References

Liu, W., Tangirala, S., Lee, C., and Parker, S. K. (2019). New directions for exploring the consequences of proactive behaviors: Introduction to the special issue. *Journal Of Organizational Behavior,* 40(1), 1–4. doi:10.1002/job.2334.

Parker, S. K., Bindl, U. K., and Strauss, K. (2010). Making things happen: A model of proactive motivation. *Journal of Management,* 36, 827–856.

Index